CONSTRUCTING A NEW AGENDA

CONSTRUCTING A NEW AGENDA

———

ARCHITECTURAL THEORY 1993–2009

———

A. KRISTA SYKES, EDITOR

Princeton Architectural Press · New York

Published by
Princeton Architectural Press
37 East 7th Street, New York, NY 10003

For a free catalog of books call: 1-800-722-6657
Visit our website at www.papress.com

Editor: Carolyn Deuschle
Cover design: Paul Wagner
Typesetting: Bree Anne Apperley

Special thanks to: Nettie Aljian, Sara Bader, Nicola Bednarek, Janet Behning,
Becca Casbon, Carina Cha, Tom Cho, Penny (Yuen Pik) Chu, Russell Fernandez,
Pete Fitzpatrick, Wendy Fuller, Jan Haux, Nancy Eklund Later, Linda Lee,
Laurie Manfra, John Myers, Katharine Myers, Steve Royal, Dan Simon,
Andrew Stepanian, Jennifer Thompson, Joseph Weston, and Deb Wood
of Princeton Architectural Press —Kevin C. Lippert, publisher

Library of Congress Cataloging-in-Publication Data
Constructing a new agenda for architecture : architectural theory
1993–2009 / A. Krista Sykes, editor. — 1st ed.
     p. cm.
Includes bibliographical references.
ISBN 978-1-56898-859-7 (alk. paper)
1. Architecture—Philosophy. I. Sykes, Krista.
NA2500.C598 2010
720.1—dc22
                                        2009030430

A long time ago...people used simply to drop things from time to time. But nowadays we have physicists to inform us of the laws of gravity by which objects fall; philosophers to doubt whether there are really any discrete objects to be dropped at all; sociologists to explain how all this dropping is really the consequence of urban pressures; psychologists to suggest that we are really all trying to drop our parents; poets to write about how all this dropping is symbolic of death; and critics to argue that it is a sign of the poet's castration anxiety. Now dropping can never be the same again. We can never return to the happy garden where we simply walked around dropping things all day without a care in the world. What has happened, rather, is that the practice has now been forced to take itself as its own object of enquiry. Theory is just human activity bending back upon itself, constrained into a new kind of self-reflexivity. And in absorbing this self-reflexivity, the activity itself will be transformed.

—Terry Eagleton, *The Significance of Theory*

TABLE OF CONTENTS

ACKNOWLEDGMENTS

Numerous individuals had a hand in this book. I thank Nancy Eklund Later for initiating this project and guiding it forward; Jennifer Thompson and Carolyn Deuschle for bringing the book to fruition; Lee Gray for his never-failing guidance and advice; Michael Hays, John McMorrough, and Mark Morris for their thoughts and suggestions on content; Michael Hays for generously contributing the afterword; Arie Graafland, Jeff Kipnis, John McMorrough, Roemer van Toorn, and Sarah Whiting for the extra efforts regarding their essays; and all of the authors for their permission to be included in this collection. Above all I am grateful to Joshua and Sophia for their patience, support, and enthusiasm. This work is dedicated to them.

PREFACE

This collection builds on the foundation established by Kate Nesbitt in *Theorizing a New Agenda for Architecture: An Anthology of Architectural Theory, 1965–1995*. Like its parent compilation, the present work contains a variety of texts—in this case essays, book chapters, interviews, manifestos, and questionnaires—written by architects, theorists, historians, critics, and interdisciplinary scholars. Together they offer an overview of the myriad tendencies that have characterized architectural theory in the years since the publication of Nesbitt's book.

While the two volumes share a similar intent—to gather in one place recent significant writings on architectural theory—their modes of organization differ. As opposed to the thematic divisions offered by Nesbitt, here the twenty-eight texts, each preceded by a short introduction, appear in chronological order. This reflects the lack of a single theoretical discourse during the period in question. Furthermore, the chronological organization avoids a priori classifications, which can inadvertently limit the reader's textual interpretations and forestall new thematic groupings; this can be particularly helpful for instructors eager to trace motifs tailored for specific courses. In addition to instructors and students, this collection is directed toward architectural professionals and those attentive to the ways in which contemporary architectural thought influences and is influenced by society in general. As Nesbitt noted in her preface, "the issues raised [here] are fundamental to understanding the course of architecture in the recent past, and should be of interest to all scholars involved in the analysis and critique of cultural production."[1]

We are still in the midst of a transitional period in architecture that began in the 1990s. This makes the exploration of the contemporary architectural situation—as well as any attempt to intellectually frame it—a rather difficult proposition, as there is no obvious vantage point from which to view the landscape of the recent past. Nevertheless, for this anthology I sought to select material that addresses architecture as a whole. Due to space constraints, I have largely excluded writings focused specifically on urbanism and urban planning, even though architecture and urbanism necessarily and inevitably share territory. The texts that do appear in this collection are mixed—a combination of writings that have already impacted architectural discourse and others that may prove, in retrospect, to be prescient of or decisive for our contemporary situation. In conjunction, I believe these readings will provide valuable insight into the present moment and offer a basis for future architectural thought and practice.

Notes

1   Kate Nesbitt, "Preface," in *Theorizing a New Agenda for Architecture: An Anthology of Architectural Theory, 1965–1995* (New York: Princeton Architectural Press, 1996), 13.

INTRODUCTION

The end of the twentieth century witnessed the publication of two anthologies dedicated to "architectural theory": in 1996, Kate Nesbitt's *Theorizing a New Agenda for Architecture: An Anthology of Architectural Theory, 1965–1995;* and two years later, K. Michael Hays's *Architecture Theory Since 1968.*

"Theory" as a code or framework for architectural thought has existed for centuries, often cited as originating with Vitruvius in the first century BCE. Yet the "theory" referred to by Nesbitt and Hays relates to a specific movement that began in the 1960s and strives to reconstitute the architectural discipline through mediatory concepts—derived from fields such as philosophy, linguistics, psychology, and anthropology—that simultaneously connect architecture to other social realms and (attempt to) claim for architecture its own unique territory. Architectural theory as such encompasses many overlapping and often conflicting tendencies (for example semiotics, structuralism, and phenomenology), which in turn have given rise to the more recent historicist and deconstructivist camps.

In the introduction to her volume, Nesbitt notes that "a survey of architectural theory from the last thirty years finds a multiplicity of issues vying for attention." She continues, "The lack of dominance of a single issue or viewpoint is characteristic of the pluralist period imprecisely referred to as *postmodern.*"[1] Hays, however, feels that in the midst of this pluralism one particular strain of architectural theory, which he describes as the "the coupling of Marxian critical theory and post-structuralism with readings of architectural modernism," did tend to dominate the others.[2] This brand of architectural theory—frequently referred to by the term *critical* and derived from the thought of Frankfurt School intellectuals and French philosophers—typically involves cultural critique and the desired resistance of the status quo, exposing social structures perceived as repressive and controlling. Nesbitt characterizes critical theory as a "speculative, questioning, and sometimes utopian" form of thought that "evaluates the built world and its relationships to the society it serves..., often has an expressed political or ethical orientation and intends to stimulate change."[3] At the current moment in time, mid-2009, a coupling of Hays's assertion of dominance with Nesbitt's definition of critical theory appears most helpful. This presents a notion of critical theory as an overarching and ideologically grounded practice that strives to interrogate, elucidate, and thus enhance the world in which we live.

This is a lofty goal for architecture, one that stems from and attempts to improve upon the utopian modernist quest to rescue society from its ills. Architects, historians, and critics during the so-called postmodern era recognized that to request of architecture such a wide-ranging and unattainable task put the discipline in an impossible position, poised for failure. Furthermore, figures such as Manfredo Tafuri felt that architecture was not only failing to improve society but was actually, albeit unwittingly, making things worse. As a result, architects sought ways to proceed in more limited terms that would hopefully allow architecture to be a positive force in the world at large—hence the pluralist tendencies noted by Nesbitt. Thus, during the period spanning the mid-1960s through mid-1990s, there did exist a prevailing discourse that, despite varying methods of approach, sought to reformulate the discipline and carve out a niche for architecture. What is different about the current moment is that there appears to be no overarching concept dedicated to this task, and the notion previously charged with this responsibility—

critical architectural theory—is now itself in transition, if
not in crisis.

In the past decade, a pointed critique has been leveled
against critical theory, which some see as irrelevant to architectural practice or, at the very least, dissociated from it. In his 2005
article "'Criticality' and Its Discontents," George Baird discusses
the assault on critical architecture, singling out two approaches—
that of Michael Speaks in his 2002 essay, "Design Intelligence,"
and that of Robert Somol and Sarah Whiting in their text of the
same year, "Notes around the Doppler Effect and Other Moods
of Modernism."[4] While the attitudes of their authors differ, both
of these writings characterize the critical project as exhausted and
posit new alternatives for practice that the authors feel to be more
in accordance with the uncertainty of everyday life. Yet another
text, Reinhold Martin's "Critical of What? Toward a Utopian
Realism" of 2005, critiques the propositions of Speaks and
Somol/Whiting, calling for a reconsideration of critical architecture's socio-political significance. Likewise, Arie Graafland's "On
Criticality" of 2006 investigates the recent disavowal of critical
theory, incorporating the ideas of cultural theorists to demonstrate
that theory understood as critical thinking still occupies a crucial
role in architectural discourse and design.

So why all this talk about critical theory? Why now? Indeed,
the often-cited theory-versus-practice divide has long existed,
strengthened by the intellectual density of theory itself. What is
new is the urgency of what can be described as a pro-practice
movement as it appears in the late 1990s; in most cases, this is
not a total disavowal of theory (thus the term "anti-theory" is not
quite right), but rather a mandate to focus on the realities of architecture and building (hence "pro-practice").

This pro-practice stance coalesced in 2000 with a two-part
event funded by the Skidmore, Owings and Merrill Foundation,
ending with a conference at the Museum of Modern Art in New

York, in association with Columbia University. The conference, entitled "Things in the Making: Contemporary Architecture and the Pragmatist Imagination," functioned as the public face of a workshop held the previous spring at Columbia's Temple Hoyne Buell Center for the Study of American Architecture. Incorporating architectural and interdisciplinary scholars—including philosopher John Rajchman and cultural theorist Cornel West—both proceedings focused on possible intersections of architecture and pragmatism, in all of its iterations, to potentially "serve as a lever to pry open some hardened formations in architecture,"[5] to offer alternatives to what, by that point, had become the norm of critical architectural theory. Of course, pragmatism is itself another theory (as is the call for no theory at all). But despite its philosophical origins, pragmatism, with its various emphases on experimentation and experience, holds the promise of practical application, of action, of tangible product.[6] This no doubt appealed to those frustrated with and disappointed by the more abstract conceptual processes tied to architectural theory as it has existed since the 1960s.

Another signal event, interpreted by some as a death knell for architectural theory, occurred in the year 2000. In April, the architectural periodical *Assemblage* ceased publication with its forty-first issue. Founded fourteen years earlier by editors K. Michael Hays and Alicia Kennedy, *Assemblage: A Critical Journal of Architecture and Design Culture* provided a venue for the exploration and expansion of architectural theory. Often identified as the successor of *Oppositions*—the journal, founded by editors Peter Eisenman, Mario Gandelsonas, and Anthony Vidler, associated with the Institute of Architecture and Urban Studies in New York—*Assemblage* continued the theoretical exchanges fostered by *Oppositions* during the latter's eleven-year run, from 1973 through 1984. As Hays and Kennedy stated in their solicitation for contributions to the last issue, *Assemblage* "provided a registration plane for a discourse in the process of finding its legs, developing its skills, suffering its growing pains."[7] For many, the dissolution of this "registration plane" signaled a shift away from theory that had been building in the previous years. Perhaps this is best reflected in the text Hays and Kennedy published in the final *Assemblage* issue:

> One point needs to be emphatically made one last time. The end of *Assemblage* has nothing to do with the end of theory, neither as an editorial intention nor, in our minds, as a historical symptom. Rather, the transitional moment means that theoretical activity achieves a new excitement and urgency. We hear the antitheoretical rants to be sure, and, oddly enough, coming from deep within the theoretical camp...the larger abstract ambitions and sweaty efforts of an older theory are being taken to task. But all this, too, is a problem for theory. A peculiar characteristic of theory is that it must constantly historicize itself. And the various lines of flight out of theory (the technomanagerial, the postcritical, the neopragmatist) are still products of theory's success (and perhaps, excess). They represent the sorts of revisions theory must pass through from time to time: theory taking inventory, adjusting to new demands, going through a bit of necessary retooling rather than closing down the shop altogether.[8]

The language used by Hays and Kennedy conveys the seriousness of theory's state of affairs, even if they portray the situation as well within the scope of theory's domain—as a discipline that, due to its very nature, must continually be interrogated, evaluated, and revised. Cries against theory have appeared from various corners, most notably "the technomanagerial" (Michael Speaks, Alejandro Zaero-Polo), "the postcritical" (Somol and Whiting), and "the neopragmatist" (those affiliated with the

Columbia/MoMA events, as well as Dutch architecture firms that embrace what Roemer van Toorn refers to as an "extreme realism"⁹). The primary charge against theory concerns its lack of correspondence to practice. Yet Hays and Kennedy render this disconnect as another intrinsic part of theory itself. Practice, no matter how alternative or forward thinking, is ultimately limited by the realities—economic, social, disciplinary, political—of getting something built. Indeed, "even if a building is inherently projective in the sense that it materially and conceptually changes the situation into which it is placed, it cannot ordinarily push beyond the standards of cultural acceptance and professional practice." However, as a thing apart,

> [theory] uncovers aspects of architecture practice that, while not useful or even correct for building now, may become a resource for future architectures. The theoretical text seeks out for us what we cannot otherwise imagine (this is its properly utopian vocation), but it does so not by presenting us with a concrete representation, or even a guide to one, but rather by exposing the gaps and holes in our discipline and our discourse that are our own inability to see beyond the present and its ideological closure.¹⁰

Thus, according to Hays and Kennedy, theory and practice should rightly be separate entities, despite the claims of theory's detractors. Nevertheless, the challenge put to theory at the moment of *Assemblage*'s closure—a challenge still ongoing today—is very real, real enough to prompt the editors to ardently defend theory in the final issue of their journal.

Along with the end of *Assemblage* came that of *ANY*, an architectural journal guided by editor Cynthia Davidson (wife of Peter Eisenman) from the publication's inception in 1993 through its dissolution in 2000. The conclusion of *ANY*, with its direct link to the *Oppositions* generation, strengthened the feeling that *Assemblage*'s closure related to critical theory's impending death. This sentiment was perhaps even further compounded by the appearance of multiple new architectural journals—such as *Praxis: Journal of Writing + Building* (1999), *Hunch: The Berlage Institute Report* (1999), and *306090* (2001)—that, in their own ways, foreground practice or emphasize a more direct correspondence between practice and discourse. All told, these events in the world of serial architectural publications conveyed a message that indeed a shift was occurring, and theory as understood during the previous decades was, at the very least, undergoing a process of reevaluation.

* * *

Against this background of theory's interrogation, multiple overlapping themes have emerged within the architectural realm. A variety of issues conditions the present moment—more than can be covered in this brief introduction—but nevertheless, select motifs have risen to the fore since the early 1990s. For example, recent technological advances have presented architecture with a plethora of opportunities and challenges, with implications for all aspects of the architectural discipline. In particular, the expansion of the digital domain has created a wealth of possibilities for architecture, including the rise of new modes of design (employing software and computing applications), fabrication (generating custom-built materials and building components), and representation (creating computer models and animated fly-throughs). To those outside the profession, the most obvious manifestation of digital technologies has been visible in the unprecedented formal qualities of certain contemporary buildings. The Guggenheim Museum in Bilbao (1997) by Frank Gehry and the Yokohama International Port Terminal (2002) by Foreign Office Architects

(FOA) are examples of such projects, yet they represent two very different approaches toward computer-assisted design. While the Guggenheim Bilbao's curves owe their precise appearance to aeronautical software, the forms are determined using conventional design methods: freehand sketches and small-scale models that are later mapped by CATIA (Computer-Aided Three-Dimensional Interactive Application) to render them buildable by guiding material fabrication and construction. Gehry's designs are not computer generated per se, but the software platform permits him to operate within a larger repertoire of forms that could not be constructed without this digital intervention. In opposition, FOA's design for the Yokohama Terminal was, as Charles Jencks puts it, "conceived inside the belly of a computer." That the firm's principals, Farshid Moussavi and Alejandro Zaero-Polo, "are quite proud about the way they were surprised by the emergent results"[11] suggests how different their use of the computer is from Gehry's.

The smooth, sinuous, wavelike Yokohama Terminal has elements in common with so-called blob architecture, which is perhaps most often associated with Greg Lynn.[12] The term *blob* refers to curving, biomorphic architecture that is typically reliant on computer-aided design and the exploration of complex numerical systems. Gehry's design for the Guggenheim Bilbao does not quite fit the blob designation. While the museum does offer an unconventional, swirling form (which has been compared to a flower, an artichoke, and even the unfurling skirt of Marilyn Monroe[13]), these sweeping portions collide with more traditional, rectilinear surfaces. The juxtaposition of the curved and the straight-edged foregrounds the difference of the former, something no true blob would do; the blob-architect has no need for deliberate Cartesian edges. This in part stems from the blob-architect's desire to depart from the traditional forms of architecture as well as established means of design. Indeed curvilinearity, as described by Lynn, corresponds to software-based design that utilizes flows of information—contextual, biological, mathematical, topological—to generate form.[14]

Alongside new possibilities for design, fabrication, and form, the digital era poses many questions for the architectural discipline. For example, what is architecture's role with respect to globalization, internet society, or virtual reality? How else might the architect employ new digital technologies? What might digitization mean for architecture as a discipline? Must architecture be reconceived? These issues and more accompany architecture as it navigates the contemporary digital world, affecting everything from small-scale design decisions and the ways in which structures are occupied to the actual shape and configuration of individual buildings, larger complexes, and urban developments. The digital makes up a crucial part of our present reality, one with which architecture must grapple daily.

Another reality confronting architecture concerns the environment and the part architecture can play in arresting, and perhaps even correcting, the ecological damage inflicted by modern society. In the past decade, due to global climate changes, dwindling supplies of natural resources, and pollution in general, the imperative to create sustainable and green architecture has become abundantly clear. Today it is becoming more common than not for architects to incorporate environmentally friendly strategies into their designs, including the use of local, renewable, energy-efficient, and/or salvaged materials; energy harnessing and generating devices (such as systems that capture and utilize rainwater and solar power); and living components (for example grass roofs to both insulate a structure and provide habitable green space for the occupants and wildlife). Of course, the ways in which architects address environmental concerns range widely. While architects such as Norman Foster, Richard Rogers, and Renzo Piano often employ advanced technologies to produce green designs, others such as Samuel Mockbee and Glenn Murcutt rely on combinations of local or salvaged materials, attention to geography, and awareness of proven regional solutions to create sustainable and environmentally responsive architecture. Another approach is that taken by William McDonough, who—partnered with chemist Michael Braungart—actively pursues the development of new materials and technologies that abide by a "cradle-to-cradle" philosophy, hoping to eliminate waste by employing the cast-off materials from a given process as the raw materials for another. Regardless of the methods used by architects, many appear to share a common consciousness, growing increasingly strong in the past decade, that architecture must become an environmentally responsible practice.

The rising mandate for ecologically sound architectural practices goes hand in hand with concepts of realism and the everyday. With respect to architecture, neither concept is easy to define, as they both have shifting, somewhat subjective, meanings. Despite this indeterminacy, the two ideas appear to intertwine, in that the everyday can be considered a subset of the larger realm of realism. Realism is often associated with a direct, straightforward assessment of and attitude toward the "real" (whatever the "real" may be), that which exists and must be dealt with on practical and/or symbolic levels. The everyday relates in a positive manner to the ordinary, the typical, and the local, as what constitutes "the everyday" inevitably depends on who one is and what one generally experiences. With their emphases on human experience, realism and the everyday resonate with the conversations surrounding pragmatism and regionalism, but they also exist on planes of their own. Everyday architecture is, in many ways, the antithesis of such projects as Gehry's Guggenheim Bilbao, guided not by the desire to be iconic or monumental but rather by a concern for the specificity of place, created for and by the context and population within which the building exists. While the museum's metallic exterior and billowing forms do reference Bilbao's former life as a steel and shipbuilding center, the Guggenheim bears what has become Gehry's signature—highly reflective, sheared, curving surfaces—which has appeared in numerous locations besides Spain, including Los Angeles (Walt Disney Concert Hall [2003]), Chicago (Millennium Pavilion [2004]), and Cambridge, Massachusetts (Stata Center at MIT [2004]).

Despite its relatives across the Atlantic, the Guggenheim Bilbao, perhaps even more than the famous inward-looking spiral of Frank Lloyd Wright's Guggenheim Museum in New York, is an iconic building par excellence. The millions of people, architects and others, who have been drawn to Bilbao since the museum's inception attest to this fact; whereas New York boasts many cultural delights to attract visitors, Bilbao was, before Gehry and Guggenheim Foundation director Thomas Krens' intervention, a decaying industrial town, an unlikely venue for a newfound "pilgrimage" site.[15] While the building-as-icon is not a new phenomenon—think of the Empire State or Chrysler buildings, for example—this trend appears to have reached new heights in the recent past, as the architectural critic Charles Jencks observes in his book of 2005, *Iconic Building*.[16] Immediately recognizable buildings such as the Guggenheim Bilbao (note that the museum is often referred to as "Bilbao," as if the town now exists largely because of and for the building itself) and the London Gherkin (originally Foster's Swiss Re Tower [2004]; now known as St. Mary Axe 30) act as logos, advertising the very institutions they house as well as the cities in which they reside. This represents an entirely different level of the commercialization of architecture than that lamented by architectural theorists and critics like Manfredo Tafuri.[17] Such iconic buildings are intentionally complicit with capitalist systems, employing form and visibility as a marketing technique.

While the Guggenheim Bilbao functions as an iconic building, it also highlights the related phenomenon of the star architect, or the "starchitect." In an issue dedicated to fame and architecture, the editors of *Perspecta* 37 remark that "in today's globalized marketplace of ideas, the so-called starchitect has the means to influence the wider world beyond architecture by guest-editing magazines, appearing on television shows, and collaborating with multinational corporations on everything from bathroom accessories to branding strategies."[18] Hence Rem Koolhaas guest edits an issue of *Wired* while Gehry appears on *The Simpsons* and designs jewelry for Tiffany & Co. Indeed, in contemporary society, the cultural capital generated by the starchitect is as valuable as the (often iconic) building he (or, more rarely, she) delivers. In "The Bilbao Effect," Witold Rybczynski—architect and professor at the University of Pennsylvania—discusses how, in the wake of the Guggenheim Bilbao's success, museums and municipalities are increasingly turning to renowned architects like Gehry, Steven Holl, Daniel Libeskind, and Santiago Calatrava to create signature buildings. These works frequently arise from select design competitions, complete with eye-catching renderings and media publicity, a "charged atmosphere" that, in Rybczynski's opinion, "promotes flamboyance rather than careful thought, and favors the glib and obvious over the subtle and nuanced." He concludes that while "the 'wow factor' may excite the visitor and the journalist," it does not necessarily make for good architecture, which "should have more to say to us than 'Look at me.'"[19]

Now, roughly a decade into the twenty-first century, the trend toward iconic buildings may be winding down. Recent financial crises have left the global economy in a precarious state, halting many building projects and instigating layoffs throughout the architecture and construction industries. Such an atmosphere has prompted the architect and critic Robert Campbell to suggest that we have reached the end of an era, one he terms the "Bilbao

Decade," book-ended by the opening of the museum in the late 1990s and the current economic downturn that has affected all aspects of contemporary life. Yet, as Campbell notes, "there's an upside to recessions. They give people time to step back from the frantic pace of a boom economy and think hard about what it is they want to do."[20]

In the past two decades, however, it appears that a recession was not necessary for some to rethink, or indeed expand, the architectural arena. Architecture has never been simply a question of building; a blurred boundary has long existed between architecture and art, engineering, and other disciplines. In recent years architecture appears to have broadened its reach, though, both co-opting and infiltrating different realms. To remain with Gehry as an example, in addition to his work as a designer (of architecture, furniture, sculpture, and jewelry), in 2002 he launched Gehry Technologies, a company that offers software technologies specifically suited for architectural applications. Perhaps the paradigmatic example of architecture's broadened scope is Koolhaas, principal of the Office for Metropolitan Architecture (OMA) and founder of its research-based subsidiary AMO (Architectuur Metropolitaanse Officie), which serves as a consulting firm working on everything from business strategies to marketing and commercialization. While AMO is described as "a think tank that operates in areas beyond the boundaries of architecture and urbanism—including sociology, technology, media and politics,"[21] one could argue that, under the leadership of Koolhaas and OMA, AMO brings these realms under the purview of architecture, as both a product and a symptom of the specific moment we now occupy.

A multitude of external forces—historical, cultural, political, and economic—condition the present, and architecture, inextricably tied to such forces, has in no way been exempt from the impacts of current events, such as the sequencing of the human genome and the terrorist attacks in the early part of this decade. While significant world events are too numerous to recount here, suffice it to say that architecture as a discipline has, inevitably, responded to them all in ways that have contributed to our contemporary architectural situation, a time of enthusiasm and potential tempered by anxiety and indeterminacy. From the mid-1960s through mid-1990s, in all its different manifestations, theory led the way. Since then architecture itself has changed, in part due to various transformations in technology, means of production and fabrication, and the realities of the cultural and political landscape. Theory can no longer occupy its previous role, and thus it too has started to shift—in some cases away from utopian ideals, the declarative rejection of the status quo, and heavy-handed cultural critiques toward...what? What is the architectural end game at this moment in time? There is no clear or easy answer; indeed, the texts collected here, dating from 1993 through the present day, situate themselves along different trajectories. Auspiciously, these paths all point forward.

Notes

1 Kate Nesbitt, "Introduction," in *Theorizing a New Agenda for Architecture: An Anthology of Architectural Theory, 1965–1995* (New York: Princeton Architectural Press, 1996), 16.

2 K. Michael Hays, "Introduction," in *Architecture Theory Since 1968* (Cambridge, Mass.: MIT Press, 1998), xiv n. 1.

3 Nesbitt, "Introduction," 18.

4 George Baird, "'Criticality' and Its Discontents," *Harvard Design Magazine*, no. 21 (Fall 2004/Winter 2005): 16–21.

5 Joan Ockman, "The Idea of the Workshop Project," in *The Pragmatist Imagination: Thinking about "Things in the Making,"* ed. Joan Ockman (New York: Princeton Architectural Press, 2000), 17.

6 For more on the pragmatism workshop and conference, see Ockman, *The Pragmatist Imagination.*

7 K. Michael Hays and Alicia Kennedy, letter calling for contributions, published in *Assemblage* 41 (Apr. 2000).

8 K. Michael Hays and Alicia Kennedy, "After All, or the End of 'The End of,'" *Assemblage* 41 (Apr. 2000): 6.

9 See Roemer van Toorn, "No More Dreams? The Passion for Reality in Recent Dutch Architecture...and Its Limitations," reprinted here.

10 Hays and Kennedy, "After All, or the End of 'The End of'": 7.

11 Charles Jencks, "The New Paradigm in Architecture," *Hunch* 6/7 (Aug. 2003), http://www.charlesjencks.com/articles.html.

12 See Greg Lynn, *Folds, Bodies & Blobs: Collected Essays* (Brussels: La Lettre Volée, 1998).

13 Herbert Muschamp, "The Miracle of Bilbao," *New York Times*, September 1997.

14 See Greg Lynn, "Architectural Curvilinearity: The Folded, the Pliant and the Supple," reprinted here.

15 See Muschamp, "The Miracle of Bilbao."

16 Charles Jencks, *Iconic Building* (New York: Rizzoli, 2005).

17 See Manfredo Tafuri, *Architecture and Utopia: Design and Capitalist Development*, trans. Barbara Luiga La Penta (Cambridge, Mass.: MIT Press, 1976); originally published as *Progetto e Utopia* (Bari: Laterza & Figli, 1973).

18 Brendan M. Lee, DaeWha Kang, Justin Kwok, and Robert McClure, "Editorial Statement," *Perspecta 37, Famous* (2005): 4. See this entire issue for comments on issues surrounding architecture and celebrity.

19 Witold Rybczynski, "The Bilbao Effect," *The Atlantic* (Sept. 2002), http://www.theatlantic.com/doc/200209/rybczynski.

20 Robert Campbell, "Marking the End of 'The Bilbao Decade,'" *Boston Globe*, January 11, 2009, http://www.boston.com/ae/theater_arts/articles/2009/01/11/marking_the_end_of_the_bilbao_decade/.

21 See http://www.oma.nl/ for this description of AMO.

INTRODUCTION
Architectural Curvilinearity: The Folded, the Pliant
and the Supple / *Greg Lynn*

In 1993, Greg Lynn guest-edited an issue of *Architectural Design*
dedicated to an emerging movement in architecture: folding.
Lynn, a Los Angeles-based architect/educator with a background
in philosophy and an attraction to computer-aided design, was
the ideal person to organize this publication and, in effect, define
the fold in architecture, a concept that generated intense interest
during the remainder of the decade.

In his contributory essay, "Architectural Curvilinearity: The
Folded, the Pliant and the Supple," Lynn ties together a variety
of sources—including the work of Gilles Deleuze, René Thom,
cooking theory, and geology—to present an alternative to
existing architectural theory and practice. He states that since
the mid-1960s architecture has been guided by the notion of
contradiction, whether through attempts to formally embody
heterogeneity or its opposite; in short, postmodernism and deconstructivism can be understood as two sides of the same coin. Yet,
for Lynn, "neither the reactionary call for unity nor the avant-garde
dismantling of it through the identification of internal contradictions seems adequate as a model for contemporary architecture
and urbanism." Rather, he offers a smooth architecture (in both a
visual and a mathematic sense) composed of combined yet discrete elements that are shaped by forces outside the architectural
discipline, much as diverse ingredients are folded into a smooth
mixture by a discerning chef. This new architecture, what Lynn
calls a pliant, flexible architecture, exploits connections between
elements within a design instead of emphasizing contradictions
or attempting to erase them all together. Of equal importance
is that this architecture is inextricably entwined with external
forces, both cultural and contextual. Architects deploy various

strategies—including a reliance on topological geometry and digital software and technologies—in the creation of their designs, but the resulting works tend to be curvilinear in form and inflected with the particulars of the project and its environment.

In addition to Lynn's essay, *Folding in Architecture*, as the *Architectural Design* issue was titled, included other texts by figures such as Deleuze, Jeffrey Kipnis, and John Rajchman, and representative projects by architects like Peter Eisenman, Frank Gehry, and Philip Johnson. This list of distinguished collaborators lent weight to the publication, intimating that the phenomenon of the fold was already entrenched within architectural design. If indeed it was, *Folding in Architecture* cemented the shift in architectural thought by identifying and highlighting this new architecture of smoothness. The importance of Lynn's special issue of *Architectural Design* was underscored by its reprinting in 2004 as "a historical document,"[1] complete with new introductory essays analyzing and situating the original publication as a guiding force within twenty-first-century architectural discourse.[2]

Notes

1   Helen Castle, "Preface," in *Folding in Architecture*, ed. Greg Lynn (London: Wiley-Academy, 2004), 7.

2   See Greg Lynn, "Introduction," in *Folding in Architecture*, 8–13; and Mario Carpo, "Ten Years of Folding," in *Folding in Architecture*. See also Branko Koleravic, ed., *Architecture in the Digital Age: Design and Manufacturing* (New York: Spoon Press, 2003), 3–10.

GREG LYNN

ARCHITECTURAL CURVILINEARITY: THE FOLDED, THE PLIANT AND THE SUPPLE

First appeared in *Architectural Design* 63, no. 3/4 (1993): 8–15.
Courtesy of Greg Lynn.

For the last two decades, beginning with Robert Venturi's *Complexity and Contradiction in Architecture*,[1] and Colin Rowe and Fred Koetter's *Collage City*,[2] and continuing through Mark Wigley and Philip Johnson's *Deconstructivist Architecture*, architects have been primarily concerned with the production of heterogeneous, fragmented and conflicting formal systems. These practices have attempted to embody the differences within and between diverse physical, cultural, and social contexts in formal conflicts. When comparing Venturi's *Complexity and Contradiction* or *Learning from Las Vegas* with Wigley and Johnson's *Deconstruction Architecture* it is necessary to overlook many significant and distinguishing differences in order to identify at least one common theme.

Both Venturi and Wigley argue for the deployment of discontinuous, fragmented, heterogeneous, and diagonal formal strategies based on the incongruities, juxtapositions and oppositions within specific sites and programmes. These disjunctions result from a logic which tends to identify the potential contradictions between dissimilar elements. A diagonal dialogue between a building and its context has become an emblem for the contradictions within contemporary culture. From the scale of an urban plan to a building detail, contexts have been mined for conflicting geometries, materials, styles, histories, and programmes which are then represented in architecture as internal contradictions. The most paradigmatic architecture of the last ten years, including Robert Venturi's Sainsbury Wing of the National Gallery, Peter Eisenman's Wexner Center, Bernard Tschumi's La Villette Park or the Gehry House, invests in the architectural representation of contradictions. Through contradiction, architecture represents difference in violent formal conflicts.

Contradiction has also provoked a reactionary response to formal conflict. Such resistances attempt to recover unified architectural languages that can stand against heterogeneity. Unity is constructed through one of two strategies: either by reconstructing a continuous architectural language through historical analyses (Neo-Classicism or Neo-Modernism) or by identifying local consistencies resulting from indigenous climates, materials, traditions or technologies (Regionalism). The internal orders of Neo-Classicism, Neo-Modernism and Regionalism conventionally repress the cultural and contextual discontinuities that are necessary for a logic of contradiction. In architecture, both the reaction to and the representation of heterogeneity have shared an origin in contextual analysis. Both theoretical models begin with a close analysis of contextual conditions from which they proceed to evolve either a homogeneous or heterogeneous urban fabric. Neither the reactionary call for unity nor the avant-garde dismantling of it through the identification of internal contradictions seems adequate as a model for contemporary architecture and urbanism.

[In response to architecture's discovery of complex, disparate, differentiated and heterogeneous cultural and formal contexts, two options have been dominant; either conflict and contradiction or unity and reconstruction. Presently, an alternative smoothness is being formulated that may escape these dialectically opposed strategies. Common to the diverse sources of this post-contradictory work—topological geometry, morphology, morphogenesis, Catastrophe Theory or the computer technology of both the defense and Hollywood film industry—are characteristics of smooth transformation involving the intensive integration of differences within a continuous yet heterogeneous system. Smooth mixtures are made up of disparate elements which maintain their integrity while being blended within a continuous field of other free elements.]

Smoothing does not eradicate differences but incorporates[3] free intensities through fluid tactics of mixing and blending. Smooth mixtures are not homogeneous and therefore cannot be reduced. Deleuze describes smoothness as "the continuous variation" and the "continuous development of form."[4] Wigley's critique of pure form and static geometry is inscribed within geometric conflicts and discontinuities. For Wigley, smoothness is equated with hierarchical organisation: "the volumes have been purified—they have become smooth, classical—and the wires all converge in a single, hierarchical, vertical movement."[5] Rather than investing in arrested conflicts, Wigley's slipperiness might be better exploited by the alternative smoothness of heterogeneous mixture. For the first time perhaps, complexity might be aligned with neither unity nor contradiction but with smooth, pliant mixture.

Both pliancy and smoothness provide an escape from the two camps which would either have architecture break under the stress of difference or stand firm. Pliancy allows architecture to become involved in complexity through flexibility. It may be possible to neither repress the complex relations of differences with fixed points of resolution nor arrest them in contradictions, but sustain them through flexible, unpredicted, local connections. To arrest differences in conflicting forms often precludes many of the more complex possible connections of the forms of architecture to larger cultural fields. A more pliant architectural sensibility values alliances, rather than conflicts, between elements. Pliancy implies first an internal flexibility and second a dependence on external forces for self-definition.

If there is a single effect produced in architecture by folding, it will be the ability to integrate unrelated elements within a new continuous mixture. Culinary theory has developed both a practical and precise definition for at least three types of mixtures. The first involves the manipulation of homogeneous elements; beating, whisking and whipping change the volume but not the nature of a liquid through agitation. The second method of incorporation mixes two or more disparate elements; chopping, dicing, grinding, grating, slicing, shredding and mincing eviscerate elements into fragments. The first method agitates a single uniform ingredient, the second eviscerates disparate ingredients. Folding, creaming and blending mix smoothly multiple ingredients "through repeated gentle overturnings without stirring or beating" in such a way that their individual characteristics are maintained.[6] For instance, an egg and chocolate are folded together so that each is a distinct layer within a continuous mixture.

Folding employs neither agitation nor evisceration but a supple layering. Likewise, folding in geology involves the sedimentation of mineral elements or deposits which become slowly bent and compacted into plateaus of strata. These strata are compressed, by external forces, into more or less continuous layers within which heterogeneous deposits are still intact in varying degrees of intensity.

A folded mixture is neither homogenous, like whipped cream, nor fragmented, like chopped nuts, but smooth and heterogeneous. In both cooking and geology, there is no preliminary organisation which becomes folded but rather there are unrelated elements or pure intensities that are intricated through a joint manipulation. Disparate elements can be incorporated into smooth mixtures through various manipulations including fulling:

"Felt is a supple solid product that proceeds altogether differently, as an anti-fabric. It implies no separation of threads, no intertwining, only an entanglement of fibres obtained by fulling (for example, by rolling the block of fibres back and forth). What becomes entangled are the microscales of the fibres. An aggregate of intrication of this kind is in no way homogeneous; nevertheless, it is smooth and contrasts point by point with the space of fabric (it is in principle infinite, open and uninhibited in every direction; it has neither top, nor bottom, nor centre; it does not assign fixed or mobile elements but distributes a continuous variation)."[7]

The two characteristics of smooth mixtures are that they are composed of disparate unrelated elements and that these free intensities become intricated by an external force exerted upon them jointly. Intrications are intricate connections. They are intricate, they affiliate local surfaces of elements with one another by negotiating interstitial rather than internal connections. The heterogeneous elements within a mixture have no proper relation with one another. Likewise, the external force that intricates these elements with one another is outside of the individual elements control or prediction.

Viscous Mixtures

Unlike an architecture of contradictions, superpositions and accidental collisions, pliant systems are capable of engendering

unpredicted connections with contextual, cultural, programmatic, structural and economic contingencies by vicissitude.
Vicissitude is often equated with vacillation, weakness[8] and
indecisiveness but more importantly these characteristics are _changeability_
frequently in the service of a tactical cunning.[9] Vicissitude is _of things_
a quality of being mutable or changeable in response to both
favourable and unfavourable situations that occur by chance.
Vicissitudinous events result from events that are neither arbitrary nor predictable but seem to be accidental. These events
are made possible by a collision of internal motivations with
external forces. For instance, when an accident occurs the
victims immediately identify the forces contributing to the accident and begin to assign blame. It is inevitable however, that
no single element can be made responsible for any accident
as these events occur by vicissitude; a confluence of particular
influences at a particular time makes the outcome of an accident possible. If any element participating in such a confluence
of local forces is altered the nature of the event will change. In
A Thousand Plateaus, Spinoza's concept of "a thousand vicissitudes" is linked with Gregory Bateson's "continuing plateau
of intensity" to describe events which incorporate unpredictable events through intensity. These occurrences are difficult to
localise, difficult to identify.[10] Any logic of vicissitude is dependent on both an intrication of local intensities and the exegetic
pressure exerted on those elements by external contingencies.
Neither the intrications nor the forces which put them into relation are predictable from within any single system. Connections
by vicissitude develop identity through the exploitation of local
adjacencies and their affiliation with external forces. In this
sense, vicissitudinous mixtures become cohesive through a
logic of viscosity.

Viscous fluids develop internal stability in direct proportion to the external pressures exerted upon them. These fluids

behave with two types of viscidity. They exhibit both internal cohesion and adhesion to external elements as their viscosity increases. Viscous fluids begin to behave less like liquids and more like sticky solids as the pressures upon them intensify. Similarly, viscous solids are capable of yielding continually under stress so as not to shear.

Viscous space would exhibit a related cohesive stability in response to adjacent pressures and a stickiness or adhesion to adjacent elements. Viscous relations such as these are not reducible to any single or holistic organisation. Forms of viscosity and pliability cannot be examined outside of the *vicissitudinous* connections and forces with which their deformation is intensively involved. The nature of pliant forms is that they are sticky and flexible. Things tend to adhere to them. As pliant forms are manipulated and deformed the things that stick to their surfaces become incorporated within their interiors.

Curving Away from Deconstructivism

Along with a group of younger architects, the projects that best represent pliancy, not coincidentally, are being produced by many of the same architects previously involved in the valorisation of contradictions. Deconstructivism theorised the world as a site of differences in order that architecture could represent these contradictions in form. This contradictory logic is beginning to soften in order to exploit more fully the particularities of urban and cultural contexts. This is a reasonable transition, as the Deconstructivists originated their projects with the internal discontinuities they uncovered within buildings and sites. These same architects are beginning to employ urban strategies which exploit discontinuities, not by representing them in formal collisions, but by affiliating them with one another though continuous flexible systems.

Just as many of these architects have already been inscribed within a Deconstructivist style of diagonal forms, there will surely be those who would enclose their present work within a Neo-Baroque or even Expressionist style of curved forms. However, many of the formal similitudes suggest a far richer "logic of curvilinearity"[11] that can be characterised by the involvement of outside forces in the development of form. If internally motivated and homogeneous systems were to extend in straight lines, curvilinear developments would result from the incorporation of external influences. Curvilinearity can put into relation the collected projects in this publication [*Architectural Design* 63], Deleuze's *The Fold: Leibniz and the Baroque* and René Thom's catastrophe diagrams. The smooth spaces described by these continuous yet differentiated systems result from curvilinear sensibilities that are capable of complex deformations in response to programmatic, structural, economic, aesthetic, political and contextual influences. This is not to imply that intensive curvature is more politically correct than an uninvolved formal logic, but rather, that a cunning pliability is often more effective through smooth incorporation than contradiction and conflict. Many cunning tactics are aggressive in nature. Whether insidious or ameliorative these kinds of cunning connections discover new possibilities for organisation. A logic of curvilinearity argues for an active involvement with external events in the folding, bending and curving of form.

Already in several Deconstructivist projects are latent suggestions of smooth mixture and curvature. For instance, the Gehry House is typically portrayed as representing materials and forms already present within, yet repressed by, the suburban neighbourhood: sheds, chain-link fences, exposed plywood, trailers, boats and recreational vehicles. The house is described as an "essay on the convoluted relationship between the conflict within and between forms...which were not imported to but emerged from within the house."[12] The house is seen to provoke conflict within the neighbourhood due to its public representation of hidden aspects of its context. The Gehry House violates the neighbourhood from within. Despite the dominant appeal of the house to contradictions, a less contradictory and more pliant reading of the house is possible as a new organisation emerges between the existing house and Gehry's addition. A dynamic stability develops with the mixing of the original and the addition. Despite the contradictions between elements possible points of connection are exploited. Rather than valorise the conflicts the house engenders, as has been done in both academic and popular publications, a more pliant logic would identify, not the degree of violation, but the degree to which new connections were exploited. A new intermediate organisation occurs in the Gehry House by vicissitude from the affiliation of the existing house and its addition. Within the discontinuities of Deconstructivism there are inevitable unforeseen moments of cohesion.

Similarly, Peter Eisenman's Wexner Center is conventionally portrayed as a collision of the conflicting geometries of the campus, city and armoury which once stood adjacent to the site. These contradictions are represented by the diagonal collisions between the two grids and the masonry towers. Despite the disjunctions and discontinuities between these three disparate systems, Eisenman's project has suggested recessive readings of continuous non-linear systems of connection. Robert Somol[13] identifies such a system of Deleuzian rhizomatous connections between armoury and grid. The armoury and diagonal grids are shown by Somol to participate in a hybrid L-movement that organises the main gallery space. Somol's schizophrenic analysis is made possible by, yet does not emanate from within, a Deconstructivist logic of contradiction and conflict. The force of this Deleuzian schizo-analytic model is its ability to maintain multiple organisations simultaneously. In Eisenman's project the tower and grid need not be seen as mutually exclusive or in contradiction. Rather, these disparate elements may be seen as distinct elements co-present within a composite mixture. Pliancy does not result from and is not in line with the previous architectural logic of contradiction, yet it is capable of exploiting many conflicting combinations for the possible connections that are overlooked. Where *Deconstructivist Architecture* was seen to exploit external forces in the familiar name of contradiction and conflict, recent pliant projects by many of these architects exhibit a more fluid logic of connectivity.

Immersed in Context

The contradictory architecture of the last two decades has evolved primarily from highly differentiated, heterogeneous contexts within which conflicting, contradictory and discontinuous buildings were sited. An alternative involvement with heterogeneous contexts could be affiliated, compliant and continuous. Where complexity and contradiction arose previously from inherent contextual conflicts, present attempts are being made to fold smoothly specific locations, materials and programmes into architecture while maintaining their individual identity.

This recent work may be described as being compliant; in a state of being plied by forces beyond control. The projects are formally folded, pliant and supple in order to incorporate their contexts with minimal resistance. Again, this characterisation should not imply flaccidity but a cunning submissiveness that is capable of bending rather than breaking. Compliant tactics, such as these, assume neither an absolute coherence nor cohesion between discrete elements but a system of provisional, intensive, local connections between free elements. Intensity describes the dynamic internalisation and incorporation of external influences into a pliant system. Distinct from a whole organism—to which nothing can be added or subtracted—intensive organisations continually invite external influence within their internal limits so that they might extend their influence through the affiliations they make. A two-fold deterritorialisation, such as this, expands by internalising external forces. This expansion through incorporation is an urban alternative to either the infinite extension of International Modernism, the uniform fabric of Contextualism or the conflicts of Post-Modernism and Deconstructivism. Folded, pliant and supple architectural forms invite exigencies and contingencies in both their deformation and their reception.

In both *Learning from Las Vegas* and *Deconstructivist Architecture*, urban contexts provided rich sites of difference. These differences are presently being exploited for their ability to engender multiple lines of local connections rather than lines of conflict. These affiliations are not predictable by any contextual orders but occur by vicissitude. Here, urban fabric has no value or meaning beyond the connections that are made within it. Distinct from earlier urban sensibilities that generalised broad formal codes, the collected projects develop local, fine grain, complex systems of intrication. There is no general urban strategy common to these projects, only a kind of tactical mutability. These folded, pliant and supple forms of urbanism are neither in deference to nor in defiance of their contexts but exploit them by turning them within their own twisted and curvilinear logics.

The Supple and Curvilinear

1 supple\adj [ME *souple*, fr OF, fr L *supplic-*, *supplex* submissive, suppliant, lit, bending under, fr *sub* + *plic-* (akin to *plicare* to fold)—more at PLY] 1a: compliant often

to the point of obsequiousness b: readily adaptable or responsive to new situations 2a: capable of being bent or folded without creases, cracks or breaks: PLIANT b: able to perform bending or twisting movements with ease and grace: LIMBER c: easy and fluent without stiffness or awkwardness.[14]

At an urban scale, many of these projects seem to be some-where between contextualism and expressionism. Their supple forms are neither geometrically exact nor arbitrarily figural. For example, the curvilinear figures of Shoei Yoh's roof struc-tures are anything but decorative but also resist being reduced to a pure geometric figure. Yoh's supple roof structures exhibit a logic of curvilinearity as they are continuously differentiated according to contingencies. The exigencies of structural span lengths, beam depths, lighting, lateral loading, ceiling height and view angles influence the form of the roof structure. Rather than averaging these requirements within a mean or mini-mum dimension they are precisely maintained by an anexact yet rigorous geometry. Exact geometries are eidetic; they can be reproduced identically at any time by anyone. In this regard, they must be capable of being reduced to fixed mathematical quantities. Inexact geometries lack the precision and rigor nec-essary for measurement.

Anexact geometries, as described by Edmund Husserl,[15] are those geometries which are irreducible yet rigorous. These geometries can be determined with precision yet cannot be reduced to average points or dimensions. Anexact geometries often appear to be merely figural in this regard. Unlike exact geometries, it is meaningless to repeat identically an anexact geometric figure outside of the specific context within which it is situated. In this regard, anexact figures cannot be easily translated.

DEFINITIONS OF "ANEXACT"

Jeffrey Kipnis has argued convincingly that Peter Eisenman's Columbus Convention Center has become a canonical model for the negotiation of differentiated urban fringe sites through the use of near figures.[16] Kipnis identifies the disparate systems informing the Columbus Convention Center including: a single volume of inviolate programme of a uniform shape and height larger than two city blocks, an existing fine grain fabric of commercial buildings and a network of freeway interchanges that plug into the gridded streets of the central business district. Eisenman's project drapes the large rectilinear volume of the convention hall with a series of supple vermiforms. These elements become involved with the train tracks to the north-east, the highway to the south-east and the pedestrian scale of High Street to the west. The project incorporates the multiple scales, programmes, and pedestrian and automotive circulation of a highly differentiated urban context. Kipnis' canonisation of a form which is involved with such specific contextual and programmatic contingencies seems to be frustrated from the beginning. The effects of a pliant urban mixture such as this can only be evaluated by the connections that it makes. Outside of specific contexts, curvature ceases to be intensive. Where the Wexner Center, on the same street in the same city, represents a monumental collision, the Convention Center attempts to disappear by connection between intervals within its context; where the Wexner Center destabilises through contradictions the Convention Center does so by subterfuge.

In a similar fashion Frank Gehry's Guggenheim Museum in Bilbao, Spain covers a series of orthogonal gallery spaces with flexible tubes which respond to the scales of the adjacent roadways, bridges, the Bilbao River and the existing medieval city. Akin to the Vitra Museum, the curvilinear roof forms of the Bilbao Guggenheim integrate the large rectilinear masses of gallery and support space with the scale of the pedestrian and automotive contexts.

The unforeseen connections possible between differentiated sites and alien programmes require conciliatory, complicit, pliant, flexible and often cunning tactics. Presently, numerous architects are involving the heterogeneities, discontinuities and differences inherent within any cultural and physical context by aligning formal flexibility with economic, programmatic and structural compliancy. A multitude of *pli* based words—folded, pliant, supple, flexible, plaited, pleated, plicating, complicitous, compliant, complaisant, complicated, complex and multiplicitous to name a few—can be invoked to describe this emerging urban sensibility of intensive connections.

The Pliant and Bent

pliable\adj [Me fr *plieir* to bend, fold—more at PLY] 1a: supple enough to bend freely or repeatedly without breaking b: yielding readily to others: COMPLAISANT 2: adjustable to varying conditions: ADAPTABLE, *syn* see PLASTIC, *ant* obstinate.[17]

John Rajchman, in reference to Gilles Deleuze's book *Le Pli* has already articulated an affinity between complexity, or *plex*-words, and folding, or plic-words, in the Deleuzian paradigm of "perplexing plications" or "perplication."[18] The plexed and the plied can be seen in a tight knot of complexity and pliancy. Plication involves the folding in of external forces. Complication involves an intricate assembly of these extrinsic particularities into a complex network. In biology, complication is the act of an embryo folding in upon itself as it becomes more complex. To become complicated is to be involved in multiple complex, intricate connections. Where Post-Modernism and Deconstructivism resolve external influences of programme, use, economy and advertising through contradiction, compliancy involves these external forces by knotting, twisting, bending, and folding them within form.

Pliant systems are easily bent, inclined or influenced. An anatomical "plica" is a single strand within multiple "plicae." It is a multiplicity in that it is both one and many simultaneously. These elements are bent along with other elements into a composite, as in matted hair(s). Such a bending together of elements is an act of multiple plication or multiplication rather than mere addition. Plicature involves disparate elements with one another through various manipulations of bending, twisting, pleating, braiding, and weaving through external force. In RAA Um's Croton Aqueduct project a single line following the subterranean water supply for New York City is pulled through multiple disparate programmes which are adjacent to it and which cross it. These programmatic elements are braided and bent within the continuous line of recovered public space which stretches nearly twenty miles into Manhattan. In order to incorporate these elements the line itself is deflected and reoriented, continually changing its character along its length. The seemingly singular line becomes populated by finer programmatic elements. The implications of *Le Pli* for architecture involve the proliferation of possible connections between free entities such as these.

A plexus is a multi-linear network of interweavings, intertwinings and intrications; for instance, of nerves or blood vessels. The complications of a plexus—what could best be called complexity—arise from its irreducibility to any single organisation. A *plexus* describes a multiplicity of local connections within a single continuous system that remains open to new motions and fluctuations. Thus, a plexial event cannot occur at any discrete point. A multiply plexed system—a complex—cannot be reduced to mathematical exactitude, it must be described with rigorous probability. Geometric systems have a distinct character once they have been plied; they exchange fixed co-ordinates for dynamic relations across surfaces.

Alternative types of transformation

Discounting the potential of earlier geometric diagrams of probability, such as Buffon's *Needle Problem*,[19] D'Arcy Thompson provides perhaps the first geometric description of variable deformation as an instance of discontinuous morphological development. His cartesian deformations, and their use of flexible topological rubber sheet geometry, suggest an alternative to the static morphological transformations of autonomous architectural types. A comparison of the typological and transformational systems of Thompson and Rowe illustrates two radically different conceptions of continuity. Rowe's is fixed, exact, striated, identical and static, where Thompson's is dynamic, anexact, smooth, differentiated and stable.

Both Rudolf Wittkower—in his analysis of the Palladian villas of 1949[20]—and Rowe—in his comparative analysis of Palladio and Le Corbusier of 1947[21]—uncover a consistent organisational type: the nine-square grid. In Wittkower's analysis of twelve Palladian villas the particularities of each villa accumulate (through what Edmund Husserl has termed variations) to generate a fixed, identical spatial type (through what could best be described as phenomenological reduction). The typology of this "Ideal Villa" is used to invent a consistent deep structure underlying Le Corbusier's Villa Stein at Garche and Palladio's Villa Malcontenta. Wittkower and Rowe discover the exact geometric structure of this type in all villas in particular. This fixed type become a constant point of reference within a series of variations.

Like Rowe, Thompson is interested in developing a mathematics of species categories, yet his system depends on a dynamic and fluid set of geometric relations. The deformations of a provisional type define a supple constellation of geometric correspondences. Thompson uses the initial type as a mere provision for a dynamic system of transformations that occur in connection with larger environmental forces. Thompson's method of discontinuous development intensively involves external forces in the deformation of morphological types. The flexible type is able to both indicate the general morphological structure of a species while indicating its discontinuous development through the internalisation of heretofore external forces within the system.[22] For instance, the enlargement of a fish's eye is represented by the flexing of a grid. This fluctuation, when compared to a previous position of the transformational type, establishes a relation between water depth and light intensity as those conditions are involved in the formal differences between fish. The flexing grid of relations cannot be arrested at any moment and therefore has the capacity to describe both a general type and the particular events which influence its development. Again, these events are not predictable or reducible to any fixed point but rather begin to describe a probable zone of co-present forces; both internal and external. Thompson presents an alternative type of inclusive stability, distinct from the exclusive stasis of Rowe's nine-square grid. The supple geometry of Thompson is capable of both bending under external forces and folding those forces internally. These transformations develop through discontinuous involution rather than continuous evolution.

The morphing effects used in the contemporary advertising and film industry may already have something in common with recent developments in architecture. These mere images have concrete influences on space, form, politics, and culture; for example, the physical morphing of Michael Jackson's body, including the transformation of his form through various surgeries and his surface through skin bleaching and lightening. These physical effects and their implications for the definition of gender and race were only later represented in his recent video *Black & White*. In this video multiple genders, ethnicities and races are mixed into a continuous sequence through the digital morphing of video images. It is significant that Jackson is not black *or* white but black *and* white, not male *or* female but male *and* female. His simultaneous differences are characteristic of a desire for smoothness; to become heterogeneous yet continuous. Physical morphing, such as this, is monstrous because smoothness eradicates the interval between what Thompson refers to as discriminant characteristics without homogenizing the mixture. Such a continuous system is neither an assembly of discrete fragments nor a whole.[23] With Michael Jackson, the flexible geometric mechanism with which his video representation is constructed comes from the same desire which aggressively reconstructs his own physical form. Neither the theory, the geometry or the body proceed from one another; rather, they participate in a desire for smooth transformation. Form, politics, and self-identity are intricately connected in this process of deformation.

A similar comparison might be made between the liquid mercury man in the film *Terminator 2* and the Peter Lewis House by Frank Gehry and Philip Johnson. The Hollywood special effects sequences allow the actor to both become and disappear into virtually any form. The horror of the film results not from ultra-violence, but from the ability of the antagonist to pass through and occupy the grids of floors, prison bars, and other actors. Computer technology is capable of constructing intermediate images between any two fixed points resulting in a smooth transformation. These smooth effects calculate with probability the interstitial figures between fixed figures. Furthermore, the morphing process is flexible enough that

[handwritten margin note: CONTEMPORARY CULTURE EXAMPLES THAT ARE APPLICABLE TO ARCN. DESIGN/APPROACH]

multiple between states are possible. Gehry's and Johnson's Peter Lewis House is formulated from multiple flexible forms. The geometry of these forms is supple and can accommodate smooth curvilinear deformation along their length. Not only are these forms capable of bending to programmatic, structural and environmental concerns, as is the roof of Shoei Yoh's roof structures, but they can deflect to the contours and context of the site, similar to Peter Eisenman's Columbus Convention Center and RAA Um's Croton Aqueduct project. Furthermore, the Lewis House maintains a series of discrete figural fragments—such as boats and familiar fish—within the diagrams of D'Arcy Thompson, which are important to both the morphing effects of Industrial Light and Magic and the morphogenetic diagrams of René Thom, Gehry's supple geometry is capable of smooth, heterogeneous continuous deformation. Deformation is made possible by the flexibility of topological geometry in response to external events, as smooth space is intensive and continuous. Thompson's curvilinear logic suggests deformation in response to unpredictable events outside of the object. Forms of bending, twisting or folding are not superfluous but result from an intensive curvilinear logic which seeks to internalise cultural and contextual forces within form. In this manner events become intimately involved with particular rather than ideal forms. These flexible forms are not mere representations of differential forces but are deformed by their environment.

Folding and Other Catastrophes for Architecture

3 fold vb [ME *folden*, fr. OE *foaldan*; akin to OHG *faldan* to fold, Gk di *plasios* twofold] vt 1: to lay one part over another part, 2: to reduce the length or bulk of by doubling over, 3: to clasp together: ENTWINE, 4: to clasp or embrace

closely: EMBRACE, 5: to bend (as a rock) into folds, 6: to incorporate (a food ingredient) into a mixture by repeated gentle overturnings without stirring or beating, 7: to bring to an end.[24]

Philosophy has already identified the displacement presently occurring to the Post-Modern paradigm of complexity and contradiction in architecture, evidenced by John Rajchman's *Out of the Fold* and *Perplications*. Rajchman's text is not a manifesto for the development of new architectural organisations, but responds to the emergence of differing kinds of complexity being developed by a specific architect. His essays inscribe spatial innovations developed in architecture within larger intellectual and cultural fields. Rajchman both illuminates Peter Eisenman's architectural practice through an explication of *Le Pli* and is forced to reconsider Deleuze's original argument concerning Baroque space by the alternative spatialities of Eisenman's Rebstock Park project. The dominant aspect of the project which invited Rajchman's attention to folding was the employment of one of René Thom's catastrophe diagrams in the design process.

Despite potential protestations to the contrary, it is more than likely that Thom's catastrophe nets entered into the architecture of Carsten Juel-Christiansen's Die Anhalter Faltung, Peter Eisenman's Rebstock Park, Jeffrey Kipnis' Unite de Habitation at Briey installation and Bahram Shirdel's Nara Convention Hall as a mere formal technique. Inevitably, architects and philosophers alike would find this in itself a catastrophe for all concerned. Yet, their use illustrates that at least four architects simultaneously found in Thom's diagrams a formal device for an alternative description of spatial complexity. The kind of complexity engendered by this alliance with Thom is substantially different than the complexity provided by either Venturi's decorated shed or the more recent conflicting forms of Deconstructivism. Topological geometry in general, and the catastrophe diagrams in particular, deploy disparate forces on a continuous surface within which more or less open systems of connection are possible.

⌈ "Topology considers superficial structures susceptible to continuous transformations which easily change their form, the most interesting geometric properties common to all modification being studied. Assumed is an abstract material of ideal deformability which can be deformed, with the exception of disruption." ⌉

These geometries bend and stabilise with viscosity under pressure. Where one would expect that an architect looking at catastrophes would be interested in conflicts, ironically, architects are finding new forms of dynamic stability in these diagrams. The mutual interest in Thom's diagrams points to a desire to be involved with events which they cannot predict. The primary innovation made by those diagrams is the geometric modelling of a multiplicity of possible co-present events at any moment. Thom's morphogenesis engages seemingly random events with mathematical probability.

Thom's nets were developed to describe catastrophic events. What is common to these events is an inability to define exactly the moment at which a catastrophe occurs. This loss of exactitude is replaced by a geometry of multiple probable relations. With relative precision, the diagrams define potential catastrophes through cusps rather than fixed co-ordinates. Like any simple graph, Thom's diagrams deploy X and Y forces across two axes of a gridded plane. A uniform plane would provide the potential for only a single point of intersection between any two X and Y co-ordinates. The supple topological surface of Thom's diagrams is capable of enfolding in multiple dimensions. Within these folds, or cusps, zones of proximity are contained.

As the topological surface folds over and into itself multiple possible points of intersection are possible at any moment in the Z dimension. These co-present Z-dimensional zones are possible because the topological geometry captures space within its surface. Through proximity and adjacency various vectors of force begin to imply these intensive event zones. In catastrophic events there is not a single fixed point at which a catastrophe occurs but rather a zone of potential events that are described by these cusps. The cusps are defined by multiple possible interactions implying, with more or less probability, multiple fluid thresholds. Thom's geometric plexus organises disparate forces in order to describe possible types of connections.

If there is a single dominant effect of the French word *pli*, it is its resistance to being translated into any single term. It is precisely the formal manipulations of folding that are capable of incorporating manifold external forces and elements within form, yet *Le Pli* undoubtedly risks being translated into architecture as mere folded figures. In architecture, folded forms risk quickly becoming a sign for catastrophe. The success of the architects who are folding should not be based on their ability to represent catastrophe theory in architectural form. Rather, the topological geometries, in connection with the probable events they model, present a flexible system for the organisation of disparate elements within continuous spaces. Yet, these smooth systems are highly differentiated by cusps or zones of co-presence. The catastrophe diagram used by Eisenman in the Rebstock Park project destabilises the way that the buildings meet the ground. It smoothes the landscape and the building by turning both into one another along cusps. The diagrams used by Kipnis in the Briey project, and Shirdel in the Nara Convention Hall, develop an interstitial space contained simultaneously within two folded cusps. This geometrically blushed surface exists within two systems at the same moment and in this manner presents a space of co-presence with multiple adjacent zones of proximity.

Before the introduction of either Deleuze or Thom to architecture, folding was developed as a formal tactic in response to problems presented by the exigencies of commercial development. Henry Cobb has argued in both the *Charlottesville Tapes* and his *Note on Folding* for a necessity to both dematerialise and differentiate the massive homogeneous volumes dictated by commercial development in order to bring them into relation with finer grain heterogeneous urban conditions. His first principle for folding is a smoothing of elements across a shared surface. The facade of the John Hancock Tower is smoothed into a continuous surface so that the building might disappear into its context through reflection rather than mimicry. Any potential for replicating the existing context was precluded by both the size of the contiguous floor plates required by the developer and the economic necessity to construct the building's skin from glass panels. Folding became the method by which the surface of a large homogeneous volume could be differentiated while remaining continuous. This tactic acknowledges that the existing fabric and the developer tower are essentially of different species by placing their differences in mixture, rather than contradiction, through the manipulation of a pliant skin.

Like the John Hancock Building, the Allied Bank Tower begins with the incorporation of glass panels and metal frame into a continuous folded surface. The differentiation of the folded surface, through the simultaneous bending of the glass and metal, brings those elements together in a continuous plane. The manipulations of the material surface proliferate folding and bending effects in the massing of the building. The alien building becomes a continuous surface of disappearance that both diffracts and reflects the context through complex manipulations of folding. In the recent films *Predator* and

Predator II, a similar alien is capable of disappearing into both urban and jungle environments, not through cubist camouflage[25] but by reflecting and diffracting its environment like an octopus or chameleon. The contours between an object and its context are obfuscated by forms which become translucent, reflective and diffracted. The alien gains mobility by cloaking its volume in a folded surface of disappearance. Unlike the "decorated shed" or "building board" which mimics its context with a singular sign, folding diffuses an entire surface through a shimmering reflection of local adjacent and contiguous particularities. For instance, there is a significant difference between a small fish which represents itself as a fragment of a larger fish through the figure of a large eye on its tail, and a barracuda which becomes like the liquid in which it swims through a diffused reflection of its context. The first strategy invites deceitful detection where the second uses stealth to avoid detection. Similarly, the massive volume of the Allied Bank Tower situates itself within a particular discontinuous locale by cloaking itself in a folded reflected surface. Here, cunning stealth is used as a way of involving contextual forces through the manipulation of a surface. The resemblance of folded architecture to the stealth bomber results not from a similarity between military and architectural technologies or intentions but rather from a tactical disappearance[26] of a volume through the manipulation of a surface. This disappearance into the fold is neither insidious nor innocent but merely a very effective tactic.

Like Henry Cobb, Peter Eisenman introduces a fold as a method of disappearing into a specific context. Unlike Cobb, who began with a logic of construction, Eisenman aligns the fold with the urban contours of the Rebstock Park. The repetitive typologies of housing and office buildings are initially deployed on the site in a more or less functionalist fashion; then a topological net derived from Thom's Butterfly net is aligned to the perimeter of the site and pushed through the typological bars. This procedure differentiates the uniform bars in response to the global morphology of the site. In this manner the manifestation of the fold is in the incorporation of differences—derived from the morphology of the site—into the homogeneous typologies of the housing and office blocks. Both Eisenman's local differentiation of the building types by global folding, and Cobb's local folding across constructional elements which globally differentiates each floor plate and the entire massing of the building are effective. Cobb and Eisenman "animate" homogenous organisations that were seemingly given to the architect—office tower and *siedlung*—with the figure of a fold. The shared principle of folding identified by both Eisenman and Cobb, evident in their respective texts, is the ability to differentiate the inherited homogeneous organisations of both Modernism (Eisenman's *siedlung*) and commercial development (Cobb's tower). This differentiation of known types of space and organisation has something in common with Deleuze's delimitation of folding in architecture within the Baroque. Folding heterogeneity into known typologies renders those organisations more smooth and more intensive so that they are better able to incorporate disparate elements within a continuous system. Shirdel's use of Thom's diagrams is quite interesting as the catastrophe sections do not animate an existing organisation. Rather, they begin as merely one system among three others. The convention halls float within the envelope of the building as they are supported by a series of transverse structural walls whose figure is derived from Thom's nets. This mixture of systems, supported by the catastrophe sections, generates a massive residual public space at the ground floor of the building. In Shirdel's project the manipulations of folding, in both the catastrophe sections and the building envelope, incorporate previously unrelated elements into a mixture. The space between the theatres, the skin and the lateral structural walls is such a space of mixture and intrication.

With structure itself, Chuck Hoberman is capable of transforming the size of domes and roofs through a folding structural mechanism. Hoberman develops adjustable structures whose differential movements occur through the dynamic transformation of flexible continuous systems. The movements of these mechanisms are determined both by use and structure. Hoberman's structural mechanisms develop a system of smooth transformation in two ways. The Iris dome and sphere projects transform their size while maintaining their shape. This flexibility of size within the static shape of the stadium is capable of supporting new kinds of events. The patented tiling patterns transform both the size and shape of surfaces, developing local secondary pockets of space and enveloping larger primary volumes.

So far in architecture, Deleuze's, Cobb's, Eisenman's and Hoberman's discourse inherits dominant typologies of organisation into which new elements are folded. Within these activities of folding it is perhaps more important to identify those new forms of local organisation and occupation which inhabit the familiar types of the Latin cross church, the *siedlung*, the office tower and the stadium, rather than the disturbances visited on those old forms of organisation. Folding can occur in both the organisations of old forms and the free intensities of unrelated elements as is the case with Shirdel's project. Likewise, other than folding, there are several manipulations of elements engendering smooth, heterogeneous and intensive organisation.

[Despite the differences between these practices, they share a sensibility that resists cracking or breaking in response to external pressures. These tactics and strategies are all com*pli*ant to, com*pli*cated by, and com*pli*cit with external forces in manners which are: submissive, suppliant, adaptable, contingent, responsive, fluent, and yielding through involvement and incorporation.] The attitude which runs throughout this collection of projects and essays is the shared attempt to place seemingly disparate forces into relation through strategies which are externally plied. Perhaps, in this regard only, there are many opportunities for architecture to be effected by Gilles Deleuze's book *Le Pli*. The formal character tics of pliancy—anexact forms and topological geometries primarily—can be more viscous and fluid in response to exigencies. They maintain formal integrity through deformations which do not internally cleave or shear but through which they connect, incorporate and affiliate productively. Cunning and viscous systems such as these gain strength through flexible connections that occur by vicissitude. If the collected projects within this publication do have certain formal affinities, it is as a result of a folding out of formalism into a world of external influences. Rather than speak of the forms of folding autonomously, it is important to maintain a logic rather than a style of curvilinearity. The formal affinities of these projects result from their pliancy and ability to deform in response to particular contingencies. What is being asked in different ways by the group of architects and theorists in this publication is: How can architecture be configured as a complex system into which external particularities are already found to be plied?

NEW POSITION; NOT DECONST. BUT EXAMPLES (EISENMAN + GHERY) SEEM TO BE VERY DECONSTRUCTIVIST & POST MODERN

Notes

1   Robert Venturi, *Complexity and Contradiction in Architecture* (New York: Museum of Modern Art Papers on Architecture, 1966).

2   Two ideas were introduced in this text that seem extremely relevant to contemporary architecture: typological deformation and the continuity between objects and contexts. Both of these concepts receded when compared with the dominant ideas of *collision cities* and the dialectic of urban *figure/ground* relationships. Curiously, they illustrate typological deformations in both Baroque and early modern architecture: "However, Asplund's play with assumed contingencies and assumed absolutes, brilliant though it may be, does seem to involve mostly strategies of response; and, in considering problems of the object, it may be useful to consider the admittedly ancient technique of deliberately *distorting* what is also presented as the *ideal* type. So the reading of Saint Agnese *continuously fluctuates between* an interpretation of the building as *object* and the building as *texture*...Note this type of strategy combines local concessions with a declaration of independence from anything local and specific." 77.

3   See Sanford Kwinter and Jonathan Crary, "Foreword," *Zone 6: Incorporations* (New York: Urzone Books, 1992), 12–15.

4   Gilles Deleuze, *A Thousand Plateaus: Capitalism and Schizophrenia* (Minneapolis, Minn.: University of Minnesota Press, 1987), 478.

5   Mark Wigley and Philip Johnson, *Deconstructivist Architecture: The Museum of Modern Art, New York* (Boston: Little, Brown, 1988), 15.

6   Marion Cunningham, *The Fannie Farmer Cookbook*, 13th edition (New York: Alfred A. Knopf, 1990), 41–47.

7   Deleuze, *Plateaus*, 475–6.

8   An application of vicissitude to Kipnis' logic of undecidability and weak form might engender a cunning logic of non-linear affiliations. This seems apt given the reference to both undecidability and weakness in the definition of vicissitudes.

9   Ann Bergren's discussions of the *metis* in architecture is an example of cunning manipulations of form. For an alternative reading of these tactics in Greek art also see Jean-Pierre Vernant.

10   Deleuze, *Plateaus*, 256.

11   This concept has been developed by Leibniz and has many resonances with Sanford Kwinter's discussions of biological space and epigenesis

as they relate to architecture and Catherine Ingraham's logic of the swerve and the animal lines of beasts of burden.

12   Wigley, *Deconstructivist Architecture*, 22.

13   See "O-O" by Robert Somol in the *Wexner Center for the Visual Arts*, special issue of *Architectural Design* (London: Academy Editions, 1990).

14   *Webster's New Collegiate Dictionary* (Springfield, Mass.: G&C Merriam Company, 1977), 1170

15   Edmund Husserl, *"The Origin of Geometry"* in *Edmund Husserl's Origin of Geometry: An Introduction*, trans. Jacques Derrida (Lincoln, Neb.: University of Nebraska Press, 1989).

16   See *Fetish*, ed. Sarah Whiting, Edward Mitchell, and Greg Lynn (New York: Princeton Architectural Press, 1992), 158–173.

17   *Webster's*, 883.

18   Rajchman identifies an inability in contexualism to "Index the complexifications of urban space." John Rajchman, "Perplications: On the Space and Time of Rebstock Park," in *Unfolding Frankfurt* (Berlin: Ernst & Sohn Verlag, 1991), 21.

19   A similar exchange, across disciplines through geometry, occurred in France in the mid-18th century with the development of probable geometries. Initially there was a desire to describe chance events with mathematical precision. This led to the development of a geometric model that subsequently opened new fields of study in other disciplines. The mathematical interests in probability of the professional gambler Marquis de Chevalier influenced Comte de Buffon to develop the geometric description of the *Needle Problem*. This geometric model of probability was later elaborated in three dimensions by the geologist Dellese and became the foundation for nearly all of the present day anatomical descriptions that utilise serial transactions: including CAT scan, X-Ray, and PET technologies. For a more elaborate discussion of these exchanges and the impact of related probable and anexact geometries on architectural space refer to my [A. Krista Sykes] forthcoming article in *NY Magazine no. 1* (New York: Rizzoli International, 1993).

20   Rudolf Wittkower, *Architectural Principles in the Age of Humanism* (New York: WW Norton, 1971).

21   Colin Rowe, *Mathematics of the Ideal Villa and Other Essays* (Cambridge, Mass.: MIT Press, 1976).

22 For an earlier instance of discontinuous development based on environmental forces and co-evolution, in reference to dynamic variation, see William Bateson, *Materials for the Study of Variation: Treated with Especial Regard to Discontinuity in the Origin of Species* (Baltimore: Johns Hopkins University Press, 1894).

23 Erwin Panofsky has provided perhaps the finest example of this kind of heterogeneous smoothness in his analyses of Egyptian statuary and the Sphinx in particular: "three different systems of proportion were employed—an anomaly easily explained by the fact that the organism in question is not a homogeneous but a heterogeneous one."

24 *Webster's*, 445.

25 In Stan Allen's introduction to the work of Douglas Garofalo forthcoming in *Assemblage 19* (Cambridge, Mass.: MIT Press, 1992) a strategy of camouflage is articulated which invests surfaces with alternatives to the forms and volumes they delimit. The representation of other known figures is referred to as a logic of plumage. For instance, a butterfly wing representing the head of a bird invites a deceitful detection. This differs from the disappearance of a surface by stealth which resists any recognition.

26 This suggests a reading of Michael Hays' text on the early Mies van der Rohe Friedrichstrasse Tower [unbuilt] as a tactic of disappearance by proliferating cacophonous images of the city. Hays' work on Hannes Meyer's *United Nations Competition Entry* is perhaps the most critical in the reinterpretation of functional contingencies in the intensely involved production of differentiated, heterogeneous yet continuous space through manipulations of a surface.

INTRODUCTION
Charter of the New Urbanism / *Congress for the New Urbanism*

In the later decades of the twentieth century, New Urbanism emerged as an urban design movement in favor of mixed-use, mixed-income, socially diverse, high-density, pedestrian-friendly neighborhoods, as well as sustainable and site-specific design. The focus of New Urbanism tends to be on the creation of community through a traditionally structured town center, rejecting the human dispersal and environmental damage caused by suburban sprawl and reliance on the automobile.

In 1993 a group of architects, including Andrés Duany, Elizabeth Plater-Zyberk, and Peter Calthorpe, founded the Congress for the New Urbanism (CNU). The Charter of the New Urbanism, ratified at the fourth annual conference in 1996, outlines the guiding philosophy of this planning strategy. As the charter states, "neighborhoods should be diverse in use and population; communities should be designed for the pedestrian and transit as well as the car; cities and towns should be shaped by physically defined and universally accessible public spaces and community institutions; urban places should be framed by architecture and landscape design that celebrate local history, climate, ecology, and building practice." Of utmost importance is the coordinated effort of design, public policy, and development practices; New Urbanists recognize that appropriate government infrastructure, zoning codes, and ordinances are all crucial to the success of an urban design. With this in mind, the charter details the multiple scales of our urban environment, from the metropolitan region down to the individual building, alongside concepts that should govern their growth and development.

New Urbanism has been quite controversial, due in part to what many perceive to be its prescriptive, conservative, and potentially nostalgic philosophy.[1] Nevertheless, in the past thirty years the movement has gained a respectable following, currently boasting worldwide membership of over three thousand individuals, including designers, planners, government officials, lawyers, and academics. Perhaps this popularity stems from New Urbanism offering what many architectural philosophies do not: a clear, direct mandate on possible ways to improve the built landscape and society in which we live.

Note

1   See "Seaside and the Real World: A Debate on American Urbanism," ANY 1 (July/Aug. 1993), based on an event held by the Anyone Corporation in April 1993 during which a debate on Seaside, a paradigmatic New Urbanist town, took place.

CHARTER OF
THE NEW URBANISM

First appeared at http://www.cnu.org/charter. Courtesy of
Congress for the New Urbanism, copyright 1996.

The Congress for the New Urbanism views disinvestment in central cities, the spread of placeless sprawl, increasing separation by race and income, environmental deterioration, loss of agricultural lands and wilderness, and the erosion of society's built heritage as one interrelated community-building challenge.

We stand for the restoration of existing urban centers and towns within coherent metropolitan regions, the reconfiguration of sprawling suburbs into communities of real neighborhoods and diverse districts, the conservation of natural environments, and the preservation of our built legacy.

We recognize that physical solutions by themselves will not solve social and economic problems, but neither can economic vitality, community stability, and environmental health be sustained without a coherent and supportive physical framework.

We advocate the restructuring of public policy and development practices to support the following principles: neighborhoods should be diverse in use and population; communities should be designed for the pedestrian and transit as well as the car; cities and towns should be shaped by physically defined and universally accessible public spaces and community institutions; urban places should be framed by architecture and landscape design that celebrate local history, climate, ecology, and building practice.

We represent a broad-based citizenry, composed of public and private sector leaders, community activists, and multidisciplinary professionals. We are committed to reestablishing the relationship between the art of building and the making of community, through citizen-based participatory planning and design.

We dedicate ourselves to reclaiming our homes, blocks, streets, parks, neighborhoods, districts, towns, cities, regions, and environment.

We assert the following principles to guide public policy, development practice, urban planning, and design:

The region: Metropolis, city, and town

1. Metropolitan regions are finite places with geographic boundaries derived from topography, watersheds, coastlines, farmlands, regional parks, and river basins. The metropolis is made of multiple centers that are cities, towns, and villages, each with its own identifiable center and edges.

[handwritten margin note: CITY HAS TO FIT INTO ECONOMIC SYSTEM]

2. The metropolitan region is a fundamental economic unit of the contemporary world. Governmental cooperation, public policy, physical planning, and economic strategies must reflect this new reality.

3. The metropolis has a necessary and fragile relationship to its agrarian hinterland and natural landscapes. The relationship is environmental, economic, and cultural. Farmland and nature are as important to the metropolis as the garden is to the house.

4. Development patterns should not blur or eradicate the edges of the metropolis. Infill development within existing urban areas conserves environmental resources, economic investment, and social fabric, while reclaiming marginal and abandoned areas. Metropolitan regions should develop strategies to encourage such infill development over peripheral expansion.

5. Where appropriate, new development contiguous to urban boundaries should be organized as neighborhoods and districts and be integrated with the existing urban pattern. Noncontiguous development should be organized as towns and villages with their own urban edges and planned for a jobs/housing balance, not as bedroom suburbs.

6. The development and redevelopment of towns and cities should respect historical patterns, precedents, and boundaries.

7. Cities and towns should bring into proximity a broad spectrum of public and private uses to support a regional economy that benefits people of all incomes. Affordable housing should be distributed throughout the region to match job opportunities and to avoid concentrations of poverty.

8. The physical organization of the region should be supported by a framework of transportation alternatives. Transit, pedestrian, and bicycle systems should maximize access and mobility throughout the region while reducing dependence upon the automobile.

9. Revenues and resources can be shared more cooperatively among the municipalities and centers within regions to avoid destructive competition for tax base and to promote rational coordination of transportation, recreation, public services, housing, and community institutions.

MASS
TRANSIT

The neighborhood, the district, and the corridor

1. The neighborhood, the district, and the corridor are the essential elements of development and redevelopment in the metropolis. They form identifiable areas that encourage citizens to take responsibility for their maintenance and evolution.

2. Neighborhoods should be compact, pedestrian-friendly, and mixed-use. Districts generally emphasize a special single use and should follow the principles of neighborhood design when possible. Corridors are regional connectors of neighborhoods and districts; they range from boulevards and rail lines to rivers and parkways.

3. Many activities of daily living should occur within walking distance, allowing independence to those who do not drive, especially the elderly and the young. Interconnected networks of streets should be designed to encourage walking, to reduce the number and length of automobile trips, and to conserve energy.

4. Within neighborhoods, a broad range of housing types and price levels can bring people of diverse ages, races, and incomes into daily interaction, strengthening the personal and civic bonds essential to an authentic community.

5. Transit corridors, when properly planned and coordinated, can help organize metropolitan structure and revitalize urban centers. In contrast, highway corridors should not displace investment from existing centers.

6. Appropriate building densities and land uses should be within walking distance of transit stops, permitting public transit to become a viable alternative to the automobile.

7. Concentrations of civic, institutional, and commercial activity should be embedded in neighborhoods and districts, not isolated in remote, single-use complexes. Schools should be sized and located to enable children to walk or bicycle to them.

8. The economic health and harmonious evolution of neighborhoods, districts, and corridors can be improved through

graphic urban design codes that serve as predictable guides for change.

9. A range of parks, from tot-lots and village greens to ball-fields and community gardens, should be distributed within neighborhoods. Conservation areas and open lands should be used to define and connect different neighborhoods and districts.

The block, the street, and the building

1. A primary task of all urban architecture and landscape design is the physical definition of streets and public spaces as places of shared use.

2. Individual architectural projects should be seamlessly linked to their surroundings. This issue transcends style.

3. The revitalization of urban places depends on safety and security. The design of streets and buildings should reinforce safe environments, but not at the expense of accessibility and openness.

4. In the contemporary metropolis, development must adequately accommodate automobiles. It should do so in ways that respect the pedestrian and the form of public space.

5. Streets and squares should be safe, comfortable, and interesting to the pedestrian. Properly configured, they encourage walking and enable neighbors to know each other and protect their communities.

6. Architecture and landscape design should grow from local climate, topography, history, and building practice.

7. Civic buildings and public gathering places require important sites to reinforce community identity and the culture of democracy. They deserve distinctive form, because their role is different from that of other buildings and places that constitute the fabric of the city.

8. All buildings should provide their inhabitants with a clear sense of location, weather, and time. Natural methods of heating and cooling can be more resource-efficient than mechanical systems.

9. Preservation and renewal of historic buildings, districts, and landscapes affirm the continuity and evolution of urban society.

INTRODUCTION
Thoughts on the Everyday / *Deborah Berke*

In "Thoughts on the Everyday," Deborah Berke, a New York-based architect and an associate professor at Yale, voices concern over "the usurpation of the everyday by advertising." This extends to architecture with its prevalence of "name-brand architects" and "signature buildings," trends that have grown even stronger in the twenty-first century. In place of "high-profile celebrity products," Berke advocates an architecture of the everyday that is ultimately beholden to practical realities of the discipline—a privileging of the occupants via the consideration of program and materiality.

Berke offers possible characteristics of an everyday architecture including "generic," "common," and "vulgar"—terms that recall Robert Venturi and Denise Scott Brown's pleas for "ugly and ordinary architecture."[1] Yet, in a crucial way, Berke's position differs quite dramatically from that of Venturi and Scott Brown, namely in their respective approaches to popular culture. Scott Brown (like Alison and Peter Smithson before her) looked to advertising as a source of information about what people desire.[2] Berke, however, refuses to equate "successful marketing" with "'popular' culture," questioning the relationship between the everyday and mass culture.

The concluding essay of *Architecture of the Everyday*, Berke and Steven Harris's edited collection of 1997, "Thoughts on the Everyday" reads as part journal entry, and part manifesto, echoing the candor of the former without the pretension of the latter. While espousing the potential virtues of an architecture of the everyday, Berke's text also serves as a critique of the "paper architecture" of the previous decades as well as theoretical musings on architecture that remain conceptual. The language used throughout her "thoughts" leaves little doubt as to Berke's allegiance; for while architecture of the everyday "may" be "banal," "crude,"

70

and "visceral," such architecture "is functional." Above all, "the architecture of the everyday is built."

An architecture of the everyday, while attractive in its rejection of star architecture, megalomaniacal architects, and rampant commercial culture, is also problematic in that, aside from generalities, such an architecture is difficult to define; indeed, to outline a prescriptive code for an architecture of the everyday runs counter to the desired result. Berke acknowledges as much, leaving the reader to struggle with the lingering—and perhaps unanswerable—question of "what, indeed, is an architecture of the everyday?"

Notes

1   See Robert Venturi, Denise Scott Brown, and Steven Izenour, *Learning from Las Vegas*, rev. ed. (1972; Cambridge, Mass.: MIT Press ,1977).

2   Denise Scott Brown, "Learning from Pop," *Casabella* 359/60 (Dec. 1971): 15–23; and Alison Smithson and Peter Smithson, "Today We Collect Ads," *ARK* 18 (Nov. 1956).

DEBORAH BERKE

THOUGHTS ON
THE EVERYDAY

First appeared in *Architecture of the Everyday* (New York: Princeton Architectural Press, 1997), 222–26. Courtesy of Deborah Berke.

We exist in a culture where heroes have been replaced by celebrities, and fifteen minutes of fame are valued over a lifetime of patient work. In this climate the architect must become a celebrity in order to gain the opportunity to build (or else must loudly proclaim a refusal to build in order to become established as a critical force). Those who do build tend to produce signature buildings designed to attract the attention of the media and sustain the public's focus, for under these rules architecture can only emanate from the hand of the name-brand architect. The built environment is strewn with these high-profile celebrity products—heroic gestures neither made nor commissioned by heroes.

What should architects do instead? A simple and direct response: acknowledge the needs of the many rather than the few; address diversity of class, race, culture, and gender; design without allegiance to *a priori* architectural styles or formulas, and with concern for program and construction.

We may call the result an architecture of the everyday, though an architecture of the everyday resists strict definition; any rigorous attempt at a concise delineation will inevitably lead to contradictions. Nonetheless, here are some points that may be related to it.

An Architecture of the Everyday May Be Generic and Anonymous.

Much like the package in the supermarket with the black letters on the white ground that does not carry a brand name—but is still a perfectly good container for its contents—the generic does not flaunt its maker. It is straightforward. Unostentatious, it can lurk, loiter, slip beneath the surface, and bypass the controls of institutionally regulated life.

An Architecture of the Everyday May Be Banal or Common.

It does not seek distinction by trying to be extraordinary, which in any case usually results in a fake or substitute for the truly extraordinary. In its mute refusal to say "look at me," it does not tell you what to think. It permits you to provide your own meaning.

An Architecture of the Everyday May Therefore Be Quite Ordinary.

It is blunt, direct, and unselfconscious. It celebrates the potential for inventiveness within the ordinary and is thereby genuinely "of its moment." It may be influenced by market trends, but it resists being defined or consumed by them.

An Architecture of the Everyday May Be Crude.

There is a freshness to things that are raw and unrefined. Buildings that are conceived without polish may be rough, but "rough and ready."

An Architecture of the Everyday May Be Sensual.

The everyday world is sensual. It not only provokes sight but also touch, hearing, smell. The architecture of the everyday encompasses places known by their aroma, surfaces recognizable by their tactile qualities, positions established by echo and reverberation.

An Architecture of the Everyday May Also Be Vulgar and Visceral.

While vulgarity may seem the opposite of anonymity, both are often oblivious to external standards. This is not necessarily bad: standards of taste serve to legislate and perpetuate an approved set of objects. The vulgar rejects good taste and the unthinking obedience it demands.

In architecture, standards of good taste seem to dictate that the presence of the body not be acknowledged in or by buildings. Architectural photographs rarely show people, and the true user is often ignored by the architect. The result is sterility. Visceral presence cannot be denied.

An Architecture of the Everyday Acknowledges Domestic Life.

There is poetry and consolation in the repetition of familiar things. This is not to romanticize dreary and oppressive routine; events need not be dictated and programmed by architects. An architecture of the everyday allows for personal rites but avoids prescribing rituals.

An Architecture of the Everyday May Take on Collective and Symbolic Meaning but It Is Not Necessarily Monumental.

Without denying the need for monuments, it questions whether every building need be one.

An Architecture of the Everyday Responds to Program and Is Functional.

It is a form of design in which program contributes meaning, and function is a requirement to satisfy rather than a style to emulate. It resists debasement into winsome reproductions of another time in the name of "the vernacular" or simplistic contextualism.

An Architecture of the Everyday May Change as Quickly as Fashion, but It Is Not Always Fashionable.

If the idea of an architecture of the everyday currently seems both a little too fashionable and a little too much like fashion, note that the real architecture of the everyday is subject to different forces of change from those that drive fashion. The forms, materials, and images of innovation in everyday life are often unpredictable. The next everyday cannot be discovered through focus groups and market analysis.

The Architecture of the Everyday is Built.

* * *

The initial impetus to search for a definition of an architecture of the everyday evolved from an ongoing conversation I had with Steven Harris as we traveled together to New Haven from New York City and back, twice a week, for nine years. Having been friends for almost twenty years, our conversations were familiar and comfortable, often filled with gossip or reminiscences. Our commute took us on Interstate-95, the easternmost north–south run of the grid of interstates that define long-distance automobile travel in the United States.

In retrospect, I-95 was a pretty good place to have a twice-a-week conversation on the everyday, it being such an everyday condition itself; a wide asphalt line on the ground for the transport of people and goods. Over the years of our shared commute, the nameless food and fuel stops became McDonald's and Mobil stations—a transformation to name-brandness apparently sanctioned by some turnpike authority. Similarly, the exclusive suburban residential developments just off the highway grew evermore extravagant as the ready dollars of the 1980s purchased houses that were absurd amalgams of aspirational imagery and bombastic size. Our ongoing observation seemed to find that the banal landscape, the fuel for our conversation on (and subsequent teaching of) the everyday, was each day becoming less anonymous and certainly less banal.

We realized that the replacement of the ordinary by the brand-nameable was not an innocent transformation of the everyday, but rather the usurpation of the everyday by advertising. To confuse ubiquitous logos with generic identity was to mistake successful marketing for "popular" culture. Indeed, today even the idea of popular culture bears an ambiguous relationship to the everyday. So often it seems to be merely the way the everyday appears on high culture's radar screen.

Of course, every aspect of reality is mediated in some way. But the everyday may still be the place that is least mediated by the forces that seek to limit or absorb its vitality. This is the promise it holds. For architects this is a cautionary tale and a genuine opportunity. We are invited to enter into the real and the good aspects of everyday life, but we must do so without destroying it.

In the opening paragraphs of her 1964 essay "Notes on Camp," Susan Sontag writes: "It's embarrassing to be solemn and treatise-like about Camp. One runs the risk of having, oneself, produced a very inferior piece of Camp." I feel that the same could be said of trying to make or write about an architecture of the everyday. The difference between an "architecture of the

everyday" and everyday buildings lies precisely in the consciousness of the act of making architecture. This is precisely where
the strategy I am proposing is most susceptible to criticism, a
fact of which I am well aware. An architect cannot pretend to
be naive. Architecture is not innocent. Likewise, the making of
architecture is a highly conscious, indeed a self-conscious, act.
But the everyday is also not naive. To assume so would be to confuse it with a sugary and debased notion of the vernacular—with
nostalgia for some state of original purity or innocence. The
everyday flirts, dangerously at times, with mass culture. But the
everyday remains that which has not yet been co-opted.

INTRODUCTION
Mach 1 (and Other Mystic Visitations) / *Sanford Kwinter*

Few buildings in the past decades have been greeted with as much adulation as was Frank Gehry's Guggenheim Museum in Bilbao, Spain. The building opened in October 1997, but as *New York Times* architectural critic Herbert Muschamp noted that fall in an article entitled "The Miracle of Bilbao," "people [had] been flocking to Bilbao for nearly two years, just to watch the building's skeleton take shape." Muschamp further commented on the phenomenon of the building's popularity: "'Have you been to Bilbao?' In architectural circles, that question has acquired the status of a shibboleth. Have you seen the light? Have you seen the future?"[1] Indeed, both the public and many within the architectural community praised Gehry's latest work. However, Sanford Kwinter, an architectural theorist, writer, and professor, offers an alternative reading of the Guggenheim Bilbao. In "Mach 1 (and Other Mystic Visitations)," Kwinter argues that while the museum may be an accomplishment in its own right, the fanfare surrounding its reception conveys a larger truth about the complacent and normative state of the architectural discipline in the late twentieth century.

In the early 1900s, modern architects' imaginations were captured by the ocean liner—its efficiency, the correspondence between form and function, the technology that made its production possible. (Recall Le Corbusier's enthrallment with the ship as discussed in 1923's *Vers une Architecture*: "our daring and masterly constructors of steamships produce palaces in comparison with which cathedrals are tiny things, and they throw them on to the sea!"[2]). This fascination accompanied an experimental era of architectural design. Yet, at the turn of the twenty-first century, Kwinter feels that this sense of exploration—adventurousness that pushes the boundaries of accepted norms—thrives only in other contemporary realms of design. Architecture may borrow materials, software programs, and production systems from the aeronautical industry, but the "experimental" spirit of the architectural discipline has been subsumed by "pseudo-innovation," and architecture is left rehearsing "variations on familiar themes." Indeed, is not the Guggenheim Bilbao often compared to a ship, its metallic form soaring above the Nervión River? Titanium cladding and radical curvature aside, how far has architecture actually come from Le Corbusier's ship adoration?

Bilbao may be a remarkable social phenomenon, but in Kwinter's opinion, it is not an architectural masterpiece, nor is it architecture's future. Rather, Bilbao is by omission a reminder of what architecture currently is not, and what he hopes it can eventually become.

Notes

1   Herbert Muschamp, "The Miracle in Bilbao," *New York Times Magazine* (September 7, 1997): 54–59, 72, 82.
2   Le Corbusier, *Towards a New Architecture*, trans. from 13th French edition (1931; Mineola, N.Y.: Dover, 1986), 92.

SANFORD KWINTER

MACH 1 (AND OTHER MYSTIC VISITATIONS)

First appeared in *ANY* 21 (1997), reprinted in S. Kwinter, *Far from Equilibrium: Essays on Technology and Design Culture* (Barcelona and New York: Actar, 2008), 36–45. Courtesy of Sanford Kwinter.

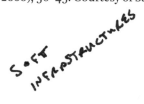

Architects do not lack for work these days, yet still they fret, and it is small wonder. Powerful and disturbing millennial forces are everywhere afoot and their failure to be adequately discharged or convincingly absorbed is making mincemeat of the perennially nervous profession. The prestige of architectural ideas and practices, about to achieve self-confidence as it rises to a par with that of other arts and disciplines for the first time since the Renaissance, is again having its thunder stolen almost daily. The efficient but one-dimensional marketplace world in which we live, fraught to the exclusion of almost everything else with relations of exchange and driven by forces of unrelenting supplication, is a world, one could say, in which we are hectored mercilessly by design, swathed in its miasma of artificial affectation, hyperstyle and micro-human-engineering that anticipates, like a subtle reflex arc, our every move and gesture.

80

Design has now penetrated to, even threatens to replace, the existential density, the darkness, the slow intractable mystery of what was once the human social world. In its place it is installing a shrill new immediacy, a garish transparency of postures, glances, and address. Design has become us; it is, alas, what we are, and there is no way (for now at least) to separate ourselves from it. Even formerly lumpen cultural sectors such as the commercial fashion world now exercise a grip on minds and sensibilities, postures and moods, producing figures of genius (Rei Kawakubo, Martin Margiela, Hussain Chalayan), and heroes of popular notoriety (Alexander McQueen, John Galliano and the consumer house-cults of Prada, Chanel, and Gucci) from within a system of dissemination so vast and inclusive that architects would not even know how to dream of competing. Amid the shameless ersatz novelty of the fashion world there are flickers of true innovation—and most critical of all for our purposes here, there is evidence of an undeniable purchase on the life of the city, the street, and the popular imagination.

Yet fashion is trifling when compared to the explosive influence of media design. Brat pack heroes and role models today are as likely to include graphic designers and typographers as sports figures, rock stars, and film idols (the once de rigueur electric guitar, former pivot of the male adolescent household (and psyche), may already have been replaced by webmaster software packages, crossplatforms, and high-speed IP connections). Graphic design, filling the void carved in the 1980s by the disappearance of both high art and serious popular music, has resulted in a full-blown but still incompletely acknowledged, post-boomer rock 'n' roll revolution, although this time for the eyes and no longer the ears. The phenomenal proliferation of art direction in sports, music, and lifestyle magazines, youth-targeted advertising, CD packaging, film title sequences, homepages, MTV programming, lifestyle-gear logos, and related clothing and paraphernalia together form a seamless performative mesh, a cultural project in the fullest sense of the word, one of nonstop modulation and adrenalated *display*. The design heroes of the popular imagination today—and one might fix the incept date of this new regime as recently as 1992, birthtime of Aldus Corporation's Fontographer software <font merge> command,[1] of *Ray Gun* magazine and the emergence to "school" status of its niche-making R&D department, the *Emigré* collective—are those whose task it is to bestow the queasy, modern, disaffected "look" of our digitally poisoned, post-literate world: the communications systems shape-givers. Even cinema is losing ground to the invasion of the real-time total graphical interface and the video game.

Will there even be architects in thirty years? This is a question that no other generation has ever had to consider. The falsely assured still maintain that, economically, buildings quite simply are like food—irreducible facts of life that no transformation of social or market forces can ever change. They may well be wrong. Despite the customary, fashionable genuflection toward infrastructural questions and concerns today, little attention is being paid to the more radical, more disturbing reality: that infrastructural demands are not only becoming exponentially more importunate today but that these infrastructural demands *are breeding and mutating in kind and not only degree.* We have no choice today but to deal with the new "soft" infrastructures: knowledge infrastructure, program infrastructure, cultural infrastructure, virtual infrastructure. The demand for design—and de-design—in our over-engineered, over-mediated world is both enormous and pervasive, yet the majority of architects still respond to it with the medieval language of the stoic, autonomous building. Today's design world is stratified, with an emerging class structure, its associated embedded conflicts, and an emerging new proletariat increasingly separated from the principle means of production. Architects smile from behind their bow ties, for they have not yet seen that this new proletariat is themselves. And yet, surely they must know.

Our environment is being reworked in depth, no one denies this. Buildings, however, are not oases from history (unless explicitly and brutally organized to be so, and then at best only incompletely) but rather *relays* in a comprehensive cultural system of management, administration, and engineering of human affect and historical unfolding. Like the coils of an anaconda, loop after loop of the soft-infrastructural mesh is drawn daily around us, not to crush, but merely to restrict expansion in unsanctioned directions, to guide all movements subtly but uncompromisingly toward other ends. Architecture imagines itself regal, leonine and sovereign, but today it is the anaconda that rules.

How long has it been since buildings could claim—from a simple historical-materialist point of view—to represent the principle greatest repository of accumulated capital in our culture? Or more simply, when were buildings first displaced by public works projects and private industrial initiatives as the largest and most expensive things? Is not the answer—of which we all nurture our favorite chapters—the real secret history of the present, the noir narrative in which architecture figures as the delusional, vertigo-struck, and now tumbling anti-hero? The simplest answer of all, of course, is that architecture has never been the vastest, most intensive, form-giving cultural enterprise; that position has always been occupied by war. In war the soft-infrastructural enterprises at once find their model, their origin, and their reason for being. To the classic military triumvirate or C^3—Command/Communications/Control—correspond not some but perhaps all of the new design environments and milieus that have started to appear around us with such force and energy this past decade. This is not to say that such practices have anything evil, murderous, or destructive about them, only that the citadel/fortress obsession—the well-known "edifice complex" of architecture, source of its hubristic claim to preeminence in the design world—has finally completed its inevitable, de facto evolution to a *logistics* operation. In other words, it has assumed its modern destiny as an informational regime oriented to performative environments, to protocols, and, *in extremis*, to psychological operations. This partial evolution also suggests that a hilarious spectacle is now preparing itself as our Big Building Field Marshals polish their chest medals in proud anticipation of their next Patton-like tour of what they believe to be today's architectural battlefield. If they listen, they'll hear some gunfire in the far distance, but just barely. Mostly they'll simply hear the rattling of their own medals.

* * *

CRITIQUE
of GEHRY
& OBJECT
BUILDINGS

In 1997 in Bilbao, amid the machinations of an endless political chess match, a building of undeniable beauty and exuberance rose up before a hungry if cynical world. (Nothing could have been more calculated than Guggenheim director Thomas Krens's corporate "acquisitions and mergers" gambit, or the Spanish government's tactical engagement with the powder keg of historical and geopolitical forces (an unconcealed mixture of potlatch and détente), and no one more willing to oblige these exercises in realpolitik than an architect—"I only do buildings!" he says, disingenuously.) Yet the unveiling of the dancing behemoth of Bilbao, like an electrical shimmer on the twenty-first century's terrifying horizon, has been greeted with a hysteria redolent of nothing less than a mystic visitation. I myself once believed that Frank Gehry's Walt Disney Concert Hall in Los Angeles might well become the great architectural project of the end of the twentieth century, and I was untroubled for a time to state so in just those millennial terms. Today I feet less naive. The Bilbao museum, however, and more important, the critics' and public's neurotically euphoric reception of it, seem to wish it to stand in as the fulfillment of the earlier project's lost promise. But the shortfall is simply too great. Not, of course, in relation to the earlier Disney, for Bilbao represents a significant accomplishment in its own right, though it vies for stature within a radically different context of meaning. The Basque (offshore) setting both isolates and intensifies the architectural gesture in intellectual, existential, and historical terms, but it also banalizes it significantly. This shiny new museum for the Common Market (the strident European demand for political stability, driven by the requirements of monetary interactions, need observe no boundaries as it carpetbags its way to internationally admired means of social control via architecture) simply does not qualify as a summary statement on the relations of society, form, and modernization at the end of the great modern century. Of course, many will argue that even the idea of such a summary statement is precluded by the very lessons and predicaments that characterize the thought and history of the last hundred years. That, however, depends on how one places oneself in relation to history.

It would behoove many of a certain generation to celebrate Bilbao as a concluding dance and a death rattle (a sound so eerie and unlike any other that it often leads loved ones to imagine the dying are momentarily coming back to life—whence the raptures of the mystic visitation). While Frank Lloyd Wright's New York Guggenheim is certainly among the most radical buildings ever built in the West, Bilbao is rather at best a lyrical *son et lumiéres* show on an all-too-classical theme (though to be fair, innovation of the former kind has not been attempted often in this generation by anyone, and Gehry himself has never made claim to ambitions beyond the way buildings merely look).

The pilgrimage that so many made to the museum's opening in 1997 was admirable, large-spirited, and certainly invigorating for the design profession, though deep in every pilgrim's subconscious, it also covered over an undeniably morbid, complacent, and self-congratulatory act. I myself, for example, would have been as fascinated, and troubled, to have wandered the haunted chambers of the submerged *RMS Titanic*.

In the era of the ships, when architects and intellectuals were spellbound by the technical revolutions of mass travel, by the cult of speed and the plastic deformations of time, by synthetic total environments and their emancipatory possibilities for stale and weary "historical man," by the machine and its possibilities for human and collective transformation at once political, economic, aesthetic, and sexual, the *Titanic* represented an accomplishment—a polemical and aesthetic summary—of everything good, bad, and unforeseeable that modernity might become. The event of its sinking was probably the only modification that could have further intensified it as a focus of cultural longing, speculation, and fantasy. It already figured among the greatest engineering feats, technical and even social accomplishments in the popular and social imaginary. Important buildings of the era—the Fagus Works, the Monument to the Third International, later the Dymaxion House, the Empire State Building, the villas of Le Corbusier, etc.—could articulate their greatness convincingly only in humble reference to the *Titanic* and its ilk. Once long ago, ocean liners had all but stolen architecture.

As architects were preparing their valises and black ties for the Bilbao opening extravaganza, some of us, on this side of the Atlantic, were deliberately heading in the opposite direction, westward to the Mojave Desert to celebrate one of the major barrier-shattering acts of the modern world. For that weekend in October also represented the fiftieth anniversary, and the commemorative re-enaction, of perhaps the second most significant accomplishment in the history of twentieth-century space. Between 1905 and 1917 the Newtonian model of rigid, absolute space fell at the hands of Einsteinian relativity and plasticism. But on October 14, 1947, the limitations of speed and altitude (or, for those living on a round planet, cosmic *distance*) with which humans were able physically to converse and interact with their world were eliminated. General Chuck Yeager's accomplishment—flying an aircraft faster than the air could carry its sound alongside it—not only opened the supersonic realm to technological manipulation but made it possible to imagine thrusting guided objects beyond the earth's atmosphere, indeed, beyond even the influence of its gravitational field. Space had for the first time come within practical human reach. The modern world, as I have argued elsewhere, was in a peculiarly American sense reborn after World War II in relation to these events.[2] But the focus and intensity, due to the abstract nature of Mach 1 and the esotericism of its technological apparatus, did not penetrate collective consciousness in the same way as did the cult of the great liners of the early century. Had architects been less obsessed by their precious "modern movement" in the 1940s they'd surely have seized on one of the strangest, and related, experiences of modern times: the incremental destruction of London by the V2 rockets, or buzzbombs, missiles that could penetrate the urban space and wreak their destruction several seconds before they could even be heard! The World War II supersonic rockets, like the trenches and no-man's-land of the first Great War, penetrated cultural consciousness deeply, yet passed over the architectural imagination (and conscience) almost entirely.

Today we are not so easily spared, or rather we are not granted our innocence with the same casual impunity. The editor of an American design magazine, introducing a special issue on Buckminster Fuller in 1997, was compelled to described a mystic visitation of her own experience that occurred while attending Pasadena's Rose Bowl parade.[3] As the parade began, a United States Air Force stealth bomber flew overhead and buzzed the stands—"silent…alien…primitive…" in her words. The crowd gasped as the aircraft's implausible, inscrutable image and muted terror engraved itself indelibly in each of the spectators minds. Weeks later when recalling the event in her editorial, its power to trouble not only the mind but also the complacencies of the architectural discipline remained undiminished: "What astonishes today is aeronautical design [not architecture]" (her own son dreams of designing Boeings, not buildings). What characterizes the history of aircraft design, as well as current industrial, product, equipment, and communications design, but which can almost no longer ever be said to be true of architecture, is the astonishing flexibility and transformability of the tolerance *envelope*, that is, of the system of givens within which design takes place and whose parameters are accepted as a priori and fixed. In other words, the ethos of these practices is *experimental* in the fullest and most dangerous sense. We should therefore, in relation to the field of architecture, allow ourselves to be amused, but certainly not so easily be duped, by pseudo-innovation, by the mere variations on familiar themes of which we see so much around us today, variations that only become more extreme and strident as the envelope within which they are designed becomes increasingly brittle and stale.

As we made our way to Edwards Air Force Base we moved liked animals.[4] We neither expected, nor wished, to actually see anything (military security, in anticipation of our arrival, had in any case seen to that). We came rather to listen, to hear the sound of our century reaching back to communicate with itself, to hear the sonic boom from Yeager's F-15 roll across the high desert floor, roll across the last half-century like an auditory territorial marking, calling out to the savagely dangerous and primitive X-1 winged rocket bomb in which he first tore through the sonic wall and changed the shape and dynamics of our world. We came because we believe in shock waves, we believe them to be part of the music of modernity; not something to watch a ribbon be cut from, but something to feel with our diaphragms, eardrums, genitals, and the soles of our feet. We wanted to be in the desert badlands that day with nothing but the sun, the baked dirt, the pneumatic tremors, and the unbroken horizon. We came because out there somewhere we knew was the zero-degree and the future, and that in Bilbao was the past.

Notes

1   Acquired by Macromedia Corporation in 1994. The merge and crash capabilities were introduced in release version 3.5 (1991).
2   Sanford Kwinter, "Flying the Bullet, or When Did the Future Begin?" in Rem Koolhass, *Rem Koolhaas: Conversations with Students*, ed. Sanford Kwinter (New York: Princeton Architectural Press, 1996).
3   Cynthia Davidson, "Dear Reader," *ANY* 17, *Forget Fuller?* (1997).
4   I was traveling with Jesse Reiser.

INTRODUCTION
A New Pragmatism? / *John Rajchman*

In "A New Pragmatism?" John Rajchman, a philosopher and
educator who focuses on architecture and art, employs William
James's notion of "things in the making"[1] in an attempt to propel
the architectural discipline beyond the stagnation of the "theory
versus practice" divide. First presented at the Anyhow conference
in Rotterdam in June 1997, this essay begins with a brief discussion of pragmatism as explored by thinkers from Kant through
Foucault. Rajchman evokes Deleuze's reading of the latter—
specifically Foucault's notions of the diagram and the archive—
to propose a new method of architectural thought grounded in a
"new pragmatism," characterized as "a pragmatism of diagram
and diagnosis." Rajchman poses the diagram (a heavily touted
architectural term in late twentieth- and early twenty-first century discourse) as a "diagnostic tool,"[2] a way of interpreting the
Foucauldian archive of the present, linking multiple (often unac-
knowledged) forces coursing through, generating, and impacting
contemporary life, making way for an unknown, unpredictable,
unprogrammable future. In short, Rajchman hopes that such a
pragmatism of diagram and diagnosis will open new avenues of
exploration that move beyond the implicit negativity of criticality
while not abandoning theory all together.

Following Rajchman's proposal, pragmatism served as a platform for discussions of architecture's possible future. Indeed, others also felt that "pragmatism seem[ed] to potentially offer a fresh
point of departure" for considerations of architecture.[3] Perhaps
the most significant discussions occurred at a two-part event sponsored by the Skidmore, Owings and Merrill Foundation in 2000:
in May, a multidisciplinary workshop at Columbia University; and
in November, a conference called "Things in the Making" at the

Museum of Modern Art in New York. Yet, despite the fanfare surrounding these occasions, talk of pragmatism had largely faded
out within a few years.

Notes

1 William James, "Bergson and His Critique of Intellectualism," *A Pluralistic Universe* (1908; Lincoln, Neb.: University of Nebraska Press, 1996).

2 John Rajchman, "Discussion Five," in *Anyhow*, ed. Cynthia Davidson (Cambridge, Mass.: MIT Press, 1998), 252.

3 Joan Ockman, "Pragmatism/Architecture: The Idea of the Workshop Project," in *The Pragmatist Imagination: Thinking about "Things in the Making,"* ed. Joan Ockman (New York: Temple Hoyne Buell Center for the Study of American Architecture, Columbia University; Princeton Architectural Press, 2000), 18.

JOHN RAJCHMAN

A NEW PRAGMATISM?

First appeared in *Anyhow*, ed. Cynthia Davidson (Cambridge, Mass.: MIT Press, 1998), 212–17. Courtesy of the MIT Press.

I would like to suggest a kind of pragmatism. One might say a "new pragmatism," as it takes up lines started by the classical pragmatist philosophers, but under new conditions. I will call it a pragmatism of diagram and diagnosis. Its role in this session of the conference is odd, for it supposes a relation to a future that we can neither program nor project. It is about forces that we can't predict, with which we can only experiment—about what William James once called "things in the making." My larger question is how to engage in pragmatism at a time when we are told with an air of self-evidence that we have entered the brave new world of "global information societies." I think we need to break a bit with this self-evidence. What I have in mind is not a pragmatics of communication or information typical in such societies, but rather a manner of questioning, of seeing unforeseen singularities that those societies serve to unleash.

Of course there are more familiar senses of "pragmatism" that fit better with the erosion of the powers of the state in which globalization discourse delights. For example, in opposition to Mao Zedong, Deng Xioping is called a pragmatist. He declared practice to be the sole criterion of truth, though the pronouncement derives authority from the Party—an odd destiny for what the first pragmatist Charles Sanders Peirce said was incompatible with any party, any church, since it works through dissent and divergence. Today a pragmatist is often thought to be someone proud to have nothing to do with ideological program, theory, position, or larger vision, content to devise efficient ways of solving specific local problems. My "diagrammatic pragmatist," while concerned with a future that one can neither program nor project, while working outside anything like a party bureaucracy, is quite different from this. Let's take an example. We might talk of "diagramming and diagnosing" the new geographies that emerge with the crisis in the great invention that is Imperial Europe, the national-social-state, as it was overdetermined by colonialism and then the Cold War.[1] For globalization is more than a "transnational" homogenization of conditions; it is, at the same time, a loosening, a vacillation of borders shown in mixtures or "hybridities" and the questions they pose. We might thus talk of "diagramming" spaces in Europe in contrast to inserting them in the old geopolitical map of the "great nations" of the last century or even in that supranation called "Europe" with its unelected Brussels administrators. We might thus diagnose new forces of a European racism: focused on immigrants, assuming different guises according to the different "imagined communities" or nationalisms of the states in which it figures. But what then does such "diagrammatization" mean—what does it do? I'll start with some conceptual distinctions.

In some philosophical circles, words like "functional," "instrumental," "operational," and "utilitarian" have gotten a bad name—what Max Weber called *Zweckrationalität*.[2]

Immanuel Kant elaborated a strong view in relation to the "disinterest" that he thought was required by moral imperative, political reason, or aesthetic judgment. One consequence is the place that falls to architecture in Kant's hierarchical classification of the beaux arts. He thought architecture the most "interested" of the free liberal arts—the most tied to money, market, government, and instrumentality, hence the lowest, the least free, the least beau of all. Of course, there would be many avatars of this idea of disinterest that Kant took to be freedom. It is found in the heroic linage of a reductive or self-critical formalism railing against an increasing functional society, in the "critique of instrumental reason" proposed by Max Horkheimer and Theodor Adorno, and again when Martin Heidegger, reacting to Friedrich Nietzsche's diagnosis of the "ascetic ideal" in Kant's doctrine of aesthetic disinterest, proposed to "retranslate" it as mystical *Gelassenheit* ("letting be").

It is therefore interesting that the term *pragmatisch* (pragmatic), which Kant introduced into philosophy, had another purpose or "point of view" that expresses another kind of question. That in any case was the thesis of Michel Foucault's *thèse*, which consisted of a translation of Kant's *Anthropology from a Pragmatic Point of View* lectures. Foucault stressed that *pragmatisch* is neither instrumental nor practical and may even problematize the exclusive division between the two. It is rather "experimental" in the sense of that word found in writings of pragmatists and in Nietzsche when Zarathustra declares, "Society is an experiment, o my brothers—and not a contract!" Foucault associated the "pragmatic" in Kant with a problem that even Jürgen Habermas would later agree besets much post-Kantian critical philosophy: that of the empirical and the transcendental. Looking back we can now see that the various "transcendental conditions," subjective or objective, which the post-Kantian philosophers would propose, were in fact all patterned on some element from empirical domains that they were supposed to condition or ground. The "pragmatist" way out of this dilemma was then to rethink the very sense of "critical." The critical question becomes how to see and to conceive new forces that exceed and problematize assumptions that normally function as "transcendental." It becomes a question of how, in the absence of a priori or transcendental conditions, prior to what "determines" us as subjects, objects, members of communities, we may yet "invent ourselves" and our worlds. Peirce derived his word "pragmatism" from Kant; and in all of the philosophers whom we today call pragmatists we find formulations of this basic question—in Peirce's attempt, against Laplacian determinism, to introduce chance into the question of how, in Dewey's attempt to introduce "contingency" into social history, and again in what James called "the problem of novelty"—the problem of how to deal with "things in the making," how to see and respond to the emergence of things for which we have no preset manner of seeing or responding.

Foucault himself went on to develop this pragmatist question in a new way when, following the events of 1968 in Paris and Prague, his work took a more explicitly political turn. He then tried to elaborate a "strategic" (not to be confused with "instrumental") conception of the workings of power and the role of critical philosophy in them—power as strategy, philosophy as conceptual toolbox. I'd like to look at one aspect of this process that focuses on the word *diagram*, as when Foucault said of Bentham's *Panopticon* that it is a "diagram of power reduced to its ideal form." When Deleuze called Foucault a new cartographer, a new archivist in the city, we might then say he was a man with a diagram rather than a plan, a program, or a project.[3] He was someone who had worked out a diagram of a partially unseen kind of power or power strategy at work in many different institutions and situations—an ingenious "abstract machine" functioning in many ways, not to be found on the official map of policies and prescriptions, planned as such by no one. The basic problem to which the machine was addressed was a problem of population—in Foucault's words, what to do about "the accumulation of men."[4] In effect it was a machine to "individualize a population" by dividing up the space and time of its activities, which would gradually prove useful for a wide range of things and in a great variety of settings. We see it, for example, in new differentiations of domestic space, in the emergence of worker cities, and in colonial modernizations.

Of course, to sketch a diagram of a "disciplin*ary* society" was not to say everything was completely, hopelessly "disciplin*ed*." It was only to say that this partially unseen "abstract machine" was still at work in it. But what then was the point of drawing this diagram? One answer comes from Foucault's conception of the archive. What is the point, for example, of establishing the archive, which lets us see why "prisons resemble factories, schools, barracks, and hospitals which all resemble prisons?" Foucault said he wanted such an archive to function as a sort of "diagnostic"—he wanted it to suggest an untimely future that we can't program or project, but with which we can only experiment. Thus he declares that the archive is not concerned to "sketch in advance what we will look like" but, on the contrary, with breaking with such continuities, to confront us with the fact that we are in the process of becoming something other, we know not yet what.[5] With the archive would go a "pragmatic" sense that we are made up of "differences," or processes of complexification and differentiation of futures unknown. Deleuze proposed this precept for the Foucauldian archive: "not to predict but to be attentive to the unknown that is knocking at the door." In this sense, it is through the archive that Foucault tried to introduce a "time of the diagrammatic" into history; in Deleuze's words, he wanted to turn history into the "negative condition for an experimentation." Such was the pragmatism of his diagram, his diagnosis.

Put another way, we may say that Foucault's diagram and diagnosis came at a time when the great abstract machine of the disciplines was in fact not working so well, when it was entering into a crisis in relation to new forces that it was no longer able to contain. Having advanced it, Foucault himself entered into a crisis. He came to a fresh conjecture concerning the "failure of political theories nowadays." He thought we could analyze the various strands of "liberalism," whether they appeal to markets or to civil society, as attempts on the part of the modern state deliberately to limit itself so as to better perform its characteristic functions with respect to populations and their relations with territories and resources; one outcome of such a "reason of state" was the geopolitical confrontations of the great nations of Europe that began in the 19th century. In other words, in the mid-1970s Foucault "diagnosed" that we were living through a crisis in the "welfare-warfare-state" as a basic matrix of our "political rationality" and were in the process of becoming something else, we could not yet quite say what; and I think that our worries and divisions twenty years later over how much of the welfare apparatus to retain while insuring that we are "competitive in global markets" would have seemed for Foucault only to confirm and extend this diagnosis.

In any case, we might distinguish two aspects of the "diagram of discipline" that Foucault had worked out archivally in the 1970s, both emphasized by Deleuze. The first is that it came at a "diagnostic" or critical moment, a pragmatic interval between the disciplinary formation and something as yet undefined such that we must experiment, and experiment with ourselves, in order to see it. The second is that among the "new forces" of this "critical moment" were those of biotechnology and digital devices and the new arrangements or assemblages that they help create in and among us—forces now taken for granted as part and parcel of "globalization." These forces or arrangements called for new diagrams, new diagnoses, new experiments. Of course, the diagram of the disciplines had been, among other things, one of architectural and urban spaces, and the question thus arises whether we might find something like this "pragmatic cartography" of new assemblages or arrangements in what is called "the new urbanism." I think several features of this urbanism might usefully be seen in this light.

First, the crisis of the decline in the centrality of Taylorism and factory discipline might also be seen urbanistically in the relics of declining industrial sectors photographed, for example, by Bern and Hilla Becher. The new forces that displace the diagram might then be found in formations that tend in one way or another to depart from the "reason of state" with which the disciplines came to be tied up, leading to a new kind of problem. The problem is not so much of environments or spaces that are excessively organized, controlled, or "rationalized" in the Weberian sense but rather of ones that are increasingly random, diffuse, disparate, thin, often even surreal, ones that therefore *work* through other forms of the accumulation and interconnection of men and women—through other "diagrams." To see what is at work in them, we need to readjust our mapping techniques. In particular, in the ultrarapid, large-scale developments that we see in Asia and may yet see in Africa, we need to draw new diagrams, which, in the absence of fixed models or maps, suggest discrete possibilities of intervention.

Second, this cartographic readjustment requires new ways of thinking about space and time or about *espacement* (spacing). For the disciplinary diagram basically worked through segmentations of space-time in interlocking closed environments, and against it arose the protest of another time, another memory, and "duration" prior and irreducible to it, as for example in the waves of Virginia Woolf, where a life is imagined to be composed of multiple irregular bits combined in ways that can never be turned into a perfect narrative continuity—what Foucault at one point called a revolt of time against space. Now, however, we have formations that look rather different from the segmented assemblages of the mechanical city as depicted, for example, by Fernand Leger in his 1919 painting *Men in the City* or in Fritz Lang's 1927 film *Metropolis*. We have other "smoother" sorts of accumulation and interaction, and the question of how to diagram and creatively or experimentally deal with them arises, as earlier with the critical question of a duration irreducible to segmentation.

Third, to "diagram" these new kinds of *espacement* is in effect to deal with them through something akin to the pragmatism I am trying to sketch; one might say that a "gay science of the city" works through diagram and diagnosis rather than through a plan, program, or project. It is a style of analysis, thinking, perhaps even of design, in which a city-diagram-experimentation relation replaces the older state-program-ideology relation typified by Marxism, in which the old mystico-literary theme of allegory and utopia is replaced by the pragmatic one of diagram and diagnosis of new urban conditions.

Understood in this way, the "diagrammatic" in the gay science of the city brings us back to the old questions of form and meaning. They are formulated in one way in Deleuze's attempt, in contrast to the assumptions of classical perspective, to envisage looser and more dynamic sorts of "spacing"; at the close of his study of the "images" in postwar cinema, he drew a contrast between the mechanical city and a new "brain-city" that displaces it. Different diagrams, different "automatisms" go with each city; and they serve in turn to bring out the differences between the mechanical and energetic or the mechanical and digital or smart kinds of machines and machinic arrangements.

In particular we see relations between brain and city, nervous systems and environments unlike those we previously imagined through the classical paradigms defined by relations of eye to nature or figure to landscape. Problems of "diagramming information" take over from the problems, tied up with earlier techniques of drawing and painting, of inserting distinct objects or figures into compositional wholes, as if seen through a classical Italian window or located within an existing frame or fixed set of coordinates. The question then becomes: What kinds of images, signs, meanings are thus made possible?

Pragmatism is not opposed to the question of how things, including buildings, make sense. Perhaps one could say it is a matter of introducing a certain indefiniteness, multiplicity, vagueness (or, as it is now said, a certain "complexity") into it. Thus Peirce, inventor of pragmatism, experimenter, and philosopher of chance, also helped start semiology; with his transformation of the idea of truth went an altered "logic of sense." Today Peirce is admired for a semiology that is directly visual and not subordinate to language as in Ferdinand de Saussure's work; Peirce's concept of the "index" is still alive in art-historical debate. But if we then think of signs or images as specific to "mediums" and their possibilities, their conditions of invention and reinvention, what about architecture—what about "diagrammatic" signs or images in it?

The diagram was of course part of Deleuze's own semiology. He worked out a contrast between diagram and code in the pictorial arts as well as in music. It was part of his general attempt to envisage an interstitial "spacing" prior to Albertian procedures to depict distinct figures in perspective and recount illustrative stories about their interrelations. Thus in contrast to Vasily Kandinsky's dream of a pure pictorial code of shapes and colors, there would be the diagrams of "other movement" in Paul Klee, the contourless abstract lines in Jackson Pollock, and the "a-signifying marks" in Francis Bacon, which suggest other possibilities within a given "pictorial fact." But can we then conceive of such an uncoded "diagrammatic" dimension in architecture or the specific ways that it acquires its meanings? Today's talk of "dynamic topologies" and "vectoral images" seems to suggest one idea.

We might recast the diagram-code distinction in architecture in this way. We might call "diagrammatic" those images or spaces that introduce other "possible movements" not predetermined by an overall program; they are those that, in contrast to classical composition of fixed elements in well-formed or organic wholes, work through connections in multiple disparate spaces, allowing for relations of mixture, hybridity, contamination, simultaneity; they thus let unforeseen things happen rather than trying to insert everything into an over-arching plan, system, or story. The diagrammatic dimension thus helps free an older idea of "function" from absorption or negation by a purist aestheticism while undoing its identification with the preprogrammed stories or sets of intercorrelations. One might thus talk of a "new functionalism" concerned with the complex insertion of architecture into an environment, characterized by a new problem: that of "re-singularizing" a milieu or environment by releasing something unforeseen, as yet "pre-subjective" or "a-signifying" into it. The "sense" of a building would then no longer be given through an "embodiment" of something that predates it, not even a "world" in the phenomenological sense of the word; it would "make sense" in ways that depart from monumentalizing or commemorative impulses traditional to architecture. For where a monument conserves and makes public something one is supposed to remember, a diagram sets into motion unforeseen connections and the new possibilities that they release or introduce. It is thus concerned with accumulations and connections of people in another way and through a different kind of "spacing," which Deleuze suggests when he talks of an architecture of *trajets et parcours*—not "the pharaoh's tomb in a central chamber at the bottom of the pyramid," he writes, but rather "more dynamic models: from the drift of continents to the migration of peoples."[6]

What then does the "new pragmatism"—the pragmatism of diagram and diagnosis that I have been trying to imagine— involve? What does it do? In the first place, the diagrammatic supposes a pragmatic relation to a future that is not futuristic, not imagistic. It is concerned in the present with those multiple unknown futures of which we have no image just because we are in the process of becoming or inventing them. It follows that the diagrammatic requires and excites different kinds of solidarity or "movement" among us that those of the traditional avant-garde group, the organization of a political party, or even a nice progressive social-democratic public sphere, inasmuch as those forms rest on the presumption of a future we are able to know and master. The diagrammatic "mobilizes and connects" us in other, indirect ways that work more through linkages, complicities, and alliances that grow up around new questions or in response to new conditions or forces than through adherences to the prior supervenient generalities of a theory, a project, or a program. Perhaps in this way the pragmatism of diagram and diagnosis might help transform the sense of what is "critical" in our thought and our work. It might help move beyond the impasses of older images of negative theology, transgression, or abstract purity and introduce a new problem: that of resingularizing environments, of living an indefinite "complexity," prior to set determinations, which questions the simplicities and generalities of our modes of being and suggests other possibilities. Such a pragmatism would differ from the "communicational" or "informational" pragmatics promoted by globalization discourse—it ties creation and resistance to the present.

Notes

1 For all of these issues see Etienne Balibar, *La crainte des masses* (Paris: Galilée, 1997), especially the essay on what a border is, what the borders of Europe are, and what European racism means.

2 By this Weber meant the kind of rationality set by goals or ends in contrast to the kind concerned with deciding which ends or goals one ought to pursue.

3 See Gilles Deleuze, *Foucault*, trans. Brian Massumi (Minneapolis, Minn.: University of Minnesota Press, 1988). In *Politics/Poetics: documenta X—The Book*, Daniel Defert describes in some detail how architects close to Tafuri helped make the theme of "heterotopia" seem basic to Foucault's analysis of space; as such it would later be introduced into geography by Edward Soja and others. Perhaps Deleuze's focus on "diagram" (around the same time) might today indicate another direction.

4 Michel Foucault, "The Eye of Power," in *Power/Knowledge*, trans. Colin Gordon (New York: Pantheon Books, 1980), 151.

5 See Gilles Deleuze, "What is a *dispositif?*" in *Michel Foucault, Philosopher*, ed. and trans. T. J. Armstrong (New York: Routledge, 1992), 164ff. Deleuze draws attention to the relevant passages concerning "diagnosis" from the *Archaeology of Knowledge*, saying that they fit with all of his work. For example, the "diagnosis" consists in asking what new "subjectivization" we might yet invent given that there is a sense in which, in relation to sex, we are no longer Greek, no longer Christian, no longer even Freudian. "Diagnosis" is one sense of the world *krisis*, from which we get our term *critical*. It belongs to the link between "critical" and "clinical" that Nietzsche helped introduce into philosophy.

6 Gilles Deleuze, "Ce que dissent les enfants," in *Critique et Clinique* (Paris: Minuit, 1993), 81ff. What children say (that they try to explore the milieu through dynamic *trajets*, and draw out the map or diagram) is shown in particular by Fernand Deligny's diagrams of odd movements of autistic children. They might well be read in tandem with Klee or Bacon. The terms *trajet* and *parcours* often occur together in Deleuze's late writings in *Essays clinical and critical*, notably in the introduction, where they are used to say what a work or "oeuvre" is. For example, the expression "architecture of parcours and trajets" is used to describe Nietzsche's labyrinthine notion of Earth in the essay

"Ariadne's Mystery" first published in English in ANY, no. 5 (March/April 1994). "Trajet" means passage, crossing, journey, way; as a verb, "parcourir" means to travel through or traverse, and so see or look-over; and a "parcours" is then such a course, line, way. The conceptual use Deleuze makes of the pair of terms seems to be connected with two problems: (i) the "trajectories" or "goings-through" suggested by the terms may be said to *make* or *show* a space, or to involve a time, that is not pregiven or predetermined as by a prior plan. (ii) the "jet" in "trajets" comes from the sense of "throwing" that Latin puts into such words as "subject" and "object"; one might say thus that "trajets" here refer to a kind of "throwing-through" space and time prior to one given by the traditional sense of objects represented for subjects.

INTRODUCTION
The Rural Studio / *Samuel Mockbee*

"All architects expect and hope their work will act in some sense as a servant for humanity—to make a better world." For Samuel Mockbee, this hope became a reality through the creation of the Rural Studio, a design/build program that introduces architecture students at Auburn University to the cultural, economic, and social situations of poor communities in the rural South. In the early 1990s, Mockbee and groups of students began working with individual families and neighborhood residents in need of housing and public facilities. The studio projects, ranging from smokehouses to playgrounds to chapels, are inexpensive, sustainable, and innovative in design, drawing inspiration from regional tendencies and unconventional materials such as salvaged car windshields and tires, old railroad ties, and hay bales. The resulting buildings demonstrate that inventive and creative design need not be technologically advanced or prohibitively expensive.

In his essay "The Rural Studio," Mockbee discusses his view of the architect's role in contemporary society. He writes of the necessity for "subversive leadership," of the need to recognize the interconnectedness of spheres of life, of the architect's responsibility to disrupt normative and accepted social relationships. "People and place matter," Mockbee declares, and it is the architect's responsibility to keep both in mind despite increasing pressure from late-capitalist culture.

His language is undeniably humanist and is at times tinged with mysticism: "there is something divine in a work of architecture," he declares, "and we must maintain faith in the wonder of architecture to bring us into accord with the natural world, the supernatural world, with our fellow human beings and the great unknown." This emotional view carries over into Mockbee's architectural process, which begins with the sketch and relates closely

105

to drawing and painting. Thus Mockbee appears as an architect/artist in the tradition of the Renaissance man, yet he rejects the model of the gentleman architect in favor of the hands-on builder.

In an era of "starchitects" and signature buildings, Mockbee's approach to architecture stands out as remarkably different, a difference that has garnered much positive attention. Even after Mockbee's death in 2001, the Rural Studio has continued to thrive, inspiring professionals, academics, and students to strive for what he called "an architecture of honesty."

SAMUEL MOCKBEE

THE RURAL STUDIO

First appeared in *Architecture Design* 68, no. 7/8 (1998), 72–79.
Courtesy of Jackie Mockbee and Wiley Publishing.

For every architect there is a creative moment when he or she plugs into the Muse and generates, from Chaos, a sketch that builds order. The sketch is a mark that suggests the possibility of an idea and an ideal. Taking this act further and applying it to all of us is about making some mark in one's lifetime that can be given the title of Architecture; a mark that will remain after the power of one's living imagination is gone.

All architects expect and hope their work will act in some sense as a servant for humanity—to make a better world. That is the search we should always be undertaking and, again, there are no clear-cut definitions or assumed pathways. Therefore it is important to give critical attention to some basic issues that every architect, regardless of time and place, will have to face. Issues that Alberti called choosing between fortune and virtue. Issues not as questions of judgment but questions of value and principle. What I am going to try and show is my own search in dealing with these issues.

Architects are by nature and pursuit leaders and teachers. If architecture is going to inspire a community, or stimulate the status quo into making responsible environmental and social structural changes now and in the future, it will take what I call the "subversive leadership" of academicians and practitioners to remind the student of architecture that theory and practice are not only interwoven with one's culture but with the responsibility of shaping the environment, of breaking up social complacency, and of challenging the power of the status quo.

Last year, I was asked to participate in an AIA (American Institute of Architects) Design Conference, along with two other architects and the English architect Michael Hopkins. Each of us gave lectures during the day and then participated in an after-dinner panel discussion that evening. Primarily, the question-and-answers session that evening settled around questions about how an architect receives and executes major commissions. Each of the other architects were giving their answers to this question when Michael Hopkins interjected somewhat matter-of-factly that the evening before he had received a "fax on his pillow" informing him that he had just received yet another commission from one of his major clients in England. Later on someone made the observation that Hopkins was working for the richest woman in the world—the Queen of England—while I was working for the poorest man in the world, Shepard Bryant (the client and recipient of The Rural Studio's first charity house, the Hay Bale House in Mason's Bend, Alabama). They noted at the same time that my work and the work of Michael Hopkins represented two very different approaches to the practice of architecture. They wondered what the implications of this were. The question was directed at me and I answered that it probably had more to do with our nature than with any convictions—more to do with our own private (and somewhat selfish) desires rather than any commitment to public virtue.

But as far as my own convictions went, I believe that architects are given a gift of second sight and when we see something that others can't we should act, and we shouldn't wait for decisions to be made by politicians or multinational corporations. Architects should always be in the initial critical decision-making position in order to challenge the power of the status quo. We need to understand that when a decision is made, a position has already been taken. Architects should not be consigned to only problem-solving after the fact.

People then turned to Michael Hopkins for his answer. He replied, "Maybe architects shouldn't be in the position to make those kinds of decisions." I took this to mean issues affecting social, economic, political or environmental decisions, and also staying away from making subversive decisions!

At first I was somewhat stunned by his answer and then reflected that perhaps here was a man who could be speaking for most practising architects.

I do not believe that courage has gone out of the profession, but we tend to be narrow in the scope of our thinking and underestimate our natural capacity to be subversive leaders and teachers. In other words, the more we practise, the more restricted we become in our critical thinking and our life styles. Critical thought requires looking beyond architecture towards an enhanced understanding of the whole to which it belongs. Accordingly, the role of architecture should be placed in relation to other issues of education, healthcare, transportation, recreation, law enforcement, employment, the environment, the collective community that impacts on the lives of both the rich and the poor.

The political and environmental needs of our day require taking subversive leadership as well as an awareness that where you are, how you got there, and why you are still there, are more important than you think they are.

Architecture, more than any other art form, is a social art and must rest on the social and cultural base of its time and place. For those of us who design and build, we must do so with an awareness of a more socially responsive architecture. The practice of architecture not only requires participation in the profession but it also requires civic engagement. As a social art, architecture must be made where it is and out of what exists there. The dilemma for every architect is how to advance our profession and our community with our talents rather than our talents being used to compromise them.

We must use the opportunity to survey our own backyards either to see what makes them special, individual and beautiful, or to note the unjust power of the status quo, or the indifference of the religious or intellectual community in dealing with social complacency or the nurturing of the environment. Peering out at your contemporary landscape is required before commitments to inspire can be started, accomplished and finished.

People and place matter. Architecture is a continually developing profession now under the influence of consumer-driven culture. The profession is becoming part of the corporate world and corporations (citizens of no place or any place) increasingly resemble nation states. Of the world's largest 100 economies, 49 are countries and 51 are corporations. The 200 largest corporations employ only three-quarters of one percent of the world's work force.

During the next twenty-five years forces in the world of politics, economics and the environment will be driven by two factors: a demographic explosion that will double the population in undeveloped countries; and a technological explosion of robotics, biotechnology, lasers, optics and telecommunication in developed countries. These two factors will have a major impact on the natural environment. The architect's role will be to make architecture labour under the given conditions of a particular place, whether it is Winston County, Mississippi; Mason Bend, Alabama; or Mascot, Australia. It is not prudent to sit back as architects and rely on the corporate world's scientists and technology experts to decide which problems to solve. It is in the architect's own interest to assert his or her values—values that respect, we should hope, the greater good.

It is also obvious that the place one is inspired by is of profound importance. The chance of not being from that place is not a crippling deficiency that will render one incapable of inspiration. What is important is using one's talent, intellect and energy in order to gain an appreciation and affection for people and place.

Architecture will make itself understood. There is something divine in a work of architecture, and we must maintain faith in the wonder of architecture to bring us into accord with the natural world, with the supernatural world, with our fellow human beings, and with the great unknown.

I'd like to explain a little about my background—about being blessed and cursed as a Southerner. Coleman Coker, my partner, and I grew up in North Mississippi. We are first cousins, six generations removed. As Southerners our heritage is part of our character. My great grandfather rode with the Mississippi Partisan Rangers under Colonel WC Falkner and later General Forrest. These were my heroes growing up in the segregated South of the 1950s and the early 1960s. I grew up recreating the great battles of Brice's Crossroads and visiting the battlefields of Vicksburg and Shiloh.

Later I came to realise the contradictions that existed in my world. That I came from an isolated area where lies were being confronted with the truth. That I came from the American South which was attached to fiction and false values and a willingness to justify cruelty and injustice in the name of those values.

Years ago, I was outside my home at Meridan, Mississippi, and I had to pull over and stop for a road grader. While I was waiting I noticed a graveyard and a particular grave. It was the grave of James Chaney. James Chaney was one of three civil-rights workers killed in the summer of 1964. He would be a man of about my age today, but, more importantly, I have now come to believe and know that he defines who I am and who I am not. For me, he represents one of the true heroes of the South. And he is a true hero by the fact that he had the courage to risk his life and accept responsibility. His courage was a gift to me and to all of us. As architects we are given a gift and with it, a responsibility, though certainly more passive than James Chaney's. But the question for us is the same: do we have the courage to make our gift count for something?

The professional challenge, whether one is an architect in the rural American South or elsewhere in the world, is how to avoid being so stunned by the power of modern technology and economic affluence that one does not lose sight of the fact that people and place matter.

For me, drawing and painting are the initial influences for the making of architecture. The sketch is always out front. It sees ahead and deeper into what is already on the paper.

The initial sketch is always an emotion, not a concept. In the beginning, it is important to allow the imagination to move freely without any influence from a preconceived form. It's a mark that suggests the possibility of an idea. For me, it's the act of drawing that allows the hand to come into accord with the heart. When that happens, there comes a moment when the marks of the sketch—it can be a pen mark or a computer mark—utter the first deeper knowledge of what will come later.

This brings us to the present phase in my quest as an architect. Even though my career had been developing successfully, I did not feel that I was maturing as a responsible architectural citizen. I believe what the poet William Carlos Williams pre-scribed about the best architect being the person "with the most profound insight into the lives of the community." So I applied to, and received, a Graham Foundation Grant to execute a series of large murals in an attempt to extend the study of architec-ture into what I hoped would be a wider human landscape. I am interested in what might prompt and make possible a process of entering a taboo landscape, in my case, the economic poverty of the Deep South; also in developing a discourse beyond merely looking at the effects of poverty but also at how architects can step over the threshold of injustice and address the true needs of a neglected American family and particularly the needs of their children. Of all Southerners, young children are the most likely to be living in poverty. In Mississippi, one in four lives below the poverty level. These children don't have the same advantages as the rest of America's children. They will come of age without any vision of how to rescue themselves from the curse of poverty.

Physical poverty is not an abstraction, but we almost never think of impoverishment as evidence of a world that exists. Much less do we imagine that it's a condition from which we may draw enlightenment in a very practical way. The paintings which began the work of the Rural Studio try to establish a dis-course between those of us who have become mentally and mor-ally stalled in modern obligations and these families who have no prospect of such obligations. The paintings are by no means an attempt to aestheticise poverty. It's about stepping across a social impasse into an honesty that refuses to gloss over ines-capable facts. It's an honesty that permits differences to exist side by side with great tolerance and respect. Just as those of us who have had advantages can learn from this resilience, so can architecture learn something from an architecture of hon-esty. It is about stepping into the open and expressing the sim-ple and the actual rather than the grand and the ostentatious.

It's not about your greatness as an architect but about your compassion. These paintings are an attempt at becoming an agency of understanding what is common and universal for all families. Architecture won't begin to alleviate all of these social woes. But what is necessary is a willingness to seek solutions to poverty in its own context, not outside it. What is required is the replacement of abstract opinions with knowledge based on real human contact and personal realisation applied to the work and place.

This brings me to Auburn University's Rural Studio. It had become clear to me that if architectural education was going to play any socially engaged role, it would be necessary to work with the segment of the profession that would one day be in a position to make decisions: the student. The main purpose of the Rural Studio is to enable each student to step across the threshold of misconceived opinions and to design/build with a "moral sense" of service to a community. It is my hope that this experience will help the student of architecture to be more sensitive to the power and promise of what they do, to be more concerned with the good effects of architecture than with "good intentions." The Rural Studio represents an opportunity to be real in itself. The students become architects of their own education.

For me, these small projects have in them the architectural essence to enchant us, to inspire us, and ultimately, to elevate our profession. But more importantly, they remind us of what it means to have an American architecture without pretence. They remind us that we can be as awed by the simple as by the complex and that if we pay attention, this will offer us a glimpse into what is essential to the future of American Architecture: its honesty.

"Love your neighbour as yourself." This is the most important thing because nothing else matters. In doing so, an architect will act on a foundation of decency which can be built upon. Go above and beyond the call of a "smoothly functioning conscience"; help those who aren't likely to help you in return, and do so even if nobody is watching!

INTRODUCTION
Field Conditions / *Stan Allen*

In 1972, Peter Eisenman wrote an editorial for *Oppositions*
entitled "Post-functionalism" in which he stated that, unlike art
and music, architecture had yet to break free from the anthropo-
centric model established during the Renaissance. Functionalism,
Eisenman asserted, was just another form of humanism. With
this in mind, Eisenman called for an architecture beyond functionalism that would be based on the specific techniques of the
architectural discipline, concerned with the process of creation
and the resulting object.

Stan Allen's "Field Conditions" serves as a complement
to Eisenman's "Post-functionalism" in that Allen, an architect
and dean of the School of Architecture at Princeton University,
also calls for an architecture that departs from an accepted
Renaissance model, namely the quest for the unified whole.
"Form matters, but not so much the forms of things as the forms
between things." Rather than depend on a preconceived classical
notion of form (parts combine to create a whole), Allen advocates
an architecture that is both a product of and a response to the
modern-day forces that act upon it. The consideration of such
field conditions—digital technologies, networks and systems of
communication and information, user behavior—gives rise to
designs that can accommodate the contingencies of everyday life.
An architecture based on field conditions is, Allen asserts, "inherently expandable," creating an open framework that leaves room
for change from the bottom up instead of imposed from the top
down. For inspiration he looks to postminimalist artistic techniques
and scientific theories of flocks and crowds.

While in some ways similar to Eisenman's theory of post-
functionalism—namely the desired departure from Renaissance
norms and the reliance on serialized artistic methods of the

1960s—Eisenman and Allen have two markedly different ends in mind. During the time he wrote "Post-functionalism," Eisenman fixated almost exclusively on architecture as object, without contextual or external connection. In opposition, Allen focuses on the larger picture, understanding architecture as a convergence of surrounding forces. Architecture for Allen is the ground, as it were, not the figure.

"Field Conditions" opens the fourth section of Allen's book *Points + Lines: Diagrams and Projects for the City* and is accompanied by two projects that illustrate the theoretical concepts set out in the text. Allen suggests that, due in part to contemporary technology, accepted building typologies for many social institutions have become outdated and thus are potentially limiting. It is fitting, then, that Allen's projects for the Korean-American Museum of Art in Los Angeles (1995) and the National Diet Library in Kyoto Prefecture, Japan (1996), appear as the practical counterpart to his theory of field conditions.

STAN ALLEN

FIELD CONDITIONS

First appeared in *Points and Lines: Diagrams and Projects for the City* (New York: Princeton Architectural Press, 1999), 90–103.

"The order is not rationalistic and underlying but is simply order, like that of continuity, one thing after another."
—Donald Judd

"The field describes a space of propagation, of effects. It contains *no matter or material points*, rather functions, vectors and speeds. It describes local relations of difference within fields of celerity, transmission or of careering points, in a word, what Minkowski called the *world*."
—Sanford Kwinter, 1986[1]

0.1 From Object to Field

Field conditions moves from the one toward the many, from individuals to collectives, from objects to fields. In its most complex manifestation, the concept of field conditions refers to mathematical field theory, to nonlinear dynamics, and to

118

computer simulations of evolutionary change. However, my understanding of field conditions in architecture is somewhat distinct from its more exact meaning in the physical sciences. I intend the phrase to resonate with a more tactical sense, as it would for an anthropologist or a botanist engaged in "field-work," for a general facing the field of battle, or the architect who cautions a builder to "verify in field." My concern parallels a shift in recent technologies from the analog to the digital. It pays close attention to precedents in visual art, from the abstract painting of Piet Mondrian in the 1920s to minimalist and post-minimalist sculpture of the 1960s. Postwar composers, as they moved away from the strictures of serialism, employed concepts such as "clouds" of sound or, in the case of Iannis Xenakis, "statistical" music in which complex acoustical events cannot be broken down into their constituent elements.[2] The infra-structural elements of the modern city, by their nature linked together in open-ended networks, offer another example of field conditions in the urban context. A complete examination of the implications of field conditions in architecture would necessarily reflect the complex and dynamic behaviors of architecture's users, and speculate on new methodologies to model program and space.

To generalize, a field condition could be any formal or spatial matrix capable of unifying diverse elements while respecting the identity of each. Field configurations are loosely bound aggregates characterized by porosity and local interconnectivity. Overall shape and extent are highly fluid and less important than the internal relationships of parts, which determine the behavior of the field. Field conditions are bottom-up phenomena, defined not by overarching geometrical schemas but by intricate local connections. Interval, repetition, and seriality are key concepts. Form matters, but not so much the forms of things as the forms *between* things.

Field conditions cannot claim to produce a systematic theory of architectural form or composition. The theoretical model proposed here anticipates its own irrelevance when faced with the realities of practice. These are working concepts derived from experimentation in contact with the real.

0.2 Geometric vs. Algebraic Combination

The diverse elements of classical architecture are organized into coherent wholes by means of geometric systems of proportion. Although ratios can be expressed numerically, the relationships intended are fundamentally geometric. Alberti's well-known axiom that "Beauty is the consonance of the parts such that nothing can be added or taken away" expresses an ideal of organic geometric unity. The conventions of classical architecture dictate not only the proportions of individual elements but also the relationship between individual elements. Parts form ensembles which in turn form larger wholes. Precise rules of axiality, symmetry, or formal sequence govern the organization of the whole. Classical architecture displays a wide variation on these rules, but the principle of hierarchical distribution of parts to whole is constant. Individual elements are maintained in hierarchical order by extensive geometric relationships in order to preserve overall unity.

The Great Mosque of Cordoba, Spain, constructed over a span of nearly eight centuries, offers an instructive counterexample.[3] The form of the mosque had been clearly established: an enclosed forecourt, flanked by a minaret tower, opening onto a covered space for worship (perhaps derived from market structures, or adapted from the Roman basilica). The enclosure is loosely oriented toward the *qibla*, a continuous prayer wall marked by a small niche (the *mihrab*). In the first stage of construction (c. 785–800) the typological precedent was respected, resulting in a simple structure of ten parallel walls perpendicular to the *qibla*. These walls, supported on columns and pierced by arches, defining a covered space of equal dimension to the open court. The arched walls operate in counterpoint to the framed vistas across the grain of the space. The columns are located at the intersection of these two vectors, forming an undifferentiated but highly charged field. This field generates complex parallax effects that prey on visitors as they move through the space. The entire west wall is open to the courtyard, so that once within the precinct of the mosque there is no single entrance. The axial, processional space of the Christian church gives way to a nondirectional space, a serial order of "one thing after another."[4]

The mosque was subsequently enlarged in four stages. Significantly, with each addition the fabric of the original has remained substantially intact. The typological structure is reiterated at larger scale, while the local relationships have remained fixed. By comparison with classical Western architecture, it is possible to identify contrasting principles of combination: one *algebraic*, working with numerical units combined one after another, and the other *geometric*, working with figures (lines, planes, solids) organized in space to form larger wholes.[5] In Cordoba, for example, independent elements are combined additively to form an indeterminate whole. The relations of part to part are identical in the first and last versions constructed. The local syntax is fixed, but there is no overarching geometric scaffolding. Parts are not fragments of wholes, but simply parts. Unlike the idea of closed unity enforced in Western classical architecture, the structure can be added onto without substantial morphological transformation. Field configurations are inherently expandable; the possibility of incremental growth is anticipated in the mathematical relations of the parts.

It could be argued that there are numerous examples of classical Western buildings that have grown incrementally and have been transformed overtime. St. Peter's Basilica in Rome, for example has an equally long history of construction and rebuilding. But there is a significant difference. At St. Peter's, additions are morphological transformations, elaborating and extending a basic geometric schema, and tending toward compositional closure. This contrasts with the mosque at Cordoba where each stage replicates and preserves the previous stage of construction by the addition of similar parts. And at Cordoba, even in later stages when the mosque was consecrated as Christian church and a Gothic cathedral was inserted into the continuous and undifferentiated fabric of the mosque, the existing spatial order resisted the central or axial focus typical of the Western church. As Rafael Moneo has observed: "I do not believe that the Cordoba Mosque has been destroyed by all these modifications. Rather, I think that the fact that the mosque continues to be itself in face of all these interventions is a tribute to its own integrity."[6]

To briefly extend the argument to a more recent example, Le Corbusier's Venice Hospital (1964–65) employs a syntax of repeated self-same parts, establishing multiple links at its periphery with the city fabric. The project develops horizontally, through a logic of accumulation. The basic block of program, the "care unit" formed of twenty-eight beds, is repeated throughout. Consulting rooms occupy open circulation spaces in the covered areas between. The rotating placement of blocks establishes connections and pathways from ward to ward, while the displacement of the blocks opens up voids within the horizontal field of the hospital. There is no single focus, no unifying geometric schema. As in the mosque at Cordoba, the overall form is an elaboration of conditions established locally.[7]

0.3 Walking Out of Cubism

Barnett Newman, it has been said, used a sequence of plane/line/plane to "walk out of the imperatives of cubist space and close the door behind him."[8] The story of postwar American painting and sculpture is in large part a story of this effort to move beyond the limits of cubist compositional syntax. Sculptors in particular, working under the shadow of the achievements of abstract expressionist painting, felt that a complex language of faceted planes and figural fragments inherited from pre-war European artists was inadequate to their larger ambitions. It is out of this sense of exhaustion that minimalism emerged in the mid-sixties. Robert Morris's refusal of composition in favor of process, or Donald Judd's critique of "composition by parts" evidence this effort to produce a new model for working that might be as simple and immediate as the painting of the previous decades they so admired.

Minimalist work of the sixties and seventies sought to empty the artwork of its figurative or decorative character in order to foreground its architectural condition. The construction of meaning was displaced from the object itself to the spatial field between the viewer and the object: a fluid zone of perceptual interference, populated by moving bodies. Artists such as Carl Andre, Dan Flavin, Morris, and Judd sought to go beyond formal or compositional variation to engage the space of the gallery and the body of the viewer. In written statements, both Judd and Morris express their skepticism toward European (i.e., cubist) compositional norms. They place their work instead in the context of recent American developments. As Morris wrote: "European art since Cubism has been a history of permuting relationships around the general premise that relationships should remain critical. American art has developed by uncovering successive premises for making itself."[9] Both Morris and Judd single out Jackson Pollock for his decisive contribution. Judd notes that "Most sculpture is made part by part, by addition, composed." For Judd, what is required is consolidation: "In the new work the shape, image, color, and surface are single and not partial and scattered. There aren't any neutral or moderate areas or parts, any connections or transitional areas."[10] The aspirations of minimalist work are therefore toward unitary forms, direct use of industrial materials, and simple combinations: a "pre-executive" clarity of intellectual and material terms. Minimalism's decisive tectonic shift activated the viewing space and reasserted the artwork's condition as "specific object."

And yet if minimalism represents a significant overturning of prewar compositional principles, it remains indebted to certain essentializing models in its reductive formal language and use of materials. Its objects are clearly delimited and solidly constructed. (Judd's later architectural constructions confirm this essential tectonic conservatism.) Minimalism develops in sequences, but rarely in fields. It is for this reason that the work of artists usually designated "postminimal" is of particular interest here.[11] In contrast to Andre or Judd, the work of artists such as Bruce Nauman, Lynda Benglis, Keith Sonnier, Alan Saret, Eva Hesse, and Barry Le Va is materially diverse and improper. Words, movement, technology, fluid and perishable materials, representations of the body—all of these "extrinsic" contents that minimalism had repressed—return. Postminimalism is marked by hesitation and ontological doubt where the minimalists are definitive; it is painterly and informal where the minimalists are restrained; it remains committed to tangible things and visibility where the minimalists are concerned with underlying structures and ideas. These works, from the wire constructions of Alan Saret to the pourings of Lynda Benglis to the "nonsites" of Robert Smithson, introduce chance and contingency into the work of art. They shift even more radically the perception of the work, from discrete object to a record of the process of its making in the field.

The artist who moves most decisively in the direction of what I am calling field conditions is Barry Le Va. Partly trained as an architect, Le Va is acutely aware of the spatial field implicated by the sculptural work. Beginning in the mid-sixties, he began making pieces, some planned in advance, others incorporating random process, that thoroughly dissolve the idea of "sculpture" as a delimited entity, an object distinct from the field it occupies. He called these works "distributions": "Whether 'random' or 'orderly' a 'distribution' is defined as 'relationships of points and configurations to each other' or concomitantly, 'sequences of events.'"[12] Local relationships are more important than overall form. The generation of form through "sequences of events" is somewhat related to the generative rules for flock behavior or algebraic combination. Le Va signals a key compositional principle emerging out of postminimalism: the displacement of control to a series of intricate local rules for combination, or as a "sequences of events," but not as an overall formal configuration. In the case of postminimalism, this is often related to material choices. When working with materials such as wire mesh (Saret), poured latex (Benglis), or blown flour (Le Va), the artist simply cannot exercise a precise formal control over the material. Instead the artist establishes the conditions within which the material will be deployed, and then directs its flows. In the case of Le Va's pieces of felt cloth, it is a matter of relating fold to fold, line to line. In later works from the sixties, the materials themselves become so ephemeral as to function as a delicate registration of process and change.

0.4 Thick 2D: Moirés, Mats

All grids are fields, but not all fields are grids. One of the potentials of the field is to redefine the relation between figure and ground. If we think of the figure not as a demarcated object read against a stable field, but as an effect emerging from the field itself—as moments of intensity, as peaks or valleys within a continuous field—then it might be possible to imagine figure and field as more closely allied. What is intended here is a close attention to the production of difference at the local scale, even while maintaining a relative indifference to the form of the whole. Authentic and productive social differences, it is suggested, thrive at the local level, and not in the form of large scale semiotic messages or sculptural forms. Hence the study of these field combinations would be a study of models that work in the zone between figure and abstraction, models that refigure the conventional opposition between figure and abstraction, or systems of organization capable of producing vortexes, peaks, and protuberances out of individual elements that are themselves regular or repetitive.

A moiré is a figural effect produced by the superposition of two regular fields. Unexpected effects, exhibiting complex and apparently irregular behaviors result from the combination of elements that are in and of themselves repetitive and regular. But moiré effects are not random. They shift abruptly in scale, and repeat according to complex mathematical rules. Moiré effects are often used to measure hidden stresses in continuous fields, or to map complex figural forms. In either case there is an uncanny coexistence of a regular field and emergent figure.

In the architectural or urban context, the example of moiré effects begs the question of the surface. The field *is* fundamentally a horizontal phenomenon—even a graphic one—and all of the examples described thus far function in the plan dimension. Although certain postmodern cities (Tokyo for example) might be characterized as fully three dimensional fields, the prototypical cities of the late twentieth century are distinguished by horizontal extension. What these field combinations seem to promise in this context is a thickening and intensification of experience at specified moments within the extended field of the city. The monuments of the past, including the skyscraper, a modernist monument to efficient production, stood out from the fabric of the city as privileged vertical moments. The new institutions of the city will perhaps occur at moments of intensity, linked to the wider network of the urban field, and marked by not by demarcating lines but by thickened surfaces.

0.5 Flocks, Schools, Swarms, Crowds

In the late 1980s, artificial intelligence theorist Craig Reynolds created a computer program to simulate the flocking behavior of birds. As described by M. Mitchel Waldrop in *Complexity: The Emerging Science at the Edge of Order and Chaos*, Reynolds placed a large number of autonomous, birdlike agents, which he called "boids," into an on-screen environment. The boids were programmed to follow three simple rules of behavior: first, to maintain a minimum distance from other objects in the environment (obstacles as well as other boids); second, to match velocities with other boids in the neighborhood; third, to move toward the perceived center of mass of boids in its neighborhood. As Waldrop notes:

> What is striking about these rules is that none of them said "Form a flock"...the rules were entirely local, referring only to what an individual boid could do and see in its own vicinity. If a flock was going to form at all, it would have to do so from the bottom up, as an emergent phenomenon. And yet flocks *did* form, every time.[13]

The flock is clearly a field phenomenon, defined by precise and simple local conditions, and relatively indifferent to overall form and extent. Because the rules are defined locally, obstructions are not catastrophic to the whole. Variations and obstacles in the environment are accommodated by fluid adjustment. A small flock and a large flock display fundamentally the same structure. Over many iterations, patterns emerge. Without repeating exactly, flock behavior tends toward roughly similar configurations, not as a fixed type, but as the cumulative result of localized behavior patterns.

Crowds present a different dynamic, motivated by more complex desires, and interacting in less predictable patterns. Elias Canetti in *Crowds and Power* has proposed a broader taxonomy: *open* and *closed* crowds; *rhythmic* and *stagnating* crowds; the *slow* crowd and the *quick* crowd. He examines the varieties of the crowd, from the religious throng formed by pilgrims to the mass of participants in spectacle, even extending his thoughts to the flowing of rivers, the piling up of crops, and the density of the forest. According to Canetti, the crowd has four primary attributes: "The crowd always wants to grow; Within a crowd there is equality; The crowd loves density; The crowd needs a direction."[14] The relation to Reynolds' rules outlined above is oblique, but visible. Canetti, however, is not interested in prediction or verification. His sources are literary, historical, and personal. Moreover, he is always aware that the crowd can be liberating as well as confining, angry and destructive as well as joyous.

Composer Iannis Xenakis conceived his early work *Metastasis* as the acoustical equivalent to the phenomenon of the crowd. Specifically, he was looking for a compositional technique adequate to express powerful personal memories:

> Athens—an anti-Nazi demonstration—hundreds of thousands of people chanting a slogan which reproduces itself like a gigantic rhythm. Then combat with the enemy. The rhythm bursts into an enormous chaos of sharp sounds; the whistling of bullets; the crackling of machine guns. The sounds begin to disperse. Slowly silence falls back on the town. Taken uniquely from an aural point of view and detached from any other aspect these sound events made out of a large number of individual sounds are not separately perceptible,

but reunite them again and a new sound is formed which may be perceived in its entirety. It is the same case with the song of the cicadas or the sound of hail or rain, the crashing of waves on the cliffs, the hiss of waves on the shingle.[15]

In attempting to reproduce these "global acoustical events," Xenakis drew upon his own considerable graphic imagination, and his training in descriptive geometry to invert conventional procedures of composition. That is to say, he began with a graphic notation describing the desired effect of "fields" or "clouds" of sound, and only later reduced these graphics to conventional musical notation. Working as he was with material that was beyond the order of magnitude of the available compositional techniques, he had to invent new procedures in order to choreograph the "characteristic distribution of vast numbers of events."[16]

Crowds and swarms operate at the edge of control. Aside from the suggestive formal possibilities, with these two examples architecture could profitably shift its attention from its traditional top-down forms of control and begin to investigate the possibilities of a more fluid, bottom-up approach. Field conditions offers a tentative opening in architecture to address the dynamics of use, behavior of crowds, and the complex geometries of masses in motion.

0.6 Distributed Institutions

There exists a strong historical connection between the precise rules of axiality, symmetry, and formal hierarchy that govern classical architecture and the traditional type-forms of Western institutions. The library, the museum, and the concert hall, as much as the bank, the city hall, or the capitol all appeal to the stability of classical order to signify their status as durable institutions. In the twentieth century, the utopian programs of early modern architecture sought to render the institutions of liberal democracy as transparent bodies. Lightweight steel skeletons and glass curtain walls signaled literal transparency, while a functional and compositional dynamic made visible the separate elements of these increasingly complex programs.

However, the extent to which compositional shifts are capable of refiguring these institutions reaches a limit. On the one hand, it should be noted that while the rules of combination may be new in these modernist compositions of fragments, the classical assumption that composition is concerned with the arrangement of and connections among those parts persists. As Robert Morris has put it, "European art since Cubism has been a history of permuting relationships around the general premise that *relationships should remain critical.*"[17] Perhaps a more radical shift is required. This is all the more urgent given that, under the pressure of technological or societal shifts, institutions are changing from within. As the social, political, and technical roles of those institutions are called into question, the corresponding typologies lose their special capacity to order and represent the space of these institutions. In the case of the library or the museum, what was once a place of certainty, an orderly deposit of knowledge arranged in familiar and agreed-upon categories, has been eroded by the onrush of media, consumer culture, and telecommunications. Architecture's capacity to represent and shelter that collective memory has in turn withered. To design a library or a museum today is to contend with an entirely new set of expectations. Above all, it means to recognize an ever increasing uncertainty about what constitutes knowledge, who has access to it and how it is distributed.

There are no simple equations of organization and behavior, of politics and form. As Michel Foucault has pointed out, while there are constraining architectures, there are no specifically "liberating" architectures. "Liberty," he says, "is a practice."[18]

Nonhierarchical compositions cannot guarantee an open society or equality in politics. Democracy, it has been said, has less to do with the ability to do things as with the ability to undo things. The goal, therefore, in the final two projects presented in this volume [*Points and Lines*; the Korean-American Museum, Los Angeles, 1995; and the National Diet Library, Kyoto Prefecture, Japan, 1996] is to rethink conventional institutional form through the concept of the field. The organizational principles proposed here suggest new definitions of "parts" and alternative ways of conceiving the question of relationships among those parts. The form of these institutions does not attempt to represent, metaphorically, the new condition of the institution, nor does it attempt to directly instigate new ways of thinking or behaving. Instead, by forming the institution within a directed field condition, connected to the city or the landscape, a space is left for the tactical improvisations of future users. A "loose fit" is proposed between activity and enclosing envelope.

Michel Serres's reminder that static, accidents, and disruptions will inevitably undermine any formal system defined by points and lines is not so far from what is intended here. More than a formal configuration, the field condition implies an architecture that admits change, accident, and improvisation. It is an architecture not invested in durability, stability, and certainty, but an architecture that leaves space for the uncertainty of the real:

> Stations and paths together form a system. Points and lines, beings and relations. What is interesting might be the construction of the system, the number and disposition of stations and paths. Or it might be the flow of messages passing through the lines. In other words, a complex system can be formally described...One might have sought the formation and distribution of the lines, paths, and stations, their

borders, edges and forms. But one must write as well of the interceptions, of the accidents in the flow along the way between stations...What passes may be a message but parasites (static) prevent it from being heard, and sometimes, from being sent.[19]

Notes

1   Sanford Kwinter, "La Cittá Nuova: Modernity and Continuity" in *Zone* 1/2 (New York, 1986), 88–89, emphasis added.

2   Xenakis uses language and concepts very close to those suggested here. See Nouritza Matossian, *Xenakis* (London: Kahn and Averill, 1990), 59.

3   The following discussion was adapted from Rafael Moneo: "La Vida de los edifcios" *Arquitecture* 256 (Sept.–Oct. 1985): 27–36.

4   This phrase is taken from Donald Judd's discussion of the paintings of Frank Stella: "The order is not rationalistic and underlying but is simply order, like that of continuity, one thing after another." Donald Judd, "Specific Objects," in *Complete Writings: 1959–1975* (Halifax: Nova Scotia College of Art and Design, 1975), 184.

5   The term *algebra* derives from the Arabic *al-jebr,* "the reunion of broken parts." *Geometry*, on the other hand, is a word of Greek origin.

6   Moneo, "La Vida," 35.

7   Both the mosque at Cordoba and Le Corbusier's Venice Hospital figure in Alison Smithson's 1974 article "How to Recognise and Read Mat-Building," *Architectural Design* XLIV, 9 (1974): 573–90.

8   Cited in Rosalind Krauss, "Richard Serra: Sculpture Redrawn," *Artforum* (May 1972).

9   Robert Morris, "Anti Form," *Artforum* (Apr. 1968): 34.

10   Judd, "Specific Objects," 183.

11   In fact, postminimalism developed at nearly the same time as minimalism. "Post" here implies a certain degree of dependence and opposition rather than chronological sequence. Note, for example, the absence of women in the ranks of the minimalists; postminimalism would be unthinkable without the contributions of Lynda Benglis or Eva Hesse. A certain fluidity in these categories is also required; Robert Morris, for example, is often grouped with the postminimalists. See Robert Pincus-Witten, "Introduction to

Postminimalism" (1977) in *Postminimalism to Maximalism: American Art, 1966–1986* (Ann Arbor, Mich.: UMI Research Press, 1987).

12 Jane Livingston, "Barry Le Va: Distributional Sculpture," *Artforum* (Nov. 1968).

13 M. Mitchel Waldrop, *Complexity: The Emerging Science at the Edge of Order and Chaos* (New York: Simon and Schuster, 1992), 240–41.

14 Elias Canetti, *Crowds and Power* (New York: Farrar, Straus and Giroux, 1984), 29.

15 Matossian, *Xenakis,* cited from an interview, 58.

16 Ibid., 58–59.

17 Morris, "Anti Form": 34, emphasis added.

18 Michel Foucault, "Nietzsche, Genealogy, History" in *The Foucault Reader*, ed. Paul Rabinow (New York: Pantheon, 1984), 87.

19 Michel Serres, *The Parasite*, trans. Lawrence R. Schehr (Baltimore, Md.: Johns Hopkins University Press, 1982), 10–11.

INTRODUCTION
Junkspace / *Rem Koolhaas*

Rarely do architects receive front-cover billing on mainstream print publications; yet, in July of 2000, a portrait of Rem Koolhaas filled the cover of the *New York Times Magazine* with a headline reading "The Architect's Architect in the Architect's Time."[1] Indeed, through his built and written work, the Dutch architect—cofounder of the Office for Metropolitan Architecture (OMA) and father of its radical counterpart AMO (the theoretical and research-based armature of the design practice)—has had a tremendous impact on contemporary culture, architectural and beyond. While Koolhaas gained recognition within the discipline for his 1978 book *Delirious New York*, by the mid-1990s he had achieved wider renown: his Maison à Bordeaux and *SMLXL*, his project with Bruce Mau, both appeared on Time magazine's list of the best designs (of 1998 and 1996, respectively).[2]

Thus Koolhaas's prominence was well established when his essay "Junkspace" was published in a special edition of *A+U* in May 2000. Appearing at the turn of the twenty-first century, amid joyous anticipation of a new era and fearful predictions of impending doom (recall the hysteria surrounding the possible collapse of the digital world accompanying Y2K), Koolhaas's concept of junkspace is simultaneously fascinating and unnerving. Junkspace, "the residue mankind leaves on the planet," is characterized by Koolhaas in a sprawling and cynical diatribe that both induces and mimics—in form, structure, and substance—the mind-numbing qualities he attributes to junkspace itself. Koolhaas's text describes a bewildering, contradicting, simultaneously exciting and distressing cultural state that permeates contemporary existence: the never-ending search for the innovative, the new, the best and brightest, a quest that gives rise, from Koolhaas's perspective, to "a terminal hollowness." More chilling

134

perhaps is the assessment of architecture's recent past: "It was a mistake," Koolhaas declares, "to invent modern architecture for the twentieth century; architecture disappeared in the twentieth century; we have been reading a footnote under a microscope hoping it would turn into a novel."

What does such an analysis imply for architecture's future?[3] While Koolhaas leaves this question unanswered, "Junkspace" does imply that whatever architecture's next step may be (if architecture as such even still exists), the rules of the game have changed forever.

Notes

1 *New York Times Magazine*, July 9, 2000.

2 Recently, Koolhaas's prominence has reached amazing levels; he is listed alongside politicians, actors, corporate CEOs, and entrepreneurs as one of *Time*'s 100 most influential people (interestingly, Koolhaas's occupation is described as "Starchitect." See "The 2008 *Time* 100 Finalists," *Time*, http://www.time.com/time/specials/2007/article/0,28804,1725112_1723512_1723792,00.html.

3 In "Future City," reprinted in this collection, Fredric Jameson offers a reading of "Junkspace" that interprets the text's relationship to notions of history and history's possible future.

REM KOOLHAAS

JUNKSPACE

First appeared in *A+U Special Issue: OMA @ Work* (May 2000),
16–24. Courtesy of OMA.

"Logan Airport: a world-class upgrade for the twenty-first
century" (*Late twentieth century billboard*)

Introduction
If space-junk is the human debris that litters the universe, junkspace is the residue mankind leaves on the planet. The built
(more about that later) product of modernization is not modern architecture but Junkspace. Junkspace is what remains
after modernization has run its course or, more precisely, what
coagulates while modernization is taking place, its fall-out.
Modernization had a rational program: to share the blessings of
science, universally. Junkspace is its apotheosis, or meltdown…
although its individual parts are the outcome of brilliant inventions, hyper technical, lucidly planned by human intelligence,
imagination and infinite computation, their sum spells the end
of Enlightenment, its resurrection as farce, a low grade purga-
tory…Junkspace is the sum total of our current architecture;

we have built as much as all previous history together, but we hardly register on the same scales. Junkspace is the product of the encounter between escalator and air-conditioning, conceived in an incubator of sheetrock; (all three missing from the history books). Junkspace is the body-double of space, a territory of impaired ambition, limited expectation, reduced earnestness. Junkspace is a Bermuda Triangle of concepts, a Petri dish abandoned: it lowers immunity, cancels distinctions, undermines resolve, prefers intention to realization. It substitutes accumulation for hierarchy, addition for composition. More and more, more is more. Junkspace is overripe and undernourishing at the same time, a colossal security blanket that covers the earth, the sum of all decisions not taken, issues not faced, choices not made, priorities left undefined, contradictions perpetuated, compromises embraced, corruption tolerated…Junkspace is like being condemned to a perpetual Jacuzzi with millions of your best friends…

A fuzzy empire of blur, it fuses public and private, straight and bent, bloated and starved, high and low to offer a seamless patchwork of the permanently disjointed. Seemingly an apotheosis, spatially grandiose, the effect of its richness is a terminal hollowness, a vicious parody that systematically erodes the credibility of architecture, possibly forever…

OK, let's talk about space then. The beauty of airports, especially after each upgrade. The sparkle of renovations. The variety of shopping centers. Let's explore Public Space, discover Casinos, investigate Theme Parks. Our concern for the people has made people's architecture invisible. It was a mistake to invent modern architecture for the twentieth century; architecture disappeared in the twentieth century; we have been reading a footnote under a microscope hoping it would turn into a novel. Junkspace seems an aberration, but it is essence, the main thing. Junkspace looks as if a hurricane has rearranged a previously ordered condition, but that impression is misleading—it was never coherent and never aspired to be. When we think about space, we have only looked at its containers. All theory for the production of space is based on an obsessive preoccupation with its opposite, substance, i.e. architecture. Continuity is the essence of Junkspace; it exploits any invention that enables expansion, enlists any device that promotes disorientation, (mirror, polish, echo), deploys an infrastructure of seamlessness: escalator, sprinkler, fire-shutter, hot-air curtain, air-conditioning…Junkspace is sealed, held together not by structure, but by skin, like a bubble. Gravity has remained constant, resisted by the same arsenal since the beginning of time; but air-conditioning—invisible medium, therefore unrecorded—has truly revolutionized twentieth century architecture. Air-conditioning has launched the endless building. If architecture is what separates buildings; air-conditioning is what unites them. Air-conditioning has dictated mutant regimes of organization and coexistence that architecture can no longer follow. Like in the Middle Ages; a single shopping center is now the work of generations; air-conditioning makes or breaks our cathedrals. Because it costs money, is no longer free, conditioned space becomes inevitably conditional space; sooner or later all conditional space turns into Junkspace. Junkspace is always interior, so extensive that you rarely perceive limits; space was created by piling matter on top of matter, cemented to form a new whole. Junkspace is additive, layered and light weight, quartered the way a carcass is torn apart by predators—chunks severed from a universal condition. Walls have ceased to exist, only partitions subdivide now, shimmering membranes frequently covered in gold. Structure groans invisibly underneath decoration, or worse, is decoration: small shiny space frames that support nominal loads…

Junkspace is a domain of feigned, simulated geometry. Although strictly non-architectural, it tends to the vaulted, to the Dome. Sections seem to be devoted to utter inertness, others frantically committed to articulation: the deadest next to the most hysterical. Themes cast a pall of arrested development over interiors as big as the Pantheon, spawning stillbirths in every corner. The esthetic is Byzantine: splintered into thousands of shards: all visible at the same time, a dizzy panoptical populism. Neon signifies both the new and the old. Regressive and Futuristic, interiors refer to the Stone and the Space Age at the same time. Like the inactive virus in an inoculation, modern architecture remains essential, but only its most useless performance; Hi-Tech has been revived to celebrate the Millennium; it seemed so dead only a decade ago. It is based on the foregrounding of what previous generations kept under wraps: molluscular forms with tautly stretched skins, emergency stairs suspended in unilateral trapeze, handcrafted members propping quasi-industrial plant rooms, acres of glass hung from spidery cables, probes thrusting into space to deliver laboriously what elsewhere happens unaided, free air. Transparency only reveals everything in which you cannot partake. At the sound of midnight, all of it may revert to Taiwanese Gothic, in three years segue into Nigerian Contemporary. Murals used to show Gods; Junkspace's modules are scaled to carry Brands. Myths can be inhabited, Brands husband aura at the mercy of focus groups. Junkspace is based on cooperation. There is no design but creative proliferation. Three-dimensional graphics, transplanted emblems of franchise and sparkling infrastructures of light, LED's, and video describe an authorless world beyond anyone's claim, utterly unique, totally unpredictable, yet intensely familiar. Regurgitation instead of resuscitation. Junkspace sheds architectures like a reptile sheds skins, is reborn every Monday morning. In classical space, materiality was based on a final state that could only be modified at the expense of at least partial destruction. At the exact moment that regularity and repetition has been abandoned as repressive, building materials have become more and more modular, unitary and standardized, as if substance comes pre-digitized, (the next level of abstraction). The module becomes smaller and smaller, to the point where it becomes a mosaic. With enormous difficulty—argument, negotiation, sabotage—irregularity and uniqueness are constructed from identical elements. Instead of trying to wrest order from chaos, the picturesque now is wrested from the homogenized. All materialization is provisional: cutting, bending, tearing, coating: construction has acquired a new softness, like tailoring…The joint is no longer problematic: transitional moments are defined by stapling and taping, wrinkly brown bands barely maintain the illusion of an unbroken surface; verbs unknown in architectural history: clamp, stick, fold, dump, glue, double, fuse, have become indispensable. Each element performs its task in negotiated isolation. Where once detailing suggested the coming together, possibly forever, of disparate materials, it is now a transient coupling, waiting to be undone, unscrewed, a temporary embrace that none of its constituent parts may survive; no longer the orchestrated encounter of difference, but a stalemate, the abrupt end of a system. Only the blind, reading these faultlines with fingertips, will understand Junkspace's histories…Facetted like a formation of crystals, not by nature or design, but by default, Junkspace is like stained glass that has become three-dimensional, a buffer of colour in front of fluorescent walls that generate additional heat to raise the temperature of Junkspace to levels where you could cultivate orchids. Junkspace is hot space.

There are two kinds of density in Junkspace—the first optical, the second informational. They compete. Junkspace always changes, but it never evolves. The program of Junkspace is escalation—as in Ravel's Bolero. Assuming histories left and right, its contents are repetitive and stable; they multiply as in cloning, more of the same. Sections rot, are no longer viable, connected to the flesh of the main body via gangrenous passages. Junkspace is an ur-soup of deferment and consummation, a new form of form follows function bondage. Devoted to instant gratification, Junkspace accommodates seeds of future perfection; a language of apology is woven through its texture of basic euphoria. "Closed for your future entertainment," "pardon our appearance" or miniature yellow "sorry" billboards mark ongoing repairs or patches of wetness, announce momentary closure in return for imminent sparkle, the allure of improvement. All surfaces are archeological, superpositions of different "periods"; (what do you call the moment a particular type of wall-to-wall carpet was current?) In theory, each megastructure spawns its own sub-systems of compatible particles, tends to create a universe of rampant cohesion. In Junkspace the tables are turned: it is subsystems only, without concept, orphaned particles in search of a plan or a pattern. Traditionally, typology implies demarcation, the definition of a singular model that excludes other interpretations. Junkspace represents a reverse typology of cumulative, promiscuous identity, less about kind than about quantity. A typology of the formless is still a typology, absence of form is still form...

For instance, the typology of the dump, where successive trucks discharge their loads to form a heap, whole in spite of the arbitrariness of its contents and its fundamental incompleteness, or that of the tent—envelope that assumes different shapes to accommodate variable interior volumes. Junkspace can either be absolutely chaotic or frighteningly sterile and perfect, indeterminate and overdetermined at the same time. Junkspace is like a liquid that could have condensed in any other form. Its specific configuration is as fortuitous as the geometry of a snowflake. Patterns imply repetition or ultimately decipherable rules; Junkspace is beyond geometry, beyond pattern. Because it cannot be grasped, Junkspace can not be remembered. It is flamboyant yet unmemorable, like a screen saver, its refusal to freeze insuring instant amnesia.

Circulation

Junkspace is often described as a space of flows, but that is a misnomer; flows depend on disciplined movement, bodies that cohere. Although it is an architecture of the masses, each trajectory is strictly unique. Junkspace is a web without a spider.

This anarchy is one of the last tangible ways in which we measure our freedom. It is a space of collision, a container of atoms. It is busy, not dense. There is a special way of moving in Junkspace, at the same time aimless and purposeful. It is an acquired culture. Sometimes an entire Junkspace comes unstuck through the non-conformity of one of its members; a single citizen of an another culture—an Albanian peasant, a Portuguese mother—can hold up and destabilize an entire Junkspace, leaving an invisible swath of obstruction in its wake, a deregulation eventually communicated to its furthest extremities. When movement becomes coordinated, it curdles: on escalators, near exits, parking machines, automated tellers.

Sometimes, under duress, individuals are corralled in a flow, pushed through a single door or forced to negotiate the gap between two temporary obstacles (an invalids' bleeping chariot and a palm): the manifest ill-will such channeling provokes, mocks of the notion of flows. Flows in Junkspace lead to disaster: dead bodies piling up in front of the locked emergency doors of a disco, department stores at the beginning of sales, the stampedes of warring contingents of soccer fans: evidence of the misfit between the portals of Junkspace and the mean calibrations of the rest of the world. Each architecture now embodies two conditions: one part permanent, the other temporary. Sections age, others are upgraded. Judging the built presumed a static condition; Junkspace is always in a state of becoming. Say an airport needs more space. In the past new terminals were added, each more or less characteristic of its own age, leaving the old ones as a readable record, a progression. Since passengers have amply demonstrated their infinite malleability, the idea of rebuilding on the spot has gained currency. Travelators are thrown in reverse. The concourse becomes indescribable: former spaces of blandness suddenly turn into casbah-generic, offering vistas into a nether world of improvised locker rooms, manual labor, smoking, coffee breaks, real fires...

Screens of taped sheetrock segregate two populations: one wet, one dry, one hard, one soft, one cold, one overheated, one male, one neutered...

One shift creates new space, the other consumes old space. The ceiling is a crumpled plate like the Alps; grids of unstable tiles alternate with monogrammed sheets of black plastic, improbably punctured by grids of crystal chandeliers...Metal ducts are replaced by breathing textiles. Gaping joints reveal vast ceiling voids, (former canyons of asbestos?), harsh beams, duct, rope, cable, insulation, fireproofing, string; tangled arrangements suddenly exposed to daylight, so impure, tortured and complex that they exist only because they were never thought out. The floor is a patchwork: different textures—hairy, heavy, shiny, plastic, metallic, muddy, struggle for dominance...

The ground is no more. There are too many raw needs to be realized on only one plane. The idea of a datum level, the absolute of the horizontal, has been abandoned. Transparency has disappeared, replaced by a dense crust of preliminary occupation: kiosks, carts, strollers, palms, fountains, bars, sofas, trolleys...Corridors no longer simply link A to B, but have become arcades, destinations. Their tenant life tends to be short: the ugliest dresses, most stagnant windows, the most inexplicable flowers. All perspective is gone, as in a rain forest, (itself disappearing...)

The straight is coiled into ever more labyrinthine configurations. Only a kind of perverse modernist choreography can explain the twists and turns, ascents and descents, sudden reversals that comprise the average path from check-in (misleading name) to apron in the average contemporary airport. Because we never question or reconstruct the absurdity of our trajectories, we meekly submit to Dantesque journeys past perfume, asylum seeker, underwear, oysters, cell phone, smoked salmon...incredible adventures for the brain, the eye, the nose, the tongue, the womb, the testicles...There was once a polemic about the straight line; now the 90 degree angle has become one among many. In fact, remnants of former geometries create ever new havoc, offering forlorn nodes of resistance that create unstable eddies in newly opportunistic flows...Who would dare claim responsibility for this sequence? The idea that a profession once dictated, or at least presumed to predict, people's movements, now seems laughable. Or worse: unthinkable. Instead of design, there is calculation: the more erratic the path, the more eccentric the loops, the more efficient the exposure, the more inevitable the transaction. Postmodernism adds a crumple-zone of viral poché that fractures and multiplies the endless front-line of display, a peristaltic shrink-wrap crucial to all commercial exchange. Trajectories are launched as ramp, turn horizontal without any warning, intersect, fold down, suddenly emerge on a balcony above a large void. (Unknowingly, you always inhabit a sandwich. Space is scooped out of Junkspace as from a block of ice cream that has spent too long in the freezer: cone shaped, spherical, whatever…) An escalator takes you to an unknown destination from the sudden dead-end where you were dropped by a monumental, granite staircase, facing a provisional vista of plaster, inspired by forgettable sources.

Toilet groups mutate into Disney Store then morph to become meditation center: successive transformations mock the word "plan." In this stand-off between the redundant and the inevitable, a plan would actually make matters worse, drive you to instant despair. The plan is a radar screen where individual pulses survive for unpredictable periods of time in a Bacchanalian free-for-all.

Only the diagram gives a bearable version. Junkspace is post-existential: it makes you uncertain where you are, obscures where you go, dismantles where you were. Who are you? You thought that you could ignore Junkspace, visit it surreptitiously, treat it with condescending contempt or enjoy it vicariously. Because you could not understand it, you've thrown away the keys…but now your own architecture is infected, has become equally smooth, all-inclusive, continuous, warped, busy…

Political

Junkspace will be our tomb. Half of mankind pollutes to produce, the other pollutes to consume. The combined pollution of all Third World cars, motorbikes, trucks, busses, sweatshops, pales into insignificance compared to the heat generated by Junkspace. Junkspace is political: it depends on the central removal of the critical faculty in the name of comfort and pleasure. Entire miniature states now adopt Junkspace as a political program, establish regimes of engineered disorientation, instigate a politics of systematic disarray. Not exactly "anything goes"; in fact, the secret of Junkspace is that it is both promiscuous and repressive: as the formless proliferates, the formal withers, and with it all rules, regulations, recourse…Junkspace knows all your emotions, all your desires. It is the interior of Big Brother's belly. It preempts people's sensations. It comes with a soundtrack, smell, captions; it blatantly advertises how it wants to be read: stunning, cool, huge, abstract, "minimal," historical. Junkspace's inmates form a collective of brooding consumers in surly anticipation of their next spend, a mass of refractory periods caught in a Thousand Year Reign of Razzmatazz. Junkspace pretends to unite, but it actually splinters. It creates communities not of shared interest or free association, but of identical statistics, a mosaic of the common denominator. Ego is stripped of privacy and mystery, each man, woman and child individually targeted, spied on, split off from the rest. Fragments come together at "security" only, where a grid of video screens disappointingly reassembles magical frames into a banalized, utilitarian cubism that reveals Junkspace's overall coherence to the dispassionate glare of barely trained guards: video-ethnography in its brute form. The shiniest surfaces in the history of mankind reflect humanity at its most casual. The more we inhabit the palatial, the more we dress down. As if the People suddenly accessed the private quarters of the Dictator, a stringent dress code—last etiquette?—governs access to Junkspace: short, sneaker, sandal, jean, backpack, parka, shellsuit, fleece.

Junkspace is best enjoyed in a state of post-revolutionary gawking. There is zero loyalty toward configuration, no "original" condition, architecture as has turned into a sequence of video stills...The only certainly is conversion—continuous— followed, in rare cases, by "restoration." That is the process that claims ever new sections of history as extension of Junkspace. Just as Junkspace is unstable, its actual ownership is forever being passed on in parallel disloyalty. As its scale mushrooms— rivals and even exceeds that of the Public—its economy becomes more inscrutable. Its financing is a deliberate haze, clouding opaque deals, dubious tax breaks, "surprising" incentives, tenuous ownership, transferred air rights, joined properties, special zoning districts, public-private complicities. Junkspace happens spontaneously through natural corporate exuberance—the unfettered play of the market—or it is generated through the combined actions of temporary "Tsars" with long records or three-dimensional philanthropy, civil servants (often former leftists) that optimistically sell off vast tracks of waterfront, former hippodromes, abandoned airfields, and/or default preservation TM (the maintenance of historical complexes that nobody wants but that somehow cannot be destroyed), to real estate agents that accommodate any deficit in a futuristic glow. Funded by lottery, subsidy, charity, grant: an erratic flow of Dollars, Euros and Yens creates financial envelopes as fragile as their interior configurations. Because of a structural shortfall, a fundamental minus—a bearish bankruptcy—each square inch becomes a grasping, needy surface depending on covert or overt support, compensation and fund-raising. For culture, "engraved donor bricks," for everything else: cash, rentals, leases, chains, brands claiming "all the space that fits." Each attraction accumulates its own weaknesses; because of its tenuous viability, Junkspace swallows more and more program. Soon we'll be able to do anything anywhere...

In Junkspace old aura encounters new luster to spawn sudden commercial viability...Barcelona amalgamated with the Olympics, Bilbao with Guggenheim, 42nd with Disney. Instead of Public Life, Public Space TM: that what remains once the unpredictable has been removed. All Junkspace's prototypes are urban—the Roman Forum, Metropolis, the Future; only their synergy makes them suburban, simultaneously swollen and shrunk. Space is no longer related to density and intensification but to in- and deflation. Junkspace expands with the economy; its footprint cannot become smaller, only bigger. When it is no longer needed, it is abandoned.

REM KOOLHAAS · 147

For the third Millennium, Junkspace assumes responsibility for both entertainment and protection, exposure and intimacy, public and private. The chosen theater of megalomania, the dictatorial, is no longer polities, but entertainment. Through Junkspace, entertainment organizes hermetic regimes that are based on the same notion of "concentration" that gave us the concentration camp. Concentration Gambling, Concentration Golf, Concentration Convention, Concentration Movie, Concentration Culture, Concentration Holiday.

Entertainment is like watching a once hot planet cool off: its major inventions are ancient; the moving image, the roller coaster, sound, cartoons, clowns, dinosaurs, news, war. We have nothing to add, except stars, we recombine. Corporate-Entertainment is an empire of entropy, forced to go through the motions by ruthless Copernican laws. The secret of corporate aesthetics was the power of elimination, the eradication of excess. Abstraction as camouflage. On popular demand, Corporate Beauty has become humanist, inclusivist, arbitrary, poetic and comfortable: water is pressured through very small holes, then forced onto rigorous hoops; straight palms bent into grotesque poses, air burdened with oxygen—as if only forcing malleable substances into the most rigid behavior maintains control, satisfies the drive to exterminate surprise. Colour has disappeared to dampen the resulting cacophony; united in sedation…Junkspace is space as vacation.

Office

There once was a relationship between leisure and work, a biblical dictate on opening and closure. Now we work harder, stuck in a permanent weekend. The office is the next frontier of Junkspace. Now that you can work at home, the office aspires to the domestic; because you still need a life, it simulates the city. Junkspace features the office as the urban home: a meeting-boudoir, brave new desk sculptures, intimate downlights, monumental partitions, kiosks, mini-Starbucks on interior plazas, "wired" to all the world's other Junkspace, real or imagined. The twenty-first century will bring "intelligent" Junkspace: we will witness corporate agitprop: the CEO's suite becomes "leadership collective," the oxymoron as vision. On big digital murals: sales, CNN, NY Stock Exchange, presented in real time like a theory course at a Motoring School. "Team memory," "information persistence": futile hedges against the universal forgetting of the unmemorable. Intended for the interior, Junkspace can easily engulf a whole city in the form of Public Space TM. First, it escapes from its containers—ephemera that needed hothouse protection emerging with surprising robustness—then the outside itself is converted: danger eliminated, the street paved more luxuriously, traffic calmed. Then Junkspace spreads, consuming nature like a forest fire in L.A....Junkspace does not pretend to create perfection, only interest. It turns the existing—anything compromised—to its advantage, a new picturesque, even a new Gothic, generated by collisions between immutable objects and inchoate architectural energies, hybrids of forgetting and remembering. Its geometries are unimaginable, only doable. A new vegetal is corralled for its thematic efficiency. The outing of Junkspace has enabled the professionalization of denaturing, a benign ecofascism that positions a rare surviving Siberian tiger in a forest of slot machines, near Versace. Air, water, wood: everything is enhanced to produce a Hyperecology sanctimoniously invoked for maximum return. "Rain forest" or: Walden as farce. Outside, between the casinos, fountains project entire Stalinist buildings of liquid, ejaculated in a split-second, hovering momentarily, then withdrawn with an amnesiac competency that even Junkspace cannot yet equal. Can the bland be amplified? The featureless be exaggerated?

Airport

Through height? depth? length? variation? repetition? Sometimes not overload but its opposite, an absolute absence of detail, generates Junkspace. A voided condition of frightening sparseness, shocking proof that so much can be organized by so little. Airports, provisional accommodation for those going elsewhere inhabited by assemblies united only by the imminence of their dissolution, have turned into consumption gulags, democratically distributed across the globe to give every citizen an equal chance of admission (to become inmates)...Entire complexes are composed of three elements only, repeated ad infinitum, nothing else: one kind of beam, one kind of brick, one kind of tile, all coated in the same colour—is it teal? rust? tobacco?—Their symmetries inflated beyond any hope of recognition. Take DFW (Dallas Forth Worth Airport): in a wanton departure from the straight, the endless curve of its terminals forces its users to enact relativity theory in their quest for the gate. Its drop-off is the seemingly harmless beginning of a journey to the center of unmitigated nothingness, beyond animation by Pizza Hut, Dairy Queen...

Where culture was thinnest, will it be the first to run out? Is emptiness regional? Do wide open spaces demand wide open Junkspace? Sunbelt: huge populations where there was nothing; Indian motifs woven into wall-to-wall carpets at PHX, Public Art distributed across LAS: only what is dead can be resurrected. Death can be caused by surfeit or shortage of sterility; both conditions happen in Junkspace (often at the same time). Minimum is the ultimate ornament, the most self-righteous crime, the contemporary Baroque. It does not signify beauty, but guilt. Its demonstrative earnestness drives whole cultures into the welcoming arms of camp and kitsch. Seemingly a relief from constant sensorial onslaught, minimum is maximum in drag, a stealth repression of luxury: the stricter the lines, the more irresistible the seductions. Its role is not to approximate the sublime, but to minimize the shame of consumption, drain embarrassment, to lower the higher. Minimum now exists in a state of parasitic co-dependency with overdose: to have and not to have, to own and to crave, finally collapsed in a single emotion. Junkspace is like a womb that organizes the transition of endless quantities of the Real—stone, trees, goods, daylight, people—into the virtual.

Plastic

The constant threat of virtuality in Junkspace is no longer served by "plastic," formica or vinyl, materials that only "cheapen"; entire mountains are dismembered to provide ever greater quantities of authenticity, suspended on precarious brackets, polished to a blinding state of flash, that makes the intended realism instantly elusive. Stone only comes in flesh, light yellow, a soap-like green, the same colors as communist plastics in the fifties: wood is all pale: maybe the origins of Junkspace go back as far back as the first Kindergartens...

Colour in the real world looks increasingly unreal, drained. Colour in virtual space is luminous, therefore irresistible. The average Power Point presentation displays sudden bursts of Indian exuberance that Junkspace has been the first to translate into reality TM, a simulation of virtual vigor. The already considerable vastness of Junkspace is extended to infinity in virtual space. Conceptually, each monitor, each TV screen is a substitute for a window; real life is inside, cyberspace has become the great outdoors...

INTRODUCTION
The Cunning of Cosmetics / *Jeffrey Kipnis*

The Swiss firm of Herzog & de Meuron, founded by Jacques
Herzog and Pierre de Meuron in 1978, achieved international
recognition in the 1990s for such projects as the Ricola Factory in
Laufen, Switzerland (1989–91), and the Tate Modern in London
(1998–2000). In 2000, the year before the firm's principals
received the Pritzker Prize, an essay by Jeffrey Kipnis—an architect, critic, and educator at Ohio State University—appeared in
an *El Croquis* publication dedicated to the firm's work. In "The
Cunning of Cosmetics," a "personal reflection" with broader
implications, Kipnis identifies Herzog & de Meuron as an anomaly
within the contemporary architectural avant-garde. The radical
geometries and cross-disciplinary forays often exercised by early
twenty-first-century "cutting edge" architects have little place in
Herzog & de Meuron's work, which relies on Cartesian forms,
conventional materials (albeit used in unconventional ways),
and established architectural practices. Yet what Herzog & de
Meuron does with these seemingly normative elements defies typical expectations, giving rise to an architecture with "an urbane,
cunning intelligence and an intoxicating, almost erotic allure."
Herzog & de Meuron frequently focuses on the building's surface,
prompting Kipnis to develop the concept of the cosmetic,
as opposed to the more traditionally understood notion of ornament. Ornaments append to a body yet remain discrete objects
themselves; cosmetics act on the skin—existing only when in place
on the skin—altering its appearance surreptitiously as a veil of
sorts, not as a separate entity. In a literal sense, the cosmetic is
superficial. Its effect, however, is quite profound.

As theorized by Kipnis, the cosmetic offers an alternative
approach to enliven architecture. At a moment when the architectural avant-garde, as a whole, appears to be transgressing

the previously accepted boundaries of the discipline, Herzog & de Meuron has adopted a particular attitude (latent within architecture itself, Kipnis suggests) that engages with a very exact architectural boundary—the facade itself. This is representative of what sets Herzog & de Meuron apart, namely that the firm's operations draw from the discipline's conventions, interpreted and employed in unique ways, to create a chic, sophisticated, exhilarating architecture, what Kipnis describes as "simply...the coolest architecture around." In a realm of information flows, performance events, and blobs, might not the cosmetic be the most insightful of all?

JEFFREY KIPNIS

THE CUNNING OF COSMETICS (A PERSONAL REFLECTION ON THE ARCHITECTURE OF HERZOG & DE MEURON)

First appeared in *El Croquis* 60 + 84, *Herzog and De Meuron, 1981–2000* (Madrid: El Croquis, 2000), 404–11. Courtesy of Jeffrey Kipnis.

"During the toasts celebrating the opening of *Light Construction*, the deep-seated tension…broke out in a bristling exchange between Herzog and Koolhaas…"
—*El Croquis* 79

How long now—six years? eight?—since I tossed off my first snide dismissal of the work of Herzog & de Meuron. Of course, for a critic such as I, advocate of the architectural avant-garde, intellectual apologist for the extreme, the exotic, the subversive, was it not *de rigeur* to scorn the superficial propositions of HdM? While one branch of the avant-garde proposed exotic form as a vector of architectural resistance, HdM offered flagrantly simple Cartesian volumes. While another branch cultivated event-theory into seditious programming techniques, HdM indulged contentedly in expedient, reductive planning. HdM's fixation on the cosmetic, on fastidious details, eye-catching materials and stunning facades appeared frivolous in comparison with those other more overtly radical experiments. Even worse, the overall cast of their work seemed complicit, if not aligned outright, with the taste for Neo-Modern Confections that had already begun to emerge as the hallmark of the reactionary New Right in Europe and elsewhere.

The question more to the point, then, is when exactly did my infatuation with HdM's work begin? When did I start returning to publications to gape secretly, furtively, at the Goetz Gallery, the Signal Box, Ricola Europe, or the sublime Greek Orthodox Church like a schoolboy ogling soft porn? Did my longing for the work grow over time, or was I beguiled from the outset, my oafish snubs but the hackneyed disavowals of one discomforted by the throws of forbidden desire?

In any case, it was not until March 1996 that the utter cunning of HdM's project dawned on me in its full dimension. By then, I had already realized that their architecture's ability to insinuate itself into my psyche was a powerful effect that, like it or not, must be taken seriously. All the more so, when it occurred to me that HdM's work did not, by virtue of any polemic, force itself on me against my will; rather, like a computer virus, it slipped into my consciousness through my will, eluding any and all resistance as it began to reprogram my architectural thoughts and feelings.

In March 1996 I encountered an *Arch-Plus* special issue on HdM. What shocked me into a new awareness was not any particular essay in the issue, though it contained several excellent ones.[1] Rather, the agent of my epiphany was the unceremonious cover title: *Herzog et de Meuron: Minimalismus und Ornament.* As soon as I saw it, I knew something was wrong, very wrong; I could feel it, though I could not quite put my finger on it.

Thumbing through the magazine, I found that Nikolaus Kuhnert had, without comment, separated the firm's works into two sections: *Ornament* held all of the projects with printed surfaces, *Minimalism* everything else—a brute act of blunt taxonomy. The source of the uneasiness spawned by the cover title became apparent. How could such a coherent collection of works by one architectural intelligence lend itself so easily to partitioning into such antagonistic categories as Minimalism and Ornament?!

At first glance, the division seemed quite sensible but, as might be expected, it did not sustain closer inspection. For example, Kuhnert placed the Signal Box—a key work in the HdM oeuvre—in the Minimalist section, no doubt in respect of the simple form, the monolithic uniformity effected by the copper banding system and the functional role attributed. On the other hand, does not the luxurious field of copper bands also fit any non-trivial definition of architectural ornament, even, as we shall see, if it also undermines the concept of ornament at the same time? After all, each band was painstakingly warped to engender a mesmerizing, ephemeral gesture in light, shadow and form over a large area of the skin, one much larger than required to admit natural light to the few interior spaces. And the functional rationalization of the system as a Faraday Cage is merely a smokescreen.[2] My point, however, is not to contest the details of Kuhnert's partitioning; rather, it is to admire the insidious guile of an architecture able to infiltrate so effortlessly such irreconcilable categories, and, in so doing begin to dismantle and reform them.

Already I have touched on the most potent characteristics of HdM's architecture: an urbane, cunning intelligence and an intoxicating, almost erotic allure. It is these traits that enable it to go anywhere, to go everywhere, into site and psyche alike, to appear ever fascinating yet ever harmless even as it plies its undermining subterfuges and sly deceits. And while this constellation of themes and its attendant techniques are ancient indeed,[3] the most precise placement of HdM's work in contemporary architecture is simply that it is the coolest architecture around. All that remains for us, then, is to watch it in action, to speculate a bit on its methods, and, to begin an audit of its gains and losses. Let us return to the Signal Boxes. Would it be too much to liken them to sirens, to temptresses that lure the unsuspecting into dangerous territory? The sirens of the Odyssey, if I remember correctly, charmed sailors into hazardous waters with the sheer beauty of their voices, voices that sang but said nothing, meant nothing, promised nothing. Do you not also feel the song of the Signal Box? Are you not enticed by it, drawn to a distant train yard to drink in its presence with your eyes? What pulls you there? And why go, when the only thing certain is that there is absolutely nothing for you there, save, perhaps, peril?

In its single-minded obsession with Unspeakable Beauty, the Signal Box series is exemplary of the HdM project at its most radical. To achieve its edgy *a la mode*, HdM brushes aside the Big Questions that such a project would, today, customarily trigger. HdM ignores the fact that the signal station belongs to remote networks and inter-urban infrastructures and, therefore, that its architecture should be conceived more in terms of flows and intensities than in terms that might be likened to the visual niceties that have come to appoint bourgeois travel. Nor does HdM give a moment's thought to the inappropriateness of High Design in the harsh, dirty reality of the site, though the shrill understatement of the Signal Box is as hip to its surrounds as a gangster in colors is to South Central LA. In that regard, the Signal Box raises doubts about the subtly patronizing fantasy of a context so brutal, so unrelentingly utilitarian that it cannot even broach the cloying frippery of design.

Make no mistake about it, these are not just hypothetical interrogations made in the name of the infrastructuralists and dirty realists. In his published comments on HdM, Rem Koolhaas first remarks on the undeniable beauty of the firm's facades. Then, on the way to framing his final indictment as a question, "Is architecture reinforcement therapy or does it play a role in redefining, undermining, exploding, erasing…?" [sic], he begins to signal his misgivings by asking HdM, "Does every situation have a correct architecture?" no doubt with the Signal Box in mind.[4]

For the proponents of exotic form, the signal station series would have been an opportunity of another ilk. Largely free from the demands of human program, unencumbered by historical or formal typology, unobligated to a prevailing contextual language of architectural merit the signal station offered an ideal prospect to experiment with the very limits of form. Furthermore, because several would be built, the morphological research could have been extended to the fascinating question of non-prototypical serialization. That HdM should adhere so closely to the box, that they should even consider developing a prototype was anathema. To this group of architects, the appearance in the second Signal Box of warped surfaces will surely seem a tacit admission of the futility of the original prototypical ambition and the inadequacy of the Cartesian box. As we shall see, however, nothing could be further from truth.

In brief, the design of the Signal Box shows no concern whatsoever for flows or event-structures, for realism or new form. Its architecture is entirely a matter of cosmetics, a hypnotic web of visual seductions that emanate entirely from the copper band system, a system, it should be said, that is in fact not the building's actual skin, which lies just beneath; it only poses as the building's skin.

The point here, however, is not to diminish the architectural import of the Signal Boxes by relegating them to the cosmetic, but to embrace their irresistible intrigue, to acknowledge their vitality and in so doing, to assert the transformative power of the cosmetic. Some care must be taken here, for *the cosmetic* is not just another member of the family of decorative architectural appurtenances collectively known as ornamentation. The field of effects of the cosmetic is quite different from those of its relatives, and it is precisely in those differences that HdM's contemporary project is born.

Ornaments attach as discreet entities to the body like jewelry, reinforcing the structure and integrity of the body as such. Cosmetics are indiscreet, with no relation to the body other than to take it for granted. Cosmetics are erotic camouflage; they relate always and only to skin, to particular regions of skin. Deeply, intricately material, cosmetics nevertheless exceed materiality to become modern alchemicals as they transsubstantiate skin into image, desirous or disgusting. Where ornaments retain their identity as entities, cosmetics work as fields, as blush or shadow or highlight, as aura or air. Thinness, adherence and diffuse extent are crucial to the cosmetic effect, which is more visceral than intellectual, more atmospheric than aesthetic. Virtuosity at ornamentation requires balance, proportion, precision; virtuosity at cosmetics requires something else, something menacing: paranoid control, control gone out of control, schizo-control.

Though the cosmetic effect does not work at the level of the body, nevertheless, it requires a body—or at least a face—as a vehicle. Like veal for the saucier, or the gaunt, featureless visage of choice recently for make-up artists, the ideal vehicle for the extreme cosmetician is a body, face or form denuded of its own ability to engender affect. These days, the effects of form

as such are just too obtuse to be cool. If the attitude of the cosmetician toward the body is a minimalism, then it is of a very
different sort than the Minimalism spawned by the art world
more than two decades ago. While the two share a desire to collapse the time of impact of a work to the immediate, the former
pursued that goal by distilling form and material into an essence
that radiated (spiritual) affect through unmediated presence.
The reductions of cosmetic minimalism, on the other hand,
are anorexic, a compulsion to starve the body until it dissolves
into pure (erotic) affect, like a Cheshire cat in heat. Witness the
necrophilic charge of the anemic Rosetti Hospital Pharmacy, or
speculate on the rejection of HdM's dazzling Greek Orthodox
Church by the Bishop. Was it because he grasped the conversion
of its space from the spiritual to the erotic?

Thus, Kuhnert's bipartite distribution missed the decisive
achievement of HdM's work thus far, the sublimation of the
antithesis between ornamentalism and minimalism into a new
coherence. The most famous example of this synthesis to date is
Ricola Europe, with its renowned flourish, walls patterned with
translucent tiles silkscreened with leaf images. When backlit,
as seen in the interior during the day, the leaf pattern takes on
the empty, numbing, camp fascination of a Warholian wallpa-
per. On the exterior, the images are rarely visible, emerging only
fleetingly as hallucinations when hit at exactly the right angle by
glancing light. Photos (actually, photographers) of this building
tend to exaggerate the leaf image to the point of kitsch; its presence on the exterior is actually much rarer and more ephemeral.
But in any case this slick, eye-catching device belies the range
and depth of technique HdM exercised in realizing the full cosmetic sophistication of the work.

As usual, the form is starved to skin and bones and gutted
of any distracting conceit in plan. The silkscreened panels tile
the two long walls; starting on the underside of the cantilevered

awning, the strip paneling turns to wrap down the wall. The effect of the wrap is to subvert the integrity of the two distinct formal elements of the building, the facade and the soffit, blurring them into a single field. Ironically, this leaves the thin strip of clear glass revealing the terminal truss of the roof extensions as, strictly speaking, the only actual facade.

To further distance the thin, weightless leaf field from a wall, even a curtain-wall, it is edged like a draped veil. The edging causes the long, thin strips to seem to stream from the top to the ground, trickling so gently that the slight thickness of the upper track of the horizontal glass doors breaks the flow.

This streaming illusion on the panels blurs the front, translucent fields into the side concrete walls. On those sides, roof water flows over the concrete, causing it to reflect like glass when wet and leaving a field of parallel vertical tracks, the residue of evaporated flow. In the same device at the wraith-like echo of Ricola Europa, the Remy Zaugg studio, iron on the roof dyes the rain water rust red to create a more dramatic if somewhat disconcerting effect. At Ricola Europa, these flow tracks and the pattern of widths they delimit reiterate uncannily the field of translucent tiles and seams in form and proportion.

For all of its modes of assertiveness, its blatant use of images, its indulgence in materiality and the bluntness of its form, the genius of the Ricola Europa is that the building, in itself and as such, is never there. Its promise of stark presence withdraws to leave pure allure, a tour de force of architectural cosmetics.

As with other critical treatments of HdMs work, e.g., as neo-modernism or as applied minimal art, the question of cosmetics, with all of its allusions to makeup and scents, to skins and bodies, would have only the force of analogy were it not for the matter of HdM's technique.

With form, planning, structure and construction, even with materials, HdM technique is architectural to the point of fanaticism. In the firm's entire body of work to date, there is not a single use of form, structure or material that does not belong to the strictest canon of the architectonic. Every experiment is an effort to reanimate and update that canon, never to augment it with new entries, certainly not with new forms or programs, but not even with new materials. Even the stained water tracks and the algae, lichens and molds that grow on surfaces have belonged to the canon, albeit as nuisances, for centuries.

What makes the firm so interesting is that, unlike the avant-garde, HdM derives its critical edge from an assumption of architecture's basic adequacy and an ease with the controversial proposition that architecture has no other more profound project than to fabricate a new sensibility from its own palette. In that it pursues the new not as a matter of ideology or as a condition of marginality, but as a forthright, even aggressive assertion of the center, it is perhaps the most *au courant* practice.

If the notion of the cosmetic has any deeper purchase for HdM than mere analogy, it is because the firm does not apply cosmetics to architecture as theory or borrowed practice. HdM unleashes the destabilizing power of the cosmetic as a moment and a movement already residing within architecture's orthodoxy. In so doing, it often accomplishes timely effects *en passant* that other practices grounded more in applied theory have pursued with less success.

By working steadfastly within the protocols of architectural materiality, HdM achieves a far more convincing realization of architectural dematerialization than Peter Eisenman, who has pursued that idea in his architecture for over two decades. Eisenman, steeped in a post-structural account of architecture as an endless system of references by immaterial signs, theorized that the tradition of materiality in architecture was a perversion manifest either as fetishism or nostalgia. Accordingly, he sought to render his forms as pure signs by constructing them as empty shapes in indifferent materials, e.g., EIFS or gyp-board. As a result, more often than not, his buildings fail to insist themselves and are easily dismissed as irreal, like stage sets or amusement parks.[5]

By beginning with more traditional and tactile materials such as glass, wood or concrete and then manipulating them in non-traditional ways, HdM is able to insist on the reality of the building while never allowing it to settle as a reliable and persistent presence. In other words, they do not dematerialize a concrete form by replacing the concrete: they dematerialize the concrete itself.

The forthcoming Kunstkiste Museum for the Grohte Collection should provide an acute study in this aspect of HdM's work. As published, the project promises to be nothing short of an essay in extreme concrete, one whose rude materiality should make Ando's renowned use of the material seem hopelessly genteel, as the building will certainly do to the saccharin confections by Schultes and Peichl nearby.

The top-heavy proportions of the vertical slab make the form of the Kuntskiste seem poised to topple, the threat further intensifying the insistent weight of the materiality. But the roof water, now destined to stain every surface with its vertical striations of rust and algae, will transform the appearance of the concrete box into that of a viscous liquid in an aquarium, the image confirmed by the blackened windows floating at random like objects at neutral buoyancy. Heavy or light? Solid or liquid? Essential presence or imagistic illusion?

But as intriguing as the project is in its published form, Jacques Herzog reveals that HdM entertained an even more astonishing thought for the project. At one point they considered printing exactly positioned, full-scale photo-images of the interior of the galleries on the concrete. The photo-printing surfaces would, in effect, making the concrete appear transparent! As if the phenomenal dislocation were not enough, the idea also carried a deconstructive implication, perhaps its downfall. The photographer would have been a young artist of note from Berlin, whose presence on the surfaces would have marked his absence from the collection and raised questions about the collection itself. For whatever reason, the idea seems to have been abandoned. Nevertheless, it was a brilliant thought, and one that indicates just how aware HdM is of the eruptive force of their cosmetic techniques.

Notes

1   *Arch-Plus* 129/130 (Dec. 1995). Included in the volume is a reprint of Alezandro Zaera's excellent "Between the Face and the Landscape," from the first *El Croquis* [number 60, 1993] on HdM, and Rem Koolhaas' "Architectures of Herzog & de Meuron," republished in *Arch-Plus* under the title "New Discipline," as well as insightful comments by Mark Taylor, Terry Riley, and Hans Frei.

2   The electronic equipment in all facilities such as switching stations is already adequately shielded from interference. Thus, though the copper banding system does indeed technically produce a Faraday Cage, it is far from a functional necessity.

3   cf. *Les ruses de l'intelligence: la metis des Grecs*, by Marcel Detienne and Jean-Pierre Vemant. Translated into English as *Cunning Intelligence*.

4   From *Arch-Plus* 129/130.

5   cf. my remarks in the *El Croquis'* recent volume on Peter Eisenman (number 83, 1997).

INTRODUCTION

Green Questionnaire / *Responses by Norman Foster,*
Jan Kaplicky, Richard Rogers, Ken Yeang, and Thomas Herzog

In the past decades, the importance of green architecture has
become increasingly clear. According to the U.S. Green Building
Council, "in the United States alone, buildings account for: 72
percent of electricity consumption, 39 percent of energy use,
38 percent of all carbon dioxide (CO_2) emissions, 40 percent
of raw materials use, 30 percent of waste output (136 million
tons annually), and 14 percent of potable water consumption."[1]
These alarming numbers, combined with concerns about global
warming, diminishing natural resources, and other aspects of
environmental destruction, underlie the rising and necessary
interest in green architecture. Indeed, the American Institute of
Architects recently updated its continuing education requirements
for architects to include mandatory credits in sustainable design.[2]
This change reflects the growing sense of ecological account-
ability among practitioners and clients, as sustainable design
encompasses all aspects of a building's design, construction, and
day-to-day operation.

In "Green Questionnaire," five architects of international
prominence—Norman Foster, Jan Kaplicky, Richard Rogers,
Ken Yeung, and Thomas Herzog—share their thoughts on sustainable architecture. Their emphases vary: Foster focuses on
problems of urban sprawl; Kaplinsky highlights the importance of
materials; Rogers underscores buildings' environmental impact;
Yeang looks to the interconnectivity of natural systems; and
Herzog cites the need for renewable energies. Issues of aesthetics
feature in some answers, while technology carries more weight
in others. An intriguing point of discussion centers on the ways
in which nature can be used as a guide for sustainable design.
Despite their differences, though, the architects' responses share

an underlying tone of optimism for the future—the hope that, with the proper mentality and initiative, architecture can serve as a positive force in the natural world in hitherto unseen ways. The words of the "Green Questionnaire" architects are heartening, conveying the message that architectural responsibility extends beyond an individual building or urban plan to the environment as a whole.

Notes

1 U.S. Green Building Council, http://www.usgbc.org/DisplayPage .aspx?CMSPageID=1718.

2 American Institute of Architects, "Sustainable Design," http://www.aia.org/ education/ces/AIAS076973. This change took effect in 2009.

RESPONSES BY NORMAN FOSTER,
JAN KAPLICKY, RICHARD ROGERS, KEN YEANG,
AND THOMAS HERZOG

GREEN QUESTIONNAIRE

First appeared in *Green Architecture: An International Comparison*, *Architectural Design* 71, no. 4 (July 2001). Courtesy of Wiley Publishing.

LORD FOSTER OF THAMES BANK

What is your, or your practice's, definition of sustainable design?

Sustainable design means doing the most with the least means. "Less is more" is, in ecological terms, exactly the same as the proverbial injunction, "Waste not, want not."

It is about ideally using passive architectural means to save energy—rather than relying on wasteful mechanical services, which use up dwindling supplies of nonrenewable fuel and produce pollution that contributes to global warming. But in the final analysis, sustainability is about good architecture. The better the quality of the architecture—and that includes the quality of thinking and ideas as much as the quality of the materials used—the longer the building will have a role, and in sustainability terms, longevity is a good thing. Obviously, if a building can be long-lasting and energy efficient, that is even better.

What are your key concerns as a designer interested in sustainability?

Sustainable architecture is not simply about individual buildings, but also our ever-expanding cities and their infrastructures. Unchecked urban sprawl is one of the chief problems facing the world today. As our cities grow horizontally rather than vertically, swallowing up more and more land, people are forced to travel greater distances between home and work. Mixed-use developments within cities can help to increase density, creating lively local communities that live, work and play in the same area. The Millennium Tower that we proposed in Tokyo takes a traditional horizontal city quarter—housing, shops, restaurants, cinemas, museums, sporting facilities, green spaces and public transport networks—and turns it on its side to create a supertall building with a multiplicity of uses. It would be over 800 metres high with 170 storeys—twice the height of anything so far built—and would house a community of up to 60,000 people. This is 20,000 more than the population of Monaco, already one of the densest cities in the world. Yet the building would occupy only 0.013 square kilometres of land compared to Monaco's 1.95 square kilometres. It would be a virtually self-sufficient, fully self-sustaining community in the sky. Almost all the traffic would be internal. This sounds like future fantasy. But we have, now, all the means at our disposal to create such buildings.

How would you judge the success of a building in the "green" age?

A "green" building will use as little energy as possible and will make the most of the embodied energy required to build it. Ideally, a building should create its own energy by burning renewable fuels such as vegetable oil and harvesting solar energy. If possible it should create more energy than it uses so that it can provide energy to other buildings. The building should have a structure that allows for flexibility so that it will have a long life. We have already proved these concepts in the Reichstag—the new German parliament in Berlin.

In what way do you use nature as a guide?

We look to vernacular traditions that are specific to the area in which we are working. Very often there are rich architectural traditions that work with, and not against, nature which have been forgotten over time. In two projects in the Mediterranean we are using pergolas—large cable trellises covered with plants to provide natural shading and integrate the building visually within the landscape. In the American Air Museum at Duxford in Cambridgeshire and the Glass House at the National Botanic Garden of Wales near Cardiff, we partially buried the structures in the ground, again to integrate them within the landscape, but also to make passive use of the thermal mass of the soil to help save energy.

Our Chesa Futura in St. Moritz in Switzerland uses timber construction, which makes environmental sense for a number of reasons. It is culturally sympathetic, reflecting local architectural traditions, and it contributes to the established ecology of felling older trees to facilitate forest regeneration. Furthermore, wood is an entirely renewable resource; it absorbs carbon dioxide during its growth cycle; and if indigenous timber is used, little or no energy is expended in its transportation.

Finally, in traditional towns and villages in Switzerland buildings are clustered tightly together rather than sprawling over the landscape. Chesa Futura is a reminder of the importance of building more intensely in existing urban concentrations to preserve the natural world.

JAN KAPLICKY OF FUTURE SYSTEMS

What is your, or your practice's, definition of sustainable design?

The major aspects of sustainable design are choice of materials and the performance of a building once it is built. Buildings have to be self-sufficient in energy—80 per cent or more. It is even now possible to be selling energy back into the electricity grid overnight. Long-term performance, however, is very difficult to quantify. There is as yet no real unit of measurement. Energy also has to be considered in the construction of a building: how much will be consumed during construction and before that in the production of the materials. This also means that the quantity and weight of materials have to be given serious consideration for the first time. The fewer materials a building uses the greener it is—less resources and energy are used to produce it.

What are your key concerns as a designer interested in sustainability?

Materials, as I have suggested, are absolutely top priority. The impact sustainability is going to have on design, however, is going to be much more revolutionary. At the moment, people are trying to pretend that the need to produce sustainable architecture is going to have no effect on the form of buildings. It is like when the car was first invented and it imitated the form of the horse-drawn carriage. It took a certain amount of time for it to take on its own form. Rather than just being kosher, green architecture needs to find its own form. Airflow and cross ventilation will, for instance, have an important impact on the form of buildings.

How would you judge the success of a building in the "green" age?

As yet there have been no truly green buildings built. The buildings that are currently being constructed aren't even prototypes for a "green" age. They are only minor attempts at sustainability.

The law as it stands doesn't give significant changes, especially in the United States and United Kingdom. There is very little room for green architecture in architecture schools. An American lecturer at a well-known U.S. school recently referred to it merely as fashion. It is evident that completely new thinking is required. The motorcar didn't happen until the engine existed. Intelligent buildings don't as yet exist.

In what way do you use "nature" as a guide?

Nature can be used as a model at many different levels. For instance, termites' nests have two skins with natural ventilation. In between nature's structures also have a tightness not presently found in man-made constructions. They are far lighter in weight than those made by man and comparably far greater in strength. The thread in a spider's web, for instance, is twice as strong as steel. There is so much to learn from a more efficient use of materials. In general, organic forms are far more efficient than man's.

LORD ROGERS OF RIVERSIDE

What is your, or your practice's, definition of sustainable design?

Sustainable design aims to meet present needs without compromising the stock of natural resources remaining for future generations. It must include a concern for the principles of social and economic sustainability as well as the specific concerns of the energy use and environmental impact of buildings and cities. The key issues are: low energy; loose fit; resource efficiency.

What are your key concerns as a designer interested in sustainability?

Buildings are responsible for 50 per cent of the world's generation of CO_2.

Richard Rogers Partnership has a longstanding concern with environmental performance, reflecting the personal interests of the directors. The practice sees issues of energy use and environmental impact as a critical part of the building and urban design process. True sustainability, in terms of building design, is dependent on maximum energy efficiency coupled with the use of replenishable materials. Specialist analysis and research inform design and encourage innovation in environmental systems and technologies.

RRP has pioneered the development of "intelligent" buildings that can contribute substantially (up to 75 per cent) to reducing the running and maintenance costs during the life cycle of a building. Our aim is that the new building for the National Assembly for Wales in Cardiff will have zero CO_2 emission, for example.

The practice also has evolved an approach to civil, accessible and ecological urban design. The masterplans for Shanghai and for ParcBIT in Mallorca are key examples that demonstrate a strong ecological framework. Sustainable planning is a key feature of the practice's work, in particular the Greenwich Peninsula, where the practice produced a masterplan and redevelopment strategy for English Partnerships, including one of a handful of "Millennium" villages that will encourage good sustainable design in the twenty-first century.

How would you judge the success of a building in the "green" age?

The practice has an ongoing commitment to the development of "intelligent" buildings that can contribute to a substantial reduction in the running and maintenance costs during the life cycle of a building.

Greater sustainability is achievable through:

1. Intelligent design—harnessing the benefits and efficiencies of integrated passive environmental design through orientation, building form and organisation.

2. The use of an intelligent building fabric—responsive facades can maximise natural daylight, optimise natural ventilation, control solar gain and loss.

3. The appropriate use of materials—concern for the "hidden" environmental costs of building materials (embodied energy and life-cycle issues), the benefits of transferring technology from other industries and the use of advanced, clean means of production.

4. Intellectual capital—the analysis of the behaviour of buildings, application of CFD modelling and, especially, close collaboration with specialist consultants leads to the intelligent use of thermal mass, buffer zones, thermal flywheels, efficient airflows, etc.

In what way do you use nature as a guide?
Nature provides inspiration, information and analogy.

KEN YEANG

What is your, or your practice's, definition of sustainable design?
Sustainable design can be defined as ecological design—design that integrates seamlessly with the ecological systems in the biosphere over the entire life cycle of the built system. The buildings materials and energy are integrated, with minimal impact on the environment from source to sink.

What are your key concerns as a designer interested in sustainability?
My key concerns are that designers should be aware of the connectivity of all systems in nature and that these should be integrated as part of the built system's processes. Designers should also beware of making excessive claims about the sustainability of their designs because ecological design is still in its infancy.

*How would you judge the success of a building in the
"green" age?*

A successful "green" building is one that integrates seamlessly with the natural systems in the biosphere, with minimal destructive impact on these systems and maximum positive impact.

In what way do you use nature as a guide?

Nature should be imitated and our built systems should be mimetic ecosystems.

THOMAS HERZOG OF HERZOG AND PARTNER

*What is your, or your practice's, definition of sustainable
design?*

Sustainability in architecture has to be regarded as one of the key issues of our profession, since almost half of the energy consumed in Europe is used to run buildings. A further 25 per cent is accounted for by traffic which—in part—is influenced by urban planners. The role of architecture as a responsible profession is of far-reaching significance in this respect. In this context, sustainable design can be defined as a working method, aimed at the preservation of our natural resources while using renewable forms of energy—especially solar energy—as extensively as possible.

*What are your key concerns as a designer interested in
sustainability?*

There are various topics linked to the issue of sustainability, such as the choice and the provenance of materials, the energy needed for their transport and refinement, the process of construction, the degree of a building's thermal performance, expenditure for the operation and sustenance of buildings, their life span, flexibility with regard to the use, the adaptability of the building services, the suitability for assembly, dismantling and reassembling of the building components, and the possibility to convert or recycle. But one of the main issues is the integration of technologies and components to use renewable energies—especially solar energy—in a satisfying way, especially one that controls the impact on, and potential for, the appearance of the building.

How would you judge the success of a building in the "green" age?

The success of a building is dependent on its overall performance, including its utility value, which has largely to do with the very complex topics that have been summarised under the term "sustainable." But the beauty and the design of a building is as important as its usability and function. Only beautifully made buildings contribute to our built environment in a sustainable way and will be regarded as worthwhile to be preserved. Here, the careful integration of technologies for the use of renewable energies offers the chance to generate new forms of architectural expression which are closely linked to the local condition, such as the microclimate and topography, the natural resources and the cultural heritage of a certain region.

In what way do you use nature as a guide?

In general I do not think that architecture can be deduced immediately from nature, since the design process and function of our buildings are quite different from what is found in most plants and animals. Nevertheless, there are a lot of lessons to be learnt from nature, especially with regard to the efficiency, performance, adaptability, variety and tremendous beauty which most organisms display under close observation. Considering that nature has to obey the same physical laws as man-made objects this should be seen as very encouraging for us, making it well worthwhile to study its principles and mechanisms.

INTRODUCTION
Scale and Span in a Global Digital World / *Saskia Sassen*

Digitization affects all areas of architecture; perhaps the most obvious changes during the late twentieth century have involved building design and fabrication, notably clear in the work of architects such as Greg Lynn and Frank Gehry. Yet the impact of digitization extends to concepts of space, place, and materiality—influencing the type, features, and organizations of a given design. With respect to phenomena such as telecommuting and videoconferencing, the traditional workplace has been irreparably altered; what kind of office (if any) is necessary if a physical location is no longer needed? Questions of this order have led to speculations that digitization will negate architecture and urbanism as they are conventionally understood.

In "Scale and Span in a Global Digital World," Saskia Sassen—a professor of sociology at Columbia University and a member of the university's Committee on Global Thought—counters the idea that digitization will "neutralize" the need for architecture and the city's established role as the center of human activity. Digitization, Sassen asserts, creates circumstances that require new conceptual categories, as our everyday experiences are no longer (if ever they were) adequately described by notions such as digital versus nondigital, mobile versus fixed. Indeed, such historically constructed concepts leave little room for the inevitable and ubiquitous overlap of the digital and the material, nor do they account for the ways in which something like real estate, for example, can be both a physical entity and a liquid commodity. Furthermore, digitization promotes globalization, which leads to a reconsideration of scale and span; national, regional, and local divisions still exist, yet they are overlaid by a complex system of transnational networks. The result is "the global city," "the synthesis…of the old and the new." This layering and merging leads not to the supplanting of architecture and urbanism by digitization and globalization, but to an intertwining of the digital and the material; the two are dependent on each other, albeit in ways that depart from previous conceptions of architectural and urban space. Thus Sassen calls for a reevaluation of what architecture and the city are and may be with respect to this new digital era.

SASKIA SASSEN

SCALE AND SPAN IN A GLOBAL DIGITAL WORLD

First appeared in *Anything*, ed. Cynthia Davidson (Cambridge, Mass.: MIT Press, 2001). Courtesy of the MIT Press.

I want to discuss the questions of scale and span under conditions of digitalization and globalization. In her introduction to the Anything conference, Cynthia Davidson cited William Gibson's comment that the impact of the digital might well be to eliminate and neutralize everything that architecture has historically represented.[1] In parallel to what Gibson anticipated in 1991, today we read and hear a lot of comment and analyses arguing that the impact of the digital on cities will be to neutralize what cities have traditionally represented. In abstract terms, one could see this representation as centrality—a centrality dependent upon and influenced by different cultures, different places, different times, and different articulations of urban space.[2]

My effort here is to examine the impact of digitalization and globalization on the architectural, the urban, and the city in a way that resists the dominant interpretations, which posit that digitalization (and to a large extent, globalization, as in electronic markets) entails an absolute disembedding from the material world. With this type of interpretation comes, then, the neutralization of such conditions as the architectural and the urban—not in general terms, however, but as conditions that are produced, articulated, and inflected by crucial instantiations of the embeddedness of the digital. Mine is a particular kind of reading of digitalization: it seeks to detect the imbrications of the digital and nondigital domains and thereby to insert the condition of the architectural and urban in mappings, both actual and rhetorical, from which this digitalization can be easily excluded.[3] I use notions of *scale* and *span* (or *scope*) to capture the precise locations of this insertion. The risk in this type of effort, it seems to me, lies in generalizing, in using metaphors and figurative language—in brief, to hover above it all. Rather, we need to go digging.

The difficulty that analysts and commentators have had in understanding the impact of digitalization on cities and architecture—indeed, on multiple configurations—essentially is the result of two analytic flaws. The first (and this is especially evident in the United States) restricts interpretation to a technological reading of the capacities of digital technology. This would be the required and proper reading for engineers, but if one is trying to understand the impact of a technology, such a reading becomes problematic. The difficulty is that a purely technological reading inevitably leads one to a place that is a nonplace, where one announces with absolute certainty the neutralization of many of those configurations marked by physicality and place-boundedness, including architecture and the urban.[4] The second flaw, I would argue, is a continuing reliance on analytical categorizations that were developed under other spatial and historical conditions—that is, conditions preceding the current digital era. Thus the tendency is to conceive of the digital as simply and exclusively digital, and the nondigital, whether represented in terms of the material or the actual (both conceptions are equally problematic), as simply and exclusively that, nondigital. These either/or categorizations filter out alternative conceptualizations, thereby precluding a more complex reading of the impact of digitalization on material and placebound conditions.

One such alternative categorization captures these imbrications. Let me illustrate this through the case of finance. This is certainly a highly digitalized activity, yet it cannot simply be considered exclusively digital. To have electronic financial markets and digitalized financial instruments requires enormous amounts of matériel, not to mention human talent (which has its own type of physicality). This matériel includes conventional infrastructure, buildings, airports, and so on. Much of this matériel is, then, inflected by the digital. Conversely, much of what takes place in cyberspace is deeply inflected by the cultures, material practices, and imaginations that take place outside cyberspace. Much, though not all, of what we think of as cyberspace would lack any meaning or referents if we were to exclude the world outside cyberspace. In brief, therefore, digital space and digitalization are not exclusive conditions that stand beyond the nondigital. Digital space is embedded in the larger societal, cultural, subjective, economic, and imaginary structurations of lived experience and the systems within which we exist and operate.

So in terms of the impact of the digital on architecture, on urbanism, and on the city, yes, there has been a profound transformation, but it is one not necessarily marked by the neutralization of capital fixity or of the built environment or, in the end, of the city. Rather than being neutralized, these emerge with renewed and strategic importance in some of their features, that is to say, not as a generalized condition but as a very specific condition. A first impact, then, is a particular type of built environment—a conventional communication system, a city, in essence, a particular type of spatiality—that accommodates and furthers the new digital dynamics.

A second impact is the complex overlapping of the digital (as well as the global) and the nondigital, which brings with it a destabilizing of older hierarchies of scale and often dramatic rescalings. As the national scale loses significance, along with the loss of key components of the nation-state's formal authority over that scale, other measures gain strategic importance. Most especially among these are subnational scales, such as the global city, and supranational scales, such as global markets or regional trading zones. Older hierarchies of scale (emerging in the context of the ascendance of the nation-state) continue to operate and are typically organized in terms of institutional scope: from the international, down to the national, the regional, the urban, and the local. Today's rescaling cuts across institutional scope and, through policies such as deregulation and privatization, negates the encasements of territory produced by the formation of national states. This does not mean that the older hierarchies disappear, but rather that rescalings emerge alongside the old ones, and that they can often trump the latter.[5]

These transformations, although resulting from digitalization and globalization, and continuing to entail complex imbrications of the digital and nondigital and between the global and the nonglobal, can be captured in a variety of instances. For example, much of what we might still experience as the "local" (an office building or a house or an institution right there in our neighborhood or downtown) is actually something I would rather think of as a "microenvironment with global span" insofar as it is deeply internet-worked.[6] Such a microenvironment is in many senses a localized entity—something that can be experienced as local, immediate, proximate. It is a sited materiality.

But it is also part of global digital networks, which lend it immediate far-flung span. To continue to think of this simply as local is not especially useful or adequate. More importantly, the juxtaposition between the condition of being a sited materiality and having global span captures the enfolding of the digital and nondigital and illustrates the inadequacy of a purely technological reading of the capacities of digitalization. This would lead us to posit the neutralization of the place-boundedness of that which precisely makes possible the condition of being an entity with global span.

A second example is the bundle of conditions and dynamics that marks the model of the global city. To single out one key dynamic: the more globalized and digitalized the operations of firms and markets, the more their central management and coordination functions (and the requisite material structures) become strategic. It is precisely because of digitalization that simultaneous worldwide dispersal of operations (whether factories, offices, or service outlets) and system integration can be achieved. And it is precisely this combination that raises the importance of central functions. Global cities are strategic sites for the combination of resources necessary for the production of these central functions.[7]

Conceptualizing digitalization and globalization along these lines creates operational and rhetorical openings for recognizing the ongoing importance of the material world, even in the case of some of the most dematerialized activities.

One could examine, for example, the digital through one of its most powerful capabilities: the dematerializing and liquefying of that which was material and/or hardly mobile. (I would also argue that this capability still contains a complex imbrication with the nondigital.) Digitalization brings with it an amplification of those capacities that make possible the liquefying of that which is not liquid. Thereby, digitalization raises the mobility of what we have customarily thought of as immobile, or barely mobile. At its most extreme, this liquefying dematerializes its object. Once dematerialized, it becomes hypermobile—instantaneous circulation through digital networks with global span. It is important to underline that the hypermobility gained by an object through dematerialization is but one moment of a more complex condition. Representing such an object as simply hypermobile is, then, a partial representation since it includes only some of the components of that object, i.e., those that can be dematerialized but achieve that condition as a function of what we could describe as highly specialized materialities. Much of what is liquefied and circulates in digital networks and is marked by hypermobility remains physical in some of its components.

Take, for example, the case of real estate. Financial services firms have developed instruments that liquefy real estate, thereby facilitating investment and circulation of these instruments in global markets. Yet, part of what constitutes real estate remains very physical. At the same time, however, that which remains physical has been transformed by the fact that it is represented by highly liquid instruments that can circulate in global markets. It may look the same, it may involve the same bricks and mortar, it may be new or old, but it is a transformed entity. We have difficulty capturing this multivalence through our conventional categories: if it is physical, it is physical; and if it is liquid, it is liquid. In fact, the partial representation of real estate through liquid financial instruments produces a complex intertwining of the material and the dematerialized moments of that which we continue to call real estate.

Hypermobility, or dematerialization, is usually seen as a mere function of the new technologies. This understanding obscures the fact that it takes multiple material conditions to achieve this outcome. Once we recognize that the hypermobility of the instrument, or the dematerialization of the actual piece of real estate, had to be produced, we introduce the overlapping of the material and the nonmaterial. It takes capital fixity to produce capital mobility, that is to say, state-of-the-art built environments, conventional infrastructure—from highways to airports and railways—and well-housed talent. These are all at least partly place-bound conditions, even though the nature of their place-boundedness is going to be different from what it was one hundred years ago, when it might have been marked by immobility. Today, it is a place-boundedness that is inflected and inscribed by the hypermobility of its components. Both capital fixity and mobility are located in a temporal frame where speed is ascendant and consequential. At the level of the material, speed alters such dynamics as obsolescence and the value of investment.[8]

For example, the new transnational professional class is hypermobile. We conduct ourselves as if we could download our bodies, but at any given moments, part of the task and part of what takes us around the globe have to do with things that are place-bound, and our interventions—which justify what we are, who we are, and why we are here or there—are also place-bound. So again, we are confronted with conventional categories that polarize: Is it hypermobile? Is it fixed? Is it place-bound? Is it mobile? All of these questions typically miss much of what is happening. One example that captures the essence of this polarization is the private digital network that MCI Worldcom has created, connecting 4,000 buildings in Europe with 27,000 buildings in the United States. By connecting with these buildings—which are not just any buildings—this digital network creates a spatiality that in some ways is a local event. It is a microenvironment; it connects across the Atlantic a set of buildings that are scattered over two continental territories where the space itself becomes a kind of space for mobility that might as well be a microspace or a local space. The firms that are locating to those buildings are also paying premium rates. We have, then, a digitally connected space among select, very fixed entities.

A corollary to these microenvironments is the redefinition and reconfiguration of ideas of the center. The MCI Worldcom network spans a huge geographic distance, yet it is constructed as a space of centrality. The enormous agglomeration of buildings that physically characterizes this digital network, despite being manifest in all our major cities, cannot be read in the same ways that we looked at urban centers twenty or even ten years ago. A new urban history is being constructed, even though it is deeply embedded and almost camouflaged by the older social spatial histories within which it is taking place. For us to more fully understand the impact of the digital and of globalization, we need, therefore, to suspend the category "city." Rather, we need to construct a more abstract category of centrality and of spaces of centrality, that, ironically, could allow us to recover the city, albeit a recovery as just one instantiation within a much broader set of issues.[9]

If we begin to unpack the impact of the digital and of globalization through these kinds of questions, and not simply confine our analysis to the technical capacities of technologies, we can chart an enormously interesting conceptual map with which we can explore these issues. Through this mapping of globalization and digitalization, one can also see the extent to which we have existed in a consciousness deeply embedded in the idea of the national: territories, administration, identities, citizenship—all formed in national terms. One of the impacts of the rescaling described earlier is the removal of layers of institutional encasing "constructing" the national, and the freeing up subnational systems of circulation.

The global city is precisely the synthesis of these two scales—the old and the new. It overrides and neutralizes older hierarchies of scale and functions as enormously complex sited materiality with global span. In the era of globalization, the state also participates in the neutralization of these national encasings. The state, therefore, is not just a victim of globalization. It actively participates in producing laws that facilitate the partial denationalization of the global city, creating opportunities for foreign actors, foreign markets, foreign firms, and foreign cultural institutions to be operative in what was once constructed as the national. In this combination of elements, I would argue, lies a very different reading of the impact of the digital on architecture and the city. The direction in which it takes us could lead to a rich and complex agenda for research, theorization, and argument.

Notes

1 "While the advent of nanotechnology promises to render architecture a dead technology, something akin to its traditional practice already flourishes in the virtual landscape of the computer. Our century's only crucial architectures are structures of information. The microchip is a cathedral. A library is something on the other end of a modem. The Postmodern, in retrospect, will seem a breathing space prior to the advent of the Posthuman." William Gibson, "Letter to Anyone," in *Anyone*, ed. Cynthia C. Davidson (New York: Rizzoli, 1991), 264.

2 The variety of dynamics that I am describing are all located on edges, borders, and frontier zones. As a researcher, I find these thresholds particularly interesting because it is precisely at the points of transaction between new and old spatial modes that all kinds of things appear to happen. This has a whole series of implications for very specialized research agendas in several fields, as well as for the city itself.

3 For a development of some of these ideas see "Digital Networks and Power" in *Spaces of Culture: City, Nation, World,* ed. Mike Featherstone and Scott Lash (London: Sage, 1999); and "The Virtual House," *ANY* 19/20, 1997.

4   Another consequence of this type of reading is to assume that a new technology will inevitably replace all older technologies that are less efficient or slower, at executing those tasks that the new technology is best at. We know that inevitable replacement is historically not the case.

5   I develop some of these issues in *Losing Control? Sovereignty in an Age of Globalization* (New York: Columbia University Press, 1996) and in the book I am currently working on, *De-Nationalization*.

6   See Saskia Sassen, "Geographies and Countergeographies of Globalization" in *Anymore*, ed. Cynthia C. Davidson (Cambridge, Mass.: MIT Press, 2000), 110–19.

7   There are other dimensions that specify the global city; see the fully updated edition of my book *The Global City* (Princeton, N.J.: Princeton University Press, 2001).

8   Much of my work on global cities has looked to conceptualize and document the fact that the global digital economy requires massive concentrations of material conditions in order to be what it is. Finance is an important intermediary in this regard; it represents a capability for liquefying various forms of nonliquid wealth and for raising the mobility (i.e., hypermobility) of that which is already liquid, a subject I developed in "Juxtaposed Temporalities: Producing a New Zone" in *Anytime*, ed. Cynthia C. Davidson (Cambridge, Mass.: MIT Press, 1999), 114–21.

9   See Saskia Sassen, "Reconfiguring Centrality" in *Anywise*, ed. Cynthia C. Davidson (Cambridge, Mass.: MIT Press, 1996), 126–32.

INTRODUCTION
Notes around the Doppler Effect and Other Moods
of Modernism / Robert Somol and Sarah Whiting

In 2002, Robert Somol and Sarah Whiting published "Notes around the Doppler Effect and Other Moods of Modernism" in *Perspecta* 33, an issue entitled *Mining Autonomy*. With this article, Somol—an assistant professor at UCLA and co-founder of the firm Pollari x Somol (P XS)—and Whiting—dean of the Rice School of Architecture and a principal in WW Architects—offer a critique of the "now dominant paradigm of criticality," suggesting as an alternative the concept of projective practice. "Disciplinarity," Somol and Whiting assert, "has been absorbed and exhausted by the project of criticality." The authors elaborate with a discussion of disciplinarity that traces two trajectories stemming from 1970s discourse. The first is associated with critical architecture as developed by Michael Hays and Peter Eisenman, building in part on the thought of historian-critics Manfredo Tafuri and Colin Rowe. Concerned with "autonomy and process" (resistance to reification and indexical representation), criticality is juxtaposed to the second 1970s-derived concept of disciplinarity, which Somol and Whiting associate with Rem Koolhaas, concerned with ideas of "force and effect." This latter understanding of disciplinarity provides an example of the projective.

Somol and Whiting posit the Doppler effect—"the perceived change in frequency of a wave that occurs when the source and receiver of the wave have a relative velocity"—as a mediatory concept to explain how a projective architecture functions: "a Doppler architecture acknowledges the adaptive synthesis of architecture's many contingencies. Rather than isolating a singular autonomy [as does the critical], the Doppler focuses upon the effects and exchanges of architecture's inherent multiplicities: material, program, writing, atmosphere, form, technologies,

188

economies, etc...The Doppler shifts the understanding of disciplinarity as autonomy to disciplinarity as performance or practice."
Importantly, Doppler architecture depends on both the object—the
architecture—and the subject—the occupant—for the production
of effects. Thus, the experience of a given work changes based on
the subject's personal knowledge and history. Such "atmospheric
interaction" Somol and Whiting align with the "cool," building on
Marshall McLuhan's notions of "hot" and "cool" media, employed
here to characterize the difference between the critical ("hot")
and the projective ("cool"). The authors declare "while cooling
suggests a process of mixing (and thus the Doppler Effect would
be one form of cool), the hot resists through distinction, and connotes the overly difficult, belabored, worked, complication. Cool
is relaxed, easy." As a final stroke, Somol and Whiting underscore the difference between "hot" and "cool" through reference
to David Hickey's comparison of Robert DeNiro's and Robert
Mitchum's performances in their respective versions of Cape
Fear. They conclude that, like the critical, "'De Niro architecture'
is hot, difficult, and indexes the processes of its production..." In
contrast, like the projective, "'Mitchum architecture' is cool, easy,
and never looks like work: it's about mood or the inhabitation of
alternative realities."

   Since its publication, "The Doppler Effect" quickly has become
a staple of architectural discourse throughout the United States
and abroad, frequently cited in discussions on the contemporary
state of theory and even prompting a symposium, "Projective
Landscape: A Conference on Projective Practice," at the Delft
University of Technology in March 2006.

ROBERT SOMOL AND SARAH WHITING

NOTES AROUND THE DOPPLER EFFECT AND OTHER MOODS OF MODERNISM

First appeared in *Perspecta* 33 (2002). Courtesy of the authors and of the Yale School of Architecture.

No matter how often I tell myself that chance happenings of this kind occur far more often than we suspect, since we all move, one after the other, along the same roads mapped out of for us by our origins and our hopes, my rational mind is nonetheless unable to lay the ghosts of repetition that haunt me with ever greater frequency. Scarcely am I in company but it seems as if I had already heard the same opinions expressed by the same people somewhere or other, in the same way, with the same words, turns of phrase and gestures...Perhaps there is in this as yet unexplained phenomenon of apparent duplication some kind of anticipation of the end, a venture into the void, a sort of disengagement, which, like a gramophone repeatedly playing the same sequence of notes, has less to do with damage to the machine itself than with an irreparable defect in its programme.
—W. G. Sebald, *The Rings of Saturn*

I would like to show that these unities form a number of
autonomous but not independent domains, governed by
rules, but in perpetual transformation, anonymous and without a subject, but imbuing a great many individual works.
—Michel Foucault, *The Archaeology of Knowledge*

From Critical to Projective
In 1984, the editors of *Perspecta*, Carol Burns and Robert Taylor,
set out an ambitious agenda for issue 21: "Architecture is not an
isolated or autonomous medium, it is actively engaged by the
social, intellectual, and visual culture which is outside the discipline and which encompasses it…It is based on a premise that
architecture is inevitably involved with questions more difficult
than those of form or style." While this orientation bears a curi-
ous connection to the "realist" or "grey" tradition of an earlier
Yale generation, it also serves as a sign of the nascent mixture
of a critical, neo-Marxism with a celebration of the vernacular
or everyday with which Yale would soon become synonymous.[1]
Published in that same issue, K. Michael Hays's canonic essay
"Critical Architecture: Between Culture and Form" offered a useful corrective to the editorial position of the issue by indirectly
implying that the editors were insufficiently dialectical in their
understanding of engagement and autonomy. Hays's sophistication has always been to recognize that autonomy is a precondition for engagement. Using Mies as a paradigm, Hays argued
for the possibility of a "critical architecture" that would operate
between the extremes of conciliatory commodity and negative
commentary.

Twelve issues and seventeen years later, the editors of issue
33 have returned to the theme of interdisciplinarity. This time,
however, the topic is explicitly underwritten by the terms established in Hays's 1984 essay: "*Perspecta 33* is built around the
belief that architecture stands in the critical position between

being a cultural product and a discrete autonomous discipline." Yet, while Hays was suggesting that only critical architecture operated in his privileged "between" position, the editors of 33 imply that all architecture now automatically occupies a de facto critical status. What for Hays was then an exceptional practice, has now been rendered an everyday fact of life. If nothing else, however, this inflation of critical practice by the editors of 33 has perhaps unconsciously identified a fact of the last twenty years: namely, that disciplinarity has been absorbed and exhausted by the project of criticality. As Hays's first articulation of critical architecture was a necessary corrective to the realist position of *Perspecta 21*, it may be necessary (or, at least, useful) to provide an alternative to the now dominant paradigm of criticality, an alternative that will be characterized here as projective.

As evidenced by Hays's insightful polemic, critical architecture, under the regime of textuality, required the condition of being "between" various discursive oppositions. Thus "culture and form" can alternatively be figured as "kitsch and avant-garde" (Clement Greenberg), "literal and phenomenal" (Colin Rowe), "objecthood and art" (Michael Fried), or "capitalist development and design" (Manfredo Tafuri). Within architecture, Rowe's and Tafuri's discourses most fully enable, if never completely realize, the critical project of "betweeness," whether within history/theory, as with Hays, or in terms of design, as with the work of Peter Eisenman.

It is from Rowe's and Tafuri's conceptual genetic material that architecture's critical project has been formulated. For both authors, there is a requisite assumption of contradiction or ambiguity, regardless of whether it is subsumed or sublated (dialectical materialism) or balanced (liberal formalism). Even before examining the various reconfigurations of Rowe and Tafuri, however, it is important to recognize that the opposition between them is never as clear as would be imagined: Rowe's ostensibly formal project has deep connections to a particular liberal politics, and Tafuri's apparently engaged practice of dialectical critique entails a precise series of formal a prioris as well as a pessimistic prognosis with regard to architectural production. Seen in this way, there is no more political writer than Rowe, and none more formalist than Tafuri.

The criticality of Hays and Eisenman maintains the oppositional or dialectical framework in the work of their mentors and predecessors, while simultaneously trying to short-circuit or blur their terms. In their various attempts to hybridize Rowe and Tafuri in order to fashion a critical position,[2] both Hays and Eisenman rely on dialectics—as is immediately evidenced in the titles of the journals each was responsible for founding: *Oppositions* and *Assemblage*. Despite their implicit critiques of Michael Fried's aesthetics,[3] both Eisenman and Hays ultimately fear literalism as much as Fried does; both warn against the isomorphic remapping of life and art. For both, disciplinarity is understood as autonomy (enabling critique, representation, and signification), but not as instrumentality (projection, performativity, and pragmatics). One could say that their definition of disciplinarity is directed against reification rather then toward the possibility of emergence. While reification concerns itself with the negative reduction of qualitative experience to quantification, emergence promises that serial accumulation may itself result in the production of new qualities. As an alternative to the critical project—here linked to the indexical, the dialectical and hot representation—this text develops an alternative genealogy of the projective—linked to the diagrammatic, the atmospheric and cool performance.

From Index to Diagram

In the significant production of both Hays and Eisenman, as parallel realignments of Rowe and Tafuri, the critical project is inevitably mediated; in fact, it is perpetually obsessed by, and inextricably linked to, reproduction.[4] This obsession manifests itself both in Hays's account of Mies van der Rohe's Barcelona Pavilion and Peter Eisenman's rereading of Le Corbusier's Dom-ino, where both authors adopt the technique of the index.[5] The index emerges as the most opportune mediator (or critical instigator of the between) in part because it automatically combines materialism with signification: in other words, it exists as a physically driven sign, one that is not culturally or visually determined, as are the symbol or icon. For Hays, Mies's architecture situates itself "between the efficient representation of preexisting cultural values and the wholly detached autonomy of an abstract formal system."[6] This status of being in the world yet resistant to it is attained by the way the architectural object materially reflects its specific temporal and spatial context, as well as the way it serves as a trace of its productive systems. Hays describes the Barcelona Pavilion as "an event with temporal duration, whose actual existence is continually being produced," or whose meaning is continually being decided. This act of decision is both in fact and etymologically the critical gesture par excellence.

In Eisenman's discussion of the Dom-ino, it is the design process itself that is being registered rather than the material productive and technical systems or specific context discussed by Hays. In marking the status of its existence, in its ability to function as a self-referential sign, the Dom-ino is one of the first modernist and critical gestures in architecture: "Architecture is both substance and act. The sign is a record of an intervention— an event and an act which goes beyond the presence of elements which are merely necessary conditions." For Eisenman and Hays, the Dom-ino and Barcelona Pavilion are at once traces of an event, indices of their procedures of design or construction, and objects that potentially point to a state of continual transformation. In both cases, the critical forms of self-referentiality are demonstrated via serial reproductions: be they Eisenman's redrawn axonometrics of the non-existent Dom-ino perspective, or the historical photographs Hays uses to extract the experience of the defunct, original Barcelona Pavilion. Just as the architectural artifacts are indices of a missing process or practice, the objects themselves are also significantly missing in both cases, so that a series of reproductions must stand in as their traces. This process of infinite regress or deferral is constitutive of the critical architectural project: architecture inevitably and centrally preoccupied by its status as representation, and its simultaneous commentary on that condition.

As an alternative to Eisenman's reflections on the high European frame, which situated the frame within the context of the critical-indexical project of the 1970s, one might look to Rem Koolhaas's appropriation of the mass cultural American frame at the same moment. As suggested above, Eisenman understands Le Corbusier's Dom-ino as the trace of a transformative process, and in so doing he deviates from Rowe by animating the grid. Just as the indexical project assumes or invents a particular kind of reading subject for architecture, its imagination of architectural movement relies on a narrative for the grid. Thus, although the indexical program for architecture may proceed through diagrams, it is still tied to a semiotic, representational, and sequential ambition. Koolhaas's invocation of the "cartoon-theorem" from *Life* magazine—as well as the section cut from the Downtown Athletic Club—alternatively enlists a vision of architecture as contributing to the production and projection of new forms of collectivity. These New York frames exist as instruments of metropolitan plasticity and are not primarily architecture for paying attention to; they are not for reading, but for seducing, becoming, instigating new events and behaviors. The skyscraper-machine allows the projection infinitely upward of virtual worlds within this world, and in this way extends Michel Foucault's reflections on heterotopias and prisons. Gilles Deleuze argues that Foucault understands Jeremy Bentham's Panopticon not simply as a machine for surveillance, but more broadly and productively as a diagram which "imposes a particular form of conduct on a particular multiplicity." Koolhaas's investigation of the frame structure is diagrammatic in the same way.

From these two inventions of the frame structure in mid-70s architectural discourse, one can discern two orientations toward disciplinarity: that is, disciplinarity as autonomy and process, as in the case of Eisenman's reading of the Dom-ino, and disciplinarity as force and effect, as in Koolhaas's staging of the Downtown Athletic Club. Moreover, these two examples begin to differentiate the critical project in architecture, with its connection to the indexical, from the projective, which proceeds through the diagram. The diagram is a tool of the virtual to the same degree that the index is the trace of the real.[7]

From Dialectics to Doppler

Rather than relying upon the oppositional strategy of critical dialectics, the projective employs something similar to the Doppler Effect—the perceived change in the frequency of a wave that occurs when the source and receiver of the wave have a relative velocity. The Doppler Effect explains the change in pitch between the sound of a train as it approaches and then moves away from the listener.[8] If critical dialectics established architecture's autonomy as a means of defining architecture's field or discipline, a Doppler architecture acknowledges the adaptive synthesis of architecture's many contingencies. Rather than isolating a singular autonomy, the Doppler focuses upon the effects and exchanges of architecture's inherent multiplicities: material, program, writing, atmosphere, form, technologies, economies, etc. It is important to underscore that this multiply-ing of contingencies differs greatly from the more dilute notion of interdisciplinarity, which seeks to legitimize architecture through an external measuring stick, thereby reducing architecture to the entirely amorphous role of absorber of heterogeneous life. A projective architecture does not shy away from reinstating architectural definition, but that definition stems from design and its effects rather than a language of means and materials. The Doppler shifts the understanding of disciplinarity as autonomy to disciplinarity as performance or practice. In the former, knowledge and form are based on shared norms, principles, and traditions. In the latter, a more Foucaultian notion of disciplinarity is advanced in which the discipline is not a fixed datum or entity, but rather an active organism or discursive practice, unplanned and ungovernable, like Foucault's "unities form[ing] a number of autonomous, but not independent domains, governed by rules, but in perpetual transformation."[9] Rather than looking back or criticizing the status quo, the Doppler projects forward alternative (not necessarily oppositional) arrangements or scenarios.

A projective architecture does not make a claim for expertise outside the field of architecture nor does it limit its field of expertise to an absolute definition of architecture. Design is what keeps architecture from slipping into a cloud of heterogeneity. It delineates the fluctuating borders of architecture's disciplinarity and expertise. So when architects engage topics that are seemingly outside of architecture's historically defined scope—questions of economics or civic politics, for example—they don't engage those topics as experts on economics or civic politics, but, rather, as experts on design and how design may affect economics or politics. They engage these other fields as experts on design's relationship to those other disciplines, rather than as critics. Design encompasses object qualities (form, proportion, materiality, composition, etc.) but it also includes qualities of sensibility, such as effect, ambiance, and atmosphere.

An example of a projective architecture that engages the strategy of the Doppler Effect in lieu of that of the dialectic is WW's IntraCenter, a 40,000 ft.² community center located in Lexington, Kentucky. The IntraCenter's client provided WW with a program list of dizzying operational heterogeneity: daycare, athletic facilities, social services, café, library, computer center, job training facilities, shops, etc. Rather than figuring these multiple programs so as to provide each with its own formal identification, or rather than establishing a neutral field so as to provide each with its own formal identification, or rather than establishing a neutral field so as to allow the programs to define the project, the IntraCenter elides the expected overlap between form and program. Their lack of alignment leads to a perpetual Doppler shift between the two. This strategy of nonconcentricity generates other Doppler Effects, including the many reverberations among overlapping constituencies as well as material and structural conditions. The IntraCenter is projective rather than critical in that it very deliberately sets into motion the possibility of multiple engagements rather than a single articulation of program, technology, or form (contemporary architecture's commodity, firmness, and delight).

The Doppler Effect shares some attributes with parallax, which, as Yve-Alain Bois notes, comes from the Greek parallaxis, or "change": "the apparent change in the position of an object resulting from the change in the...position from which it is viewed."[10] Claiming that Serra consciously responded to the possibilities of parallax, Bois cites as an example Serra's description of his sculpture entitled Sight Point: "[It seems at first] to fall right to left, make an X, and straighten itself out to a truncated pyramid. That would occur three times as you walked around."[11]

In other words, parallax is the theatrical effect of a peripatetic view of an object. It takes into account how the context and the viewer complete the work of art.

Where the Doppler differs from parallax is in that it is not purely optical. Predicated on waves that can be auditory or visual, the Doppler suggests that the optical and conceptual are only two of many sensibilities. Additionally, it is not a reading strategy— that is, it is not just an unfolding reading of an artwork—but an atmospheric interaction. It foregrounds the belief that both the subject and the object carry and exchange information and energy. In short, a user might be more attuned to certain aspects of a building than others. He or she might understand how the building responds to a formal history of architecture or deploys a specific technology or he or she might have particular associations with a building's material palette or site. As the novelist W. G. Sebald explains, each one of us experiences moments of repetition, coincidence, or duplication, where echoes of other experiences, conversations, moods, and encounters affect current ones. Such momentary echoes are like tracks out of alignment, hearing and seeing out of phase that generate momentary déjà vus, an overlap of real and virtual worlds.

From Hot to Cool

Someone should establish an anthropology of hot and cool...
—Jean Baudrillard

Overall, one might characterize the shift from critical to projective modes of disciplinarity as a process of cooling down or, in Marshall McLuhan's terms, of moving from a "hot" to a "cool" version of the discipline. Critical architecture is hot in the sense that it is preoccupied with separating itself from normative, background or anonymous conditions of production, and with articulating difference. For McLuhan, hot media like film are "high-definition," conveying very precise information on one channel or in one mode. By contrast, cool media, such as television, are low-definition and, since the information they convey is compromised, they require the participation of the user. In this regard, the formalist-critical project is hot in its prioritization of definition, delineation, and distinction (or medium specificity). One alternative, minimalism, would be a cool art form; it is low-definition and requires the context and viewer to complete it, lacking both self-sufficiency and self-consciousness. Minimalism explicitly requires participation and is related to Smithson's promotion of entropy. While cooling suggests a process of mixing (and thus the Doppler Effect would be one form of cool), the hot resists through distinction, and connotes the overly difficult, belabored, worked, complicated. Cool is relaxed, easy. This difference between the cool and the hot may be amplified by briefly examining a medium McLuhan does not discuss: performance.

In his obituary on the actor, Dave Hickey writes that with Robert Mitchum you get performance,[12] and performance, he says, not expressed (or represented), but delivered. The Mitchum effect relies on knowing something is back there, but not being sure exactly what it is. Hickey says that what Mitchum does, then, is always surprising and plausible. And it's exactly this trait of surprising plausibility that might be adapted as a projective effect, one which combines the chance event with an expanded realism. There are two kinds of actors, Hickey argues. First are some who construct a character out of details and make you believe their character by constructing a narrative for them. One could say that this is the school of the "Method," where the actor provides gesture and motivation, and supplies a sub-text for the text of the script. The second group of actors create plausibility by their bodies; Hickey says they are not really acting, but rather "performing with a vengeance." While Robert De Niro is an actor in the first category, Mitchum is in the second.

In the nineteen-eighties and -nineties, architecture's relationship to philosophy was like that of De Niro to his character. In other words, a kind of Method acting, or Method designing, where the architect expressed a text or where architecture represented its procedure of formation. As with the "critical project," Method acting was connected to psychoanalysis, to calling up and reenacting memories and past events. In contrast Mitchum, Hickey says, is,

> Like Coltrane, playing a standard, he is inventing the text with his own subversive vision, his own pace and sense of dark contingency. So what we see in a Mitchum performance is less the character portrayed than a propositional alternative: What if someone with Mitchum's sensibility grew up to be a sea captain? a private eye? a school-teacher?[13]

In De Niro's acting, one witnesses the struggle, not just within the character, but between the actor and the character, such that the trace of the construction of the character is visible. There is no other way to say this except that, when watching De Niro, it looks like work (think of the signature mugging and concentrated gestures). The opening scenes in both versions of *Cape Fear* are instructive in this regard. The 1991 remake begins with De Niro working out in prison, exercising or rehearsing, where the sweat rolling off his back is visible. In the original, Mitchum is in no rush: rakish, lascivious, enjoying a cigar and checking out two women as the leave the courthouse, cool as the breeze. He makes it look easy. So "De Niro architecture" is hot, difficult, and indexes the processes of its production: it's clearly labored, narrative, or representational, or expresses a relationship of the representation to the real (the provision of a psychic subtext from a real event for a fictional text). Mitchum plays a cameo role as a detective in the remake, and as he is watching

De Niro/Cady strip-searched he sees his body covered with biblical proverbs and comments with a degree of reproach (as much for the Method-acting De Niro as the character Cady?): "I don't know whether to look at him or to read him." In contrast to this narrative mode, "Mitchum architecture" is cool, easy, and never looks like work; it's about mood or the inhabitation of alternative realities (what if?, the virtual). Here, mood is the open-ended corollary of the cool-producing effect without high definition, providing room for maneuver, and promoting complicity with subject(s). With Mitchum, there are scenarios, not psychodramas. The unease and anxiety of the unhomely has been replaced with the propositional alternative of the untimely.

Within architecture, a project of delivering performance, or soliciting a surprising plausibility, suggests moving away from a critical architectural practice—one which is reflective, representational, and narrative—to a projective practice. Setting out this projective program does not necessarily entail a capitulation to market forces, but actually respects or reorganizes multiple economies, ecologies, information systems, and social groups.

Our thanks to Ron Witte, Linda Pollari, and Adam Ruedig for their help and patience with this endeavor.

Notes

1   See the collection of essays *Architecture of the Everyday*, edited by Deborah Berke and Steven Harris (New York: Princeton Architectural Press, 1997).

2   Formulating their own critical positions, both Hays and Eisenman misread Rowe and Tafuri, according to Harold Bloom's understanding of misreading as poetic influence: "Poetic influence—when it involves two strong, authentic poets—always proceeds by a misreading of the prior poet, an act of creative correction that is actually and necessarily a misinterpretation." Harold Bloom, *The Anxiety of Influence: A Theory of Poetry* (New York: Oxford University Press, 1973; 1997), 30.

3　Significantly, the "between" for Fried was a theatrical anathema that undermined modernist specificity.

4　Mediated here refers both to Fredric Jameson's theorization of mediation as an active between—that is, as an engaged interaction between two subjects or between a subject and an object, rather than a passive between that operates as pure conciliation between two terms—and to Marshall McLuhan's understanding of mediation as mass media's translatable reproducibility.

5　"Repetition thus demonstrates how architecture can resist, rather than reflect, an external cultural reality," K. Michael Hays, "Between Culture and Form," *Perspecta 21* (Cambridge, Mass.: MIT Press, 1984): 27. Also see Peter Eisenman, "Aspects of Modernism: Maison Domino and the Self-Referential Sign," *Oppositions 15/16* (Winter/Spring, 1979).

6　Hays, ibid: 15.

7　For more on this distinction, see Deleuze and Guattari: "Diagrams must be distinguished from indexes, which are territorial signs, but also from icons, which pertain to reterritorialization, and from symbols, which pertain to relative or negative deterritorialization. Defined diagrammatically in this way, an abstract machine is neither an infrastructure that is determining in the last instance nor a transcendental Idea that is determining in the supreme instance. Rather, it plays a piloting role. The diagrammatic or abstract machine does not function to represent, even something real, but rather constructs a real that is yet to come, a new type of reality." *A Thousand Plateaus* (Minneapolis, Minn.: University of Minnesota Press, 1987), 142.

8　The Doppler Effect was discovered by the Austrian mathematician and physicist Christian Doppler (1803–1853).

9　Michel Foucault, *Archaeology of Knowledge*, trans. A.M. Sheridan Smith (New York: Routledge, 1969).

10　Yve-Alain Bois citing *Webster's Dictionary*, "A Picturesque Stroll Around Clara-Clara," in *Richard Serra*, ed. Hal Foster with Gordon Hughes, (Cambridge, Mass.: MIT Press, 2001), 65.

11　Ibid, 66.

12　Dave Hickey, "Mitchum Gets Out of Jail," *Art Issues* (September/ October 1997): 10–13.

13　Ibid: 12.

INTRODUCTION
Design Intelligence—Introduction: Part 1 / *Michael Speaks*

With his assessment of contemporary architecture as operating "after theory," the educator, researcher, and writer Michael Speaks prompted some controversy within architectural discourse.[1] Indeed Speaks openly announced, "in the 1980s and 1990s theory changed the practice of architecture. But today theory has lost touch and no longer has any consequences for the practice of architecture."[2] Beginning in December 2002, he developed this view in a sequence of twelve articles and interviews titled "Design Intelligence," published in the Japanese journal *Architecture and Urbanism* (*A+U*). In this series, Speaks expounds upon his notion of intelligence, which he believes has replaced theory as a guiding architectural concept.

In this introductory essay, Speaks identifies a paradigm shift from theory to intelligence, asserting that "if...theory [was] the intellectual dominant of the late twentieth century vanguards, then intelligence has become the intellectual dominant of the twenty-first century post-vanguards." Taking his cue from the Central Intelligence Agency and other "mobile and constantly evolving global organizations," Speaks explains that in our post– September 11th world, "visionary, utopian ideas" in line with theoretical pursuits "have given way to the 'chatter' of intelligence. Philosophical, political, and scientific truth have fragmented into proliferating swarms of 'little' truths appearing and disappearing so fast that ascertaining whether they are really true is impractical if not altogether impossible." In other words, Speaks perceives critical theory's quest for cultural critique and resistance to the status quo as the search for a singular truth, an activity ill suited to the constantly changing atmosphere in which we live. After citing a few firms—such as Greg Lynn FORM, Field Operations, and SHoP—that have learned from and adapted to this condition of uncertainty, that "transform the chatter of little truths into design intelligence," Speaks concludes that "contemporary architecture is compelled by the need to innovate, to create plausible solutions to problems that have been stated but whose larger implications have not yet been formulated. This can only be accomplished with intelligence." Thus while the use of the CIA as a model for architecture may be unexpected (and the references, within an architectural text, to Al Qaeda and former Secretary of Defense Donald Rumsfeld may be even more surprising), Speaks nonetheless offers an intriguing perspective concerning the future of the discipline, a direction he elsewhere provocatively categorizes as "architectural thinking after the end of theory."[3]

Notes

1   Michael Speaks, "After Theory," *Architectural Record* (June 2005): 72–75.
2   Ibid, "No Hope, No Fear," *arq* 6, no. 3 (2002): 209.
3   Ibid: 213.

MICHAEL SPEAKS

DESIGN INTELLIGENCE PART 1: INTRODUCTION

First appeared in *A+U* (2002), 10–18. Courtesy of Michael Speaks.

Three days before the first anniversary of September 11, the day jetliners were used to bring down the towers at World Trade Center in lower Manhattan, the *New York Times Magazine* sponsored an attempt to wrestle architecture into the discussion over what might eventually be built there. *Times* architecture critic Herbert Muschamp curated "The Masters' Plan," a study authored by world renowned architects who offered a vision of what might happen if genius were allowed to play a significant role in the site's redevelopment. Following the din of criticism surrounding the official proposals sponsored by the Lower Manhattan Development Corporation (LMDC), visionary architects, Muschamp argued in an accompanying article, could make us see things that mere developers working with lesser architects could not. Recalling the bravado and naïveté of early twentieth century modernism, Muschamp's efforts, and the efforts of the architects massed in this show of architectural might, was indeed heroic. Referring to what he feared some would consider formal indulgence in several of the projects, Muschamp insisted that all were conceptually grounded.

"The history of ideas," Muschamp reassured those unfamiliar with contemporary architecture and its debates, "is the context for architecture today."

It is not at all surprising that heroic efforts such as the *New York Times Magazine* proposal curated by Muschamp have rushed to fill the vacuum created by the horrific attack on New York, on America, and on what the perpetrators saw as the architectural expression of American financial power. The defiant urge to "think BIG," as the *Magazine* suggested, or to raise the towers just as they were as many have proposed, is a natural reaction to the fear, confusion, frustration and sense of loss left by their felling. America and New York's loss was an overwhelming human tragedy, but it also marked the passing of an era for America and the rest of the world. The horrifying video of the collapsing towers taken by journalists and people on the street that day simultaneously replay and serve as the final documented moments of the twentieth, or American century, as it has been called: Certainty pierced by devastating critique giving way to carnage, chaos and speculation about an unknown future. In such circumstances, Roarkian heroism[1] is perhaps a natural impulse. The question, however, is whether it is the most intelligent response to the twenty-first century world inaugurated by the events of September 11.

The "Week in Review" section published in the same edition of the *New York Times* that featured Muschamp's proposal was devoted to an issue that has scarcely registered except in the peripheral vision of architecture's most important critics and practitioners. "Unseen: A Special Section on Intelligence" focused on terrorist networks whose global reach and operational athleticism have outpaced the agencies whose job it is to monitor, infiltrate and destroy them. The problem, as noted by Douglas Frantz in his column, "Learning to Spy with Allies,"[2] is that intelligence agencies are still largely bound and slowed by national interests while terrorist organizations such as Al Qaeda are global and free to act with speed and deliberation. As Magnus Ranstorp of the Center for the Study of Terrorism and Political Violence at St. Andrews University in Scotland, quoted in Frantz's piece observes, [the Al Qaeda] "organization mutates and transforms itself according to operational requirements." Frustrated with this very situation, United States Secretary of Defense Donald Rumsfeld noted in an interview given to the *Times* on September 4 of this year, that Al Qaeda holds many advantages over nation states because, as he said, "it learns every day." Continuing, he remarked, "It goes to school on you. It watches how you are behaving and then alters and adjusts at relatively little cost, relatively little time, relatively little training to those incremental changes we make in how we do things." Asymmetrical threats—identified by Rumsfeld as those not issuing from nation states—posed by organizations like Al Qaeda have forced national intelligence agencies to share information that during the Cold War and until very recently would have been withheld in the interests of national security. As a result, new global alliances have been established to expand the reach of intelligence agencies activated in the so-called war on terrorism. Once content to defend national interests, security agencies must now evolve into nimble, global organizations acting with preemption if they are to face the challenge posed by Al Qaeda and other asymmetrical threats.

The events of September 11 and the new focus on intelligence that has emerged in their wake underscore a transformation in knowledge and in the standards used to determine its relevance. Management pioneer Peter Drucker has pointed out, for example, that the accession of modern capitalism to world system status was enabled by a fundamental change whereby knowledge was no longer concerned with philosophical or religious truth, but with doing, with action. Knowledge was applied to tools in the first, industrial period of capitalism. As Drucker suggests, a second phase of this transformation occurs after the Second World War in which knowledge is applied not only to tools, but in addition, knowledge is applied to knowledge itself. This transformation ushered in the management revolution and signaled the emergence of what Drucker calls "the knowledge society." Taking a more pessimistic view of what they prefer to call the "society of control," Michael Hardt and Antonio Negri, authors of *Empire*,[3] the highly acclaimed neo-Marxist study of globalization and politics, nonetheless agree with Drucker's assertion that the new economic order ushered in by globalization is knowledge-based. Though states still exist as filters of power and control, Hardt and Negri argue that real command and control is now in the hands of mobile and constantly evolving global organizations—corporations, NGOs, criminal organizations and intelligence agencies—free from national obligation to roam the planet in search of affiliations that provide competitive advantage. No longer stored in national banks of metaphysical truths, today knowledge is manifest as intelligence used to manage these organizations in a world where remaining competitive is literally a matter of life and death. As Hardt, Negri and Drucker seem to suggest, and as the events of September 11 underscore, visionary, utopian ideas have given way to the "chatter" of intelligence. Philosophical, political, and scientific truth have fragmented into proliferating swarms of "little" truths appearing and disappearing so fast that ascertaining whether they are really true is impractical if not altogether impossible. No longer dictated by ideas or ideologies nor dependent on whether something is really true, everything now depends on credible intelligence, on whether something *might be true.*

In architecture as in other fields we have witnessed a shift in intellectual dominance from philosophy and its search for absolute truth, to theory and its retreat into the "truth" of negative critique. Early twentieth century architecture vanguards were dominated by the expression of ideas that emerged from national philosophical traditions. Modernisms of all variety sprang from nation states to compete for international dominance. Stripped of all national ideology (save the American ideology of the consumerism) in order to insure its universal application, a neutral "International Style" emerged after the Second World War to claim its place as the dominant form of modernism. Under the auspices of theory, a then emerging intellectual dominant that pulled the ground from under philosophy once and for all, this American inflected "International Style" was rejected in the 1960s and 1970s along with all forms of consumer culture in favor of "critical" architectures. These critical architectures, however, soon followed the same path as the International Style architecture they helped to critique and bring down. Stylized simulacra, these theoretical vanguards had none of the political or philosophical *gravitas* of their early twentieth century predecessors. Rather than asserting their own "truth," Post-modernism, Deconstructivism, Critical Regionalism and a host of other critical architectures in the late 1980s and 1990s posed instead as false pretenders to Modernism. Whether effetely Derridean or ponderously Tafurian, theoretically inspired vanguards operated in a state of perpetual critique. Stuck between a world of certainty whose demise they had been instrumental in bringing about, and an emergent world of uncertainty into which they were being thrown headlong, theoretical vanguards were incapacitated by their own resolute negativity. Tethered to a critique of Modernism and truth, they suffered its fate second hand and are today mere historical not contemporary concerns. As theory and the vanguard architectures it enabled have fallen into desuetude, there have arisen new architecture practices better suited to prosper in the uncertainty created by the new global reality that first came to our attention in the 1990s and was fully inaugurated by the events of September 11. If philosophy was the intellectual dominant of early twentieth century vanguards and theory the intellectual dominant of late twentieth century vanguards, then intelligence has become the intellectual dominant of twenty-first century post-vanguards. While vanguard practices are reliant on ideas, theories and concepts given in advance, post-vanguard practices are more entrepreneurial in seeking opportunities for innovation that cannot be predicted by any idea, theory or concept. Intelligence is today the source of all value added and consequently the source of all that is innovative. As such, it is what distinguishes one practice from another. Without intelligence, no practice can survive the hostile conditions that define the twenty-first century. Indeed, it is design intelligence, that "unseen" array of techniques, relationships, dispositions and other intangibles, that enables post-vanguard practices to innovate by learning from and adapting to instability, and in so doing to distinguish themselves from their vanguard predecessors.

Gilles Deleuze, in his little book, *Spinoza: A Practical Philosophy*, gives us a useful way to think about how these post vanguard practices become more intelligent and therefore better able to adapt to and transform their environments. He also gives us a way to understand the uniqueness of individual practices without the need of stylistic, formal, professional or even generational categories. Following Spinoza, Deleuze defines the body as any corporeal arrangement composed of an infinite number of parts or particles held together when they move in unison at the same speed. He says a body can be anything, an animal, a body of sounds, even perhaps an architectural practice. He also says that a body has the capacity to affect and be affected by other bodies. Bodies are more or less powerful, more or less able, in other words, to effect change in their environment, depending on the degree to which they are capable of being affected by their environment.

If an architecture practice is such a body, then it becomes more powerful to the degree that it transforms the chatter of little truths into design intelligence. For more formally oriented post-vanguard practices this transformation occurs through versioning, a form of rapid prototyping in which vector-based information is used to create techniques adaptable to almost any scale intervention. In offices like Los Angeles based Greg Lynn FORM and Paris based Bernard Cache of Objectile, prototypes are not considered final designs but instead create feedback loops that drive the innovation process itself. Prototypes create intelligence by generating plausible solutions that become part of a firm's distributed intelligence. Techniques and designs developed in prototyping tea sets are thus available for use in urban scale projects and vice versa. Rapid prototyping underscores the necessity to invent new techniques that then become part of the intelligence makeup of each practice. In an installation created by Hernan Diaz Alonso of Xefirotarch in Los Angeles, for example, twenty-first century forms designed with animation softwares were realized only with the aid of 19th century metal-bending tools and techniques designed specifically for the project. Prototyping also enables mass production of uniqueness in which the "final" product is both one-of-a-kind-design and the array of specialized techniques invented and deployed. There is no better example of this than Foreign Office Architects (FOA)'s recently completed Yokohama Port Terminal in Japan, a marvel of architectural and urban design that has raised FOA's design intelligence quotient to a level enviable by firms ten times their size. Combining the development of such techniques with specialized cultural and corporate expertise, offices like AMO/OMA in Rotterdam, George Yu Architects in

Los Angeles, Lang Wilson PAC in Vancouver, and SHoP in New York City, specialize in design intelligence that extends from branding and marketing consulting to product and building design. Other, less formally inclined offices like MAX.1 and Crimson, also from Rotterdam, focus on the development of what they call "orgware," the organizational intelligence that negotiates between the software of policy directives, zoning and legal codes, and building or infrastructural hardware. An example is their urban "space locator," an interactive urban gaming manual designed to allow competing urban stakeholders in Hoogvliet, a suburb of Rotterdam, to reach consensus on urban planning issues. Similarly, landscape urbanists Stan Allen and James Corner of New York/Philadelphia based Field Operations, design artificial ecologies that are deployed in interactive layers and fields rather than as single design elements. These "field operations" trigger the emergence of new forms of natural and urban life that evolve over time into self-organized artificial ecologies teaming with life.

Opening itself to being affected by the environment in which it lives impacts the organization of a body by forcing it to readjust its resting speed, creating, in turn, a more complex, variable arrangement that enables it to become more adaptable and more competitive. Indeed, it is this resting speed defined by design intelligence and not any formal, theoretical or professional identity that defines each of these architectural practices. Sharing only the ability to transform chatter into credible intelligence, post-vanguard practices cannot be categorized under any existing classification system. Some design boxes, some blobs, some everything from milled panels and coffee sets to urban parks, while others script complex ballets of urban movement. Amateurs who hold to no philosophical or professional truth, who make use of no specialized theory, these practices are open to the influence of chatter and are by disposition willing to learn.

Accustomed in ways that their vanguard predecessors can never be to open source intelligence (OSINT as it is called by the CIA) gathered from the little truths published on the web, found in popular culture, and gleaned from other professions and design disciplines, these practices are adaptable to almost any circumstance almost anywhere.

Though we live in uncertain times, one thing is certain: contemporary architecture is not driven by visionary ideas heroically realized in visionary form. Instead, contemporary architecture is compelled by the need to innovate, to create plausible solutions to problems that have been stated but whose larger implications have not yet been formulated. This can only be accomplished with intelligence. Otherwise, design is simply a matter of completing a problem given without adding anything new. Each of the offices mentioned above have developed unique design intelligences that enable them to innovate by adding something not given in the brief or the formulation of problems they have been asked to solve....

As for intelligent solutions to the problem posed by the development of the World Trade Center site in lower Manhattan: The LMDC in early September sponsored a competition in which six teams chosen from a pool of more than 400 applicants have been given $40,000 US to make proposals by November.[5] Among the six, two are notable for they allow us to draw a clear a line between the heroic vanguard and the innovative post-vanguard. The vanguard selection consists of three members of the famous 1970s era New York Five—Peter Eisenman, Richard Meier and Charles Gwathmey—and Steven Holl, also from New York. Noted for their radical rethinking of early twentieth century modernism, this is a collection of unparalleled individual genius that will offer visionary solutions for last-century problems. The other, a global team called United Architects—Foreign Office Architects, UN Studio, Reiser Umemoto,

Greg Lynn, Imaginary Forces, and Kevin Kenon—is assembled from among the most innovative practices in contemporary architecture. This is a collection of distinct intelligences moving at the same speed that combines to form a body, in the Deleuzian sense, uniquely capable of delivering innovations unanticipated in the formulation of the problem given by the brief. Whatever the outcome, this team will not be satisfied to simply solve a problem. The World Trade Center Towers were attacked because they were global symbols of modernity. Everyone agrees that any response should be tempered with respect for the hallowed site where so many lives were lost but that it should also be a reaffirmation of modernity itself. If that is so, then the real question to be answered in the development of the WTC site is whether it will be accomplished by a twentieth [century] modernism of genius or a twenty-first century modernism guided by intelligence.

Notes

1 "Roarkian" refers to Howard Roark, an architect who appeared in Ayn Rand's 1943 novel, *The Fountainhead*.
2 *Washington Post*. September 8, 2002.
3 Michael Hardt and Antonio Negri, *Empire* (Cambridge, Mass.: Harvard University Press, 2000).
4 Gilles Deleuze, *Spinoza, Practical Philosophy* (San Francisco: City Lights Publishers, 1988).
5 See LMDC website: http://www.renewnyc.com.

INTRODUCTION

From Principles to Practices: Creating a Sustaining
Architecture for the Twenty-first Century /
William McDonough and Michael Braungart

In 1992, the American architect William McDonough, in consul-
tation with the German chemist Michael Braungart, published
The Hannover Principles: Design for Sustainability,[1] strategies for
sustainable design to guide the development of the 2000 World's
Fair. The document highlighted the interaction of the built and
natural environments and basic issues of sustainability, hoping to
promote a more holistic and responsible view of design in the
service of ecology and humanity. McDonough and Braungart,
who in 1995 formed the partnership McDonough Braungart
Design Chemistry (MBDC), have continued to spread this
message through their rethinking of materials, processes, and
design, as well as written works such as *Cradle to Cradle* (2002).

The phrase "cradle to cradle" refers to the lifecycle
McDonough and Braungart envision for all manmade products,
replicating the way in which nature uses the waste from certain
processes to fuel others. For McDonough and Braungart, nature
serves as the perfect model to guide industry and inspire ingenuity. Currently environmental consciousness often focuses on
a reduction of waste; McDonough and Braungart advocate the
elimination of waste and the creation of systems that are ecologically, socially, and economically beneficial. In other words, they
feel that the concept of waste should disappear, to be replaced
by that of reusable yield.

In 2003, McDonough and Braungart issued an updated
version of *The Hannover Principles*. "From Principles to Practices,"
an article adapted from this new edition, reasserts the importance
of sustainability while reviewing the positive changes within the
fields of production and design that have occurred in the past

216

decade, including the development of various materials, buildings, and urban goals. McDonough and Braungart hope that
"the principled practice of design" as guided by the Hannover
Principles will lead to the "next industrial revolution"[2]—an era in
which interests of industry and the environment are no longer
categorized as mutually exclusive, a future in which we "create
[ecological] footprints to delight in rather than lament."

Notes

1   William McDonough, *The Hannover Principles: Design for Sustainability*
    (New York: William McDonough Architects, 1992); reprinted in *Theorizing a
    New Agenda for Architectural Theory*, ed. Kate Nesbitt (New York: Princeton
    Architectural Press, 1996), 409–10.
2   William McDonough and Michael Braungart, "Introduction," in *Cradle to
    Cradle* (New York: North Point Press, 2002).

WILLIAM McDONOUGH AND
MICHAEL BRAUNGART

FROM PRINCIPLES TO PRACTICES: CREATING A SUSTAINING ARCHITECTURE FOR THE TWENTY-FIRST CENTURY

First appeared in *green@work*, May/June 2003. Courtesy of William McDonough.

Just over a decade ago, when the City of Hannover, Germany, asked us to develop a set of design principles for the 2000 World's Fair, design for sustainability was in its infancy. While the desire to move toward a solar-powered world had gained significant momentum among the environmentally conscious by 1992, and the ideas that inform ecological design had begun to manifest themselves in encouraging innovations in "green" architecture and technology, a coherent framework for applying sustainable design to all sectors of society had yet to emerge. Imagining designs that celebrated nature and technology, human health and vibrant commerce was even further off the map.

The Hannover Principles were conceived to lay the foundation for this hopeful, new paradigm. We knew at the time that our efforts were just a first step. Though we were striving to identify universal principles based on the enduring laws of nature, we also understood that our knowledge of the world was incomplete. So, too, was our ability to predict all the many ways in which the creativity of the world's designers, architects, business leaders, and NGOs would push design for sustainability beyond the limits we could imagine in 1992. Thus, we saw the Principles as a living document—a set of enduring ideals and an open system of thought that would evolve as it was put into practice.

And evolve it has. Our firms, and many others, continue to use the Principles in their original form. Yet, as the Principles are applied in the design process or used to guide everyday decision-making, new ideas and practices emerge. The language we use is a good example. Whereas some of the Principles were originally expressed with urgent "shoulds" and "musts," today we use a more celebratory language that reflects our evolving goals. Rather than aspire to a respectful co-existence with nature, we aim to celebrate human creativity and the abundance of the living earth with designs that create mutually beneficial relationships between people and the natural world. The Principle's basic tenets, however, continue to be the standard for our designs. The result: the Principles remain an enduring touchstone, their rigor drives innovation, and our sustaining design paradigm continues to mature.

To those familiar with the Principles, they have become common sense; to those just discovering them, it might be useful to see how their application begets enormous creativity. The generative power of Principle six provides a good example. Principle six says Eliminate the concept of waste. In 1992 this was a radical new concept. Designers and engineers were typically focused on reducing waste, on trying to be "less bad." The conventional wisdom held that using less energy and fewer materials and limiting the amount of toxic chemicals released into the air, water, and soil would guarantee a sustainable world. But Principle six demands something entirely different. Rather than attempting to mitigate the destructive effects of architecture and industry, eliminating the concept of waste demands that we begin to see our designs in a wholly positive light.

Pursuing that goal over the past decade has driven the evolution of an entirely new approach to design. When one takes seriously the idea that the concept of waste can be eliminated in the worlds of architecture, commerce, manufacturing, and transportation—indeed, in every sector of society—the purview of design shifts radically. Not only are we obliged to include the entire material world in our design considerations, we are asked to imagine materials in a whole new way. In today's world of trying to be "less bad," materials typically follow a one-way path to the landfill or incinerator, and waste managers intervene here and there to slow down the trip from cradle to grave. But when we are no longer content with simply managing waste more efficiently, we can begin to create and use materials effectively within cradle-to-cradle systems, in which there is no waste at all.

Rather than seeing materials as a waste management problem, cradle-to-cradle thinking sees materials as nutrients that cycle through either the biological metabolism or the technical metabolism. In the biological metabolism, the nutrients that support life on Earth—water, oxygen, nitrogen, carbon dioxide—flow perpetually through biological cycles of growth, decay and rebirth. There are no waste-management problems. Instead, waste equals food. The technical metabolism is designed to mirror natural nutrient cycles; it's a closed-loop system in which valuable, high-tech synthetics and mineral resources circulate in an endless cycle of production, recovery and reuse.

By specifying safe, healthful ingredients, designers and architects can create and use materials within these cradle-to-cradle cycles. Materials designed as biological nutrients, such as textiles for draperies, wall coverings and upholstery fabrics, can be designed to biodegrade safely and restore the soil after use, providing more positive effects, not fewer negative ones. Materials designed as technical nutrients, such as infinitely recyclable nylon carpet fiber, can provide high-quality, high-tech ingredients for generation after generation of synthetic products—again, a harvest of value. And buildings constructed with these nutritious materials and designed to "fit" within local energy flows articulate and enhance the connection between people and nature. Already well established through the work of our firms and our clients, cradle-to-cradle thinking represents an ongoing revolution in design. Its source and sustenance: The laws of nature adapted to human design in the Hannover Principles.

When the Principles become practices, when industrial and architectural systems are modeled on the earth's flows of energy and nutrients, the notion that humanity must limit its ecological footprint is turned on its head. Indeed, as cradle-to-cradle thinking continues to be enriched by the inspired work of our colleagues, we are increasingly able to design products and places that support life, that create footprints to delight in rather than lament. This changes the entire context of the design process. Instead of asking, "How do I meet today's environmental standards," designers are asking "How might I create more habitat, more health, more clean water, more prosperity, more delight?"

Questions such as these, emerging from the daily application of the Hannover Principles, are stimulating the worldwide evolution of cradle-to-cradle design. They are driving a growing movement of principled designers who are deeply engaged in developing safe materials, products, supply chains and manufacturing processes that allow us to celebrate human creativity and the world's natural abundance. In fact, just one year after the publication of the original edition of The Hannover

Principles, we had the opportunity to develop a cradle-to-cradle upholstery fabric, Climatex Lifecycle, which is produced with completely safe ingredients and biodegrades after use. The design and production of Climatex Lifecycle transformed a factory burdened with toxic wastes into one with only positive emissions, signaling the real-world efficacy of "waste equals food."

Just so, the Hannover Principles and cradle-to-cradle thinking are moving nations as vast and influential as China to begin to apply the intelligence of natural systems to their development plans. They are guiding the design of community plans that connect people to nature and to each other. They are inspiring the design of buildings like trees, which harvest the energy of the sun, sequester carbon, make oxygen, distill water and provide habitat for thousands of species.

And more. Imagine everything we do or make as a gesture that supports life, inspires delight and expresses intelligence in harmony with nature. Imagine buildings with on-site wetlands and botanical gardens recovering nutrients from circulating water. Fresh air, flowering plants and daylight everywhere. Beauty and comfort for every inhabitant. Rooftops covered in soil and plants nourished by falling rain. Birds nesting and feeding in the building's verdant footprint. Imagine, in short, buildings as life-support systems in harmony with energy flows, human souls and other living things.

Inspired by the Hannover Principles, architects at William McDonough + Partners [WD+P] have already designed buildings such as these. From an environmental studies center on the campus of Oberlin College to the corporate offices of Gap Inc.; from the Herman Miller "GreenHouse," a factory where you feel you've spent your day outdoors, to the Museum of Life and the Environment, which explores the deep connections between natural and cultural history both in the Appalachian Piedmont and beyond—today's cradle-to-cradle designs are testaments to the lively relationship between principles and practices.

And we are now seeing the Principles influence the work of a host of influential companies. Ford Motor Company has launched the cradle-to-cradle renovation of its famous Rouge River industrial site with a new manufacturing facility, a factory with a living roof and a landscape of wetlands and swales that naturally purifies storm water runoff. Ford also introduced in 2003 the Model U, the world's first automobile designed to embrace the cradle-to-cradle vision.

Other business leaders are following suit. Shaw Industries, the largest producer of commercial carpet in the world, has begun to apply the Hannover Principles and cradle-to-cradle thinking to the company's product development process. Working with MBDC [McDonough Braungart Design Chemistry], Shaw is doing a scientific assessment of the material chemistry of its carpet fiber and backing to ensure that every ingredient is safe. The result: an infinitely recyclable, completely healthful carpet tile made from true technical nutrients that eliminate the concept of waste.

Clearly, cradle-to-cradle design makes good sense economically and socially. This is especially visible in the workplace. When designs for large-scale factories and offices are modeled on nature's effectiveness, they generate delightful, productive places for people to work. This not only encourages a strong sense of community and cooperation, it also spurs enormous leaps in productivity and allows efficiency and cost-effectiveness to serve a larger purpose.

Consider: Ford's living roof and constructed wetlands revitalize the landscape while filtering storm water runoff for $35 million less than conventional technical controls. Herman Miller's GreenHouse generated increased worker satisfaction and productivity gains of 24 percent, which paid for the $15 million building in a single year. The Gap Inc. building, maximizing local energy flows, exceeds California's strict energy requirements by 30 percent. By aiming to maximize positive effects, these designs outperformed buildings that set efficiency as their highest goal.

The principles of cradle-to-cradle design can be applied to entire cities and regional plans. Working with the City of Chicago, WM+P drew upon the example of the Hannover Principles to serve Mayor Richard Daley's quest to make Chicago "the greenest city in America." The Chicago Principles, which will be announced in 2003, will provide a reference point as the city develops community plans and cradle-to-cradle systems that will make it a national model of how industry and ecology, nature and the city can flourish side by side.

Looking ahead, we see Chicago becoming a hub of green manufacturing and transit, energy effectiveness, and cradle-to-cradle material flows. A place in which every material moves in regenerative cycles, from city to country, country to city, all the polymers, metals, synthetic fibers and communications software flowing safely in the technical metabolism, all the photosynthetic nutrients flowing in the biological metabolism. All of which adds up to flourishing human communities, places that generate and enjoy an abundance of ecological, economic and cultural wealth.

There is really no end in sight—and that's the point. As we seek constant improvement by the sharing of knowledge, as our understanding of the world evolves, the Hannover Principles will continue to be our touchstone and inspiration for new designs. This process, merely a decade old, has already created hopeful changes in the world and is transforming the making of things into a regenerative force. Ultimately, we believe the principled practice of design will lead to ever more places and ever more products that honor not just human ingenuity but harmony with the exquisite intelligence of nature. And when that becomes the hallmark of good design, we will have entered a moment in human history when we can truly celebrate our kinship with all life.

INTRODUCTION
Boundaries/Networks / *William J. Mitchell*

In *City of Bits* (1996) and *e-Topia* (1999), William J. Mitchell—
professor of architecture and media arts and sciences at the
Massachusetts Institute of Technology—examines the relationship between information technology and contemporary
culture. Mitchell's text of 2003, *Me++: The Cyborg Self and the
Networked City*, offers a continuation on this theme. More specifically, in the book's opening chapter, "Boundaries/Networks,"
he provides a thought-provoking analysis of an everyday and
pervasive fact of contemporary life: the phenomenon of the network. Mitchell begins by highlighting the multiple boundaries
that surround us, from clothing to buildings to national borders.
Historically, barriers of this sort have always surrounded us,
along with points of connection between them (for example,
doors in walls and openings through city gates). Aside from the
kinds of boundaries—we now have additional artificial layers
available to us, from sunscreen to national defense systems—
what has most clearly changed in contemporary times is the
extreme proliferation of linkages. "The *network*, rather than
the enclosure," Mitchell declares, "is emerging as the desired
and contested object...Extension and entanglement trump
enclosure and autonomy." Indeed, Mitchell feels that, by the
beginning of the twenty-first century, "connectivity had become
the defining characteristic of our...urban condition."

   The ascendancy of information, communication, and
computation networks on a global scale has been accompanied by a recasting of temporality and spatiality, which we now
experience as discontinuous. Human relationships have been
altered, allowing social networks to flourish over large geographical distances and dispersed settlements. Likewise, the
built environment and our interactions with it have changed in

dramatic ways, especially in response to wireless and digital technologies. In short, in this world of divisions and separations, we are enmeshed in overlapping, complex worldwide networks that impact all aspects of daily life.

WILLIAM J. MITCHELL

BOUNDARIES / NETWORKS

First appeared in *Me++: The Cyborg Self and the Networked City*
(Cambridge, Mass.: MIT Press, 2003), 7–17. Courtesy of the
MIT Press.

Consider, if you will, Me++.

I consist of a biological core surrounded by extended, constructed systems of boundaries and networks. These boundary and network structures are topological and functional duals of each other.[1] The boundaries define a space of containers and places (the traditional domain of architecture), while the networks establish a space of links and flows. Walls, fences, and skins divide; paths, pipes, and wires connect.

Boundaries

My natural skin is just layer zero of a nested boundary structure. When I shave, I coat my face with lather. When I'm nearly naked in the open air, I wear—at the very least—a second skin of spf 15 sunblock.

My clothing is a layer of soft architecture, shrinkwrapped around the contours of my body. Beds, rugs, and curtains are looser assemblages of surrounding fabric—somewhere between underwear and walls. My room is a sloughed-off carapace, cast into a more rigorous geometry, fixed in place, and enlarged in scale so that it encloses me at a comfortable distance. The building that contains it has a weatherproof exterior shell. Before modern mobile artillery, fortified city walls would have provided a final, hardened, outermost crust; these sorts of urban-scale skins remained reasonably effective at least until the 1871 siege of Paris, during the Franco-Prussian War.[2]

In the early years of the Cold War, outer defensive encasements reemerged, in extreme form, as domestic nuclear bunkers. The destruction of the Berlin Wall in 1989 marked the end of that edgy era. But still, if I end up in jail, an internment camp, or a walled retirement community, the distinction between intramural and extramural remains brutally literal. If I retire to a farm, a boundary fence stops my stock from straying. And if I locate myself within the homeland of a major military power, I take refuge behind a dubious high-tech bulwark that extends across thousands of kilometers; our extradermal armored layers have coevolved, with increasingly fearsome weapons systems, into invisible radar curtains and missile shields that create vast electronic enceintes. I surround myself with successive artificial skins that continually vary in number and character according to my changing needs and circumstances.[3]

All of my boundaries depend, for their effectiveness, upon combining sufficient capacity to attenuate flow with sufficient thickness. If I want to keep warm, for example, I can use a thin layer of highly insulating material or a thicker layer of a less effective insulator. If I want acoustic privacy, I can retreat behind a closed door, or I can simply rely on the attenuation of sound waves in air and move out of earshot. If I want to create a jail, I can construct escape-proof walls, or I can remove the prisoners to a sufficiently distant place—like the eighteenth-century British convicts transported to Australia. In sparsely populated territories, distance creates many natural barriers, while in buildings and cities, efficient artificial barriers subdivide closely packed spaces.

Connections

But I am, as Georg Simmel observed, a "connecting creature who must always separate and who cannot connect without separating."[4] My enclosures are leaky. Crossing the various boundaries that surround me there are paths, pipes, wires, and other channels that spatially concentrate inflows and outflows of people, other living creatures, discrete goods, gases and fluids, energy, information, and money. I am inextricably entangled in the networks of my air, water, waste disposal, energy, transportation, and Internet service providers.

To create and maintain differences between the interiors and exteriors of enclosures—and there is no point to boundaries and enclosures if there are no differences—I seek to control these networked flows. So the crossing points are sites where I can survey what's coming and going, make access decisions, filter out what I don't want to admit or release, express desire, exercise power, and define otherness. Directly and indirectly, I employ doors, windows, bug screens, gates, cattle grids, adjustable apertures, valves, filters, prophylactics, diapers, face masks, receptionists, security checkpoints, customs and immigration checkpoints, traffic signals, routers, and switches to determine who or what can go where, and when they can go there. So do you, of course, and so do others with the capacity to do so in particular contexts.

Through the interaction of our efforts to effect and control transfers among enclosures and our competition for network resources, we mutually construct and constrain one another's realms of daily action. Within the relatively stable framework of our interconnecting, overlapping, sometimes shared transfer networks, our intricately interwoven demands and responses create fluctuating conditions of freedom and constraint. And as networks become faster, more pervasive, and more essential, these dynamics become increasingly crucial to the conduct of our lives; we have all discovered that a traffic jam, a check-in line, a power outage, a server overwhelmed by a denial-of-service attack, or a market crash can create as effective a barrier as a locked door. The more we depend upon networks, the more tightly and dynamically interwoven our destinies become.

Networks

The archetypal structure of the network, with its accumulation and habitation sites, links, dynamic flow patterns, interdependencies, and control points, is now repeated at every scale from that of neural networks (neurons, axons, synapses) and digital circuitry (registers, electron pathways, switches) to that of global transportation networks (warehouses, shipping and air routes, ports of entry).[5] And networks of different types and scales are integrated into larger network complexes serving multiple functions. Depending upon our relationships to the associated social and political structures, each of us can potentially play many different roles (some strong, some weak) at nodes within these complexes—owner, authorized user, operator, occupant, occupier, tenant, customer, guest, sojourner, tourist, immigrant, alien, interloper, infiltrator, trespasser, snooper, besieger, cracker, hijacker, invader, gatekeeper, jailer, or prisoner. Power and political identity have become inseparable from these roles.

With the proliferation of networks and our increasing dependence upon them, there has been a gradual inversion of the relationship between barriers and links. As the ancient use of a circle of walls to serve as the ideogram for a city illustrates, the enclosing, dividing, and sometimes-defended *boundary* was once the decisive mechanism of political geography. Joshua got access the old-fashioned way; when he blew his righteous trumpet, the walls of Jericho came tumbling down. By the mid-twentieth century, though, the most memorable ideogram of London was its underground network, and that of Los Angeles was its freeway map; riding the networks, not dwelling within walls, was what made you a Londoner or an Angeleno. And the story of recent urban growth has not been one of successive encircling walls, as it mostly would have been for ancient, medieval, and Renaissance cities, but of network-induced sprawl at the fringes.

More recently, the unbelievably intricate diagram of Internet interconnectivity has become the most vivid icon of globalization. Now you get access by typing in your password, and IT managers dissolve the perimeters between organizations by merging their network access authorization lists. Today the *network*, rather than the enclosure, is emerging as the desired and contested object: the dual now dominates.[6] Extension and entanglement trump enclosure and autonomy. Control of territory means little unless you also control the channel capacity and access points that service it.

A year after the September 11 attacks on New York and Washington, the implications of this were sinking in. The President's Critical Infrastructure Protection Board bluntly reported (to nobody's very great surprise),

> Our economy and national security are fully dependent upon information technology and the information infrastructure. A network of networks directly supports the operation of all sectors of our economy—energy (electric power, oil, and gas), transportation (rail, air, merchant marine), finance and banking, information and telecommunications, public health, emergency services, water, chemical, defense industrial base, food, agriculture, and postal and shipping. The reach of these

computer networks exceeds the bounds of cyberspace. They also control physical objects such as electrical transformers, trains, pipeline pumps, chemical vats, radars, and stock markets.[7]

Connectivity had become the defining characteristic of our twenty-first century urban condition.

Clocks

All networks have their particular paces and rhythms. Within the nested layers and recursively embedded networks of my world, my pulse—the sound of an intermediate-scale, low-speed vascular network—has been mechanized, regularized, externalized, and endlessly echoed back to me. Just as boundary, flow, and control systems subdivide my space into specialized, manageable zones, these constructed rhythms partition my time into discrete, identifiable, assignable, sometimes chargeable chunks. Bean counters are also minute counters; measurable, accountable time is money.

The miraculously monotone beat of the pendulum first established this possibility.[8] Ancient sundials and water clocks had marked the flow of time, and Benedictine monastery bells had formalized its approximate mechanical subdivision. Clock towers had provided European towns with faster communal heartbeats—essential, as Lewis Mumford pointed out, to the regulation and coordination of social and economic life, and eventually to the industrial organization of production.[9] Then, in the seventeenth century, Christiaan Huygens devised a pendulum clock that ticked precisely.

This innovation also initiated a shift in scale. Furniture-sized towers (grandfather clocks, standing in domestic hallways) soon began to associate timekeeping with the dwelling and the family rather than with the town and the larger community.

Substituting spring-driven mechanisms for pendulums allowed clocks to become even smaller, more portable, and eventually wearable—now associating time-keeping with the individual.[10] Timepieces moved to pockets, then to wrists—provocatively, the organic pulse's most obvious point of presence. Clinging tightly to flesh, they have enabled the large-scale scheduling and coordination of individual activities; during the American Civil War, for example, the Union forces depended upon them to synchronize operations.

As artificial pulse rates have accelerated, timekeeping mechanisms have continued to shrink. Today, the gigahertz, crystal oscillator hearts of tiny computer chips are embedded everywhere. (Chips without clocks are possible, and may turn out to have some important advantages, but they are not yet in widespread use.)[11] Electronic vibrations subdivide seconds into billions of parts, pace the execution of computational tasks, discipline our interactions with computational devices, calibrate GPS navigation systems, regulate power distribution and telephone systems, measure and commodify both human and machine work, and precisely construct the accelerating tempos and rhythms of the digital era—coordinated, where necessary, by a central atomic clock.[12] They not only *mark* time, they *trigger* the execution of instructions and programs. Seconds, milliseconds, microseconds, nanoseconds, picoseconds: the electronic global heartbeat keeps quickening and gathering power—so much so that, when its coordinated microrhythms threatened to falter at Y2K, there was bug-eyed panic in the technochattering classes.[13] There was talk of "spectacular explosions, nuclear meltdowns, power blackouts, toxic leaks, plane crashes, and bank failures."[14]

Processes

But there is, of course, more to the construction of time than the increasingly precise subdivision of the day. As clocks multiply and distribute themselves spatially, the relationships among them begin to matter.

Different places may simply run on their own clocks, or their timekeeping systems may be standardized and synchronized. When there was little communication between spatially separated settlements, local time sufficed, and there was no need for such coordination, but linkage by long-distance railroad and telegraph networks eventually made it imperative. In 1851 the Harvard College Observatory began to distribute clock ticks, by telegraph, to the railroad companies. As transportation and telecommunication capacities have increased, we have entered the era of globalized network time—of GMT, time zones, and sleep cycles decoupled from the solar day.[15] Once, villagers rose with the roosters to work until sunset in nearby fields; now, jet-lagged business travelers do their email at three a.m. in hotel rooms far from home.

Computers have added additional layers of complexity to the construction of time. The first computers—constructed according to the elegant principles of Turing and von Neumann—were strictly sequential machines, executing one operation at a time; programming was a matter of specifying these operations in precise order. Everything was rigorously governed by clock increments and finite (though small) durations. But as interactive computing developed, a distinction emerged between tasks that could be performed in "real" time and those that could not. For example, computer animations of three-dimensional environments could be computed and stored for later playback, or (as in today's video games) they could be computed and presented on the fly, with no perceptible time lag. In other words, if you take advantage of fast machines to compress processes, you can elide the distinction between simultaneity and sequence. "Virtual reality" would be impossible without this.

The practice of timesharing has produced a further elision. If a processor is fast enough, it can be programmed to divide its time among multiple simultaneous processes—providing the illusion that it is devoting itself exclusively to each one. In effect, a single, sequential processor divides itself into multiple "virtual machines" that seem to occupy the same space and time. The ancient, seemingly unproblematic concept of *hic et nunc*— what's here and now—begins to frazzle.

As processors have become smaller and cheaper, and as they have been integrated into networks, it has become increasingly feasible to program parallel rather than strictly sequential processes; tasks are divided up among multiple processors, which simultaneously contribute to producing the desired result. It is even possible to imagine organizing the entire Internet as a parallel computation device.[16] At this point—particularly as network speeds approach the internal bus speeds of computers—it no longer makes sense to think of a computer as a compact, discrete object, or to distinguish between computers and networks. Eventually, we will approach the physical speed limit, and its associated paradox; information cannot travel faster than light, so spatially distributed events that seem simultaneous from one node in a lightspeed network may seem sequential from another, and vice versa.

The logical endpoint of this shift to networked parallelism is the emerging possibility of quantum computing—in which every atom stores a bit, vast numbers of atomic-scale processing elements are harnessed to execute computations at unprecedented speed, and the notoriously strange spatial and temporal logic of quantum mechanics (rather than the familiar logic of our everyday world) takes over.[17] (It isn't easy to wrap your mind around the fact of quantum systems occupying several places at once, quantum bits registering 0 and 1 at the same time, and quantum computers performing large numbers of computations simultaneously.) And, maybe, the ultimate network will operate by the quantum-magical means of quantum entanglement and teleportation of quantum states from one site to another.[18]

So we have gone from local habitation and mechanical subdivision of time to a far more dynamic, electronically based, network-mediated, global system of sequencing and coordination. The early moderns measured out their lives in clock ticks (and sometimes, as Prufrock lamented, coffee spoons); now, our webs of extension and interconnection run on nanosecond-paced machine cycles that are edging into the domain of quantum logic. The more we interrelate events and processes across space, the more simultaneity dominates succession; time no longer presents itself as one damn thing after another, but as a structure of multiple, parallel, sometimes cross-connected and interwoven, spatially distributed processes that cascade around the world through networks. Once there was a time and a place for everything; today, things are increasingly smeared across multiple sites and moments in complex and often indeterminate ways.

Discontinuities

In the fast-paced, digitally mediated world that we have constructed for ourselves, what exists between 0 and 1, a pixel and its neighbor, or a discrete time interval and the next? The answer, of course, is nothing—profoundly nothing; there's no there there. The digital world is logically, spatially, and temporally discontinuous.

Our networks are similarly discontinuous structures; they have well-defined access points, and between these points things are in a kind of limbo. If you drop a letter into a mailbox, it disappears into the mail network until it shows up at the recipient's box, and if you send an email, it's just packets in the Internet cloud until it is reassembled upon receipt. Obviously it is possible, in principle, to precisely track things through networks, but in practice we rarely care about this. We experience networks at their interfaces, and only worry about the plumbing behind the interfaces when something goes wrong.

If you transfer *yourself* through a network, you directly experience this limbo. It is, perhaps, most dramatic on intercontinental night flights. You have your headphones on, there is darkness all around, and there is no sensation of motion. The video monitor constructs a local reality, and occasionally interrupts it to display current times at origin and destination. It is best not to worry too much about how to set your watch right now, precisely where you are, or whose laws might apply to you.

The discontinuities produced by networks result from the drive for efficiency, safety, and security. Engineers want to limit the number of access points and provide fast, uninterrupted transfers among these points. So you can drink from a stream anywhere along its length, but you can only access piped water at a faucet. You can pause wherever you want when you're strolling along a dirt track, but you must use stations for trains, entry and exit ramps for freeways, and airports for airline networks— and your experience of the terrain between these points is very limited. You experience the architectural transitions between floors of a building when you climb the stairs, but you go into architectural limbo between the opening and closing of the doors when you use the elevator.

Habitats

Decades ago, at the very dawn of the digital era, Charles Moore (the most thoughtful architect of emerging postmodernity) shrewdly understood what the simultaneous conditions of extension and discontinuity meant for our daily use of space;

our habitats no longer consist of single or contiguous enclo-sures, but have become increasingly fragmented and dispersed. They are no longer bounded by walls, but by the reach of our net-works. They are occupied by spatially dispersed organizations, ranging from multinational corporations and retail chains to terrorist networks. They are controlled and defended not at a continuous perimeter, but at separated and scattered access nodes. They are given order and meaning not by participation in strict spatial sequences and hierarchies, but by their global linkages. Our domains of knowledge and action cannot be defined as fixed neighborhoods, but must now be understood as dynamic, emergent, geographically and temporally fluctu-ating patterns of presence. In his influential essay "Plug It In, Rameses," he observed:

> The most powerful and effective places that our forebears made for themselves, and left for us, exist in contiguous space. They work on an organized hierarchy of importances, first dividing what is inside from what is outside, then in some way arranging things in order of their importance, so that objects give order to a location, and location gives impor-tance to objects, as at Peking, where an axis penetrates from outside through layer after layer of increasing importance (like the skins of an onion) to the seat of the emperor himself, or as in Hindu towns where caste determined location from clean to dirty along the flow of water which served everyone... Our own places, however, like our lives, are not bound up in one contiguous space. Our order is not made in one discrete inside neatly separated from a hostile outside...We have, as we all know, instant anywhere, as we enjoy our capacity to make immediate electronic contact with people anywhere on the face of the globe...Our new places, that is, are given form with electronic, not visual glue.[19]

Communities

Sociologists would use more technical language to make much the same point as Moore's. They would say that I—like most urbanites today—get companionship, aid, support, and social control from a few strong social ties and many weak ones.[20] These ties, which might manifest themselves, for example, as the entries in my cellphone and email directories, establish social networks. In the past, such networks would mostly have been maintained by face-to-face contact within a contiguous locality—a compact, place-based community.[21] Today, they are maintained through a complex mix of local face-to-face interactions, travel, mail systems, synchronous electronic contact through telephones and video links, and asynchronous electronic contact through email and similar media.[22] They are far less dense, and they extend around the world, coming to earth at multiple, scattered, and unstable locations.[23] As Barry Wellman has crisply summarized, "People in networked societies live and work in multiple sets of overlapping relationships, cycling among different networks. Many of the people and the related social networks they deal with are sparsely knit, or physically dispersed and do not know one another."[24]

In the years since Moore wrote, our physical habitats have grown more fragmented and dispersed as transportation networks have extended further and operated faster. Simultaneously, the electronic glue has grown much stronger; it now includes voice, video, and data channels, broadcast and point-to-point links, place-to-place and person-to-person communication, the fixed infrastructure of the bank ATM system, the sleek portable equipment of the corporate road warrior jetting between global cities, and the cheap phone card of the migrant worker.

Wherever I currently happen to find myself, I can now discover many of the same channels on a nearby television, I can access the same bank account, and I can chat with the same people on my cellphone. I can download my email and send replies almost completely independently of location. And my online world, which once consisted of ephemeral and disconnected fragments, has become increasingly persistent, interconnected, and unified; it's there again, pretty much as I left it, whenever I log in again from a new location. The constants in my world are no longer provided by a contiguous home turf: increasingly, my sense of continuity and belonging derives from being electronically networked to the widely scattered people and places I care about.

Notes

1   The duality of enclosures and networks is more than just a metaphor; it is a basic fact of graph theory—the mathematical study of network structure. Consider a floor plan as a planar graph in which corners are nodes and walls are links. Construct the adjacency graph of the plan by locating a node within every enclosed room, plus the exterior zone, then representing room-to-room and room-to-exterior adjacencies by links. The adjacency graph is the dual of the floor plan graph, and vice versa. The circulation network, created by doorways through walls, is a subgraph of the adjacency graph. For more detailed, rigorous development of this point, see Lionel March and Christopher F. Earl, "Architectural Applications of Graph Theory," in *Applications of Graph Theory*, ed. Robin J. Wilson and Lowell W. Beineke (London: Academic Press, 1979), pp. 327–56.

2   The decline of the city wall is often dated from 1494, when Charles VIII of France first deployed horse-drawn artillery pieces in his invasion of northern Italy.

3   Gottfried Semper noticed that the German word for "garment" (*Gewand*) is very closely related to the word for "partition" (*Wand*). He developed an elaborate theory of the relationships among walls, textiles, and clothing in his two great theoretical works, *The Four Elements of Architecture* (1851) and *Style in the Technical and Tectonic Arts, or Practical Aesthetics* (1860–63). (See Harry Francis Mallgrave, *Gottfried Semper: Architect of the Nineteenth Century* [New Haven,

Conn.: Yale University Press, 1996.]) In his essay "Housing: New Look and New Outlook," in *Understanding Media: The Extensions of Man* (New York:McGraw-Hill, 1964), p. 123, Marshall McLuhan repackaged the point: "Clothing and housing, as extensions of the skin and heat-control of mechanisms, are media of communication, first of all, in the sense that they shape and rearrange the patterns of human association and community." More recently, Vito Acconci has produced a series of provocative works exploring his contention that "First there is skin and bones, then clothing, then a chair, and then housing." See Sarah Boxer, "Poet Turned Antic Architect Keeps Exploring Inner Space," New York Times, F1, F5, September 12, 2002. And the discourse continues with Claudia Benthien, *Skin* (New York: Columbia University Press, 2002), and Ellen Lupton, Jennifer Tobias, Alicia Imperiale, Grace Jeffets, and Randi Mates, *Skin* (New York: Princeton Architectural Press, 2002).

4   Georg Simmel, "Bridge and Door," trans. Mark Ritter, *Theory, Culture, and Society* 11 (1994): 5–10.

5   For discussions of the pervasiveness of networks, see Albert-László Barabási, *Linked: The New Science of Networks* (Cambridge, Mass.: Perseus, 2002) and Mark Buchanan, *Nexus: Small Worlds and the Groundbreaking Science of Networks* (New York: Norton, 2002).

6   In *The Production of Space* (1974; English trans., Cambridge, Mass.: Blackwell, 1991), 38, Henri Lefebvre argued, "The spatial practice of a society secretes that society's space; it propounds and presupposes it, in a dialectical interaction; it produces it slowly and surely as it masters and appropriates it." Lefebvre's analysis is extraordinarily suggestive, but it shows little curiosity about the specific technologies of spatial production and even less about the effects of changes in those technologies. In *The Informational City: Information Technology, Economic Restructuring, and the Urban-Regional Process* (Cambridge, Mass.: Blackwell, 1989), 6, Manuel Castells extended Lefebvre's argument by identifying "the emergence of a *space of flows* which dominates the historically constructed space of places, as the logic of dominant organizations detaches itself from the social constraints of cultural identities and local societies through the powerful medium of information technologies." In *Empire* (Cambridge: Harvard University Press, 2000), Michael Hardt and Antonio Negri proposed that the irresistible and irreversible globalization of economic and

cultural exchanges" had produced "a *decentered* and *deterritorializing* apparatus of rule that progressively incorporates the entire global realm," and "manages hybrid identities, flexible hierarchies, and plural exchanges through modulating networks of command." In this volume I shall be particularly concerned with the technological infrastructure of the global space of flows, the secretion of spatial patterns by means of that infrastructure, and the specific changes that are resulting from the development of a pervasive, wireless computation and telecommunication infrastructure.

7   President's Critical Infrastructure Protection Board, *The National Strategy to Secure Cyberspace*, draft, September 2002, www .whitehouse.gov/pcipb/cyberstrategy-draft.pdf (accessed December 2002), 3.

8   For a concise history of timekeeping technologies and their increasing precision, see William J. H. Andrewes, "A Chronicle of Timekeeping," *Scientific American* 287, no. 3 (September 2002): 76–85.

9   Lewis Mumford, *Technics and Civilization* (New York: Harcourt Brace Jovanovich, 1963). See also Edward P. Thompson, "Time, Work-Discipline, and Industrial Capitalism," in *Classes, Power, and Conflict*, ed. Anthony Giddens and David Held (Berkeley, Calif.: University of California Press, 1982), 299–309; and David S. Landes, *Revolution in Time: Clocks and the Making of the Modern World*, rev. ed. (Cambridge, Mass.: Harvard University Press, 2000).

10 In his speculations on the evolution of machines, Samuel Butler suggested that large clocks would go the way of the big lizards. "Examine the beautiful structure of the little animal, watch the intelligent play of the minute members which compose it; yet this little creature is but a development of the cumbrous clocks of the thirteenth century—it is no deterioration from them. The day may come when clocks, which certainly at the present day are not diminishing in bulk, may be entirely superseded by the use of watches, in which case clocks will become extinct like the earlier saurians, while the watch (whose tendency has for some years been rather to decrease in size than the contrary) will remain the only existing type of an extinct race." (Samuel Butler, "Darwin among the Machines," in *A First Year in Canterbury Settlement and Other Early Essays* [London: Jonathan Cape, 1923], p. 210.) Butler could not anticipate, of course, that tiny vibrating quartz crystals would

one day make mechanical watches seem like bulky and expensive dinosaurs.

11 Ivan E. Sutherland and Jo Ebergen, "Computers without Clocks," *Scientific American* 287, no. 2 (August 2002): 62–69.

12 See David J. Bolter, *Turing's Man: Western Culture in the Computer Age* (Chapel Hill: University of North Carolina Press, 1984) and James Gleick, *Faster: The Acceleration of Just About Everything* (New York: Vintage Books, 1999), for discussions of accelerating subdivision and pace in the digital era.

13 In his October 1998 *Computerworld* column, for example, Edward Yourdon asked: "What if Y2K leads to massive corporate bankruptcies, heralding a long-term economic recession/depression? What if it leads to breakdowns in international communications, or a shut-down of the world's airports for six months?" This was over the top, and Y2K eventually passed with little incident. But the potential for some significant level of Y2K disruption had been real enough, and it had only been averred through a massive effort to identify and eliminate Y2K bugs.

14 Edward Yourdon, "What Comes after 1/1/00," *Computerworld* 32, no. 42 (1998): 89.

15 In 1884, at the International Meridian Conference in Washington, D.C., the globe was subdivided into twenty-four time zones, and the Royal Observatory at Greenwich was chosen as the prime meridian.

16 David P. Anderson and John Kubiatowicz, "The Worldwide Computer," *Scientific American* 286, no. 3 (March 2002): 40–47.

17 Seth Lloyd, "Quantum Mechanical Computers," *Scientific American* 273 (October 1995): 140–45; Seth Lloyd, "Quantum Computing: Computation from Geometry," *Science* 292 (2001): 1669; and George Johnson, *A Shortcut through Time* (New York: Alfred A. Knopf, 2003).

18 Carlton M. Caves, "A Tale of Two Cities," *Science* 282 (1998): 637–38.

19 Charles W. Moore, "Plug It In, Rameses, and See if It Lights Up, Because We Aren't Going to Keep It Unless It Works," *Perspecta*, no. 11 (1967): 32–43. Reprinted in *You Have to Pay for the Public Life: Selected Essays of Charles W. Moore* (Cambridge, Mass.: MIT Press, 2001), 151–60.

20 Mark Granovetter, "The Strength of Weak Ties," *American Journal of Sociology* 78 (1973): 1360–80.

21 Traditional, place-based communities were described, in many cases idealized, and contrasted with life in the big city in some of the landmark works of sociology. See, in particular, Emile Durkheim, *The Division of Labor in Society* (1893; New York: Free Press, 1964); Ferdinand Tönnies, *Community and Society* (1887; East Lansing: Michigan State University Press, 1957); and Louis Wirth, "Urbanism as a Way of Life," *American Journal of Sociology* 44 (1938): 3–24.

22 Barry Wellman, *Networks in the Global Village* (Boulder, Colo.: Westview Press, 1999).

23 There is a growing empirical literature on the role of electronic interconnections in sustaining (or weakening) social networks. See, for example, Keith Hampton, "Living the Wired Life in the Wired Suburb" (Ph.D. diss., University of Toronto, 2001); Philip E. Howard, Lee Rainie, and Steve Jones, "Days and Nights on the Internet: The Impact of a Diffusing Technology," *American Behavioral Scientist* 45, no. 3 (2001): 383–404; Robert Kraut, Vicki Lundmark, Sara Kiesler, Tridas Mukopadhyay, and William Scherlis, "Internet Paradox: A Social Technology That Reduces Social Involvement and Psychological Well-Being," *American Psychologist* 53, no. 9 (1998): 1017–31; and Norman Nie, "Sociability, Interpersonal Relations, and the Internet: Reconciling Conflicting Findings," *American Behavioral Scientist* 45, no. 3 (2001): 420–35.

24 Barry Wellman, "Designing the Internet for a Networked Society," *Communications of the ACM* 45, no. 5 (May 2002): 91–96.

INTRODUCTION
Future City / *Fredric Jameson*

In "Future City," Fredric Jameson—an American literary and
cultural critic and a professor at Duke University—offers an
analysis of two publications that stemmed from the Project on
the City, a series of research seminars lead by Rem Koolhaas at
the Harvard Graduate School of Design: *Great Leap Forward*,
which addresses the rash of building in China's Pearl River Delta
in the late twentieth century; and the *Guide to Shopping*, which
examines consumerism, the conditions that make it possible,
and its larger effects on urban areas and society. Both volumes
investigate growth and transformation within and surrounding the
contemporary city (or perhaps what was formerly known as the
city) as new phenomena, departing dramatically from historical
models. Jameson comments cursorily on the *Great Leap Forward*
but directs most of his effort to an examination of the *Guide to
Shopping*.

For Jameson, the *Guide to Shopping* differs from other studies
of consumerism in that it rests on the principle of "the mall in crisis." This is reflected in a dramatic way by Koolhaas's contribution
to the volume, "Junkspace."[1] Jameson situates Koolhaas's article
within the larger context of postmodernism ("an extraordinary
piece of writing that is...a postmodern artifact in its own right"),
and unpacks Koolhaas's language to examine the "virus" that is
junkspace. Koolhaas creates a picture of "de-differentiation," of a
world that is simultaneously new and depressingly repetitive in its
sameness: the constant quest for the larger, the more luminous,
the most luxurious. Koolhaas's essay replicates this reality, spew-
ing forth a seemingly endless stream of metaphors, each fighting
to trump its predecessors, to co-opt and surpass history.

In his reading of "Junkspace," history is the dominant concern
for Jameson, "a History that we cannot imagine except as ending,

and whose future seems to be nothing but a monotonous repetition of what is already here." The problem for Jameson involves the way forward, "breaking out of the windless present of the postmodern back into real historical time, and a history made by human beings." Koolhaas's text figures, according to Jameson, as such an attempt:

> It is the writing that is the battering ram, the delirious repetition that hammers away at this sameness running through all the forms of our existence...and pummels them into admitting their own standardized identity with each other...The sentences are the boom of this repetitive insistence, this pounding on the hollowness of space itself; and their energy now foretells the rush and the fresh air, the euphoria of a relief, an orgasmic breaking through into time and history again, into a concrete future.

Jameson's interpretation of "Junkspace" provides a lens through which we can understand the Project on the City endeavors as a whole: as research into contemporary circumstances, and the material, technological, and cultural conditions that made them possible, as a means to carve out a path along which architects, and architecture, may move forward.

Note

1 Jameson's comments pertain to the version of "Junkspace" that appears in the *Guide to Shopping*, which differs slightly from the version of "Junkspace" reprinted here, originally published in *A+U Special Issue: OMA @ Work* (May 2000): 16–24.

FREDRIC JAMESON

FUTURE CITY

First appeared in *New Left Review* 21 (May–June 2003).
Courtesy of the publisher.

The Project on the City assembles research from an ongoing graduate seminar directed by Rem Koolhaas at the Harvard School of Design; its first two volumes—the *Great Leap Forward*, an exploration of the development of the Pearl River Delta between Hong Kong and Macao, and the *Guide to Shopping*— have just appeared in sumptuous editions, from Taschen.[1] These extraordinary volumes are utterly unlike anything else one can find in the print media; neither picture books nor illustrated text, they are in movement, like a CD ROM, and their statistics are visually beautiful, their images legible to a degree.

Although architecture is one of the few remaining arts in which the great *auteurs* still exist—and although Koolhaas is certainly one of those—the seminar which has produced its first results in these two volumes is not dedicated to architecture but rather to the exploration of the city today, in all its untheorized difference from the classical urban structure that existed at least up until World War II. Modern architecture has been bound up with questions of urbanism since its eighteenth and nineteenth century beginnings: Siegfried Giedion's modernist summa, *Space, Time and Architecture*, for example, begins with the Baroque restructuration of Rome by Sixtus V and ends with the Rockefeller Centre and Robert Moses's parkways, even though it is essentially a celebration of Le Corbusier. And obviously Le Corbusier was both an architect and, with the Radiant Cities, Chandigarh and the plan for Algiers, an "urban planner." But although the Project testifies to Koolhaas's commitment to the question of the city, he is not an urbanist in any disciplinary sense; nor can the word be used to describe these books, which also escape other disciplinary categories (such as sociology or economics) but might be said to be closest to cultural studies.

The fact is that traditional, or perhaps we might better say modernist, urbanism is at a dead end. Discussions about American traffic patterns or zoning—even political debates about homelessness and gentrification, or real-estate tax policy—pale into insignificance when we consider the immense expansion of what used to be called cities in the Third World. "in 2025," we are told in another Koolhaas collective volume, "the number of city-dwellers could reach 5 billion individuals... of the 33 megalopolises predicted in 2015, 27 will be located in the least developed countries, including 19 in Asia... Tokyo will be the only rich city to figure in the list of the 10 largest cities."[2] Nor is this a problem to be solved, but rather a new reality to explore: which is, I take it, the mission of the *Project on the City*, two further volumes of which are so far projected: one on Lagos, Nigeria, and one on the classical Roman city as prototype.

Volume One of the *Project*, *Great Leap Forward*, interprets the prodigious building boom in China today—almost nine thousand high rises built in Shanghai since 1992—not so much in terms of some turn or return to capitalism, but rather in terms of Deng Xiaoping's strategy to use capitalism to build a radically different society: *infrared* rather than *red*:

> the concealment of Communist, red ideals...to save Utopia at a moment when it was being contested on all sides, when the world kept accumulating proofs of its ravages and miseries... infrared©, the ideology of reform, is a campaign to preempt the demise of Utopia, a project to conceal 19th century ideals within the realities of the 21st century.

Those who believe that the market is a reality, anchored in nature and in Being, will have difficulty grasping such a proposition, which from their perspective will be dispelled either by an outright conversion to capitalism or by economic collapse. But consider the architectural perspective: we witness thousands upon thousands of buildings constructed or under construction which have no tenants, which could never be paid for under capitalist conditions, whose very existence cannot be justified by any market standards. We here follow the outlines of housing communities in the Pearl River Delta area which are being projected for a future quite unlike those researched by Western speculators or banks and funding institutions in the capitalist world. Indeed, the four communities explored here are something like four different Utopian projections: Shenzhen, a kind of alternate or double of Hong Kong; Dongguan, a pleasure city; Zhuhai, a golfing paradise; while the old centre, Guanzhou (Canton), becomes a kind of strange palimpsest, in which the new is superimposed on an already existing traditional economic centre. It is an extraordinary travelogue into the future, and it gives a more concrete sense of China today and tomorrow than most guidebooks (and many real tours).

Proteus goes shopping

The *Guide to Shopping* is something altogether different, both
in style and intent. Consumption is, to be sure, a hot topic,
but this is no conventional study of it. Indeed, the question of
what this book is—an extraordinary picture book; a collection
of essays on various urbanistic and commercial topics; a probe
of global space from Europe to Singapore, from Disneyworld
to Las Vegas; a study of the shopping mall itself, from its first
ideologues all the way to its most contemporary forms—corresponds to the more general ambiguity of its object. Even if we
stick to the initial characterization of that object as "shopping,"
what kind of categorization is that? Is it a physical one, involving the objects to be sold? Is it psychological, involving the
desire to buy the objects in question? Or architectural, having to
do with the spatial originality of those malls—which, famously,
trace their ancestry back to Walter Benjamin's nineteenth-
century arcades; if not, as some of the time charts in this book
suggest, back to the 7000 BC "city of Catalhöyük founded for the
trade of commodities," or perhaps the "invention" of the retail
trade in Lydia in the seventh century BC? Or are we talking here
about the globalization of consumption (consumerism)? Or the
new trade routes and production and distribution networks
involved in such globalization? (Or the businessmen who organize those?) And what about the new technologies evolved for
commerce since Catalhöyük? The prodigious increase in size
of the merchandizing companies and conglomerates, some of
them larger than many foreign countries? What about shopping and the form of the contemporary city—if there is one:
significantly Koolhaas's collective project changed its name
from the "Project for what used to be the city" to the plainer
and more optimistic Project on the City. To which may be added
the question: is a new kind of space emerging—control space,
junk space? And what does all this imply for the human psyche

and human reality itself? (The first theoretician of advertising, Edward Bernays, was Freud's nephew.) What does it imply for the future and for Utopia?

I am probably forgetting some of the other modulations of this protean topic; but it will be clear that it mobilizes, alongside the obvious (and obviously anticipated) areas of architecture and urbanism, such heterogeneous disciplines as psychoanalysis and geography, history and business, economics and engineering, biography, ecology, feminism, area studies, ideological analysis, classical studies, legal decisions, crisis theory, et cetera. Perhaps this kind of immense disciplinary range is no longer quite so astonishing in a postmodern era, in which the law of being is de-differentiation, and in which we are most interested in how things overlap and necessarily spill across the disciplinary boundaries. Or, if you prefer, in the postmodern the distinction between the old specialized disciplines is constitutively effaced and they now fold back on each other, in the most interesting studies—from Deleuze/Guattari's *Thousand Plateaux* to Caro's *Power Broker*; from *Empire* to *Rembrandt's Eyes*; from Benjamin's *Arcades* to the *Geschichte und Eigensinn* of Negt and Kluge; let alone *SMXLX* or even *Space, Time and Architecture*. Theory is here mostly eschewed (although Baudrillard is mentioned once, I believe), but you must not let that tempt you into thinking that this is a non-theoretical piece of cultural journalism, let alone a coffee-table picture book. It is, as the enumeration above might also suggest, a collective volume; although not in the sense that experts of the various disciplines mentioned above are somehow judiciously assembled and their contributions sampled in turn. This makes it embarrassing for a reviewer to single out specific names, although Sze Tsung Leong has the most, and also the most philosophically reflective, chapters, with Chuihua Judy Chung a close follow-up for more concrete discussions. As for Koolhaas, his role seems to have been mostly organizational (that is to say, like certain versions of the deity, nowhere and everywhere all at once) save for an astonishing appearance in his own name, which will be discussed at the proper moment.

After the mall

I will try to put the theory back into all this; but it would first be better to work through some of the detail of the layers or strata of the book, whose alphabetical table of contents is quite misleading in this respect; and thus a veritable *tour de force* in its own right. For a few previews on the mall are the way in here: they will return, far more developed, in a variety of contexts later on. But it is as though the shopping mall is the spatial and architectural wedge into this immense topic. Few forms have been so distinctively new and so distinctively American, and late-capitalist, as this innovation, whose emergence can be dated: 1956; whose relationship to the well-known decay-of-the-inner-city-rise-of-the-suburb is palpable, if variable; whose genealogy now opens up a physical and spatial prehistory of shopping in a way that was previously inconceivable; and whose spread all over the world can serve as something of an epidemiological map of Americanization, or postmodernization, or globalization. So the mall focuses the inquiry and serves as the frame for the prodigious enlargement of all this later on. Meanwhile, pages of chronologies, colour-coded cross-referencing systems and innumerable thematic indexes already train us in the rhizomatic form of that enlargement; while a first set of comparisons between retail areas all over the world, and between national GDPs and retail revenues of the top corporations, help us begin to map the process in our minds and to form a picture, not only of the relative hierarchies of globalization, but also of a view of "shopping" that will shortly become, dare I say, not merely a political but also a metaphysical issue.

At once, however, we are pulled up short, and a fundamental difference between this work and the proliferation of new and excellent cultural-studies volumes on shopping, malls, consumption and the like, becomes clear. Before we even get to the thing itself, we come upon the mall in crisis, losing money and tenants, and on the verge of replacement…by what? Benjamin took his snapshot of the nineteenth-century arcade at the moment of its decay—and thereby developed a whole theory about history: that you could best understand the present from the standpoint of an immediate past whose fashions were already just a little out of date. Crisis puts us on notice that we have here to do, not merely with the archeology or prehistory of shopping, nor even its present but rather its future. Whatever the future of the mall as such, however, "'there's lots of trash out there.' Many cavernous old malls are dinosaurs that can't compete with the conve-nience of drive-up value retailers in power centres or strips"—to which one now needs no doubt to add eBay.

Something has evidently happened to the preconditions for the existence of malls in the first place. But what were those preconditions? As in Aristotelian causality, they come in a variety of forms and shapes: the physical or engineering preconditions are staged for us at once, in the very first letter of this ABC of shopping: namely, air-conditioning—to which we will return shortly in a more appropriate place. As for the pre-history, we have certainly been treated, in recent years, to a host of interesting predecessor forms, if not generally going as far back as Catalhöyük. Most notably the arcade itself, essentially developing in the early nineteenth century and reaching its crisis in the 1850s and 60s—exactly the moment when the next form comes along: the modern department store, whose emergence Zola immortalized in *Au bonheur des dames* (*Ladies' Delight* is a fictionalized version of real-life names like *Au printemps* and *La Samaritaine*, which have also been exhaustively studied in recent years,

for their urbanistic as much as their commercial consequences: for one thing, they are roughly contemporaneous
with Haussman's immense transformation of Paris). As for our
form—now falling into decay in its turn?—we will come to it in
a moment; indeed we will even put names and faces to it. Like a
novel or a poem, it actually has an inventor or author, although
the inventor of a whole genre is a more appropriate parallel;
something one does not come across very often.

Delirious technologies

First, we leap ahead to measure the scope and transformations
of this protean form—into airports, for example, which have
now, all the new ones, also become shopping malls; into museums; finally into the city itself. The older city centre—blighted
by suburbs and the new supermarkets, and then the malls themselves—now, with postmodernity and gentrification, catches up:
not only by housing huge new malls within itself, but by becoming a virtual mall in its own right. Indeed, something fundamental begins to happen to it (as is fitting in a volume from the
Project on the City):

> In 1994 the mall officially replaced the civic functions of the
> traditional downtown. In a New Jersey Supreme Court case
> regarding the distribution of political leaflets in shopping
> malls the court declared that "shopping malls have replaced
> the parks and squares that were 'traditionally the home of
> free speech,' siding with the protesters 'who had argued that a
> mall constitutes a modern-day Main Street.'"

But if "this return of shopping to the city has been nothing
short of triumphant," the authors find themselves obliged to
add: "To be saved, downtowns have had to be given the suburban kiss of death."

Back now to preconditions: could the bar code itself—the Universal Product Code—be one of these? Analyse its functions, and one begins to see how the statistics it immediately provides the retailer transform the whole structure of inventory, resupplying, marketing and the like. Brand names may well be more of a cultural consequence of this kind of shopping than a precondition, for their zones, the flagship boutiques, mark "the sacred precincts of the last global religion—capitalist consumerism." They also underscore a new kind of dynamic, itself consumerized under the Singapore logo "co-opetition," which celebrates the tide that lifts everybody's boats, including those of the competitors.

But with this we are off on a tour of the world, or rather shopping's world tour as it touches one spot after another and gets transformed by the local culture. Singapore is an old fascination of Koolhaas's (see *SMLXL*), but its dynamics remain an extraordinary object lesson—not only in development, but also in the way in which a city-state fits first into the region and then into the world itself. The Crystal Palace takes us back to origins once again (and to the signature of an individual, Joseph Paxton). The Depato, or Japanese department store, flings us, if not into the future, then at least into an extraordinary cultural mutation, intimately connected with the logic of Tokyo's growth along the various private railroad lines that fan out from the world's third largest city. And finally: Disney himself. For no study of any innovations in this area can be complete without a comprehensive recognition of everything—all the various things, from a new urbanism to a new kind of shopping, a new kind of globalization, a new kind of entertainment industry, even a new kind of Utopia itself—that Walt invented. Indeed, perhaps Disney and Disneyfication is better studied in this new comparatist and globalized context than as a sport or typically American singleton.

But what about the mall itself, its space for example? There is a psychology of space in the mall—the patch, the corridor, the matrix—just as there is an ecology of the thing. And here the preconditions flow back in with a vengeance: not only air-conditioning and its very interesting history (more zany inventors and creative and obsessive dreamers); but also the escalator—the elevator had been a crucial operator in Koolhaas's early book on the skyscraper landscape, *Delirious New York*—with its momentous consequences for shopping space and building possibilities; this whole rich section takes up some thirty pages. And also, somewhat later on, the skylight and the sprinkler system; not to speak of the way the new space can hide its service systems out of sight—and not even to mention the precursor "technologies": counter, display window, mirror and mannequin.

But let's get on into the ideologies of the matter, for here at last we rise from the body to the soul: poor Jane Jacobs, for example, is cast as something of a Hegelian ruse of history in her own right for defending the fundamental features of a true city experience against the various urban and architectural modernisms, and thereby enumerating "the ingredients by which shopping could stand in for urbanity and creat[ing] a 'city lite' that became the model for resuscitating America's ailing downtowns." This seems a little harsh, but it is certain that Jacobs—credited by many architects and urbanists as triggering the postmodern revolution in their field—is no anti-capitalist and lays a good deal of stress on (small) business.

But with Victor Gruen we are at origins (we can't call it "ground zero" any more; what about Harold-Bloomian genius?). For the mall was his brainchild, and it is certain that our experience of contemporary American space or non-space is to a certain degree disalienated by finding out that someone had the idea for all this, and that it is not just some weird accumulation of market-historical accidents but the result of human production. To stress Gruen's achievement, however, is also at once to set off the canonical reaction and to recall, voluntarily or not, how few of the great modernists ever designed such things, let alone theorized them in the first place (whereas they have become a staple of the postmodernists). It is also to impose some reflexion on that contemporary *auteur* who is the garish or mass-cultural equivalent of all these loftier aesthetic projects, and a true phenomenon in his own right: Jon Jerde, builder of Horton Plaza in San Diego and much else. The high art/mass culture split becomes unavoidable here too, as much as in every other contemporary cultural field.

But just as we are about to reflect a bit on that, and to go on to other related global phenomena—the Lippo Group in Indonesia; a return to the old Venturi–Scott-Brown notion of "learning from Las Vegas," and a rich interview with the authors; feminism too (women and shopping are an old and scurrilous topic); artificial landscapes; the relation of all this to psychology and psychoanalysis; the European resistance to the mall and its Americanizing consequences; and many other interesting topics raised by the second half of the alphabet—suddenly we come upon a black hole, generating prodigious energies in all directions.

Down with the junkspace virus

It is Rem Koolhaas's contribution, "Junkspace," an extraordinary piece of writing that is both a postmodern artifact in its own right, and—a whole new aesthetic perhaps? unless it is a whole new vision of history. In the light of this serried text, we must pause and rethink the entire project. But first we have to look at the writing itself, whose combination of revulsion and euphoria is unique to the postmodern in a number of instructive ways. We knew Koolhaas was an interesting writer—in this, comparable to any number of distinguished contemporary architects;

his books, in particular *Delirious New York* and *SMLXL*, combining formal innovation with incisive sentences and characteristically provocative positions. But no single text in those books prepared us for this sustained and non-stop "performance" of the built space, not just of the contemporary city, but of a whole universe on the point of fusing into a kind of all-purpose indeterminate magma.

This goes much further than the querulous culture-critical complaints about standardization (or Americanization). It starts with junk as the classical remainder (what is left over after the dialectic, or after your psychoanalytic cure): "If space-junk is the human debris that litters the universe, junk-space is the residue mankind leaves on the planet." Very soon, however, junkspace becomes a virus that spreads and proliferates throughout the macrocosm:

> angular geometric remnants invading starry infinities; real space edited for smooth transmission in virtual space, crucial hinge in an infernal feedback loop...the vastness of Junkspace extended to the edges of the Big Bang.

But this by itself could be little more than Baudrillard or television theory—the critique of virtuality as a promise (like the passing critique of Deleuzian "flows"): the point of the exercise is rather to find synonyms, hundreds upon hundreds of theoretical synonyms, hammered one upon the other and fused together into a massive and terrifying vision, each of the "theories" of the "postmodern" or the current age becoming metaphorical to the others in a single blinding glimpse into the underside:

> Junkspace exposes what previous generations kept under wraps: structures emerge like springs from a mattress, exit stairs dangle in didactic trapeze, probes thrust into space

to deliver laboriously what is in fact omnipresent, free air, acres of glass hang from spidery cables, tautly stretched skins enclose flaccid non-events.

As a tendency, Junkspace has been around for some time, at first unrecognized; again, like a virus undetected:

> Architects thought of Junkspace first and named it Megastructure, the final solution to transcend their huge impasse. Like multiple Babels, huge superstructures would last through eternity, teeming with impermanent subsystems that would mutate over time, beyond their control. In Junkspace, the tables are turned: it is subsystems only, without superstructure, orphaned particles in search of framework or pattern. All materialization is provisional: cutting, bending, tearing, coating: construction has acquired a new softness, like tailoring.

It would be too simple to say that architecture and space are here metaphors for everything else: but this is no longer architectural theory; nor is it a novel whose point of view is that of the architect. Rather it is the new language of space which is speaking through these self-replicating, self-perpetuating sentences, space itself become the dominant code or hegemonic language of the new moment of History—the last?—whose very raw material condemns it in its deterioration to extinction.

> Aging in Junkspace is nonexistent or catastrophic; sometimes an entire Junkspace—a department store, a nightclub, a bachelor pad—turns into a slum overnight without warning: wattage diminishes imperceptibly, letters drop out of signs, air conditioning units start dripping, cracks appear as if from otherwise unregistered earthquakes; sections rot, are no

longer viable, but remain joined to the flesh of the main body via gangrenous passages.

These alarming "Alzheimer-like deteriorations" are realizations of the nightmare moments in Philip K. Dick, when reality begins to sag like a drug hallucination and to undergo vertiginous transmutations, revealing the private worlds in which we are trapped beyond time. But these moments are no longer terrifying; they are in fact by now rather exhilarating; and it is precisely this new euphoria that remains to be explained.

Empire of blur

To be sure, Koolhaas means no more than perpetual renovation, and not only the tearing down of the old but also the perpetual recycling to which the once noble (and even megalomaniacal) vocation of the Master Builder has been reduced: "Anything stretched—limousines, body parts, planes—turns into Junkspace, its original concept abused. Restore, rearrange, reassemble, revamp, renovate, revise, recover, redesign, return—the Parthenon marbles—redo, respect, rent: verbs that start with *re*—produce Junkspace." This is the disappearance of all the "originals" no doubt, but along with them, of History itself:

> the only certainty is conversion—continuous—followed, in rare cases, by "restoration," the process that claims ever new sections of history as Junkspace. History corrupts, absolute history corrupts absolutely. Colour and matter are eliminated from these bloodless grafts; the bland has become the only meeting ground for the old and the new.

We are henceforth in the realm of the formless (Rosalind Krauss, out of Bataille); but "formlessness is still form, the formless also a typology." It is not quite the "anything goes" of the new generation of computer-generating "blob architects" (Greg Lynn, Ben van Berkel): "in fact, the secret of Junkspace is that it is both promiscuous and repressive: as the formless proliferates, the formal withers, and with it all rules, regulations, recourse." Shades of Marcuse and repressive tolerance?

> Junkspace is a Bermuda triangle of concepts, a petri dish abandoned: it cancels distinctions, undermines resolve, confuses intention with realization. It replaces hierarchy with accumulation, composition with addition. More and more, more is more. Junkspace is overripe and undernourishing at the same time, a colossal security blanket that covers the earth in a stranglehold of care...Junkspace is like being condemned to a perpetual Jacuzzi with millions of your best friends...A fuzzy empire of blur, it fuses high and low, public and private, straight and bent, bloated and starved to offer a seamless patchwork of the permanently disjointed.

There are no doubt still "trajectories" with their magical moments:

> Postmodernism adds a crumple-zone of viral poché that fractures and multiplies the endless frontline of display, a peristaltic shrink-wrap crucial to all commercial exchange. Trajectories are launched as ramp, turn horizontal without any warning, intersect, fold down, suddenly emerge on a vertiginous balcony above a large void. Fascism without dictator. From the sudden dead end where you were dropped by a monumental, granite staircase, an escalator takes you to an invisible destination, facing a provisional vista of plaster, inspired by forgettable sources.

There are also, in this churning pseudo-temporality of matter ceaselessly mutating all around us, moments of rare, of breathtaking beauty: "railway stations unfold like iron butterflies, airports glisten like cyclopic dewdrops, bridges span often negligible banks like grotesquely enlarged versions of the harp. To each rivulet its own Calatrava." But such moments are scarcely enough to compensate for the nightmare, or to make the hallucinations all worthwhile. Cyberpunk seems to be a reference to grasp at here, which—like Koolhaas, only ambiguously cynical—seems positively to revel in its own (and its world's) excess. But cyberpunk is not really apocalyptic, and I think the better coordinate is Ballard, the Ballard of the multiple "end-of-the-worlds," minus the Byronic melancholy and the rich orchestral pessimism and *Weltschmerz*.

For it is the end of the world that is in question here; and that could be exhilarating if apocalypse were the only way of imagining that world's disappearance (whether we have to do here with the bang or the whimper is not the interesting question). It is the old world that deserves the bile and the satire, this new one is merely its own self-effacement, and its slippage into what Dick called kipple or gubble, what LeGuin once described as the buildings "melting. They were getting soggy and shaky, like Jell-o left out in the sun. The corners had already run down the sides, leaving great creamy smears." Someone once said that it is easier to imagine the end of the world than to imagine the end of capitalism. We can now revise that and witness the attempt to imagine capitalism by way of imagining the end of the world.

Breaking back into History

But I think it would be better to characterize all this in terms of History, a History that we cannot imagine except as ending, and whose future seems to be nothing but a monotonous repetition of what is already here. The problem is then how to locate radical difference; how to jumpstart the sense of history so that it begins again to transmit feeble signals of time, of otherness, of change, of Utopia. The problem to be solved is that of breaking out of the windless present of the postmodern back into real historical time, and a history made by human beings. I think this writing is a way of doing that or at least of trying to. Its science-fictionality derives from the secret method of this genre: which in the absence of a future focuses on a single baleful tendency, one that it expands and expands until the tendency itself becomes apocalyptic and explodes the world in which we are trapped into innumerable shards and atoms. The dystopian appearance is thus only the sharp edge inserted into the seamless Möbius strip of late capitalism, the punctum or perceptual obsession that sees one thread, any thread, through to its predictable end.

Yet this alone is not enough: a breaking of the sound barrier of History is to be achieved in a situation in which the historical imagination is paralysed and cocooned, as though by a predator's sting: no way to burst through into the future, to reconquer difference, let alone Utopia, except by writing yourself into it, but without turning back. It is the writing that is the battering ram, the delirious repetition that hammers away at this sameness running through all the forms of our existence (space, parking, shopping, working, eating, building) and pummels them into admitting their own standardized identity with each other, beyond colour, beyond texture, the formless blandness that is no longer even the plastic, vinyl or rubber of yesteryear. The sentences are the boom of this repetitive insistence, this pounding on the hollowness of space itself; and their energy now foretells the rush and the fresh air, the euphoria of a relief, an orgasmic breaking through into time and history again, into a concrete future.

Such is then the secret of this new symbolic form, which Koolhaas is not the only one of our contemporaries to mobilize (but few do it better). To come back now slowly, to reenter as in a decompression chamber the more prosaic world of shopping that was the takeoff point for this delirious adventure is also to search for the occasion, for what triggered it off, what provoked such a monumental and truly metaphysical reaction. It was in fact given to us early on, in an offhand sentence of Sze Tsung Leong, at the end of a more restrained and focused account of the commercial transformation of the globe which is, after all, the topic of the present volume: "In the end, there will be little else for us to do but shop." The world in which we were trapped is in fact a shopping mall; the windless closure is the underground network of tunnels hollowed out for the display of images. The virus ascribed to junkspace is in fact the virus of shopping itself; which, like Disneyfication, gradually spreads like a toxic moss across the known universe. But what is this shopping we have been on about for so long (and the authors even longer)?

Theoretically, it comes in many packages (and predictably we can shop around for our favourite theoretical version or brand-name). The tradition of Western Marxism called it "commodification," and in that form the analysis goes back at least as far as Marx himself, in the famous opening chapter of *Capital* on commodity fetishism. The nineteenth-century religious perspective is Marx's way of foregrounding a specifically superstructural dimension in the market exchanges of capitalism. He understood "the metaphysical subtleties and theological niceties" of the commodity as the way in which the labour relationship is concealed from the buyer (the "shopper"?) and he thereby grasped commodification as an essentially ideological operation, a form of false consciousness which has the specific function of masking the production of value from the (bourgeois) consumer. Georg Lukács's philosophical classic, *History and Class Consciousness*, the inaugural text of so-called Western Marxism, develops this analysis on the larger plane of the history of philosophy itself, resituating commodification at the centre of the more general overall social process of mental as well as physical reification.

After World War II, however, the ideological orientation of this theme takes a somewhat different turn, at a moment when the sale of commodities and luxury items beyond those of simple subsistence or social reproduction becomes generalized throughout the increasingly more prosperous First World areas of Western Europe and the United States (and eventually Japan). At this point, the situationists and their theoretician Guy Debord invent a new perspective on commodification in their dictum that "the final form of commodity fetishism is the image." This is the takeoff point for their theory of so-called spectacle society, in which the former "wealth of nations" is now grasped as "an immense accumulation of spectacles." With this perspective, we are much closer to our current assumptions (or doxa), namely that the commodification process is less a matter of false consciousness than of a whole new life style, which we call consumerism and which is comparable rather to an addiction than a philosophical error or even an ill-advised choice of political parties. This turn is part of the more contemporary view of culture as the very substance of everyday life (itself a relatively new postwar concept, pioneered by Henri Lefebvre).

The images of the *Guide to Shopping* are thus images of images, and should thereby enable a new kind of critical distance, something they do conceptually by returning the notion of the commodity to its original situation in the commercial exchange. What we do with commodities *qua* images, then, is not to look at them. The idea that we buy images is already a useful defamiliarization of the notion; but the characterization whereby *we shop* for images is even more useful, displacing the process onto a new form of desire and situating it well before the actual sale takes place—when, as is well known, we lose all interest in the object as such. As for consumption, it has been volatilized altogether in this perspective; and, as Marx feared, has become altogether spiritual. Materiality is here a mere pretext for our exercise of the mental pleasures: what is any longer particularly material in the consumption of an expensive new car one drives around the local streets and has washed and polished as frequently as one can?

"In the end, there will be little else for us to do but shop." Does this not reflect an extraordinary expansion of desire around the planet, and a whole new existential stance of those who can afford it and who now, long since familiar with both the meaninglessness of life and the impossibility of satisfaction, construct a life style in which a specific new organization of desire offers the consumption of just that impossibility and just that meaninglessness? Indeed, perhaps this is the right moment to return to the Pearl River Delta and Deng Xiaoping's postmodern socialism, in which "getting rich" no longer means actually making the money, but rather constructing immense shopping malls—the secret of which lies in the fact that to shop does not require you to buy, and that the form of shopping is a performance which can be staged without money, just as long as its appropriate spaces, or in other words Junkspace, have been provided for it.

Notes

1 Chuihua Judy Chung, Jeffrey Inaba, Rem Koolhaas, and Sze Tsung Leong, eds., *Great Leap Forward*, Harvard Design School *Project on the City*, (Cologne: Taschen, 2002); and *Guide to Shopping*, Harvard Design School *Project on the City*, (Cologne: Taschen, 2002).

2 *Mutations*, Barcelona 2001.

INTRODUCTION
Architecture and the Virtual: Towards a New Materiality /
Antoine Picon

Trained as an architect, engineer, and historian, Antoine Picon
has focused his work primarily on the intersection of architecture and technology. In his article "Architecture and the Virtual:
Towards a New Materiality," Picon addresses the potential impact
of the computer and computer-aided design on materiality. While
some view the computer as a threat to architectural materiality,
an overtaking of the actual by the virtual, Picon—a professor of
architectural history and technology at Harvard Graduate School
of Design—proposes that the computer creates a new understanding and experience of materiality.

Picon begins his discussion with an examination of architectural representation, asserting that it is both ambiguous and
abstract by nature; the plan, for example, is actually quite abstract
in that we never experience a building as seen in plan. (In fact,
is not the experience of a computer-generated fly-through more
"real" than that of a two-dimensional plan?) Thoughts such as
this lead Picon to ask, "Do computer representations imply a
clear departure from the traditional practice of architecture?" His
answer is both yes and no: digitization is, in part, a tool employed
by the architect, in some ways like any other tool, just more technologically advanced; at the same time, the use of the computer
as a design tool introduces additional layers of mediation that do
not exist with pencil and paper.

Here Picon raises the analogy of the automobile, a machine
that has had tremendous ramifications for our perceptions of
space, travel, and the environment. "Rather than dematerializing
the world we inhabit, the automobile has instead transformed our
notion of it," allowing the experience of new sensations, scales,
and forms, not to mention the development of now-everyday

objects such as freeways, billboards, and parking lots. Thus, our previous understanding of materiality has been altered, but not through the dissolution of materiality itself.

A similar shift may result from the computer's ever-growing involvement in architecture. In Picon's view, recent explorations in digitized design have focused on surface and texture rather than volume, introduced unanticipated issues of scale, and rendered tectonics an increasingly complex facet of architectural representation. Flows of information, concrete data gleaned from any number of operations, often appear as influential components of architectural design, which is itself more abstract. This interaction of concrete and abstract, real and digital, suggests a new hybrid of materiality, according to Picon, that goes hand in hand with a possible new conception of what it means to practice architecture.

The computer and digitization have recast our traditional understanding of materiality, of the process of design, and of architecture as a whole, and this recasting will continue as technology matures. Picon forecasts a generalization in design on the horizon, as digital technologies allow architects to become more involved in the creation of building materials and the surrounding environment; he hopes that the expansion and hence reevaluation of the architectural discipline will lead to a increased sense of moral responsibility, guiding us toward a future in which architecture plays a greater social and political role.

ANTOINE PICON

ARCHITECTURE AND THE VIRTUAL: TOWARDS A NEW MATERIALITY

First appeared in *PRAXIS 6: New Technologies://New Architectures* (2004), 114–21. Reprinted with permission.

The development of digital design is often presented as a threat to one of architecture's essential dimensions: the concrete aspects of construction and building technologies, in a word, its materiality. Such is, for example, the concern expressed by Kenneth Frampton in his recent work, starting with his *Studies in Tectonic Culture*.[1] Despite the counterarguments posed by William Mitchell and others,[2] this concern is easily understandable, given the highly formalist nature of many digital architects' production. Computer-based design often appears to neglect the material dimension of architecture, its intimate relation with properties like weight, thrust, and resistance. On a computer screen, forms seem to float freely, without constraint other than those imparted by the program and by the designer's imagination. There is something deeply unsettling in this apparent freedom that seems to question our most fundamental assumptions regarding the nature of the architectural discipline.

However, should one accept the present stage of computer-based design as if it were setting definitive standards? As digital architecture remains in its infancy, one must be cautious not to draw conclusions about the temporary features it presents. Frampton and other detractors perhaps assume its current condition to be permanent, taking its temporary characteristics too seriously, while underestimating the real questions it raises. Its present tendency toward a certain immateriality, or rather its often-glib attitude toward materiality, may very well be ephemeral. Far from being jeopardized by the generalization of the computer and the development of virtual worlds, materiality will probably remain a fundamental feature of architectural production. One can furthermore speculate whether the use of the computer, with its web extensions, represents a substantial departure from the traditional features of architectural representation. In many respects, two-dimensional, hand-produced drawings are no more material than computer-based ones. The abstraction inherent in architectural representation does not necessarily imply a lack of materiality in its realization.

I would like to begin precisely with the general question of architectural representation, before turning to the changes brought about by the computer. Among the leads I will then follow is the idea that materiality, like almost every feature of our environment, is to a large extent a cultural construction. As has been argued by various proponents of social constructivism, physical experience is shaped partly by culture, technological culture in particular. We perceive the exterior world through the lenses provided, both literally and on a more symbolic level, by the technological culture that surrounds us. Beyond perception, our everyday gestures and movements are indebted to our machines and their specific requirements. In such a perspective the impact of the computer may more accurately be described as a reshaping of, rather than an estrangement from, physical experience and materiality.

The approach adopted here tries to avoid the pitfall of positing a naive enthusiasm with regard to the existing state of digital architecture, or the symmetrical bias of rejecting it without further examination. Rather than discussing the value of various contributions to digital architecture—hence the scarcity of the references made to them—I will concentrate on questions of a more epistemological nature. What does digital architecture, even in its present state of incomplete development, suggest regarding the changing categories of physical experience? If materiality is not endangered, how is its definition nevertheless evolving?

When we discuss computer productions, from images to web-based worlds, the term "virtual" almost immediately arises, along with an accusation of dematerialization that explicitly opposes virtual reality and true reality. Without entering into the usual philosophical debate evoking Henri Bergson or Gilles Deleuze, one may still observe that such opposition is hard to sustain in an architectural discourse. An architectural design is indeed a virtual object. It is all the more virtual that it anticipates not a single built realization but an entire range of them. There is no architectural design without some margin of indeterminacy that allows for different paths to be followed. Usually only one will be realized. Despite the attempts to improve the codification of design procedures in order to anticipate as closely as possible the built outcome, this relative indeterminacy is fundamental to the architectural project. It enables it to "speak," or rather to function as a matrix of possible narratives regarding the built reality it anticipates, without which the project would be a mere technical blueprint.

Returning to the question of materiality, one could summarize the situation by saying that while design pertains to the realities of the built environment, this relationship remains ambiguous. Again, drawings and specifications evoke a range of material effects rather than a precise, unequivocal, and unique material reality. The ambiguity of architectural design reflects on architectural representation. Even the most convincing techniques of representation do not correspond fully to the experience of the built reality. We never see buildings in plan and elevation, to say nothing of cross section or the modernist axonometric view that presupposes an observer situated ad infinitum. One would be tempted to affirm that representation in architecture, as in cartography, presupposes an impossibly located observer.

Architectural representation negotiates these contrary tendencies: the quest for verisimilitude and the desire to preserve margins of indeterminacy. Actually, the necessity to balance between these two conflicting ideals might very well account for an inherent paradox of architectural drawings: the more specific the physical effect intended, the more abstract the representation, as if this fundamental tension translated into an equilibrium between materiality and abstraction. From the Renaissance on, the drawings of architectural profiles illustrate this point. For the Vitruvian inspired architect, nothing was more material than the play of light on various moldings of a building. Yet, their representation in profile was often surprisingly distant from the effects desired. Even in canonical treatises like Palladio's *Four Books on Architecture* this representation is reduced to linear drawing.

Given this history, do computer representations imply a clear departure from the traditional practice of architecture? At this stage, the digitalization of design may very well appear as mere technological advance, a supplementary power offered to the designer, a power that does not affect the nature of its production. Digitalization does allow the architect to manipulate extremely complex forms and to more freely envision design modifications. However, are these extensions of vocabulary and the capacity to interact at every stage of the design truly revolutionary? Is this change quantitative rather than qualitative, as if contemporary designers were simply endowed with a more varied and flexible set of pencils and rulers?

This is of course not entirely true, for the computer breaks with the immediacy of the human gesture. Between the hand and the graphic representation, a layer of hard- and software introduces itself. Inherent in the software are modes of operation and preferences that constrain the designer. The machine and its programs are synonymous with a thickness absent in traditional tools.

This thickness might eventually disappear with the development of increasingly sophisticated interfaces that almost seamlessly integrate the computer into design practices. The Media Lab at the Massachusetts Institute of Technology has invested years of research into digital gloves and tactile screens as well as camera- and laser-controlled feedback systems linking physical and digital modeling. Nevertheless, the mediation of the machine and its software will not be abolished.

The difference between hand and computer produced designs parallels the contrast between a walk and a car ride. At stake in both cases is an opposition between man and the pairing formed by man and machine—a machine which cannot be reduced to a mere accessory. Both the power of the computer, and also its thickness, make it indeed different from traditional tools. Its use could be assimilable to an encounter with a "nonhuman actor," to use Bruno Latour's conceptual frame.[3] In the decades following World War II, the automobile had already led to such an encounter.

Another possibility is to consider the pairing of man and machine as a new composite subject, a hybrid of flesh and machine already realized in the automobile driver. The computer user's almost visceral relation to the screen and keyboard might be interpreted in the same light so that digital architecture comes to imply a cyborg-like author. This proposition is suggested by various contemporary reflections on computer technologies and their anthropological dimension.[4] Their influence can be traced in various architectural publications.[5]

If we leave aside these broad perspectives, the automobile analogy is still revealing. The traditional opposition of the richness of walking to the impoverishment of driving implies that materiality was at stake as seen by the contrast between the plenitude of real physical experience and the abstraction fostered by a technologically determined environment. Almost a century after the car became a mainstay of contemporary culture, we know that this opposition does not fully apply to the automobile experience. Rather than dematerializing the world we inhabit, the automobile has instead transformed our notion of materiality. My intention is not to enter here into a detailed discussion of these transformations, but to insist on some major points.

When we drive, we don't perceive exactly the same objects as when we walk. Seen from a freeway, a building is different from the vision we have when we stroll by. At the speed of the automobile, objects regroup forming new perceptual entities. The scale and form of contemporary urban skyline are manifestations of the automobile age, as are the landscapes produced by the rapid succession of billboards along major highways.

The automobile provides a series of different sensations, from accelerations and decelerations to the feeling provoked by the wind, some of which are intimately linked to the use of the engine. We have become so accustomed to acceleration that we tend to forget that the sensations it creates were almost unattainable in formerly non-mechanized societies where slow and regular movement was the rule. In a mechanized environment, between the exhilaration of speed and the prospect of accident, we have both an impression of power and a feeling of vulnerability. James Graham Ballard's famous novel *Crash* focuses on this new status of the human body, or rather of the hybrid of the body and its mechanical extension. This hybrid, both empowered and vulnerable, makes nothing of miles and is always on the verge of being bruised. In Ballard's perspective, the mélange of power and vulnerability carries heavy sexual connotations. For his characters, the accident, the fatal crash that gives its title to the novel, becomes a new technologically mediated form of coitus.[6]

The redefinition of perceptual entities that we experience while riding in a car alters our very notion of space, changing the existential status of our entire body. The most significant shift is perhaps the subtle changes that the use of the automobile infuses in our everyday experience of space. The automobile has altered but not diminished our physical perception of the world by displacing the content and boundaries of materiality.

It is tempting to use the automobile as an analogy to the computer, interpreting it as another vehicle that induces a new displacement of physical experience and materiality. The computer-assisted architect loosely parallels the driver or passenger embarking on a journey that generates a new type of experience. What are the salient features of this material experience?

The computer presents us with new perceptual entities and objects. Whereas the architect previously manipulated static forms, now she or he can play with geometric flows. Surface and volumetric deformations acquire a kind of evidence unavailable to traditional graphic means of representation. They can indeed be generated and followed in real time on the screen. In that respect, the use of the computer is strangely close to practices like clay modeling, and it is no coincidence that various attempts have been made to couple its use with three-dimensional shaping in places like MIT's Media Lab.

The new evidence acquired by geometric flows may account for the multiplication of projects that look like fluid surfaces. For example, Reiser + Umemoto's "West Side Convergence" appears as a geometric flow that has been frozen into architectural form.[7]

In addition to deformation and flows, the computer enables the manipulation of non-material phenomena, such as light and texture, so that they acquire the status of quasi-objects to the architect. Numerous parameters of light can be manipulated: it can be intensified or dimmed, made direct or diffuse. Similarly, surfaces can be adjusted with an almost infinite combination of factors of roughness and smoothness, of reflectivity and transparency to an extent that makes them almost tactile. These manipulations have widely different manifestations, from superficial effects like the "hypersurface" projections made possible by the digital world's capacity for any form to be textured with any image,[8] to the mathematically substantiated creations of Bernard Cache's Objectile practice.[9] What they have in common is an emphasis on surface and tactile conditions, as opposed to abstract volumetric considerations.

While some dimensions of digital architecture, like the surface condition I just mentioned, become essential, others appear more problematic. In the case of the automobile, the emergence of new pertinent objects is accompanied by the loss of the ordinary sense of distance in favor of the notion of accessibility. In a similar way, with digital architecture, scale no longer seems evident. What is the true scale of the forms that appear on computer screens? Despite the inclusion of scale figures in photomontages, it is often difficult to answer this question. The standard presentation of a project like Nox's "Beachness" is highly revealing in this respect.

One first perceives a complex maze of lines, then a twisted form that looks like a crumpled piece of paper or cloth. Subsequent images reveal that one is actually looking at a huge, almost megastructural, design.[10] Computer imagery is in profound accordance with a world organized by fractal rather than traditional geometry in which information and complexity are found at every level. In such a world, there is no fixed scale at which things must be deciphered.

In addition to challenging ideas of scale, digital technologies make the relation between architectural representation and tectonics less clear than in the past. This dissociation between representation and tectonics is evident in Frank Gehry's CATIA-designed complex surfaces, the forms of which owe little to structural considerations.[11] Despite the discourse of the architect, a similar distance separates Toyo Ito's transparent luminous competition model for the Sendai Mediatheque from the structural reality of the heavy steel plates used to construct the building.[12] Foreign Office Architects' Yokohama Terminal reveals a similar tension between the fluidity of the original design and the techniques mobilized to realize it. The world shaped by digital technologies is not only complex at every level; it is also full of surprises because of the gap that often separates computer modeling and tectonics.

The antagonism of critics like Kenneth Frampton is directly related to the recognition of this gap between digital representation and traditional tectonics. However disturbing it may be, such a gap is not necessarily synonymous with a dematerialization of architecture. The computer redefines materiality rather than abandoning it in favor of the seduction of pure images.

This displacement demands a redefinition of design objectives and procedures. The digital world requires a new visual practice able to follow the complex maze of interactions between the global and the very local, between the general definition of the project and the sometimes minute, sometimes dramatic changes brought by parametric variations. In this world, the smallest change may affect the design as a whole, as in the well-known claim of chaos theory that the fluttering of a butterfly in one part of the world may cause a storm in another.[13] The sensibility generated by this dependence on parametric variations is again not without analogy to the heightened sensory experience of driving at full speed on an uneven surface where the tiniest obstacle can cause dramatic consequences. Marcos Novak has compared the digital and liquid states: "the operations associated with the idea of the liquid suggest that parameterization leads to radical variability within a continuum implied by a thing and its opposite."[14] Computers immerse us into a fluid, eminently variable world that gives a special intensity to some of our sensations and the decisions to which they lead us.

The automobile is only a metaphor, and as such it shouldn't be taken too literally. Contrary to the automobile's linear trajectory, the digital world that unfolds under the eyes of the designer is multi-dimensional. It flows theoretically in all directions; it is also theoretically reversible. These characteristics are at odds with the necessity for the design process to follow a particular sequence from preliminary sketches to the ultimate technical specifications, and to involve various consultants, from the architect's collaborators to the engineers and builders in charge of specific technological developments. In other words, computer-aided design cannot be a labyrinthine exploration of the almost infinite possibilities offered by the machine. While form can vary endlessly, choices have to be made; decisions have to be enforced in order to break with the theoretically reversible nature of digital manipulation.

The importance of these choices fosters a new attitude based on the strategic evaluation of the potential for design evolution at critical stages of development. It has been often noted that computers imply a scenario-based kind of reflection. Besides the use of scenarios, diagrams may orient the designer among the various paths of evolution made possible by digital media. Because of their proximity to concept, and the suppression of unnecessary concrete details to which they proceed, diagrams are often perceived as pure mental schemes. This approach is inconsistent with the true nature of diagrams, namely the fact that they are inseparable from courses of action. They possess a physicality of their own, similar to the seemingly abstract notations that choreographers use to note the steps of a ballet. There is a striking parallel between the contemporary, often Dutch-inspired, architectural diagram and geopolitical diagrams produced at the beginning of this century.[15] Both are based on a schematic description of the world that tends to neglect differences in scale and geographical complexity, to say nothing of historical specificity. Geopolitics loves blocs, alliances, and other global entities. Dutch-inspired diagrams are also based on massive aggregates and global data.[16] In both cases, the world appears as a field in which forces are manifest rather than a static geography. Like geopolitics, contemporary architectural diagrams make extensive use of charts and arrows attempting to make these forces visible. They converge on nodes that can be likened to objectives or targets. In both cases, what seems at stake is the apprehension of a mobile and fluid environment, requiring continuous action.

More generally, the computer has often been understood as an extension of the mind, a super memory or an enhanced tool for logical exploration. The French anthropologist Leroi-Gourhan, for example, tracks a spectacular evocation of human progress through the use of technological tools in *Le Geste et la Parole*. This book spans the Neolithic period to the twentieth century, from the first trimmed and polished stones to early computers.[17] For Leroi-Gourhan, human progress was marked by the gradual externalization of functions, from stone knives and axes that extended the capacity of the hand to the externalization of mental functions with the computer.

The computer indubitably can be related to an extension of the mind, but it also alters our perception of objects by extending the realm of our sensations. New interfaces currently being developed will soon affect our motor skills. Already the mere use of a mouse has created new kinds of gestures. Among teenagers, the development of video games has fostered even more specific kinds of reflexes.

Our very perception of space will in its turn be affected by these physical changes. Films like *Johnny Mnemonic*, *The Matrix*, or *Minority Report* have envisaged changes in the perception of ordinary space brought about by the development of sophisticated interfaces between ordinary and digital space. The notion of enhanced or increased reality suggests a different materiality made possible by the hybridization of the physical and the digital. While this hybridization is not fully developed, some features of the displacement of materiality are already evident.

Similarly, visual codes are changing at a surprising speed. We no longer marvel, for instance, at digital media's capacity for effects like zooming in and out. Rather, we tend to perceive our ordinary three-dimensional world in similar terms, as if ordinary reality were the result of a provisional compromise, or rather a middle-range lens accommodation, between the very small and the extremely large, between atoms, or rather pixels, and galaxies. Immediately recognizable forms and objects are suspended between closely observed surfaces and textures that evoke some kind of abstract art and the less abstract, satellite-like views that give precedence to surface and texture effects. In both cases, the perception of volume relies upon the relationship of two kinds of surfaces or skins.

One could also relate the new status of form and object to the cultural context created by globalization. Globalization can indeed be characterized as a strange short-circuit between the local and the general that destabilizes middle-range institutions and practices.[18] In our global world we see things either from very close or from an extremely distant point of view. It is certainly no coincidence that the computer has been instrumental in the process of globalization. Zooming might be a mere consequence of the crisis of the traditional notion of scale implied both by computer use and globalization, a crisis that generates a specific form of perceptive instability.

This instability blurs the distinction between abstraction and concreteness, for nothing is at the same time more abstract and concrete than a view that challenges interpretations based on the ordinary categories of form and object. More generally, in the age of the computer and with the physics of solids and DNA manipulations, materiality is increasingly defined at the intersection of two seemingly opposed categories. On the one hand is the totally abstract, based on signals and codes; on the other hand is the ultra concrete, involving an acute and almost pathological perception of material phenomena and properties such as light and texture as they are revealed by zoom-like practices. This hybridization between the abstract and the ultra-material represents the new world of sensations and movements that we are entering today.

In the architectural domain, the coexistence of reflections of a diagrammatic nature with a renewed interest in some of the most concrete aspects of materials is typical of this situation. At an urban level, the GPS also represents the immediacy between abstraction and concreteness. Using a GPS, we are both plugged into a global, abstract geodesic grid and confronted with our immediate surroundings.[19] As the computer is beginning to affect the design of buildings, the digital environment will eventually modify urban design, if only because old problems like the legibility of the urban sequences are now redefined by tools like the GPS.

But how are the intuitions of the architect or the urban designer conveyed to a public that inhabits his projects? In other words, can the new materiality desired by computer aided designers concern a larger public unaware of the various and often contradictory reflections developed by figures like Greg Lynn, Marcos Novak, Jesse Reiser, and others? Their architecture of blobs and topological geometrical forms seems distant from the common definition of architecture. At the level of the city, the same gap separates the world of computerized urban simulations from the ordinary perceptions of the people.

At least two reasons may be invoked in favor of an optimistic answer. The first one lies in the way the computer permeates everyday life, so that this alteration of materiality can be understood as a general phenomenon. We are all about to inhabit both the ordinary and the virtual worlds— hence Toyo Ito's famous statement that architects should indeed design for subjects imparted with two bodies, a real and a virtual one. "We of the modern age are provided with two types of bodies," writes Ito. "The real body which is linked with the real world by means of fluids running inside, and the virtual body linked with the world by the flow of electrons."[20] Actually, these two bodies are not separated, but rather they are part of what constitutes today's physical presence. The Sendai Mediatheque epitomizes this contemporary physical status: simultaneously densely material, reminiscent of heavy-duty naval construction with its massive steel plates, and fluid, translucent like a precious electronic gem. Thus, in this case, the gap between tectonics and architectural representation, far from being accidental, is actually rooted in the core intention of the architect.

Earlier I mentioned video games and their impact on a whole generation, the behavior of which has been shaped by bizarre figures of dwarves, princes, and ogres running and jumping on Gameboy and computer screens. This generation has developed physical and mental attitudes that call for a different kind of space, a space that can be deciphered through systems of clues and series of unfolding scenarios, instead of traditional holistic mapping. This generation's spatial expectations might very well be fulfilled only by digital-oriented architecture.

The second reason to be confident in the new architectural materiality enabled by the computer lies in the fact that, contrary to the automobile, the computer is not an isolated machine of the kind that the French philosopher George Simondon called a "technological individual,"[21] or a super prosthesis adding to man's physical capacity. The computer is only a part of a global digital universe that includes entire worldwide networks as well as millions of personal digital assistants. One could of course argue that the automobile was already inseparable from a world populated with roads, traffic lights, gas stations, and parking lots.[22] The automobile world was, however, comparable to a denumerable system rather than to a seamless fabric. The density and the high degree of interconnection and redundancy that characterize the digital universe make it difficult to describe it in terms of systems. Environmental categories such as landscape seem more appropriate. We are more and more immersed in this landscape.

Regarding the question of materiality, the digital landscape provides numerous new opportunities like the possibility to design materials, to shape their properties and appearance, instead of using them in a passive manner. As various authors have pointed out, the digital revolution is contemporary with a revolution in the materials we produce and use.[23] At the Harvard Design School, a group of professors and students led by

Toshiko Mori recently has been exploring the potential for architectural expression of materials by design, a potential already mobilized by designers like Mack Scogin or Sheila Kennedy.[24]

Computer-aided material production seems to abolish the distance between representation and materiality, provided that one defines materiality in other terms than traditional tectonics. But this collapse is actually an illusion provoked by the elimination of the complex series of interfaces necessary to bridge the distance between architectural representation and material by design. The computer doesn't abolish the distance between representation and reality, far from it. It simply creates the possibility of a continuously documented process between pure architectural representation and technical specifications. In his revolutionary descriptive geometry course, Gaspard Monge began by distinguishing between the objects that were susceptible to receive a rigorous definition and those that were not.[25] The digital age enables every object and every material, at each stage of its elaboration, to be rigorously defined. True novelty might very well lie ultimately in the generalization of design, as a practice regarding not only buildings and their various technological systems, but also materials and beyond them nature as an engineered reality. Many contemporary landscape proposals, such as the Fresh Kills landfill competition entries,[26] no longer address nature as an external resource to be drawn upon. Increasingly, it appears as something the production of which can be shaped by adequate design. The increasing use of the term "landscape urbanism" in regard to situations like Downsview or Fresh Kills appears as a consequence of this trend.[27] In this technological nature, materiality is totally permeated by design. Despite the dissociation between architectural representation and tectonics, the true novelty is not a growing gap between design and materiality, but rather their intimate interaction that might eventually challenge the traditional professional identities of the architect or the engineer. Both identities were indeed based on the assumption of a distance between the intellectual and the physical world, a distance that design was meant to bridge. If one takes seriously the hypothesis of a blurring between abstraction and concreteness, these identities must be altered. Cecil Balmond's claims to cooperate fully in the design process, instead of being confined to mere structural calculations, is representative of the new perspectives that arise from a world blurring the distinction between mathematical abstraction and spatial concreteness.[28]

This potential generalization of design procedures makes us more liable than ever for its consequences, since the world appears more and more as our creation, from nature to artifacts, from materials to building. Thus, a new political responsibility is at stake. For architects, this implies a departure from the traditional posture of the professional indifferent to the large issues raised by his realizations. To inscribe oneself in current economic and cultural trends is probably no longer enough, considering, as Sanford Kwinter once put it, that the task of architecture is to take "the flow of historical conditions as its privileged materiality."[29] As we have seen, materiality means much more today than the mere understanding of the forces that shape the global market. Toshiko Mori has said, "Architects and other citizens must actively make choices about where to build, what to build, how to build, and with what to build."[30] One should probably add to the list "when not to build" in a world where the environment and sustainable development have become crucial issues. To refrain from building is more and more often a better solution than to engage in developments that may eventually prove damaging. The real problem of today's architectural scene is, in my opinion, not so much its possible dematerialization as its lack of clearly defined political and social agenda despite the greater than ever need for it.

The growing success of designers of sustainable structures like Shigeru Ban might very well lie in their articulation of both a concern for materiality and technological innovation and a more clearly articulated political and social concern.

Instead of representing an endangered dimension of architectural design, materiality will remain a pervasive concern. But this concern is now synonymous with a new responsibility. Its content is changing, and its meaning is yet undecided. One of the tasks of architecture might very well be to throw some light on its present potential.

Notes

1 See among others Kenneth Frampton, *Studies in Tectonic Culture* (Cambridge, Mass.: MIT Press, 1995).

2 William J. Mitchell, "Antitectonics: The Poetics of Virtuality," in *The Virtual Dimension,* ed. J. Beckmann (New York: Princeton Architectural Press, 1998), 205–17.

3 See Bruno Latour, *Nous n'avons jamais été modernes: Essai d'anthropologie symétrique* (Paris: La Découverte, 1997); Bruno Latour, *Politiques de la nature* (Paris: La Découverte, 1999).

4 Cf. Donna Haraway, "Manifesto for Cyborgs: Science, Technology, and Socialist Feminism in the 1980s," *Socialist Review* 15:2 (1985): 65–107; Donna Haraway, *Simians, Cyborgs and Women: The Reinvention of Nature* (New York: Routledge, 1991); Paul N. Edwards, *The Closed World. Computers and the Politics of Discourse in Cold War America* (Cambridge, Mass.: M.I.T. Press, 1996).

5 See Antoine Picon, *La ville territoire des Cyborgs* (Besançon, France: Editions de l'Imprimeur, 1998).

6 James Graham Ballard, *Crash* (London: Cape, 1973).

7 For a reproduction of this project, see for instance *Città: Less Aesthetics More Ethics* (La Biennale di Venezia: Marsilio, 368–69).

8 Stephen Perrella, "Electronic Baroque, Hypersurface II: Autopoeisis," *Architectural Design* 69: 9–10 (1999): 5–7.

9 Bernard Cache, *Earth Moves: The Furnishing of Territories* (Cambridge, Mass.: MIT Press, 1995).

10 See for instance the presentation given in Peter Zellner, *Hybrid Space, New Forms in Digital Architecture* (New York: Rizzoli, 1999), 114–17.

11 For a general discussion of the tension between surface and tectonics that epitomizes Gehry's work, see Mark Burry, "Between Surface and Substance," *Architectural Design* 72:2 (2003), 8–19.

12 Cf. Ron Witte and Toyo Ito, eds., *Mediatheque of Sendai* (Munich: Prestel, 2002).

13 Cf. James Gleick, *Chaos* (New York: Viking Press, 1987).

14 Marcos Novak, "Eversion: Brushing against Avatars, Aliens and Angels," *Architectural Design* 69:9–10 (1999): 72–76, 72 in particular.

15 On the diagrams produced by geopolitics, see for instance Claude Raffestin, *Géopolitique et histoire* (Lausanne: Payot, 1995).

16 Among the publications typical of this practice, see Richard Koek, Winy Maas, and Jacob van Rijs, *Farmax: Excursions on Density*

(Rotterdam: 010 publishers, 1994) and Rem Koolhaas, Stefano Boeri, and Sanford Kwinter, *Mutations* (Bordeaux, Arc en Rêve, 2001).

17   André Leroi-Gourhan, *Le geste et la parole, I. Technique et Langage, II. La mémoire et les rythmes* (Paris: Albin Michel, 1964, 1991).

18   Cf. Pierre Veltz, *Mondialisation, Villes et territoires: L'economie d'archipel* (Paris: P.U.F., 1996).

19   GPS art is actively exploring this short circuit between abstraction and concreteness. See for instance *GNS Global Navigation System* (Paris: Editions Cercle d'Art, 2003).

20   Toyo Ito, "Tarzans in the Media Forest," *2G* 2 (1997): 121–44, 132 in particular.

21   George Simondon, *Du mode d'existence des objets techniques* (Paris: Aubier, 1969).

22   Cf. Gabriel Dupuy, *Les territoires de l'automobile* (Paris: Anthropos, 1995).

23   See for instance Bernadette Bensaude-Vincent, *Eloge du mixte: Matériaux nouveaux et philosophie ancienne* (Paris: Hachette, 1998).

24   Toshiko Mori ed., *Immaterial/Ultramaterial* (Harvard Design School: George Braziller, 2002).

25   *Programmes de l'enseignement polytechnique de l'école centrale des travaux publics*, reproduced in Janis Langins, *La république avait besoin de savants. Les débuts de l'école polytechnique et les cours révolutionnaires de l'an III* (Paris: Belin, 1987), 116–98, 142 in particular.

26   See these projects in *Praxis* 4 (2002).

27   Charles Waldheim, "Landscape Urbanism: A Genealogy," *Praxis* 4 (2002): 10–17.

28   Cecil Balmond, with Jannuzzi Smith, *Informal* (Munich: Prestel, 2002).

29   Sanford Kwinter, contribution to *Flying the Bullet, or When Did the Future Begin?* (New York: Princeton Architectural Press, 1996).

30   Toshiko Mori, Immaterial/Ultramaterial,\ xv.

INTRODUCTION
No More Dreams? The Passion for Reality in Recent Dutch Architecture...and Its Limitations / *Roemer van Toorn*

In "No More Dreams," the Dutch educator, writer, and critic Roemer van Toorn characterizes various forms of projective practices—autonomy, *mise-en-scène*, and naturalization— that compose the contemporary architectural landscape in the Netherlands. Van Toorn, whose work focuses on the intersections of architecture, urbanism, and culture, begins to unpack the projective by examining its theoretical precursor, critical architecture, which for van Toorn includes architectures such as deconstructivism and critical regionalism that offer a critique of late capitalism. He locates critical architecture's failure in its insistence on "reject[ing] and react[ing] to the positive things that have been achieved in contemporary society, such as the vitality of much popular culture, including its hedonism, luxury, and laughter." Van Toorn prefers the "proactive" approach of the projective, particularly that these practices seek to work within the reality of modern life instead of repudiating its existence or attempting to avoid it. Yet he feels that despite their different manifestations—whether they fixate on pragmatics, technology, or aesthetics—these projective architectures falter in their "addiction to reality," forestalling political and social agendas in architecture. Instead of using design to stake a political claim or push ethical principles, these architects adhere to an "extreme realism...that is intended to show no theoretical or political mediation, a kind of degree zero of the political, without thought about the consequences of the social construction it would lead to in reality." Thus, while these practices accept reality, they consciously do very little to alter it in a utopian sense.

The concept of utopia, as van Toorn implies, is out of vogue— "utopian dreams are rare," he asserts. "Late capitalism is the only

game in town." Nevertheless, van Toorn has "larger ambitions,"
hope that utopia can still serve a purpose, that the "interaction
between the dream of utopia and reality [can] help a projective
practice develop a new social perspective." Specifically, he looks
for an architecture that, in our era of global capitalism, is "prepared to rethink the now eroded concept of democracy or to carry
out research into what democracy could mean today in spatial
terms." This alternative frame of thought is not, for van Toorn,
a way of presaging the future; rather, he hopes that we will "be
attentive to the unknown knocking at the door" and hence
discover new paths forward.

ROEMER VAN TOORN

NO MORE DREAMS?
THE PASSION FOR REALITY
IN RECENT DUTCH
ARCHITECTURE...
AND ITS LIMITATIONS

First appeared in *Harvard Design Magazine* 21 (Fall 2004/Winter 2005), 22–31. Courtesy of the author and the publisher.

It was once not considered foolish to dream great dreams. Imagining a new, better world energized thinkers and spurred their resistance to the status quo. Now utopian dreams are rare. Instead of chasing after elusive ideals, we prefer to surf the turbulent waves of free-market global capitalism. In our wildly prosperous First World—brimful of computerized production, technological and genetic applications, and commercial and cultural entertainment—reality can seem more exciting than dreams. Some even maintain that the ideals we strove for in the past have now become reality: according to Third Way politics, the neoliberal economic engine simply needs a bit of fine-tuning; late capitalism is the only game in town: although social rights and a measure of equality are needed, corporate globalism can only be accommodated.[1]

According to this free market fundamentalism, utopian attempts to change society lead to dictatorships. Not only conservatives think this. Neo-Marxists Michael Hardt and Antonio Negri argue that the organization of resistance in the margins is no longer necessary now that resistance is active in the very heart of society.[2] They believe that late capitalism is so complex and dynamic that it is capable of switching automatically from an alienating equilibrium of control into a potentiality for multiple freedoms. Everything is changing much faster than we ever imagined it could. Until the 1980s, mainstream cultural institutions condemned the transgressive operations of the avant-garde, whereas today they support and favor trangressive works, because they gain publicity from scandal. Time and time again, global capitalism has shown itself capable of transforming its initial limitations into challenges that culminate in new investments. One important consequence of this is that earlier forms of social criticism and social engagement are outmoded. Thus many reflective architects believe that it no longer makes any sense to spend time constructing new ideologies or criticizing "the system." Instead, they draw inspiration from the perpetual mutations of late capitalism.[3]

During a symposium on "The State of Architecture at the Beginning of the Twenty-first Century" held at Columbia University, Sylvia Lavin, chair of the UCLA graduate department of architecture, uttered the provocation that architecture ceases to be "cool" when it clings to the critical tradition.[4] Nor is hers a lone voice; a whole cohort of American commentators is anxious to move beyond critical architecture.[5] One form of critical architecture—exemplified by the work of Peter Eisenman, Daniel Libeskind, Diller + Scofidio, and Bernard Tschumi—offers comments within architectural-social discourse and avoids looking for better alternatives in reality. The Frank House by Eisenman, for example, forces the couple living in it to think about the psychology of their cohabitation by placing a slot in the floor between their beds. Robert Somol and Sarah Whiting have argued provocatively that we should stop burning our fingers on this kind of "hot" architecture that insists on confrontations. Whiting and Somol discourage an architecture born out of pain or the need to sabotage norms. Instead architects should initiate "projective" practices that are "cool."[6] (Why the word projective? "Because it includes the term project—that is, it is more about an approach, a strategy, than a product; it looks forward [projects], unlike criticality, which always looks backwards," according to Sarah Whiting in an email.)

While Whiting and Somol focus foremost upon American critical architecture that has been valorized by theories of deconstruction, Critical Regionalism in Europe, Asia, and Australia—exemplified by the works of Ando, Hertzberger, Siza, and Murcutt—tries, out of disgust with contemporary society, to overcome estrangement, commodification, and the destruction of nature.[7] Critical Regionalism does not strive to make difficult or playful comments on society but to invest in alternative spaces far from the wild city of late capitalism. It hopes to locate moments of authenticity—to calm the mind and the body—in order to survive in our runaway world. While critical architecture deconstructs the discourse of architecture, demystifies the status quo, and/or locates alternative worlds in the margin, it believes that constructing liberating realities in the center of society is impossible.

In contrast to both deconstruction and Critical Regionalism, Whiting and Somol's proposed "projective practices" aim to engage realities found in specific local contexts. Instead of hanging ideological prejudices (derived from utopian dreams or from criticism) on built form, the architectural project, in their view, must be rendered capable of functioning interactively. With a projective practice the distancing of critical theory is replaced by a curatorial attitude. This new paradigm in architecture, to paraphrase Dutch writer Harm Tilman, presupposes a continuous focus on the method (the "how") that leaves the "what" and the "why" undefined.[8] By systematically researching reality as found with the help of diagrams and other analytical measures, all kinds of latent beauties, forces, and possibilities can, projective architects maintain, be brought to the surface.[9]

These found realities are not only activated by the projective project, but also, where possible, idealized. If all goes well in the realization of a projective design, the intelligent extrapolation of data, the deployment of an aesthetic sensibility, the transformation of the program, and the correct technology may activate utopian moments. But the utopianism is opportunistic, not centrally motivating.

Whereas projective projects are chiefly discussed in the United States, architects in the Netherlands, in other European countries, and in Asia have for some time pursued them in practice. Before we look at some examples, we must pause to consider the nature and failure of it predecessor, critical architecture. On the one hand, projective practice is inspired by personal and strategic motives. After all, if you want to succeed in a new generation, it's a good idea to contrast your own position with that of the preceding generation. On the other hand, the critical tradition has itself handed projective architecture the arguments against dreaming totalizing dreams, against designing speculative systems that offer a comprehensive picture of what reality should be.

Disenchantment

Between the end of the Second World War and the beginning of the 1970s, many architects came to the conclusion that Modern architecture, rather than fostering emancipation, encouraged repression and manipulation.[10] The depressing discovery that hopeful dreams can end in nightmares prompted prominent members of the architectural community—Kenneth Frampton,

Manfredo Tafuri, Aldo Rossi, and Aldo van Eyck, among others—to mount a recalcitrant opposition to the commercial and populist city. They believed that instead of being a prisoner of modernity, architecture should mount continuous opposition to capitalist society. Quite apart from the fact that it operates in the margins of society and is often reserved for the elite, the creativity of critical architecture depends on dealing with the very things it finds repugnant.

As Theodor Adorno remarked, "Beauty today can have no other measure except the depth to which a work resolves contradictions. A work must cut through the contradictions and overcome them, not by covering them up, but by pursuing them."[11] The void in the Jewish Museum by Daniel Libeskind in Berlin memorializing the Holocaust is an example of the beauty Theodor Adorno is after. The horror of Fascism as a dark shadow of disaster present in this void gives the museum its symbolic meaning. Jean Nouvel avoids critique through the creation of symbolic meaning conveyed obliquely through form. Nouvel wants to break the enchantment of our mediatic world with a strong and strange presence that leads to a kind of seductive contemplation. His objects are unidentifiable, inconsumable, strange. This uncanny architecture must be developed, according to social theorist Jean Baudrillard, to reach the inexplicable, a reality so ineffable that it can counteract the oversignification of everything in our culture of transient junk images.[12] The alien language of Nouvel's architecture has the aura of nothingness, or, in the words of Paul Virilio, of a mute and silent space in radical opposition to the surfeit of our design culture. Instead of the negation of our broad cultural situation found in the work of Daniel Libeskind or Jean Nouvel, Diller + Scofidio, as analyzed by Michael Hays, "produce a kind of inventory of suspicion. They capture the salient elements of a given situation 'or problem,' register them, and slow down the processes that motivate them long enough to make the working perceptible, just before the whole thing again slips back into the cultural norm, beyond our critical grasp."[13]

Critical Regionalism, another form of critique, is a reaction against the rootlessness of modern urban life. It seeks durable values in opposition to our culture of mobility (it is no coincidence that Critical Regionalists see the car as a horror). Critical Regionalism locates its resistance in topography, anthropology, tectonics, and local light. It doesn't look for confrontation, as do Eisenman, Libeskind, Nouvel, or Diller + Scofidio, but is critical in its withdrawal from urban culture, and in its self-questioning and self-evaluating. According to Alexander Tzonis and Liane Lefaivre, its place-defining elements have to create a distance, have to be difficult, and should even be disturbing to overcome the regional illusions of the familiar, the romantic, and the popular.[14] Critical architecture supposedly does not compromise itself since it tries to dismantle or distance itself from the logic that leads to exploitation. Yet, because of its constant need to unmask the forces to which it is opposed, it is condemned to engage at the scenes that threaten its effectiveness. As such, critical architecture is more reactive than proactive.

Critical architecture in general rests on a self-affirming system of theoretical and ideological convictions: "Look at me! I'm critical! Read me!" Somol and Whiting rightly remark that critical architecture proceeds from a preconceived legibility.[15] It is an architecture that brooks no alternative interpretations. Unless the critical theory and vision are legible in the object, the object fails. Critical architecture is opposed to the normative and anonymous conditions of the production process and dedicated to the production of difference. Criticism reveals the true face of repressive forces, and this view of power is supposed to promote political awareness. Criticism is critical architects' only hope. Much of this criticism is concentrated in formalist and deconstructive theory and has a textual and linguistic bias. Other critical positions, such as those of Aldo van Eyck and the early Herman Hertzberger, and of Critical Regionalism, try to create alternative worlds, "utopian islands" floating in seas of anonymity and destruction.

Although I have much sympathy for Critical Regionalism, it is too nostalgic for a lost, mainly rural landscape, too comfortable and marginal, too much in love with architecture (rather than the life that architecture can help script). Preferable, it seems to me, are works that operate with and within society at large and that set a collective and public agenda in direct communication with modernization. The victimology of critical theory leaves no room for plausible readings capable of completing a project in the mundane context of the everyday (including that of alienation and commodification). Estrangement must not be thought of as something to overcome, but as a position from within which new horizons can open. Although the urban, capitalist, and modern everyday is pushing toward increased homogeneity in daily life, the irreconcilable disjunctions born in a postindustrial city full of anachronistic interstices make it impossible to think of modernization as only negative. Michel de Certeau's work confirmed the impossibility of a full colonization of everyday life by late capitalism and stressed that potential alternatives are always available, since individuals and institutions arrange resources and choose methods through particular creative arrangements. Often critical experts and intellectuals prefer to think of themselves as outside everyday life. Convinced that it is corrupt, they attempt to evade it. They use rhetorical language, meta-language, or autonomous language—to paraphrase Henri Lefebvre—as permanent substitutes for experience, allowing them to ignore the mediocrity of their own condition. Critical practices reject and react unsubtly to the positive things that have been achieved in contemporary society, such as the vitality of much popular culture, including its hedonism, luxury, and laughter.

After Critique

Instead of assailing reality with a priori positions or resistance, as critical architecture does, projective practices analyze the facts and, in the process of creation, make micro-decisions capable of transforming a project in concrete and surprising ways. The architect waits and sees in the process of creation where information leads him or her. As Michael Rock recently remarked, "Much of the strange shapes of recent Dutch architecture can be attributed to the devotion to the diagram, and the authorial absolution it grants. By taking traditional Dutch pragmatism to absurd, deadpan extremes, the designer generates new, wholly unexpected forms. Some of Droog Design embodies this absurdist-hyper-rationalism. The designer simply continues to apply the system until the form appears in all its strangeness. Dutch design seems intent on erasing the sense that any designer imposed any subjectivity."[16]

The touchstone here is not subjective vision but an addiction to extreme realism, a realism that is intended to show no theoretical or political mediation, a kind of degree zero of the political, without thought about the consequences of the social construction it would lead to in reality. The extreme realities the projective is obliged to confront are the cyborg; the information society; the global migration of money, people, and imagination; shopping; fashion; media; leisure; and the coincidence of the enormous effectiveness and absolute abstraction of digitization. In other words, this practice brings to its extreme the consequences of the processes of commodification, alienation, and estrangement that constitute the contemporary motor of modernity.

For projective practices, dreaming is no longer necessary, since even our wildest dreams are incapable of predicting how inspiring, chaotic, liberating, and dynamic reality can be. The intelligence which a project is able to embody in negotiation with reality is what matters. According to the proponents of projective practices, involvement, even complicity with given conditions, rather than aloofness, is more productive than dreaming of a new world. Projective practices respect and reorganize the diverse economies, ecologies, information systems, and social groups present during the process of creation. Projective architecture also promotes a return to the discipline in a pragmatic and technical approach that takes account of the interdisciplinary influences that play a role in the realization of projects. Central to projective practice is the question of what architecture is able to express as material reality. The paternalistic "we know best" attitude that has long hindered critical architecture is a thing of the past. And architecture is allowed to be beautiful without any tortured worrying over accompanying dangers of superficiality or slickness.[17] We no longer have to say "sorry," according to Robert Somol.[18] Often projective architects, like Foreign Office Architects, have no idea what they seek except apolitical architectural knowledge driven only by technology and instrumentality. Others speak about beauty (the theme of the 2007 Documenta exhibition in Kassel), technical knowledge, and in some cases bottom-up self-organizing systems.[19]

The question now is what projective practices can affect in actuality. From my perspective, they come in three basic types in many recent realized projects in the Netherlands, types that display "projective autonomy," "projective mise-en-scène," and "projective naturalization." As we shall see, projective autonomy confines itself primarily to models of geometry. Projective mise-en-scène and projective naturalization, by contrast, experiment with architecture as infrastructure. Projective autonomy tries to restore contact with the user and the contemplator through passive experience, while projective mise-en-scène and projective naturalization seek interaction. While projective autonomy is interested in form—what the aesthetic by its own means is able to communicate—the projective mise-en-scène seeks the creation of theatrical situations, and projective naturalization seeks strictly instrumental and operational systems.

In the practices in the Netherlands I am about to discuss, architects are not theorizing their work as "projective"; rather they are practicing and making in ways that fit this American concept.

Projective Autonomy

The architecture of Claus & Kaan, Rapp + Rapp, and Neutelings Riedijk reveals what I am calling "projective autonomy." The meticulously crafted forms (a return to the discipline) characteristic of their projective strategy offer comfort and reassurance. Projective autonomy revolves around the self-sufficiency of tasteful, subdued form, which, notwithstanding the vicissitudes of life or passing dreams, is in theory capable of enduring for centuries. In many cases it appears as a modest architecture that combines functional, economic, and representational requirements in an efficient, aesthetic, and sustainable manner. The preference for tranquility and harmony, for aloofness from change, means that in projective autonomy we are dealing with a conventional or limited projective practice. Projective autonomy is not concerned with movement, complexity, or any of the other dynamic processes that can be used to legitimize projects, but with relatively stable cultural and economic values.

Rapp + Rapp work with received architectural language, with the internal structure of architectural typologies as the residuum of the historical and the contemporary city, very much in the spirit of the early less figurative work of Aldo Rossi,

Hans Kollhoff, and Colin Rowe. Thus the foyer in Amsterdam's Bos en Lommer district is a variation of the classic atrium typology. For Claus & Kaan, the organizing principal is not historical typology but the typographic autonomy of a building—I am referring not so much to the architects' fondness for letters and numbers as to the way they "interspace" the building—to the rhythm of thick and thin spaces by which the individual elements, from the smallest detail to the entire volume, are ordered. Just as the typographer selects his typeface and searches for the most appropriate spacing, so Claus & Kaan deal in a craftsmanly and repetitive manner with windows, columns, doors, facade panels, and volumes. They pursue a conventional architecture that inspires confidence and eschews controversy, that is about mass, boxy volumes, light, beauty, and style.[20] Radical chic and subversion are definitely not goals for them, but their buildings do possess some minimalist chic. The abstract language and meticulous detailing lend their buildings a self-satisfied, stylish gloss. The floating black bar with its sleek banded pattern in the main facade of the Municipal Offices in Breda reveals a certain kinship with the elegant profiling of Bang & Olufsen design. Minimal chic glosses over vulgarities with its abstract perfection.

While the buildings of Rapp + Rapp and of Claus & Kaan behave decorously and seriously, fun is given plenty of running room in the work of Neutelings Riedijk. No puritanical architecture for them, but instead good strong shapes that tell a story. Architecture, like television, comics, and other manifestations of popular visual culture, must communicate with the public. In the case of Neutelings Riedijk it is once again possible to speak of "buildings with character." Neutelings Riedijk strive for dramatic effects that offer the viewer an "everyday architectural surrealism."[21] Their buildings are dramatis personae that have stepped into our carpet metropolis, turning their heads to survey their surroundings. Buildings in the landscape become part of the theater of life, although the leading player here is not the user but the architecture. Neutelings Riedijk are interested not in life itself, but in the autonomy of the decor against which it is played out. Their buildings may be brooding, robust, humorous, even bizarre. A critical architecture would use these powerful characteristics to sabotage the language of architecture or the norms and values of society. The "Pop art" of Neutelings Riedijk, unlike that of Andy Warhol for example, is free of ulterior motives. Their buildings are intended to be autonomous characters, to radiate a unique and subversively entertaining identity that we will not easily forget. Such narrative sculpture is ideally suited to the branding game so loved by clients and cities.

Projective Mise-en-scène

In the projective mise-en-scène approach favored by MVRDV and NL Architects, the user becomes an actor invited to take an active part in the theater choreographed by the architects. In these projective practices, projects are not to be contemplated; rather they throw reality forward through the help of scenarios inspired by the theatrical programs the architects write based upon the data they find within contemporary "extreme reality." Because nobody really knows what the "appropriate" response is to the unprecedented degree of innovation and uncertainty in this reality, observing its many mutations "neutrally" is seen as essential.

In the projective mise-en-scène, the city is one huge datascape. The architects use a method based on systematic idealization, an overestimation of available clues in which it is possible to integrate even mediocre elements. The program of requirements, which sometimes seems impossible to comply with, is followed to the letter, as are the complex and stringent Dutch building regulations. But an experiment with the real world remains the basic aim: in the margins and gaps of late capitalism these architects hope to foreground unclassified realities easily seen as parts of the ordinary world, while turning them upside down by means of theatrical performances.

Usually theatrical performances allow us to dream of other worlds. Not so the theatre of MVRDV and NL Architects: after observing and charting our dynamic society, they go in search of new shapes that, with the help of an inventive program and a fresh aesthetic, cater to actual and everyday demands of use. They turn life into an optimistic and cheerful play that generates new solutions while making jokes about our constantly mutating reality. Giving the flat roof of the bar in Utrecht an added function is not just a clever use of space; by putting a basketball court on the roof of this student bar, NL Architects also achieves a delightfully absurd juxtaposition of two quite different milieus. MVRDV makes "endless" interiors in which diverse programs are compactly interwoven. The architects call them "hungry boxes," boxes hungry to combine different programs in a continuous landscape.[22] Whereas Neutelings Riedijk create representational forms that tell a story at one remove from the user/observer, MVRDV translate the program into a carefully choreographed spatial experience that incorporates the user into science fictions hidden in the everyday. When you stack all the village libraries from the province of Brabant in one huge skyscraper with the looks of an updated tower of Pisa and make individual study rooms into elevators zipping up and down the facade of books, the user suddenly takes part in a futuristic mise-en-scène.

With NL and MVRDV, we can justifiably speak of spectacular effects, of "scripted spaces" that steer experience (especially via the eye) in a particular direction. While NL makes jokes and develops a trendy lifestyle typology without bothering too much about providing the design with a data-based, pseudo-scientific alibi, MVRDV looks for new spatial concepts capable of giving our deregulated society the best imaginable spectacular shape.

In projective mise-en-scène, it is not the autonomous force of the type, of chic minimalism, or of expressive decor that is given free rein—as in projective autonomy—but the daydreams alive in society. Objects are not important as things in a projective mise-en-scène; they are there to be used as a screen onto which fragments of our extreme reality can be projected. (On the Dutch pavilion at the Hannover world expo, MVRDV projected all kinds of Dutch data clichés—the artificial landscape, the dunes, tulip fields, a forest, and windmills.) As in the social sciences, objects are seen as the carriers of everyday culture and lifestyle. The architecture is a co-producer in the embodiment of cultural and social meaning. In projective mises-en-scène, everyday life is magnified by the spectacular decor that the architect assembles from data that reproduce the hidden logic of contemporary society. Instead of continuing to hide the more than sixteen million pigs in thousands of pitch-roofed bioindustry barns spread over the picturesque countryside of the Netherlands, MVRDV proposes that it is more efficient and animal-friendly to house pigs in high-rise flats in the harbor of Rotterdam. Suddenly—without any value judgment—the facts that there are more pigs than people in the Netherlands and that pigs can be happy in high-rises with a view—looks plausible. The shock effect of such a surreal and pragmatic mise-en-scène—like the Benetton billboards by Olivier Toscani with an AIDS patient dying in a living room—will immediately grab our attention. But if this bewildering realistic mode of representation is interested in either a better world or in exposing our Brave New World remains uncertain. The fables that lie hidden in the everyday are made visible by MVRDV's opportunistic imagination and make users into leading actors, as in the "Medical Center Pajama Garden" in Veldhoven. Instead of hanging around the sterile corridors and other introverted spaces typical of a hospital, patients can relax in their pajamas daydreaming of the Mediterranean among olive trees and other surreal "Mediterranean" set pieces.

Dreaming about utopias has lost its appeal. The everyday is so rich in fantasies that dreaming of a different world outside the existing one is no longer necessary. Like Steven Spielberg, architects must provide new representations that everyone can enjoy.[23] Entertainment first confronts you with dystopias (e.g., sixteen million stacked pigs), then guarantees a happy ending by glossing them over with "pragmatic solutions" ensuring conformity. The attitude is the putatively cool "Whatever."

Projective Naturalization

The limitation of projective mise-en-scène is that, while it is busily projecting meaning onto things, it forgets that things can themselves convey meaning, can be sensitive and active, and can activate processes in both the eye and the body. That performative capacity is at the heart of practices that follow the route of what could be called "projective naturalization." In the Netherlands, projective naturalizations have been developed by, among others, Oosterhuis.nl, UNStudio, Maurice Nio, and NOX Architekten. They featured largely in the recent "Non-Standard Architectures" exhibition in Paris.[24] Projective naturalization is not about signs, messages, codes, programs, or collages of ideas projected onto an object, but about technologies that allow matter to be performative.

Architect Lars Spuybroek of NOX is not interested in technology as a way of regulating functions and comfort. He sees it as a destabilizing force whose function is to fulfill our craving for the accidental by providing a variety of potentialities and events. "With the fluid merging of skin and environment, body and space, object and speed, we will also merge plan and volume, floor and screen, surface and interface, and leave the mechanistic view of the body for a more plastic, liquid, and haptic version where action and vision are synthesized," he writes.[25] What geology, biology, and even history have taught the architects of projective naturalization is that mutable processes generate far more intelligent, refined, and complex systems than ready-made ideas ever can.[26] This nonconventional architecture comprehends many shapes and schools.[27] What these manifestations have in common with nature is that the shapes they produce exhibit similarities with the structures, processes, and shapes of biology. The properties of these buildings change in response to changing conditions, just as nature does. A facade is not simply a shell, but a skin with depth that changes in response to activity, light, temperature, and sometimes even emotions.

A blobbish interactive "D-tower" designed by NOX is connected to a website at which the city's inhabitants can record responses to a questionnaire, designed and written by artist Q.S. Serafijn, about their everyday emotions: hate, love, happiness, and fear. The answers are graphed in different "landscapes" on the website that show the valleys and peaks of emotions for each of the city's postal codes. The four emotions are represented by green, red, blue, and yellow, and they determine the colors of the lamps illuminating the tower. Each night, driving through the city of Doetinchem, one can see which emotion is most deeply felt that day. A host of measurable data and technologies gives rise to a sophisticated metabolism that, as in Foreign Office Architects' Yokohama Terminal, channels the flows of people, cars, ships, and information like blood cells through and near the organism of the building. The project tries to function without obstacles or other complications and avoids communicating cultural meaning through shock, as does the work of MVRDV.

Projective naturalization projects are not rough or unfinished like many projective mise-en-scènes, but smooth and fluid. It is not ideology but the (wished for) instinct of artificial organisms that ensures that complex processes are operating appropriately. Buildings are intended to function like bodies without heads following complex biomechanical logic. When Foreign Office Architects exhibited their Yokohama Terminal at the Venice Biennale, they showed sections of a body scan parallel to one of the terminals, suggesting that the logic of a building should resemble the body's. The foreign presence of forms generated by the "genetic manipulation" of data and technology in projective naturalizations helps prevent instant categorization of these projects as good or bad, beautiful or ugly. Judgment is deferred. The building rebuffs immediate consumption as symbol or myth; instead it invites people to use it, to interpret, to enter into relations, to step into a stream of stimuli organized by matter. More than ever a building is able—by means of the new digital design methods and computer-controlled production of complex 3D elements ("advanced prototyping")—to behave like an organism.

In contrast to projective mises-en-scène, projective naturalizations are not interested in projecting scenarios onto objects related to society, religion, power, politics, globalization, or individuals. Projective naturalizations possess a super-functionality that revolves around movement, self-organization, and interactivity.[28] The intelligence of the project does not reside in a capacity for reflection, in offering a representation for or against something, but in activating open processes that can supposedly function automatically in accord with the flows of the status quo. Projective naturalizations are about modulating precise and local decisions from a mechanistic perspective interested in open, self-organizing systems that allow flows of consensus to follow their different trajectories with the aid of an advanced construction processes. Grand dreams and other paradigms— except those of advanced technology and design expertise—

are of little relevance. While concentrating on organic abstractions, projective naturalizations totally neglect the fact that every
appropriation of a project depends on narratives of use and is
about the interaction between social behavior and a given objective condition. What projective naturalizations tend to forget is
that our social actions and behavior, not our biological bodies,
constitute our identities.[29]

Larger Ambitions

Breaking with criticism, a passion for reality and a return to what
architecture as a discipline is capable of projecting are essential
to make the most of the many possibilities inherent in the "second modernity."[30] Instead of predicting the future, we have to be
attentive to the unknown knocking at the door. Projective practices also demonstrate that the question is not whether architecture should participate in late capitalism. That is a given.
But what form this relationship with the market should take is
an ethical and political question that cannot be curated only in
pragmatic, technical, or aesthetic terms.

The projective practices described here create spaces cut
from the same cloth as the garments of the ruling systems. As
such they confine themselves to forms of comfort enjoyed in
particular by the global middle class. Apart from fear of confrontation with the unknown, the chief concerns of this middle class
are the smooth processes that guarantee its rights to power,
individualism, career, identity, luxury, amusement, consuming,
and the infrastructure that makes all this possible.

This totalitarianism of difference, of individual rights—celebrated as the "multitude" of neoliberalism—overlooks the fact
that it is essential to pay attention to the collective interests of
the world population (including that of the transnational middle class). Instead of the paradigm of difference, we should viv-
ify a paradigm of sameness and supra-individual responsibility.

Culture is now all about diversity, flexibility, and the search for permanent novelty and effect that a project initiates, about how an object can relate to the market as an open supposedly neutral platform. This is a strategy without political ideals, without political or socio-historical awareness, that is in danger of becoming the victim of a dictatorship of aesthetics, technology, and the pragmatism of the blindly onrushing global economy. Instead of taking responsibility for the design, instead of having the courage to steer flows in a certain direction, the ethical and political consequences arising from the design decisions are left to market realism, and the architect retreats into the givens of his discipline.[31] In that way, all three projective practices described here are formalistic.

The positive thing about projective practices is that in the making of a project, under the influence of the material, the economy, the construction, the form, the program, the specific context, and with the help of architectural knowledge and instruments, projections can be tested and developed. In the very act of walking, projective practices create their paths. In the making of work, reality projects itself.

What these projective practices fail to see, however, is that utopian dreams are necessary in order to develop in a project a perspective that reaches beyond the status quo. I am not suggesting that utopian dreams can be realized, but that such dreams provide frames of reference for political action. Utopian dreams also enable us to make a detached diagnoses of the present. This moment of exile from the addiction to reality could make us aware of our own inevitable and implicit value judgments, of the fact that excluding political and social direction itself sets a political and social direction. It is the interaction between the dream of utopia and reality that could help a projective practice develop a new social perspective. What should fascinate projective practice is how it might inflect capitalism toward democracy.

The only problem is that so far almost nobody has been prepared to rethink the now eroded concept of democracy or to carry out research into what democracy could mean today in spatial terms.[32] Talking about democracy is simultaneously a taboo and a fetish. We treat the word democracy as a palliative that relieves us from having to think hard about its realization.

If we were to dream about new forms of democracy, we would develop visions that shake off the current political ennui, the blind pursuit of the market, and our incessant navel-gazing. But instead it looks as if we have nodded off. Do we really derive so much enjoyment from the addictive consumption of comfort, design trends, technology, and countless mutually indifferent differences? Isn't it time to wake from our deep sleep and again dream of utopias?

Acknowledgments: Thanks to William S. Saunders and Dave Wendt for their input and remarks about this essay. An abridged version of this article was published in Architecture in the Netherlands Yearbook, 2003–04 *(Rotterdam: Nai Publishers, 2004).*

Notes

1   See Francis Fukuyama, *The End of History and the Last Man* (New York: Free Press, 1992); Anthony Giddens, *The Third Way: The Renewal of Social Democracy* (Malden, Mass.: Polity Press, 1999); and Anthony Giddens, ed., *The Global Third Way Debate,* (Cambridge, U.K.: Polity Press, 2001).

2   Michael Hardt and Antonio Negri, *Empire* (Cambridge, MA: Harvard University Press, 2000); Gopal Balakarishnan, ed., *Debating Empire* (London and New York: Verso, 2003).

3   See also *Latent Utopias: Experiments within Contemporary Architecture,* ed. Zaha Hadid and Patrik Schumacher (Vienna and New York: Springer Verlag, 2002).

4   Symposium held to mark Bernard Tschumi's retirement as dean of Columbia University, New York City, March 28–29, 2003, now published in a book, *The State of Architecture at the Beginning of the 21st Century,* ed. Bernard Tschumi and Irene Cheng (New York: Monacelli Press, 2003).

5   More information about "post-critical" can be found in: Sanford Kwinter, "Who is Afraid of Formalism?" *ANY* 7/8, 1994; "Equipping the Architect for Today's Society: the Berlage Institute in the Educational Landscape" (dialogue between Wiel Arets, Alejandro Zaero-Polo, and Roemer van Toorn), Stan Allen, "Revising Our Expertise," Sylvia Lavin, "In a Contemporary Mood," and Michael Speaks, "Design Intelligence" in *Hunch*, 6/7, 2003; Jeffrey Kipnis, "On the Wild Side" (1999) in *Foreign Office Architect: Phylogenesis, FOA's Ark*, ed. Farshid Moussavi and Alejandro Zaera-Polo (Barcelona: Actar Editorial, 2004), 566–80. A robust debate about criticism among Hal Foster, Michael Speaks, Michael Hays, Sanford Kwinter, and Felicity Scott can be found in *Praxis: Journal of Writing and Building 5: Architecture after Capitalism*, 2003, 6–23.

6   Sarah Whiting and Robert Somol, "Notes around the Doppler Effect and Other Moods of Modernisms," *Perspecta: The Yale Architectural Journal 33, Mining Autonomy*, 2002, 72–77, reprinted here.

7   See Kenneth Frampton, "Towards a Critical Regionalism: Six Points for an Architecture of Resistance," in *The Anti-Aesthetic: Essays on Postmodern Culture*, ed. Hal Foster (New York: New Press, 1999) and Liane Lefaivre and Alexander Tzonis, *Critical Regionalism: Architecture and Identity in a Globalized World* (New York: Prestel USA, 2003).

8   Harm Tilman, "Architectuur onder globalisering" editorial, *De Architect*, January 2004.

9   All data regarding location, program, use, and infrastructure as well as the economy, politics, art, fashion, the media, the everyday, technology, typology, and materials that might conceivably help to advance a specific "found" reality are documented in diagrammatic form, especially charts and graphs. Of course, ideology is implicit in the science of measurement and the way the hidden qualities of reality are communicated. Most projective practices are, however, not aware of this ideological dimension. In addition they are ideologically "smooth" because the veil of fashion and style hides the many contradictions through the deployment of the design. For more information on the ideological dimension of contemporary Dutch architecture see my article "Fresh Conservatism: Landscapes of Normality," in *Artificial Landscape: Contemporary Architecture, Urbanism*, ed. Hans Ibelings (Rotterdam: NAi Publishers, 2000).

10 Manfredo Tafuri managed to convince the architectural world that the modern avant-garde, in overthrowing the past with its radical modernizing technology, had not only contributed to a progressive avant-garde program but had also and more particularly helped to accelerate capitalist modernization. The avant-garde's principle of montage anticipated—according to Tafuri—the assimilation process of the dynamic and mechanical capitalist revolution that every individual must undergo: permanent anxiety prompted by urban living and the loss of values.

11 Theodor Adorno, quoted in Hilde Heynen, *Architecture and Modernity: A Critique* (Cambridge, Mass.: MIT Press, 2000), 4.

12 For an excellent explication of the work of Jean Nouvel, see K. Michael Hays's introduction and the interview between Jean Baudrillard and Jean Nouvel in *The Singular Objects of Architecture* (Minneapolis, Minn.: University of Minnesota Press, 2002).

13 K. Michael Hays, "Scanners," in *Scanning: The Aberrant Architectures of Diller + Scofidio*, ed. Aaron Betsky, K. Micheal Hays, and Laurie Anderson (New York: Whitney Museum of Art, 2003), 129–36.

14 See note 7.

15 Various observations on criticism versus the projective are set out clearly by Somol and Whiting in "Notes around the Doppler Effect and Other Moods of Modernisms."

16   "Mad Dutch Disease," Premsela Lecture by graphic designer Michael
     Rock at Premsela Dutch Design Foundation, Amsterdam, February 11,
     2004, available from the Premsela Foundation <www.premsela.org>.

17   As long ago as 1995, Hans van Dijk noted a tendency in Dutch
     architecture toward a kind of "aestheticized pragmatism" that
     combines realism (with respect to the terms of reference, regulations,
     budget, etc.) with a desire to produce a good looking building
     (but without reference to any particular aesthetic theory). See "On
     Stagnation and Innovation. Commentary on a Selection," in Ruud
     Brouwers et al., *Architecture in the Netherlands. Yearbook 1994–1995*
     (Rotterdam: NAi Publishers, 1995), 138–52.

18   See also Robert Somol, "12 Reasons to Get Back into Shape," in
     Content, ed. Rem Koolhaas and OMA-AMO (Cologne: Taschen, 2004),
     86–87.

19   Research done by the offices like Stefano Boeri and Multiplicity,
     and Raoul Bunschoten and CHORA, investigate the territorial
     transformations taking place in contemporary society. With the help
     of new observing, representing, and curating tools, they map and
     work with the processes of self-organization of inhabited space rather
     than in typological prototypes. The inherent rule in their design
     projects aims at constructing itself in relation to the dynamics already
     operating in the territory, which are not all necessarily controllable
     by centralized planning practices. See also Stefano Boeri, "Eclectic
     Atlases," in Multiplicity, *USE: Uncertain States of Europe* (Milan: Skira
     Editore, 2003) and Raoul Bunschoten and Chora, *Urban Flotsam*
     (Rotterdam: 010 Publishers, 2001).

20   "We do not believe in designing aesthetic objects with complicated
     forms that can only be built through craftsmanship. Instead, we use
     standard industrial materials, spans, and constructions: ordinary
     products and ordinary techniques." Claus & Kaan, *Hunch* 6/7, 2003,
     140.

21   Willen Jan Neutelings and Michael Riedijk, *At Work: Neutelings Riedijk
     Architects* (Rotterdam: Uitgeverij 010, 2003), 7.

22   "The Hungry Box," a traveling exhibition about the work of MVRDV,
     at the Netherlands Architecture Institute from November 2, 2002, to
     January 5, 2003.

23 Winy Maas mentioned Spielberg in a call to architects during
    the presentation of a research studio at the Berlage Institute,
    March 2, 2004.

24 See *Non-Standard Architectures*, catalogue and exhibition curated
    by Zeynep Mennan and Frédéric Migayrou in the Centre Pompidou,
    Paris (December 10, 2003–March 1, 2004), which featured work by
    Asymptote, dECOi Architects, DR_D, Greg Lynn FORM, KOL/MAC
    Studio, Kovac Architecture, NOX Architekten, Objectile, Oosterhuis.nl,
    R&Sie, Servo, and UNStudio.

25 Lars Spuybroek in a 1998 essay outlining the philosophy of NOX
    Architekten at www.archilab.org.

26 See also Manuel de Landa, *A Thousand Years of Nonlinear History*
    (New York: Zone Books, 2000) and *Intensive Science and Virtual
    Philosophy* (London and New York: Continuum, 2002).

27 The pavilions by Oosterhuis.nl and Asymptote in the Floriade
    Park (in *Architecture in the Netherlands: Yearbook 2002–2003*, ed.
    Anne Hoogewoning, Roemer van Toorn, Piet Vollaard, and Arthur
    Wortmann [Rotterdam: NAi Publishers, 2003], 38–40) and the
    saltwater pavilion by Kas Oosterhuis and the freshwater pavilion by
    Lars Spuybroek at Neeltje Jans (in *Architecture in the Netherlands:
    Yearbook 1997–1998*, ed. Hans van Dijk, Hans Ibelings, Bart Lootsma,
    and Ron Verstegen [Rotterdam: NAi Publishers, 1998], 42–47).

28 Projective naturalizations also aspire to be operational. See also what
    Rem Koolhaas has to say about this in a reaction to the manifesto of
    Ben Van Berkel, Sanford Kwinter, Alejandro Zaera-Polo, and Greg Lynn
    (during the 1997 Anyhow conference in Rotterdam). "They had fresh
    and new ambitions and postures—antisemantic, purely operational
    represented in virtuoso computer (in)animation. I remember being
    critical of their claim, then, that they had gone beyond form to sheer
    performance, and their claim that they had gone beyond the semantic
    into the purely instrumental and strictly operational. What I find
    (still) baffling is their hostility to the semantic. Semiotics is more
    triumphant than ever—as evidenced, for example, in the corporate
    world or in branding—and the semantic critique may be more useful
    than ever." Rem Koolhaas, in "Spot Check: A Conversation between
    Rem Koolhaas and Sarah Whiting," *Assemblage* 40, December 1999,
    46. See also Felicity D. Scott, "Involuntary Prisoners of Architecture,"
    October 106 (Fall 2003): 75–101.

29   I am always surprised when Ben Van Berkel and Caroline Bos
     (UNStudio) show their "Manimal" metaphor for a new architectural
     practice—an image hybridizing a lion, a snake, and a human—and
     only talk about the process of generating the Manimal but never
     about its cultural, ideological, and symbolic implications. For them
     it's all about form and not how social practices of use unlock such a
     metaphor.

30   The idea of a "second" or "reflexive" modernity was first developed
     in Ulrich Beck's *Risikogesellschaft: auf dem Weg in eine andere
     Moderne* (Frankfurt am Main: Suhrkamp, 1986), translated as *Risk
     Society: Towards a New Modernity* (London; Newbury Park, Calif.: Sage
     Publications, 1992).

31   For the role of the market in architecture see also Roemer van Toorn,
     "Lost in Paradise" in *Architecture in the Netherlands: Yearbook 2001–
     2002*, ed. Anne Hoogewoning, Piet Vollaard, and Roemer van Toorn
     (NAi Publishers: Rotterdam 2002) and "Propaganda" in *Architecture in
     the Netherlands: Yearbook 2002–2003*.

32   At times, the practice of Rem Koolhaas (although he refuses to talk
     about it) seems to experiment with new notions of democracy in
     space. Alongside the three projective practices mentioned in this
     article are also "projective juxtapositions," in which the permanent
     crisis of late capitalism is a source of inspiration. Projective
     juxtapositions are characterized by an indefinable critical detachment
     that continually places the program and with it the organization of
     society in a state of crisis. In projective juxtapositions—such as those
     of OMA—a project never reaches a conclusion but instead provokes
     a never-ending subjective interpretation and inhabitation. The early
     projective juxtapositions of OMA were a vessel to experiment with
     new freedoms, as for example in the Kunsthal resisting the current
     idea that a museum needs to be a temple with quasi-neutral white
     exhibition spaces. There a projective juxtaposition is combined with
     what Immanuel Wallerstein calls Utopistics (Immanuel Wallerstein,
     Utopistics, Or, Historical Choices of the Twenty-First Century [New
     York: W.W. Norton, 1998]). With Utopistics, Wallerstein is not
     referring to a progressivism that already knows what is to come, but
     is pleading for a science that seriously assesses liberating historical
     alternatives—what best possible path for a far (and uncertain) future
     can be followed. Reassessing Utopistic examples—which proved

successful in creating freedom in the past—can help in the creation of new situations of freedom. Such an approach can be found in the OMA's Seattle library, which to a large extent reworks the public library of Hans Sharoun in Berlin (among other examples from the catalogue of Utopistic examples). When Utopistics are combined with a projective juxtaposition, we come close to what I am after. But the OMA experiments with Prada and the Guggenheim in Las Vegas went no further than a projective mise-en-scène which Salvador Dalí would have loved: "It is not necessary for the public to know whether I am joking or whether I am serious, just as it is not necessary for me to know it myself" (Salvador Dalí, *Diary of a Genius* [London: Creation Books, 1964]).

INTRODUCTION
Architecture's Expanded Field / *Anthony Vidler*

In 1979 "Sculpture in the Expanded Field," a classic article by
the art critic/theorist Rosalind Krauss, appeared in the journal
October. In this essay, Krauss discusses sculpture's tendency,
beginning in the early 1960s, to reach beyond the previously
accepted boundaries of the discipline toward various interactions
with both the landscape and architecture. She identifies three
categories in addition to sculpture—marked sites, axiomatic structures, and site-constructions—that can be used to understand the
works of certain "sculptors" during the late 1960s and 1970s.[1]

  In "Architecture's Expanded Field," published in the conference proceedings of "Architecture Between Spectacle and Use,"
held at the Clark Art Institute in spring 2005, Anthony Vidler
builds upon Krauss's theorization of postmodern sculpture to
explore architectural trends in the early twenty-first century.[2] In his
text, Vidler—architectural historian, theorist, and dean of the Irwin
S. Chanin School of Architecture at The Cooper Union—examines
an expanded field for architecture that involves conceptions of
both landscape and sculpture; the former in relation to nature,
site, and urbanism; and the latter with respect to notions of
monumentality. These considerations, Vidler asserts, give rise to
an architecture that is "not-exactly-architecture. Or at least 'not-
exactly-architecture' as we have experienced architecture up to
the present."

  According to Vidler, four paradigms—combinations of
architecture–landscape, architecture–biology, architecture–program, and architecture–architecture—characterize the prevailing
developments in recent architectural thought. These principles
all appear as reactions to what has come before them: "Against
neorationalism, pure language theory, and postmodern citation
fever, architecture—like sculpture some decades earlier—has

found new formal and programmatic inspiration in a host of disciplines and technologies, from landscape architecture to digital animation." Typically these new architectures differ in physical appearance and generative codes, yet they are joined, Vidler asserts, by the use of the diagram (albeit in multiple manifestations) as a method of operation and a conceptual device. Vidler hopes that architects working within this broader architectural realm, armed with ingenuity, contemporary technology, and the lessons of their predecessors, will move beyond the stale dichotomies of twentieth-century architecture (such as form versus function) to address issues raised but not resolved by modernist architects, especially those concerning crises of the population explosion and the environment.

Notes

1   Rosalind Krauss, "Sculpture in the Expanded Field," *October* 8 (Spring 1979): 41.

2   A version of "Architecture's Expanded Field" originally appeared in *Artforum* 42, no. 8 (Apr. 2004).

ANTHONY VIDLER

ARCHITECTURE'S
EXPANDED FIELD

First appeared in *Architecture Between Spectacle and Use*, ed. A. Vidler (Sterling and Francine Clark Art Institute: Williamstown, Mass., 2008), 143–54. Courtesy of the author and publisher.

The first who compared painting and poetry was a man of the most exquisite taste who felt that the two arts produced in him the same effects. He saw that the one and the other restituted the presence of absent things by substituting appearance for reality; both finally please us by tricking us. A second wished better to understand our pleasure and discovered that in both arts, it sprang from the same source. Beauty, the notion of which comes to us in the first place from material objects, has general rules that are applied to different domains: to actions, to thoughts, as well as to forms. A third, reflecting on the value and the distribution of these general rules, noted that some dominate painting, others poetry, and that in this way in certain cases, poetry could support painting in the same way that in others, painting could support poetry, through commentaries and examples. The first was an amateur; the second, a philosopher; the third, a critic.
—Gottfried Lessing

Attacking the fashion for the comparison and interpenetration of the arts of painting and poetry, and stressing the special role of each art as it depended on its means of representation—poetry as a narrative form, and painting as a capturing of a moment— Lessing initiated, with what Hubert Damisch has characterized as a great cultural shock to eighteenth-century theory, a discussion that has continued to this day. What is it that is specific to each art, and what would it be if it corresponded to the special media of each art?

If it is true that the painter uses for his imitations means and signs different from those of the poet, that is to say forms and colors extended in space, while poetry is served by articulated sounds that follow each other in time, and if it is incontestable that signs should have a natural and simple relation with the object signified, then signs that are juxtaposed can express only juxtaposed objects, in the same way that successive signs can only translate objects or their successive elements. Objects or their elements that are juxtaposed are called "bodies." Thus bodies with their evident characters are the objects proper to painting. Objects, or their elements, disposed in order of succession evoke, in the widest sense, actions. Actions are thus the proper object of painting.

Nearly two and a half centuries after Gottfried Lessing published his *Laocöon* (1766), an essay in which he attempted to define the arts of painting, sculpture, and literature in relation to the specificity of each one's medium and its inherent ability to represent space and time, and over sixty years since Clement Greenberg wrote his own reply to Lessing in "Towards a Newer *Laocöon*" (1949), the issue seems still unresolved, and most particularly in the case of architecture.[1] While Lessing did not speak of architecture in his essay, the question has always hovered around this special case of the arts, bound as it is to an art that is neither painting nor sculpture, and, of course, neither poetry nor prose, but that nevertheless partakes of and participates in all of the arts in question.

What I want to do here is to place in perspective a few of the issues surrounding debates over architecture, its characteristics of display, representation, and, as has been advanced, spectacle. For in the face of the increased blurring of the distinctions among painting, sculpture, and architecture, through practices from performance art, installation art, site-specific art, land art, and the rest, "media specificity" has once again emerged as a critical watchword. How do we define, and thereby ensure the individual integrity of each art as a practice when there no longer seems to be any division between the spatial and the textual, or more problematically in the case of sculpture and architecture, between the aesthetically constructed spatial and the functionally constructed spatial? When artists like Vito Acconci are experimenting with architecture and architects like Frank Gehry seem as preoccupied with the sculptural form of building as with its functional role, it seems that what Rosalind Krauss once termed the "expanded field" of sculpture has invaded architecture,[2] or, as the experimental constructions of Dan Graham and others demonstrate, architecture has invaded sculpture.

Yet there still remains the suspicion that there is a fundamental distinction inherent in the kinds of uses appropriate to each art that goes beyond simple questions of function versus form, use versus uselessness. And, as Kant intuited, such distinctions have been sought since the Enlightenment. In architecture, the question was construed as a dual conflict between art and life. The philosopher and mathematician Jean le Rond d'Alembert put the problem most concisely when he defined architecture as "the embellished mask of our greatest need," which meant that to the philosophic eye architecture was little more than the aesthetic or "rhetorical" supplement to shelter. One could interpret all the attempts to define the "essence" of architecture since then as struggles to reduce this dualism to a singularity. Thus the appeals to an architecture of pure metaphysical uplift (John Ruskin through Louis I. Kahn) or one of pure functionalism (Jean-Nicholas-Louis Durand through Hannes Meyer) and all the shades of functionalist aesthetic in between. Each phase of modernism has juggled the equation according to its own standards of politics or aesthetics. Thus "function" has been reduced to structural integrity or spatial economy while "metaphysics" has been defined as spiritual uplift or sublime effect. Other, more recent theories have posited the primacy of the "program," the power of the "sign," or the return to "tradition." More recently, debates on the nature of architecture, while not as acerbic and more eclectic than in the period of high modernism, turn around the instrumental role of the "diagram"—an attempt to propose function and space as a singular entity, and the *effect* of the surface—in an aesthetic appeal to the effects of new cast and molded materials subject to the sculpting of digital programs.

The real ambiguity between sculpture and architecture emerged, of course, with the modernist adoption of abstraction as the formal language of both. While sculpture was representational of the figure and architecture representational of historical styles, there was little debate about their interface until Auguste Rodin's merging of the surface of the door with the space of his sculptural forms, and until Constructivism and Neoplasticism determined that the abstract forms in space would serve architecture, sculpture, painting, and the graphic arts equally. Greenberg, trying to save painting from the invasion of reliefs following Vladimir Tadin's *Corner Relief*, attempted to define flatness—the mark on the canvas—as the determining factor.

This ambiguity has been present at least since the 1960s, when it was equally possible to see Dan Graham taking his inspiration from architectural theory and practice as it was to see Louis I. Kahn constructing a "minimalist" aesthetic akin to that developed by Donald Judd and his peers. But with the current exploration of digital form common to the architecture of Frank Gehry and his younger contemporaries and to sculptors like Richard Serra, the distinctions seem to have come to rest in the narrow territory of "use" versus "uselessness."

Such neo-Kantian terms, which stem from the philosopher's celebrated separation between the arts of pure objective pleasure and those of social usefulness, may well have been operative in moments when the social occupation and spatial experience of sculpture was a question of exterior perception. Now, with the installation of sculpture in the public realm as a spatial construction and the necessary occupation of, say, Richard Serra's *Torqued Ellipses* by the moving body as well as the perceiving eye, questions of "use" as traditionally defined are thrown into doubt. How do we distinguish, for example, between the "use" of a public square as a spatial and recreational experience and that of the same square inhabited by a work such as Serra's *Tilted Arc*? Both would seem to occupy a realm once defined as architectural, and together they make up a spatial entity very different from that once provided by a freestanding sculptural figure at the center of the square. A *Tilted Arc* is at once sculptural and architectural, even as contemporary architects would hold that the exterior and interior forms of their buildings are both equally architectural and sculptural. Both in the end are experienced not only haptically by projection but also optically through vision; both are equally imposing on, and respondent to, the body; both fulfill a combination of experiential, aesthetic, and functional "use."

Here it might be useful to return to Rosalind Krauss's first exploration of sculpture's "expanded field" in 1979. In this groundbreaking article Krauss set up a diagram of relations and distinctions that for the first time placed the "sculpture" of the 1960s in its relationship to other non-sculptural arts—landscape and architecture. For her, sculpture proper was not a universal but a specifically historical quality defined by its monumental and memorial characteristics; its gradual loss of such specificity began with Rodin's *The Gates of Hell* and was completed by modernist abstraction's final loss of "site." Modernist sculpture, then, was nomadic. By the 1950s this avant-garde nomadism had grown exhausted, and sculpture began to explore domains outside itself—developing into something that was not sculpture but also "not-landscape" and "not-architecture." These "non-sites" were then elaborated into more specific "not-sculptural" categories—"site constructions" (Robert Smithson's *Partially Buried Woodshed*), "marked sites" (combinations of "landscape" and "not-landscapes" such as Smithson's *Spiral Jetty* and Michael Heizer's *Double Negative*), and "axiomatic structures" (combinations of "architecture" and "not-architecture" such as the work of Richard Serra, Robert Irwin, and others).

It is this last category, which conjoins architecture and its opposite, that is of interest here. For, as Krauss argues, "in every case of these *axiomatic structures*, there is some kind of intervention into the real space of architecture . . . the possibility . . . of mapping the axiomatic features of the architectural experience—the abstract conditions of openness and closure—onto the reality of a given space."[3]

If such holds true for the destiny of sculpture in its postmodernist field, might we not be able to construe a similarly expanded field for architecture in its present exploratory condition? For it is true that both "landscape" and "sculpture," or rather "not-landscape" and "not-sculpture," have been emerging as powerful metaphors to construe a new condition of architecture. "Landscape" emerges as a mode of envisaging the continuum of the built and the natural, the building and the city, the site and the territory, and "sculpture" figures as a way of defining a new kind of monumentality—a monumentality of the *informe*, so to speak, that at once challenges the political connotations of the old monument, yet nevertheless preserves a "not-monumental" role for architecture.

Following several decades of self-imposed autonomy, architecture has recently entered a greatly expanded field. Against neorationalism, pure language theory, and postmodern citation fever, architecture—like sculpture some decades earlier—has found new formal and programmatic inspiration in a host of disciplines and technologies, from landscape architecture to digital animation. Where former theorists attempted to identify single and essential bases for architecture, now multiplicity and plurality are celebrated, as flows, networks, and maps replace grids, structures, and history. Where arguments once raged between Corbusian and Palladian sources, now Henri Bergson and Gilles Deleuze are studied for their anticipation of non-formal processes. Blobs, swarms, crystals, and webs proliferate as paradigms of built form, while software has replaced traditional means of representation with dynamic effect. Nearly two and a half centuries after Gottfried Lessing inaugurated the search for medium specificity in his *Laocöon* and more than fifty years after Greenberg articulated a self-reflexive definition of modern painting and sculpture, the boundary lines of architecture remain unresolved.

And yet, underlying the new formal experimentation is a serious attempt to reconstrue the foundations of the discipline, not so much in singular terms but in broader concepts that acknowledge an expanded field, while seeking to overcome the problematic dualisms that have plagued architecture for over a century: form and function, historicism and abstraction, utopia and reality, structure and enclosure. Over the last decade, four new unifying principles have emerged as the most dominant: ideas of landscape, biological analogies, new concepts of "program," and a renewed interest in exploring the formal resources to be found inside architecture itself. It is not, of course, accidental that these apparently new conceptual models are themselves deeply embedded in the history of architectural modernism, some from as early as the Renaissance, and that each has already been proposed as a unifying concept at one time or another over the last two centuries.

The first, the notion of landscape, which derives from eighteenth-century picturesque gardens, with their narrative walks and framed views, has now been extended to include questions of regional and global visions of urban form. Given the early development of the genre of landscape painting in Holland and the Netherlands' experience in engineering the national landscape, it is perhaps appropriate that many Dutch architects, including Ben van Berkel and Caroline Bos of UNStudio and Winy Maas of MVRDV, have found inspiration in the idea of landscape, using it to construe digital models of new cities and regional plans out of data flows, and, on a smaller scale, new topological forms for the interior landscapes of houses.

Questions of biological form strongly influenced architecture and design in the later nineteenth century, especially after the popularization of Charles Darwin's theories, leading to the experiments characteristic of Art Nouveau. Later in the twentieth century, the development of cybernetics and early research into DNA, including the discovery of the double helix, led architectural theorists like Reyner Banham in the 1960s to propose biological form as the next revolution in architecture. Charles Jencks followed up this proposition in his 1974 book *Architecture 2000*, in which his chart of architectural "movements" presciently ended in the year 2000 with a prediction of "bioform." Contemporary architects like Greg Lynn have built on these theories and have developed a new repertoire of form using the techniques pioneered by animation software: beginning with the idea of the "blob" and more recently experimenting with the forms of complex organisms from butterflies to jellyfish, Lynn has designed coffee sets that interlock like the carapaces of insects and turtles and institutions that unfold from the ground like giant colorful orchids and artichokes.

Yet another model, the idea of "program," was transformed in the first age of the avant-gardes from its eighteenth-century meaning as a design exercise for student architects into an overriding concept that regulates and generates form according to a detailed understanding of its function. In the 1950s the idea was extended by theorists like Sir John Summerson to assume a central place as a single "source of unity" for modern architecture, but it was quickly forgotten in the rush to bury functionalism under postmodern historicism. Now, architects like Rem Koolhaas have taken up an expanded idea of program as a means to explode every convention of traditional architectural modernism and to create the basis for an architecture that realistically confronts the present global political, social, and economic reality.

Finally, the internal exploration of architectural form, the search for a language of architecture that is not applied, so to speak, from the outside but rather developed out of the constituents of its own practice—a kind of formalist Lessing—has its distinguished roots in avant-garde modernism and especially in the interpretation of pure abstract art, from Piet Mondrian and Theo van Doesburg through to Peter Eisenman, who has himself expanded his precedents by transforming architects such as Giuseppe Terragni, and later Andrea Palladio and Francesco Borromini, into paradigms of formal transformations. These paradigms, however apparently different on the surface and hotly debated among their protagonists (presumably in search of fame), are nevertheless joined by their common reliance on a device that they have each called, in different ways, a "diagram," at once a way of working and an attempt to go beyond the binary concepts of modernism in order to frame a new field of action for architecture that subsumes form and function within a matrix of information and its animation.

Recently, this word "diagram" has become quite a magic wand of a word in the United States; something like the word "type" in the 1970s, "postmodern" in the 1980s, and "blob" in the 1990s. Everyone, but everyone, is doing the diagram. The diagram is in fact the dance of the moment, which is, on one level, strange, since the word was first introduced into architectural criticism in 1996 by Toyo Ito. When discussing the architecture of Kazuyo Sejima he wrote, "You (Sejima) see a building as essentially the equivalent of the kind of spatial diagram used to describe the daily activities for which the building is intended in abstract form. At least it seems as if your objective is to get as close as possible to this condition."[4] For such an architecture, Ito coined the term "diagram architecture." Since then, all hell has broken loose around this little, apparently insignificant word, and everybody has jumped to say that they, too, let it not be forgotten, are doing diagram architecture. So important has it seemed to be a diagram architect that Eisenman himself has published a book, called *Diagram Diaries*, that proves conclusively that not only has he been doing diagrams longer than anyone else but he has been doing diagrams his whole career; indeed he, not anyone else, invented the diagram.[5]

I have explored elsewhere the different iterations of diagram procedures and traced the epistemology of diagrams out of Charles Pierce's investigations into the nature of icons, as well as showed the way in which diagrams proper have entered a field already littered with types of drawing, from the sketch to the *parti*, and have transformed it into a domain ready for advanced computation. For, as deployed by landscapists, bio-blobists, programmatic ironists, and autonomistic formalists, the diagram has been fabricated as a ready way to access and to motivate the iteration of architecture through digital means. This diagram might take the form of maps—reframed and abstracted through different types of information about the "ground;" it might incorporate topologies drawn from natural structure, from skins to DNA; it might bring together in a single composite form a range of information, from the technical to the social, hitherto impossible to synthesize in the traditional *parti*; it might allow for the complex exploration of layered forms taken from the analysis of sites, buildings, or objects in order to produce new form.

In terms that echo Krauss's sculptural field, then, we may find combinations of architecture and landscape, architecture and biology, architecture and program, architecture and architecture producing new versions of the "not-landscape" and the "not-sculpture" that is nonetheless not-exactly-architecture. Or at least "not-exactly-architecture" as we have experienced architecture up to the present. And now, with the availability of new digital technologies, this expanded field, as many critics have noted, is confronting technologies that have been all-too subservient to the software aesthetic that arrives with every new program, whether AutoCAD or Rhino or Maya. At the same time, these new models open themselves up to accusations of being new dogmas, utopian totalizers, or apolitical formalists.

Nevertheless, I feel that they represent more simply a moment in the experimental exploration of languages and techniques that, if intelligently deployed, could offer, and sometimes already has offered, critical responses to questions placed on the agenda by modernism but not yet satisfactorily answered, in either political or architectural terms: the housing question that still haunts architecture and development on a global scale; the question of density raised by population explosions and land scarcity; the ecological crisis in resources and modes of conservation that, with radical shifts in climate and diminishing energy sources, presents more fundamental problems for architecture than those addressed by developments in materials and "green building" alone.

The posting of such questions is aided by new modeling techniques for assimilating, integrating, and ultimately forming data of all kinds so that the consequences of programmatic decisions might be evaluated in terms of design alternatives. These alternatives do not simply appear as random choices among beautiful surfaces or shaped blobs. Rather, they take shape as arguments in forms that propose political, social, and technological interventions and, in turn, imply a critique of business as usual. In sum, this new modernity continues to address the questions of the present with an avant-garde imagination, but now with the wisdom of hindsight and a truly historical understanding of the modern. It is perhaps not too much of an exaggeration to state that this expanded field for architecture owes greatly to the previous expansion of the sculptural field. Thus, the spatial arts now come together in their superimposed expanded fields, less in order to blur distinctions or erode purity than to construct new versions that, for the first time, may constitute a truly ecological aesthetics.

Notes

A version of this essay first appeared in *Artforum* 42, no. 8 (April 2004).

1   Clement Greenberg, "Towards a Newer Laocöon," *Partisan Review* 7, no. 4 (July–August 1940): 296–310.

2   Rosalind Krauss, "Sculpture in the Expanded Field," *October* 8 (Spring 1979): 30–44.

3   Krauss, "Sculpture in the Expanded Field," 41.

4   Toyo Ito, "Diagram Architecture," *El Croquis* 77, no. 1 (1996).

5   Peter Eisenman, *Diagram Diaries* (New York: Universe, 1999).

INTRODUCTION
Architecture by Numbers / K. Michael Hays

"Architecture should no longer be understood as an object but rather as a condition and construction."[1]

In spring 2004, the Whitney Museum of American Art at Altria mounted an exhibition entitled "Architecture by Numbers." In this show, K. Michael Hays—professor of architectural theory at Harvard University Graduate School of Design and adjunct architectural curator for the Whitney—gathered works that, in various ways, arise from numerical operations. Each project is unique in its use of mathematical information, exposing or engineering patterns latent within the given objects of study, whether they are extreme landscapes, keyboard diacritics, or Abrahamic religions. These pieces, developed by "artists-architects," move beyond conventional concepts of architecture to fixate on the field's relationship with numbers, not to create a built entity, but as a way to think outside the current boundaries of the discipline. Indeed, "architecture exists in these projects not as a practice of object making—or even as a process of design in a conventional sense—but as a frame for thinking specific artistic problems... Architecture here is a particular kind of activity, but also a particular frame of mind—a conscious decision to think in this way rather than some other."

For Hays the works' aesthetic manifestations matter less than the underlying attitudes that gave birth to them. In an era reportedly "after theory," Hays argues for a method of thought that exceeds the practical, the pragmatic, and the concrete. Theory in the sense here proposed is neither prescriptive nor interpretive; "rather, theory is...an act of recasting something already known." Hays offers the infinitive to architect as a means to initiate this recasting, a way to "seek after architecture as a specific mode of knowledge; to perform presently a specific activity for the purpose of prolonging or continuing the practice historically authorized as architecture, but which cannot now be done in the same way; to select from among other possible practices (dancing, writing, filming, designing, etc.) this particular course of action; to set it next to other systems; to intend architecture; to desire architecture."

The concept of desire, stemming from Lacan's investigations of the structuring of the human psyche, does more for Hays that simply characterize the work presented in "Architecture by Numbers"; it also functions as a way to reconceptualize the architecture of the neo-avant-garde operating in the late 1960s through early 1980s. Elsewhere Hays suggests that in place of a model based on linguistics, "we rewrite the analytical model of architecture into something that [he calls] architecture desire, or in a zone that we might call the architectural Imaginary and Symbolic."[2] This alternative theoretical framework demarcates a potential future for architecture; indeed, "an architecture modeled on desire marks the sharp edge of intellectual passion that opens up what you can't control; it welcomes the risk of formlessness, the unpredictable consequences of ideas…Truisms are cut into, things come undone, and 'provisional generalizations' make new contexts for knowledge. Maybe in considering again the neo-avant-garde we might stumble upon a genuinely *new* architecture."[3]

Notes

1   K. Michael Hays in Deborah Hauptmann, "Critical Thought and Projective Practices: An Interview with K. Michael Hays," in *The Architecture Annual 2005–2006, Delft University of Technology*, ed. Henco Bekkering, Deborah Hauptmann, Alexandra den Heijer, Julius Klatte, Ulrich Knaack, and Sanne van Manen (Rotterdam: 010 Publishers, 2007), 59.
2   Ibid.
3   Ibid.

K. MICHAEL HAYS

ARCHITECTURE BY NUMBERS

First appeared in/ *Praxis 7: Untitled Number Seven* (2005), 88–99.
Reprinted with permission.

Architecture is fundamentally involved with numbers. From the very beginnings of architectural theory, as it emerged out of Pythagorean-Platonic philosophies of harmony and proportion, architecture has been understood as a fulcrum between the material world of things and their construction and the transcendent mathematics of the cosmos itself. In the spring of 2004, I curated a show for the Whitney Museum of American Art at Altria called "Architecture by Numbers." The premise of the show was simple: to juxtapose examples of contemporary practices that regard architecture's ongoing involvement with numbers as more fundamental than architecture's involvement with building.

Obviously, many mainstream architectures, both of empirical datascapes (MVRDV, UNStudio, and others) and of digitally animated topographies (Greg Lynn and others), are deeply and directly dependent on numbers. But at a time when it seems the entirety of our experience has become digitized, this involvement might be regarded as part of an inevitable and primarily practical absorption of the numerary into the center of the discipline. The five artists-architects[1] in this exhibition seek out numerical information in architectures at the highly impractical margins of the discipline—in objects, places, or ideas of such singularity that some may see their projects as aberrations or even obsessions. The obsessions include the numerology of labyrinths, the digital record of extreme landscapes, self-reflexive and self-negating geometrical transformations, numerical patterns generated by the surface of the human body, and the landscapes of information that can be derived from punctuation marks. Architecture exists in these projects not as a practice of object making—or even as a process of design in a conventional sense—but as a frame for thinking specific artistic problems such as authorship and production; the abstract calculations endemic to contemporary space versus the sensuous particularity of spatial experience; and sociological representation versus individual expression. Architecture here is a particular kind of activity, but also a particular frame of mind—a conscious decision to think in this way rather than some other.

It will be obvious that an interest in number, pattern, iterations, singularities, and the like, as presented in these projects, can be sustained only at a level of investigation that has recently once again come under suspicion—namely the theoretical. The current dogma seems to be that the complexity of the purely practical demands on architecture and the undeniable cleverness of architects' responses to those demands, exhaust the cultural interest in architecture in our own time. We are "after theory," the conventional locution goes. With the ability to process massive amounts of information and push it through sophisticated graphic software, we no longer have need of the slow and cumbersome ideas and abstractions that theory traffics in. The massive movements and sheer speed of the world system make theoretical supplements to real-time technocracy no more than ornaments, detours, and perversions of real progress and immediacy of effect. Not only gritty professionals, but students too are encouraged to avoid theory's opaque air and stay on the ground where things are clear, concrete, and ostensive. One of the things I find interesting about the museum exhibition, as a setting distinct from the profession and the academy, is its availability as a site for a new practice of theory, and perhaps the only site where works like these could be made to interact.

What is right about the post-theoretical turn is the recognition that architecture, more than any of the other arts, is subject to vast forces beyond the control of any design intention. In addition to economic and constructional limitations, and the demands of client, program, and policy, architecture is constrained by disciplinary conventions, cultural expectations, and the movement of history itself—as different trends and styles come and go. What is more, recent developments in technologies of media have blurred traditional boundaries between architecture and other visual and spatial arts, further challenging architecture's autonomy and specificity. No theory can guide or control design practice in this context the same way that, say, semiotics or typology drove certain practices in the 1970s. But this overemphasis on the practical seems to me, at least partly, a mark of the refusal to imagine something beyond the limits of the present—whether in architecture's past, in some future project, or indeed in our midst. For all the capability and sophistication in the body and mind of the current architectural endeavor, there is a surprising provincialism of spirit. The works of interest here are less shy of the larger range of experience and thought.

In calling the works grouped together here theoretical investigations, I mean something different from theory that guides and controls design practice. I intend rather the more fundamental, but also more limited activity of conceptualizing experiences that are irreducibly architectural—experiences that belong to none other than architectural objects or events in general and to numerary organizations or patterns in particular. This entails that architecture be understood as both an enabling condition and a restraint on thought and action—a condition, not a thing; a condition very close to Riegl's *Kunstwollen*, or Edward Said's notion of "beginning intention."[2] For example, a dance performance is not architecture, but a dance performance can be framed as an enabling condition for the production of architectural knowledge, as in Bernard Tschumi's *Manhattan Transcripts* or Diller + Scofidio's *Delay in Glass*. Music is not architecture, but a "willing" of music to become architecture can proliferate connections of music and architecture to even other practices, as Sanford Kwinter and Jeffrey Kipnis have demonstrated. Film is not architecture, but to read film architecturally enlarges both, as Giuliana Bruno does. And theory, as I intend it here, is neither a method (as in a design technique for generating form) nor a procedure for delivering form to interpretation (as in criticism and historiography). Rather theory is a first step in the intentional production of a present difference out of pre-existing traditions, a refunctioning and reforming of disciplinary concepts. It is an act of recasting something already known, or what Said calls a "molestation," that at the same time must be informed by an inaugural logic that authorizes it along with the subsequent texts it sponsors. In a sense, theory is something rather like desire.

Italian speakers have the advantage of the term *progettare* to designate the irreplaceable and untranslatable action required to design a project or project a design. Here I would like to suggest the infinitive *to architect* as an analogous term for the intention and the desire I am attributing to the artists-architects exhibited here. To architect then, comes to mean something different from to make or even to plan—different because the categories produced in architecting cannot be objects in their own right. To architect means rather to seek after architecture as a specific mode of knowledge; to perform presently a specific activity for the purpose of prolonging or continuing the practice historically authorized as architecture, but which cannot now be done in the same way; to select from among other possible practices (dancing, writing, filming, designing, etc.) this particular course of action; to set it next to other systems; to intend architecture; to desire architecture. The works here are the multiple signature of the socially symbolic system that is architecture. They track its impulse in difference bandwidths of experience and perception, and at vastly different scales—from the microcosms of Ben Nicholson to the territories of Laura Kurgan. And what they share is the conviction that architecting is an activity and a process of the imagination.[3]

With this, one will immediately suspect that I am making an essentialist claim, that I attribute to each of this group some special truck with Architecture (capital A)—an isolated and hermetic enterprise that presupposes that you must already know about its essence; and if you don't, then no one can tell you. But take Preston Scott Cohen as an example, and his use of projective geometry as a specifically demarcated set of codes and procedures that when used in ways initiated and developed in architecture's own disciplinary history, conserves and extends this particular field of activity, giving it a constantly permutating shape and identity. The technicalization of the geometric system and its historically articulated laws and programmed expressiveness are also an elimination of any essentialism. For they attest most emphatically not to an unchanging canon of architectural objects, but rather to the present effort to keep architecture going in a contemporary situation of its almost implacable "backgroundization." Further, they maintain and proliferate architecture not so much against other contemporary forms of cultural production as together with them, adjacent to other configurations of aesthetic and social expectations, but nevertheless distinct. Cohen therefore understands that to architect is necessarily to repeat; the repetition of certain geometric procedures contains experience, and experience accumulates as architecture demonstrates its present capacity for transformation, elaboration, and reconnection with other cultural materials. This procedural repetition is an appetite, the effort by which architecture strives to preserve itself. And the consciousness of that appetite is just what I mean by the desire to architect.

Or consider Ben Nicholson—part architect, part historian, part mystic—who explores the numerology of labyrinths in obsessively meticulous pencil drawings bound in notebooks. His ultimate goal is to correlate number, geometry, and concepts from religion—in particular the three Abrahamic religions that have made such important contributions to architecture's history. For Nicholson, the meander—and the labyrinth that derives from a meander folded back on itself—are the most basic traces of bodily movement through time and space: the architectural *Ursprung*, an original pure first appearance of a beginning intention. But from an elaboration of the rules of the meander, Nicholson finds a certain numerical isomorphism in what initially seems to be exceedingly unlikely places—such as the seven-day movement of the Hajj, the Hebrew Alef-Beit, and the structure of St. John's *Book of Revelation*. The sheer apartness-from-architecture of these examples is important. For Nicholson, different from Cohen, number deconstructs architecture in that number is both necessary for architecture and absolutely heterogeneous to it. Number is not architecture; number is an effect on architecture of the force exerted by the Abrahamic tradition—what in Freudian language would be called a displacement of that originary desire wherein the activity of architecting is analogous to a dreamwork. Or in more contemporary language, the Abrahamic system is a kind of infrastructure in the architectural assemblage Nicholson has discovered and constructed (for the machinery of desire must always be constructed). In the adjacencies and crossings of the disparate forces that Nicholson brings together, we again find desire.

Laura Kurgan's work, in its move from number and geometry to number and geography, makes it apparent, perhaps even more than the others, that a kind of foreign material is always necessarily woven in to the visual-spatial patterns of architecture by number (in the same way that heterogeneous spaces and codes are blocked together in the dreamwork, to stay a moment longer with that analogy). Her four *Monochrome Landscapes* (2004) are from a distance strikingly similar to Ellsworth Kelly's monochrome paintings of the late 1950s and early 1960s (one of which, *Green Blue Red*, is owned by the Whitney). But Kurgan's are digital images of extreme landscapes—the Cameroon rain forest, the Alaskan tundra, the Atlantic Ocean, or the Iraqi desert—acquired by the privately owned Ikonos and QuickBird satellites. Each pixel within each image is expressed as a number and corresponds to a specific latitude and longitude—a unique geographic area of about sixty-one square centimeters per pixel that the satellite's sensors are instructed to record. The heat value of each position is first expressed as a number that is in turn assigned a standard false color. This visible rendition of purely numerical information includes parts of the electromagnetic spectrum normally invisible to human eyes. (Scientist use standard false color images to map all sorts of landscape conditions from deforestation to military movements.) Kurgan then transposes the standard false colors into "true" colors (which are visible to humans), producing four images with an extraordinary internal informational structure concerned entirely with architecture's perennial struggle to understand and manage territories, but which could have technically or conceptually been produced only in the present. At the same time, she redirects the deconstruction of categories (painting, photography, landscape, etc.) onto ideological apparatuses that are the work's original frames: museum, science, and the commercialization of information (all of which become part of the work's infrastructure). And yet, there is a singularity to the work, a radical specificity of its experience that defies any descriptive information. Even our most successfully interpretations and references are disrupted by the sheer unthinkability of this visual occasion.

The digital information behind Marsha Cottrell's work originates from keyboard characters—all the punctuation marks and diacritics, but not the letters—that have been strewn, layered, repeated, scaled, spliced, and organized into countless configurations. The typewritten units—altered in stages and subjected to an untraceable series of improvisational actions—are the foundation of a vast and expanding digital library. Cottrell extracts from and adds to this repository of virtual debris as she builds the drawing. Mark becomes image in search of a code. It is of interest that Cottrell is not strictly an architect. Hers is a procedure whereby, on first encounter of her work, the architectural codes and categories which the "trained" viewer brings to the work are of no use in unraveling its problematics; all existing interpretive frames available to our critical consciousness that might help us read the work in question brings us up short against the visual evidence. What has to happen is that the reading practice itself must change. Architectural clichés must be cleared away to find something vital, something new. The mental circuitry required for viewing must now include shunts that relate keyboarding, drawing, and printmaking to numeracy, landscapes, and meteorology. In *Garden, Gale, and Math*

Dreaming Future, architecture merges, or one might say architecture "events itself" as that which is out of place in printmaking; it was neither foreseen nor preconceptualized, but rather discovered and produced—anachronistically and anamorphically—entirely in the architectural imaginary itself.

If Duchamp considered his *Three Standard Stoppages* to be "a joke about the meter,"[4] a stab at the accepted authority of that standard unit of measurement, then Michelle Fornabai's work may be a similar play on the authority that the human body has had in architecture as a presumed natural and unimpeachable standard. In the project *Body Roll Sheath Chaise*, a body is rolled across a flat surface; the folds, creases, points, and pressures of its motion are marked on a planar register that is then mutated into a complex three-dimensional form and woven by a computer numerically controlled loom—it can then be worn as a robe or inflated and used as a chair. In *Interference* screen, Fornabai begins with a module of six feet (the average height of a human body) by six inches (the average span of a human hand), and distorts twelve of these units according to a mathematical algorithm, producing a reiterative series of mirrored loops. A resulting screen converts anthropometrics into optics—visual effects of fluctuating interference and pulsating pattern. In Fornabai's work, the materials and techniques of couture meet the serial variability potential of advanced building component fabrication, but again the singularity of the visual event operates to change the rules for the pragmatics of architectural knowledge.

As I return again and again to think about this group of works, I am continually reminded of the opening scene of *The Matrix*, in which numbers slide down the computer screen, liquefied and pulsating as if with some digitized life—unencoded particles swirling in a kind of informational plasma. I imagine that this realm provisionally mapped onto the screen is the Real (I mean it in Lacan's sense as that which resists symbolization, can never be experienced immediately, and yet whose effects constantly erupt in to the mediating realms of the Symbolic and the Imaginary). I imagine that intersecting our world at every point are infinite vectors of digital information that we cannot represent, but whose materiality nevertheless determines our world. I then think that the works groped here are like the various programs imbricated in the matrix, that allow us to give image to the Real. It seems right that these projects reside in the register of Lacan's Imaginary, as small-other objects, marks of desire, or the objects of desire as such (whose visual, spatial, and indeed algebraic connotations spelled out the mirror stage Lacan surely intended us to retain). The works intend to restrict and organize the numerary, to conceptualize it, to ideologize it, and to architect it. Their variously patterned and calibrated surfaces differently diagram the complex of information out of which everything arises—the cultural unconscious itself, denizen of the socially Symbolic, now structured numerically rather than linguistically like Lacan's.

A more full account of the activity named by the intransitive verb "to architect," and a more complete theory of architecture desire as a kind of energy field or, indeed, the Real of constantly connecting, unconnecting, and reconnecting architectural quanta, could make an important contribution to our understanding of contemporary architecture practice. But it is more than I can do here. In the present context, an issue of *PRAXIS* that considers the practice of curating generally, something must be offered (however brief) about the relation of these objects collected in an exhibit and my account of them. Suggesting that these objects are constituted by something I'm calling architecture desire, or in a zone I'm calling the architecture imaginary, I mean to claim for them a material space and experience distinct from the language and concepts that are the tools of conventional interpretive theory. The Freudian machinery of desire gives us the primary processes of the unconscious as figures that cannot be reduced to the rational and conceptual workings of the secondary processes of conscious discourse. My claim is that the projects reserve an analogous dimension for architecture insofar as their primary processes appear as figural disruptions and distortions that critical thought and critical writing about them can never fully contain. "Le Travail du rêve ne pense pas," declared Lyotard (The Dreamwork does not think).[5] Of course, there is a kind of writing that itself produces the same sort of nonconceptualizable experience that I have claimed for these projects; but let's leave that for another time and say here that typically theoretical writing about architecture seeks to produce evermore discriminating concepts for the objects and events that are its subject—mediating, but not (one hopes) reducing them. Of course, theory, as a para-doxa, should be disruptive, should fold together objects and ideas in an attempt to forever keep things open. Still, to pick out and gauge the workings and qualities of our subject matter, we provisionally stabilize and structure it, hoping that a temporary halt can produce the possibility of further movement. But then is curating not a third activity between making objects and making theories? Is to curate not to further act on architecture desire (by simply juxtaposing objects primarily), displacing the rules of discourse and conceptualization and testifying to the architecture event without recourse to the concept that would fix it? Curating must hold out the possibility that a concept for the curatorial project exists and could be provided by theory. But it does not give the concept in language; rather it seeks to produce it as an event.

The architecture sought for by the various practices of architecting—including theorizing and curating—exceeds all these activities, but could not have emerged without them. It is, as I have suggested, peculiar, excessive, exorbitant, and everywhere open to reading and rereading; indeed, all its readings are rereadings. And it demands new thoughts constantly. It is as though the ungraspable totality of architecture desire inscribes itself as the limit condition of all mere practices of architecture, but also inflicts an unassuaged need for something else.

Notes

1   Preston Scott Cohen, Michelle Fornabai, Laura Kurgan, and Ben Nicholson all have been trained as architects and continue to teach architectural design, but they also have exhibited in art galleries. Marsha Cottrell is an artist in whose works I detected fundamental architectural operations. I shall refer to the group as artists-architects.

2   In *Beginnings* (1975), Said distinguishes between "origin (as divine, mythical, and privileged) and "beginning" (as secular and humanly produced). An "origin," as in classical and neo-classical though, is endowed with linear, dynastic, and chronological eminence—centrally dominating what derived from it. A "beginning," in contrast, especially as embodied in much modern thought, encourages orders of dispersion, adjacency, and complementarily (xii, 373). For Said, the novel is a major beginning in Western literary culture.

3   Here I understand imagination in the Kantian sense of *die Einbildungskraft*, which is an activity in an intermediary zone between intuition and the understanding. On one hand, imagination imposes a spatial and temporal structure on the sensuous manifold, while on the other hand it relates the domain of the sensuous to the cognitive laws of the understanding. Its essential activity in instances of aesthetic judgment, then, is schematization—the sensuous presentation of conceptual determinations. What is particularly interesting is the nature of this activity in the judgment of the sublime when the capability of the understanding is exhausted, when judgment is both necessary and impossible, when the sensuous object exceeds conceptual comprehension.

4   Theirry de Duve, *The Definitively Unfinished Marcel Duchamp* (Cambridge, Mass.: MIT Press, 1991), 55.

5   This is a title of a chapter of Jean-François Lyotard's *Discours* (Paris: Klinckseick, 1971) which relies heavily on the Freudian system of desire to develop the concept of the heterogeneous singularity of figure.

INTRODUCTION
Critical of What? Toward a Utopian Realism /
Reinhold Martin

The contemporary critique of criticality has been portrayed in
part as a generational divide, characterized by the up-and-
comers' Oedipal impulse to overcome their father (namely,
Peter Eisenman). Even the terminology of Somol and Whiting's
article—talk of the projective's "cool," "relaxed," "easy" attitude
as opposed to criticality's "hot," "belabored," "difficult" nature—
alludes to the new-versus-old, progressive-versus-conservative
mentality that the proponents of the projective foreground over
the critical. Yet in his 2005 article "Critical of What? Toward a
Utopian Realism," Reinhold Martin—a partner in Martin/Baxi
Architects, an assistant professor at Columbia University, and a
member of this younger generation—champions criticality, or
at least a revived version of it, based on his notion of utopian
realism.

Martin begins by echoing George Baird's inquiry of the projective or "post-critical" project: "by what criteria," Martin asks,
"is the 'post-critical' to be judged, beyond mere acceptance
and accommodation of existing societal, economic, or cultural
norms?" He then briefly rehearses the history of criticality, identifying two strains of the concept—the first focused on political
critique (developed by historian-critics such as Manfredo Tafuri),
and the second involved with aesthetic critique (associated with
architects such as Eisenman). Martin fears that post-critical practice risks the evacuation of all critique from architecture's domain.
He offers as an example practitioners associated with designs
for the World Trade Center, specifically the group collectively
known as United Architects, comprised of figures such as Farshid
Moussavi and Alejandro Zaera-Polo of Foreign Office Architects
(FOA) and Greg Lynn. Despite the "visionary" image projected

346

by these architects, in Martin's estimation, their design ultimately was conservative, in keeping with the political status quo; their proposal did not challenge socially accepted norms, and Martin feels that it even reinforced the ideas of American imperialism and capitalist growth. He cites the United Architects design as an illustration of "aesthetics as politics," a case where a seemingly progressive architectural project prefigures an objectionable political project—the war in Iraq. "Just what sort of world," he asks, are the "affirmative, projective practitioners of the 'post-critical'... projecting and affirming in their architecture and their discourse?"

In response, Martin proposes an alternate form of practice grounded in the concept of utopia, where utopia is "read literally, as the 'non-place' written into its etymological origins that is 'nowhere,' not because it is ideal and inaccessible, but because... it is also 'everywhere.'" Such a utopia, he continues, "is what Derrida called a 'specter,' a ghost that infuses everyday reality with other, possible worlds, rather than some otherworldly dream." The concept of utopia, then, can open new avenues of thought and provide the foundation for an architectural practice Martin terms "utopian realism." In his own "cool" maneuver, Martin shies away from precisely defining utopian realism or identifying architects practicing in such an idiom (as "naming them or their work would blow their cover"). Indeed, this lack of prescriptiveness is an essential part of utopian realism, which "recognizes 'reality' itself as... an all-too-real dream enforced by those who prefer to accept a destructive and oppressive status quo." The beauty of utopian realism is the open-ended reconsideration of reality that it affords, allowing architecture to hold a potentially powerful and efficacious position in the socio-political realm.

347

REINHOLD MARTIN

CRITICAL OF WHAT?
TOWARD A
UTOPIAN REALISM

First appeared in *Harvard Design Magazine* 22 (Spring/Summer 2005), 104–9. Courtesy of the author and publisher.

There has long been a tendency in architecture to erect straw figures only to knock them down. In his article "Criticality and its Discontents," published in the Fall 2004/Winter 2005 issue of *Harvard Design Magazine* dedicated to "Realism and Utopianism," George Baird admirably—and, I think, accurately—summarizes recent efforts to do just that.[1] These entail the identification of and subsequent assault on something called "the critical" or "critical architecture," usually accompanied by a collateral assault on something called "theory." At the risk of erecting yet another straw figure that tramples on the subtleties of Baird's analysis, it might be fair to characterize such practices, variously named "post-critical" or "projective," as sharing a commitment to an affect-driven, non-oppositional, nonresistant, nondissenting, and therefore nonutopian, forms of architectural production. But as Baird notes, these efforts have thus far failed to deliver an actual, affirmative project, settling instead for vague adjectives like "easy," "relaxed," and—perish the thought—"cool." Baird therefore concludes his article by asking (with critical overtones?) what they expect to yield in the form of discourse or what he calls "critical assessment." In other words, by what criteria is the "post-critical" asking to be judged, beyond mere acceptance and accommodation of existing societal, economic, or cultural norms?

This question seems worth pursuing but also, perhaps, rephrasing. Since, as with all the other "posts" that preceded it, the "post-critical" (or "relaxed" or "projective") assumes the existence of what it denounces or, in any event, criticizes. Here Baird offers a useful, fair summary of the official history of "critical architecture." To this, however we might append another question: critical of what? Since, it must also be noted that this history actually collapses two opposing positions into one, largely through generational iteration. In the first instance, the "critical" in architecture is assumed to have been defined by a Frankfurt School-style negative dialectics associated with historians and theorists such as Manfredo Tafuri and his American readers, such as Michael Hays. This position usually winds up testifying not to the existence of a critical *architecture*, but to its impossibility, or at most, its irreducible negativity in the face of the insurmountable violence perpetrated by what the economist Ernest Mandel called, some time ago, "late capitalism." Meanwhile—as the story goes—architects like Peter Eisenman have explicitly professed their disinterest in either resisting or affirming such violence at the level of academic and professional practice, preferring instead to dedicate themselves to a vigorous negation and revision of the *internal* assumptions of the discipline, in the form of the so-called autonomy project. Thus Eisenman's provocative turn to Giuseppi Terragni's work for the Italian fascists as a model, under the argument that its formal syntax could be separated definitively from its political semantics. (This example is dutifully replicated—minus the theory—by post-critics such as Michael Speaks, in their championing of jargon and techniques associated with right-wing think tanks and the CIA.) Whereas, the traditional ground on which the two "critical" approaches have met is that of a dialectic, in which aesthetic autonomy acts as a kind of temporary stand-in for the autonomy of the Enlightenment subject pending the arrival of concrete social transformation, or as Theodor Adorno would have it, a negative mirror that reflects that subject's ineluctable demise.

Baird observes that most of the proponents of a "post-critical" position whom he names have passed through academic or professional circles associated with these other older names. But more importantly, we might add, they seem to have accepted rather obediently a central proposition implied by Eisenman's use of the word *critical* with respect to his own work: that the stakes of an internal critique of a supposedly autonomous architecture, and the attendant pursuit of a "new" architecture that continually reinvents its own autonomy are somehow equivalent to—rather than dialectically engaged with—a critique of architecture's tragic, a priori collaboration with the external forces it appears to resist, as elaborated by Tafuri with respect to the modernist avant-gardes. In other words, the assumption hidden in naming Eisenman the father of a "critical architecture" that a subsequent generation now chooses to kill off is that there is somehow an equivalence between a *political* critique (as adumbrated by historians and theorists like Tafuri) and an *aesthetic* critique (as adumbrated by architects like Eisenman).

On the other hand, it is somewhat surprising to find the "paranoid-critical" Rem Koolhaas taken up as a more positive role model by the post-critics, despite the time he may or may not have spent surfing on the late capitalist beach. But either way, whether the name of the father is Peter or Rem, the post-critical project is deeply Oedipal. This is a point worth making less on the grounds of institutional history (however substantial the evidence may be), than on the theoretical philosophical grounds that continue to haunt even the most resolute of anti-theorists. Since a number of those named by Baird, as well as their immediate ideological colleagues, have at one time or another also invoked the name of the philosopher Gilles Deleuze as a comrade in arms—at least before this became too embarrassing, since it was pointed out time and again that in doing so they were distorting the Deleuzian politico-philosophical project so as to render it unrecognizable. And yet, folds and rhizomes aside, one source of such embarrassment persists, in the form of another, "difficult" book that Deleuze co-authored with Félix Guattari—the *Anti-Oedipus* (1972), which is nothing less than a frontal assault—epistemological, philosophical, psychoanalytical, historical, political—on the parochial family trees and "generations" so dear to those who compulsively fetishize "criticality" in order to kill it off for good.

It has been said many times that the *Anti-Oedipus* is a book of the '60s. And, given that Baird explicitly situates the front lines of the "post-critical" debate in the United States, it is worth noting that contemporary American electoral politics—down to the most recent, bloody skirmish in the culture wars—has often been said to amount to a referendum on the countercultural radicalism associated with that decade. So, is it possible that the "post-critical" polemic is, like the more general rightward swing in American politics, actually a rather thinly disguised effort to bury the utopian politics of the 1960s once and for all? In other words, is it possible that all of the relaxed, "post-critical" Oedipality is—in direct opposition to the antiauthoritarian *Anti-Oedipus*—actually an authoritarian call to order that wants once and for all to kill off the ghost of radical politics by converting political critique into aesthetic critique and then slowly draining *even that* of any dialectical force it may have inadvertently retained?

I ask this question with some regret, since it is addressed mainly to those who rush to denounce serious critique (whether political or aesthetic) as an inconvenient obstacle to professional advancement at the very moment that the very possibility of *any* critique of the status quo must be defended more vigorously than ever. But as an architect, I am also well aware of the very real difficulties of actually practicing architecture (and getting paid for it) while voicing even the most mild of objections. Thus the usual response is this: architecture is in any case so thoroughly disempowered, so culturally marginal, as to render any critique emanating from within its walls, so to speak, ineffectual if not entirely irrelevant. What must be sought is a more "robust," more "effective" architecture. This is said to apply in extra measure to academic theory, to say nothing of history, which together are judged to be doubly irrelevant by virtue of their supposed obscurity. So why bother?

But these assertions amount to a category error, since the problem is not that architectural discourse is too academic to have any political relevance, but that it is not academic enough. There is nothing "irrelevant" about the very real politics of the universities that post-critics still depend on for their livelihood, where very real professors are regularly denounced by very real cultural conservatives, often prompting anguished symposia on academic freedom (a relevant political concept if there ever was one) in response. The heroic efforts of the late Edward Said and many other such intellectuals are testimony to the significance of academic practice in the international arena of *realpolitik*. Likewise Jacques Derrida, whose recent passing drew a shameful, defensive "obituary" from the *New York Times* that specifically projected academic discourse onto politics. But perhaps the most telling of such episodes recently was the roundtable of distinguished academics convened in 2003 by the editors of the aptly named journal *Critical Inquiry* to assess the "future of theory." That meeting also drew the attention of the *New York Times*, which concluded that "The Latest Theory is That Theory Doesn't Matter."[2] While for its part, *Critical Inquiry* published the results of all the fractiousness—coming mainly from the political *left*—while concluding editorially that "theory" does matter after all, just not in the way we might have thought.

But perhaps of greater interest to architecture here are two longer articles not directly associated with the conference that appeared in the same issue. The first, by the philosopher of science Bruno Latour, was titled "Why Has Critique Run out of Steam? From Matters of Fact to Matters of Concern."[3] It summarized Latour's recent efforts to replace an epistemology infused by the spirit of revolt and radical politics with a new realism founded on ever-contestable "matters of concern" rather than indisputable "facts." For Latour, "critique" is basically code for Marxism, which, along with other modernisms and their denunciatory tendencies, he is at pains to denounce and replace with a vaguely postmodern version of American pragmatism oriented toward renovating the institutions of parliamentary democracy. Thus, if architecture's self-proclaimed "post-critical" party still resides in the so-called blue states, those of its members still willing to be identified as liberals might find some solace in Latour's method of resolving what used to be called capitalism's "contradictions"—i.e., doing "critical" architecture and still getting paid for it.

For those of firmer constitution, that particular issue of *Critical Inquiry* also offered a text by the theorist Slavoj Žižek, titled "The Ongoing 'Soft Revolution.'"[4] There, Žižek, an unapologetic (if unorthodox) Marxist, conjures the particularly poignant image of "a yuppie reading Deleuze," through which he provocatively claims certain affinities between the apparatus of desire exemplified by advertising and affect-producing Deleuzian "desiring machines." Žižek is well aware of the reductivism of this claim, and he goes on here and elsewhere to give Deleuze and Guattari their full due as philosophers of radical social transformation. Still, the image of a "yuppie reading Deleuze" stays with us, and it is with this image that I want to offer a brief, concrete response to Baird's call for a critical assessment of an avowedly "post-critical" architecture.

Perhaps the most obvious demonstration of contemporary, theoretically informed architecture's all-too-relevant political efficacy has been in the ongoing debate over the future of the former World Trade Center site in lower Manhattan. From the myriad dimensions in which this has unfolded, I want to excerpt one specific example: the proposal designed by the group of "post-critical" fellow travelers (some of whom represent that tendency's European version) that called itself the United Architects.[5]

The story really begins with the exhibition organized in New York by the gallerist Max Protetch titled "A New World Trade Center" that ran from January 17 through February 16, 2002. There, a mere four months after the attacks, the public was presented with fifty-eight proposals by architects, designers, and artists that, according to the gallery, together represented "a landmark opportunity both for architects and the general public to explore the possibilities for the World Trade Center site."[6] On the one hand (and running parallel with the increased swagger of American foreign policy), this was a raw, unvarnished effort to exploit the "landmark opportunity" offered by 9/11's presumptive clearing of the decks—a chance to fulfill a heroic vision (post-Saddam and post-postmodern?) already prepared in think tanks and universities but theretofore preempted by the exigencies of professional realism. While on the other hand, the Protetch exhibition was also the first real evidence of the capacities of a neomodern aesthetics to channel the will to power in directions inaccessible to the more literal conformisms of architecture's corporate, contextualist mainstream.

Symptomatic of things to come on this front was the project submitted by Foreign Office Architects (FOA) for an undulating tower of bundled tubes, accompanied by these remarks: "Let's not even consider remembering...What for? We have a great site in a great city and the opportunity to have the world's tallest building back in New York. Ground Zero used to host 1.3M m² of workspace, and that is a good size to attempt to return to New York what it deserves."[7]

Though it remains unclear what New York "deserves" to forget, it is abundantly clear that such willful amnesia refers not only to a salutary rejection of the often sanctimonious imperatives of memorialization, but also to an active blindness to the historical conditions of which 9/11 was only one component. Hardly disguised, this "end of history" argument for a new historical type—a new type of skyscraper—exploits its own contradictions to monumentalize, in exemplary "post-critical" fashion, the neoliberal consensus regarding new "opportunities" opened up by techno-corporate globalization. Accordingly, the responsibility of professionals in the new world order is confined to facilitating the arrival of the "new," while washing their hands of the overdetermined historical narratives—and the dead bodies—through which this new is named.

Comparable in posture here was the project submitted by Greg Lynn FORM for a prototypical defensible skyscraper insightfully premised on "the collapse of boundaries between global military conflict and everyday life."[8] Rather than dissent, however, the prototype and its author naturalize this state of affairs—which was long ago given the name "total war"—in a collapse of even the most rudimentary critique into an excited monotone. The resulting hymn to total war only makes sense when seen against the backdrop of Lynn's ongoing commitment to the supposed inner, digital logic of the instruments of production and consumption associated with Hollywood's military-entertainment complex, with overtones of the German military aesthete, Ernst Jünger. Thus Lynn asserts, with a lucid cynicism, "The transfer of military thinking into daily life is inevitable."[9]

In September 2002 the United Architects, an international collection of relatively young designers including Lynn and FOA, were among the six teams chosen by the Lower Manhattan Development Corporation (LMDC) to produce what the LMDC called "innovative" designs for the site. In support of their selection, the LMDC press release referred to the team as "visionaries" in possession of an expertise in, among other things, "theory," an official characterization that uncannily reproduces Žižek's hilarious image of a "yuppie reading Deleuze."

Also included in the team of young professionals that called itself the United Architects was the Hollywood-based entertainment, design, and marketing firm Imaginary Forces. And indeed, at Ground Zero the public relations message emanating from the team began with their name, which resourcefully morphed the United States into the United Nations, a hybrid that itself dissolved into a transnational becoming-Benetton in the team's group portrait—assembled multiracial faces in a field of colored squares. In support of the implied theme of resolute unity-within-diversity (in the face of a "faceless" enemy?), the project statement offered rhetoric about solemnly moving forward, while images of the scheme proclaimed the result—the crystalline "United Towers"—a "bold vision of the future" dedicated to "returning pride to the site."[10]

And the Deleuzianism? Difference within continuity: a "single continuous building" that differentiated itself into five linked towers built in five phases. A monument to corporate "diversity," the project internalized the naturalized growth fantasies of global capitalism in the form of a relentless, evolutionary development of the site. Affective, nationalist unity ("pride") was shown not to preclude "difference"—a basic premise of the kinder, gentler imperialism recently ratified by the American electorate. An architectural avant-garde thus switches sides in the ongoing culture wars that brought (critical, post-structuralist) "theory" into the discipline with a vengeance in the 1980s. Since by responding obediently to the call for architectural "vision" while remaining utterly blind to the violence of the package they served up, these architects and others put themselves in a position of docile compliance with the imperatives of a nation at war.

Likewise for the proposal's symbolism, which in many ways crossed nationalism with theological pathos more systematically than did Daniel Libeskind's expressionist winning entry. It required only a little "imaginary force" to see the corporate, crypto-Gothic "cathedral" (their term) designed by United Architects as a baldly symbolic response to an act associated with militant Islam. The skyscraper—Cass Gilbert's "cathedral of commerce"—meets Philip Johnson's Crystal Cathedral. But by melting such ruthlessly "meaningful" religious symbolisms into a dynamic series of visual effects that had the buildings dissolving into a majestic forest in an accompanying video while simultaneously allowing the more unconscious impression of a family of skyscrapers holding hands in the absence of the missing "twins," the project also set in motion a fluid dynamics comparable to that which organized subsequent militarization, as American political fantasies morphed Osama into Saddam. In the architecture of becoming that mixed spirituality with marketing offered up by the United Architects, the particular, violent irony of the United States claiming to act morally on behalf of the United Nations (to *become*, in effect, the United Nations) in invading Iraq was prefigured, affectively and aesthetically.

Though their project was apparently not his favorite, then-*New York Times* architecture critic Herbert Muschamp proposed renaming the United Architects (using rhetoric reminiscent of Dave Hickey, a favorite "post-critical" aesthetic theorist) "The International House of Voluptuous Beauty" in recognition of their apparent efforts to realize "form for form's sake,"[11] while elsewhere in the *Times*, theologian and erstwhile architecture theorist Mark C. Taylor was enlisted into the cause. Surprisingly, Taylor complied by offering the extraordinary exhortation to avoid "becoming obsessed with a past we will never understand" and instead turn optimistically toward the future. Though aimed primarily at the memory industry, such collateral (if unintentional) dismissals of any effort to *articulate* the historical dimensions of 9/11 as so much backward-looking nostalgia continued to confuse images of "progress" with positive historical change and mystification with critical reflection. Chillingly, as if to underline the elision, Taylor approvingly concluded his summary with the message he heard coming from the United Architects: "*e pluribus unum.*"[12] Again, what looks progressive fades into its opposite.

The subsequent chapters in the story are well known, down to the made-for-television struggle between Libeskind and David Childs for control of the project's architectural image that Childs eventually won. Like the distorted smatterings of "theory" in the discourse of those who would eventually become the United Architects, it is possible that Libeskind's emotionalism simply became redundant, as images of "progressive" architecture—including Libeskind's—circulating in the winter of 2002–2003 were replaced on American television screens that spring with images of the "shock and awe" bombing campaign in Baghdad. Total war had been waged in the aesthetic training camp called Ground Zero, only to be projected back outward, in near-perfect symmetry.

This, then, was not merely a sordid rerun of what Walter Benjamin once famously called the aestheticization of politics. It was aesthetics *as* politics. By enthusiastically accepting the protocols of cultural (and architectural) "progress" for its own sake, "post-critical" architects showed themselves all too willing to assist politically in the prosecution of a virtual war that was soon to go live. While even today, many prefer to misrecognize the demand for "vision" as an "opportunity" that was later betrayed by the back room deals of developers and politicians, rather than the overexposed intensification of neoimperial desires that it represented from the beginning. Thus, the global city prepared itself to market an image of supposedly enlightened rationality symbolized in a "visionary" architecture. The dilemma, simply put, was that this gesture was made *in the service of* an emboldened sense of empire and war on all fronts, and not against it.

To be sure, for more sober practitioners of the "post-critical," the liberal-humanist idea of the "project" supplants theological vision as a guide. Hence, architecture and/or architects who are merely critical (or "merely" antiwar?) are judged to have insufficiently fulfilled the old, modernist mission of being "projective" and of thereby affirming an enlightened alternative. But just as we can justifiably ask of the straw figure called critical architecture, "critical of what?" we might ask the affirmative, projective practitioners of the "post-critical" just what sort of world they are projecting and affirming in their architecture and in their discourse?

If the answer is anything close to that offered by the United Architects, then I vote "No"—despite its many legitimate claims to an authentic, technologically enabled urbanity.[13] Still, those who lament the relentless negativity of much critique (such as, perhaps, that offered above) are at least partly right, since, the problem is not that critical discourse is too difficult and therefore ineffectual. The problem is that it is often too easy. Bruised by the complicities of what Tafuri called "operative criticism," much critical work does not risk intervening in the future in the systematic manner for which, I think, many architects rightly yearn. Similarly, the need to engage directly with messy realities called for by some post-critics is indeed urgent. The question is which realities you choose to engage with, and to what end. In other words: what's your project? This also means avoiding the elementary mistake of assuming that reality is entirely real—that is pre-existent, fixed, and therefore exempt from critical re-imagination. For this, alliances are necessary.

So, what is to be done? To begin with, rather than lapse into the post-utopian pragmatism of that grandfather of the "post-critical," Colin Rowe, the question of utopia must be put back on the architectural table. But it must not be misread as a call for a perfect world, a world apart, an impossible totality that inevitably fades into totalitarianism. Instead, utopia must be read literally, as the "non-place" written into its etymological origins that is "nowhere" not because it is ideal and inaccessible, but because, in perfect mirrored symmetry, it is also "everywhere." Utopia is both glamorous and boring, exceptional and prosaic. Among its heralds is another, earlier denizen of lower Manhattan, Herman Melville's Bartleby the Scrivener, an anonymous, modest clerk who, when asked literally to reproduce what the '60s would later call "the system," simply and politely refused, declaring "I would prefer not to."

Utopia, then, is what Derrida called a "specter," a ghost that infuses everyday reality with other, possible worlds, rather than some otherworldly dream. And if another name for the so-called post-critical is "realism," we have already seen at Ground Zero how architecture's realist fantasies of twisting, dancing skyscrapers have worked systematically to exorcise utopia's ghost with crystal cathedrals dedicated to a fundamentalist oligarchy. But like all ghosts, that specter is never quite dead, returning to haunt architectural projects already quietly among us and others coming soon. We can call these projects the first evidence of a "utopian realism" (details to follow). Meanwhile, utopian realism must be thought of as a movement that may or may not exist, all of whose practitioners are double agents. Naming them, or their work, would blow their cover. (They may or may not all be architects.) Those who could voted for Kerry. (So you, too, could be a utopian realist.) Utopian realism is critical. It is real. It is enchantingly secular. It thinks differently. It is a style with no form. It moves sideways, instead of up and down the family tree. It is (other) worldly. It occupies the global city rather than the global village. It violates disciplinary codes even as it secures them. It is utopian not because it dreams impossible dreams, but because it recognizes "reality" itself as—precisely—an all-too-real dream enforced by those who prefer to accept a destructive and oppressive status quo. Utopia's ghost floats within this dream, conjured time and again by those who would prefer not to.

Notes

1   George Baird, "'Criticality' and its Discontents," *Harvard Design Magazine* 21 (Fall 2004/Winter 2005): 16–21.

2   Emily Eakin, "The Latest Theory is that Theory Doesn't Matter," *New York Times*, D9, April 19, 2003.

3   Bruno Latour, "Why Has Critique Run out of Steam? From Matters of Fact to Matters of Concern," *Critical Inquiry* (Winter 2004): 225–48.

4   Slavoj Žižek, "The Ongoing 'Soft Revolution,'" *Critical Inquiry* (Winter 2004): 292–323.

5   For a more detailed analysis of the architectural discourse surrounding the World Trade Center projects, see Reinhold Martin, "Architecture at War: A Report from Ground Zero," in *Angelaki* (August 2004): 217–25. My account here of the United Architects project is adapted from that article.

6   Max Protetch, "A New World Trade Center: Exhibition Overview,"
    www.maxprotetch.com/site/previous/andewwtc/foa.index.html.

7   Foreign Office Architects, "A New World Trade Center: Foreign Office
    Architects Bunch Tower," www.maxprotetch.com/site/previous/
    andewwtc/foa .index.html.

8   Greg Lynn FORM, "A New World Trade Center: Greg Lynn FORM,
    A New World Trade Center," www.maxprotetch.com/site/previous/
    andewwtc/foa .index.html.

9   Ibid.

10 Lower Manhattan Development Corporation, "Introduction," www
    .renewnyc.com/plan_des_dev/wtc_site/new_design_plans/firm_f/
    default.asp.htm.

11 Herbert Muschamp, "The Latest Round of Designs Rediscover and
    Celebrate Vertical Life," *New York Times*, B10, December 19, 2002.

12 Mark C. Taylor, "Beyond Mourning, Building Hope on Ground Zero,"
    New York Times, December 29, 2002.

13 It must be noted that two other projects in the LMDC study, associated
    with other figures in the current debate over criticality, played out
    somewhat more convincing endgames: the mute, negative symbol
    of architecture-as-such (a grid turning a corner) produced by Peter
    Eisenman, Charles Gwathmey, Steven Holl, and Richard Meier; and
    the equally mute field of leaning towers (Hilberseimer with a twist?)
    produced by Stan Allen and James Corner in collaboration with
    Skidmore, Owings & Merrill and others. Neither project, however,
    offered a systematic alternative to the politically charged demand for
    symbolism in which the LMDC study was framed.

INTRODUCTION
Technology, Place, and Nonmodern Regionalism/
Steven A. Moore

Contemporary discussions of regionalism in architecture trace
back to the writings of figures such as Lewis Mumford and
Harwell Hamilton Harris in the mid-twentieth century.[1] The
phrase "critical regionalism," first introduced by Liane Lefaivre
and Alexander Tzonis in 1981, achieved widespread attention
through the writings of Kenneth Frampton, who co-opted the
term and discussed his concept of Critical Regionalism in many
essays, including "Towards a Critical Regionalism: Six Points for
an Architecture of Resistance" (1983).[2] In this article Frampton
addresses the perceived opposition between culture and civilization, as well as the universalizing tendencies of the latter to
override the former. In his view, negative characteristics such as
the scenographic and the visual have come to dominate positive
aspects such as the tectonic and tactile. As examples of design
addressing specific place and the preservation of local culture,
Frampton offers the work of architects such as Alvar Aalto,
Alvaro Siza, and Tadao Ando. In another essay, "Ten Points on
an Architecture of Regionalism: A Provisional Polemic," Frampton
concludes by positing this version of regionalism as "a critical
basis from which to evolve a contemporary architecture of resistance—that is, a culture of dissent free from fashionable stylistic
conventions, an architecture of place rather than space, and a
way of building sensitive to the vicissitudes of time and climate.
Above all, it is a concept of the environment where the body as
a whole is seen as being essential to the manner in which it is
experienced."[3]

As Canizaro notes, while Critical Regionalism "is the most
recent" theory of regionalism, "it is by no means alone."[4]
Indeed, Canizaro's anthology includes a series of essays that

363

offer renewed notions of regionalism for the twenty-first century. "Technology, Place, and Nonmodern Regionalism" is such an essay. Authored by Steven A. Moore—an architect, an educator, and the codirector of the Center for Sustainable Development at the University of Texas at Austin—this article questions the aesthetic emphasis of Frampton's Critical Regionalism, and building on the thought of cultural theorists such as Bruno Latour and Henri Lefebvre, portrays architecture as a political practice. In his own eight points ("generalizations stated as practice-based *attitudes*, not as deductive propositions"), Moore offers a manifesto for a "regenerative regionalism" as a framework for future architectural thought.

Notes

1   For more on regionalism, see Vincent B. Canizaro, ed., *Architectural Regionalism: Collected Writings on Place, Identity, Modernity, and Tradition* (New York: Princeton Architectural Press, 2007). For a historical sketch of regionalism beginning with the ancient Greeks, and then a discussion of critical regionalism since the mid-twentieth century, see respectively Alexander Tzonis, "Introducing an Architecture of the Present: Critical Regionalism and the Design of Identity," 8–21, and Liane Lefaivre, "Critical Regionalism: A Facet of Modern Architecture since 1945," 22–55, both in *Critical Regionalism: Architecture and Identity in a Globalized World*, ed. Liane Lefaivre and Alexander Tzonis (New York: Prestel, 2003).

2   Kenneth Frampton, "Towards a Critical Regionalism: Six Points for an Architecture of Resistance," in *The Anti-Aesthetic: Essays on Postmodern Culture*, ed. Hal Foster (Port Townsend, Wash.: Bay Press, 1983), 16–30.

3   Kenneth Frampton, "Ten Points on an Architecture of Regionalism: A Provisional Polemic," *Cente 3: New Regionalism* (1987), 20–27. Reprinted in Canizaro, ed., *Architectural Regionalism*, 385.

4   Vincent B. Canizaro, "Preface: The Promise of Regionalism," in Canizaro, ed., *Architectural Regionalism*, 10.

STEVEN A. MOORE

TECHNOLOGY, PLACE, AND NONMODERN REGIONALISM

First appeared in *Architectural Regionalism: Collected Writings on Place, Identity, Modernity, and Tradition*, ed. Vincent B. Canizaro (New York: Princeton Architectural Press, 2007), 432–42.

In the 1980s and early 1990s, the topic of regionalism enjoyed considerable attention within architectural discourse. The prospect of a progressive, or *critical* regionalism seemed an antidote to both the regressive fantasies of postmodern historicism and the various proposals for a deconstructivist architecture inspired by European linguistic theory. Since the mid-1990s, however, the regionalist moment has waned. The progenitors of the discourse, Kenneth Frampton, Alexander Tzonis, and Liane Lefaivre, have moved on to other topics, and the projects of those architects who embodied the critical regionalist attitude have been re-framed by other discourses.

This is a natural, if not satisfying, development. In the maturation of any discourse, some possibilities are suppressed just as others are amplified by the exigencies of the situation. The purpose of this article, then, is to reconstruct possibilities that reflect our current situation. To do so I argue that *technology* and *place* should be understood as the suppressed core concepts that are contained within regionalist architectural production. These are central to our understanding of what a "region" might be, and their interrogation is an opportunity to reconsider the history of regionalism as a concept.

Place & Region

The geographer John Agnew has argued that, in modernist thought, the traditional concept of place is devalued for two reasons: first, modern social science has confused, or conflated, the distinction between "place" and "community." "Community" in the modern view, argues Agnew, has been assumed to be both "a physical setting for social relations" and "a morally valued way of life."[1] Because of this modern logic, place has been erroneously equated with the concepts of morality. Modernist logic, in Agnew's analysis, fails to understand society as a dynamic process that transforms places and regions. As a result, moderns have tended to reify moral concepts as places so that their characterization of big cities as dens of iniquity and small towns as the vessels of morality is clearly ideological, not empirical.[2]

Second, beginning in the nineteenth century—a period that witnessed the dramatic evaporation of traditional communities—social scientists attempted to predict the trajectory of history. Common to all of these a priori predictions was the polarity of "community" and "society." Writers as dissimilar as Herbert Spencer and Karl Marx saw community as being coercive and intellectually limiting, or even idiotic, whereas national societies were characterized as liberative.[3] Conservatives, such as Auguste Comte, saw the loss of traditional village forms as the loss of the ideal social type. In contrast, the politics of nation building and the liberative project of Enlightenment became an ideology of "antitraditionalism." To free humans from feudal bonds to the land, and the hierarchical relations inscribed there, was understood by moderns to be the grand scheme (or teleology) of history. The German sociologist Max Weber popularized this historical tension as the transformation of *gemeinschaft* into *gesellschaft*.[4]

This logic suggests that the modern reification of moral codes and the teleology of history conspired to devalue place as a concept relevant to the conditions of contemporary life. "'Becoming modern' involves casting off ties to place (in work, recreation, and sense of identity) and adopting an 'achievement oriented' or 'class conscious' self that is placeless."[5] Agnew argues, in concert with the postmodern geographer Edward Soja, that the devaluation of place was most vigorously promoted by Marxist ideology.[6] For traditional Marxists to consider social behavior as determined in any way by the conditions of place would have been to subvert the dialectic order of causality. Marxist logic has traditionally held that material order arises from a dialectic relationship with social activity. But if Marxists devalued the concept of place on ideological grounds, there is considerable irony in the recognition that it has been market forces that have most effectively devalued real places.[7]

In the eyes of the Left, the doctrine of environmental determinism (which opposes a dialectic understanding of place by holding that societies owe their unique character to the conditions of their territory) amounts to nothing less than racism and the fetishization of place.[8] We will return to this logic shortly.

In a renovation of this Marxist position, Agnew argues that places cannot be understood within the limited dimensions of architecture or physical geography.[9] Rather, Agnew argues that the variables that characterize places are multivalent. He offers three elements, or scales, by which we might understand the phenomenon of place: location, sense of place, and locale.[10]

By "location," Agnew intends that a place can be understood as a geographic area encompassed by the objective structures of politics and economy. In this sense, places are linked together, for example, by the interests of the European Union or the Monroe Doctrine. Using the same logic, one might argue that Houston is closer to the cities of Aberdeen, Scotland, and Stravanger, Norway, than to Austin, Texas, because the same corporate structures manage the oil fields of the North Sea and Texas. It is these structural conditions of political economy at the macro-scale that most concern Marxist scholars.

At the other end of the spectrum Agnew argues for the existence of a "sense of place." By this term he means the local "structure of feeling" that pervades being in a particular place. This dimension of place includes the inter-subjective realities that give a place what conventional language would describe as "character" or "quality of life." For example, the reverence that the citizens of Austin reserve for a swim in Barton Springs and that New Yorkers reserve for food, fashion, and style are ontological, rather than objective, dimensions of place. It is at this scale that the complex human poetics of place are experienced. It is the inter-subjective construction of conditions experienced as a sense of place that most concern constructivist scholars and phenomenologists.

Between objective location and the subjective sense of place, Agnew establishes a middle ground, or "locale." This quality of place is the setting in which social relations are constituted. Locale includes the institutional scale of living to which architecture contributes so much: the city, the public square, the block, and the neighborhood. By considering the concept of place, or region, from this meso-scale we avoid two problems. First, we can appreciate the insights of Marxists but avoid the over-determination that results from their preoccupation with the seemingly objective conditions of political economy. Second, we can appreciate the insights of constructivists and phenomenologists but avoid the under-determination that results from their preoccupation with the subjective conditions of atomized reality.[11] It is the "elastic" scale of all three dimensions, viewed from the meso-scale of the city-state, that best describes a place. By understanding the concept of place as a dynamic process that links humans and nonhumans in space at a variety of scales, we might get beyond the opposition between those who see it as a set of objective structures and those who see it as a set of romantic myths tied to subjective experience.

Technology and Society

Just as place is typically thought of as primarily physical in quality, technology is commonly understood to be physical hardware—radios, refrigerators, or computers. This materialist definition discounts the social construction of such objects and assumes these "objects" are constructed based solely on technical measures.[12] Similarly, in the positivist tradition, technology is understood as the asocial application of scientific truths. In the philosophical tradition of Heidegger, technology is understood as an ontological practice, meaning that it comes to define who and how we are. In contrast to both of these traditions, the literature of science and technology studies has demonstrated that technology is a social system that is inextricably part of society.[13] Technology, like place, is a field where the struggle between competing interests plays out.

The sociologists Donald MacKenzie and Judith Wajcman have argued that technology, like place, includes three qualities: "human knowledge," "patterns of human activities," and "sets of physical objects."[14] I find it helpful to examine technology as a process of social construction. Knowledge is required not only to build the artifact, but to relate the natural conditions upon which the artifact works and to use it. The second quality, "patterns of human activity," or human practices, refers to the institutionalization, or routinization, of societal problem solving. In the practices of architecture, carpentry, or masonry are examples of these "routines." Lastly, "sets of objects" takes us back to the things themselves. The point is that computers, hammers, or tractors are useless without the human knowledge and practices that engage them.

What I want to argue here is that the definition of place offered by Agnew and the definition of technology offered by MacKenzie and Wajcman are similar to that shown in Figure 1. From it I propose three related ideas: first, that places and technologies are both spatial concepts with related structures; second, that these qualities are dialogically related; and third, that modern forms of knowledge, like the economics of location, tend toward the abstract and over-determined (meaning that the outcome of events is strongly tied to structural conditions), while our understanding of objects and sense of place tends toward the under-determined (meaning that the outcome of events is weakly tied to structural conditions). These points serve only to magnify the centrality of locale and act as the glue that holds the discourse of places and technologies together.

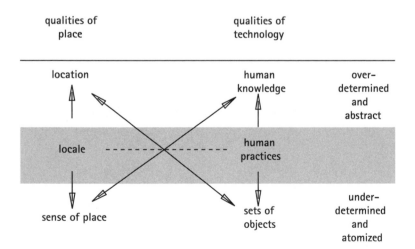

Fig. 1

To argue that place is a spatial concept is a tautology and requires no further backing. However, to argue that technology is a spatial concept requires some explanation. Bruno Latour's term *technological network* is helpful in this regard. Latour has argued that "technological networks, as the name indicates, are nets thrown over spaces."[15] By "technological network," Latour refers not just to "sets of objects," but to the social networks that construct relationships between human knowledge, human practices, and nonhuman resources—the latter being the stuff—steel, wood, water, etc.—from which the objects themselves are made. His point is that technology is essentially a spatial concept because its operation depends upon the mobilization of human and nonhuman resources that exist in different places.[16] For example, architects, clients, contractors, and bankers make up a social network of building producers. Their relationship has a social and spatial quality to it. Advances in communications technology, many now argue, have radically collapsed the spatial reality of these social relations. When one recognizes, however, that lumber from Oregon, windows from Pittsburgh, carpet from Mobile, and compressors from Taiwan are required to realize the material intentions of the producers, the concrete qualities of their purely social network are materialized as a global technological network. A technological network produces spatial links that tie the social network of producers to those nonhuman resources required for construction. This is a central argument of this study that has important implications for how we understand an architecture of place in a contemporary context.

My argument is that technology is best understood not through history, but through geography. History interprets reality as human events in time. Through temporal interpretation we might better understand the causal sequence in which humans construct artifacts. In contrast, geography interprets reality as human events in space. Through spatial interpretation we are more likely to understand how technological networks dominate the places inhabited by humans and nonhumans.

Henri Lefebvre has argued two points that reinforce this dynamic relationship between technology and place. First, that social spaces are produced by technology acting upon nature.[17] Lefebvre's second point is that each society—or each mode of production—makes its own peculiar type of space.[18] What architects might extract from Lefebvre's logic is that the differing qualities of places are more a matter of technological practices than aesthetic choices because such practices are always already spatial. For example, carpentry requires not only forests and citizens in need of housing, but also the spatial mechanisms that link them. This is the heart of what I will characterize as the *dialogic* relation of technology and place.[19]

The Nonmodern Thesis

In reconsidering Frampton's critical regionalism hypothesis, it is necessary to examine the unresolvable conflict between his mix of modernism, as it is embodied in the doctrines of critical theory, and postmodernism, as it is embodied in the place-bound doctrines of Martin Heidegger. The simplest way to illustrate this conflict is demonstrated in Figure 2. Here I have plotted the way that modernism and postmodernism value the concepts of place and technology.[20]

The point of the diagram is to argue, as did Agnew, that moderns have generally held a negative attitude toward place because the social hierarchies inscribed there restrict human liberty. Conversely, moderns have held a positive attitude toward technology because machines, science claims, will free us from the drudgery of place-bound tyrannies.

The flip side of the diagram in Figure 2 is to recognize that postmoderns, far from constructing a new worldview,

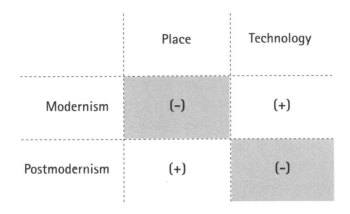

	Place	Technology
Modernism	(–)	(+)
Postmodernism	(+)	(–)

Fig. 2

have merely inverted the relationships constructed by modern thought. Where postmoderns desire to recuperate the propinquity of place and value it positively, they have become ever-more skeptical of modern technologies and the unintended consequences that have followed in their wake. The malignant promises of atomic power and industrial agriculture are salient examples of the fears nurtured by postmoderns like Heidegger or the American poet-farmer Wendell Berry. Another way to argue this point is to claim that conservative postmoderns, at least in their attitude toward place and technology, are only *anti*-moderns. In the world of architecture, a figure like Leon Krier exemplifies this position—his drawings value the premodern city as the place that embodies ideal civic relations, but he employs technology only as a scenographic, or instrumental, tool to realize those social relations.

The problem, or the opportunity, found in Frampton's critical regionalism hypothesis, then, is that it relies upon assumptions drawn from opposing philosophical traditions.

Critical regionalism proposes to value both technological means and the propinquity of place as positive forces in history, an admirable goal. By relying alternately upon the opposing assumptions of critical theory, which are modern, and those of Martin Heidegger, which are postmodern, critical regionalism leads to philosophical confusion.[21]

I argue that the doctrines of critical regionalism are better served by non-modern assumptions, as Figure 3 demonstrates. Bruno Latour has used the term "nonmodern" to argue that we have, in practice, never been modern at all.[22] If being modern means the isolation of subjects from objects, and the isolation of humans from nonhumans, then I agree with Latour that we have been modern in *theory*, but never in *practice*. It is a condition like pregnancy—one is never "sort of" modern. In this sense, modernity has been a convenient license to plunder nature, not an anthropological fact.

The nonmodern thesis proposes to erode the Cartesian distinctions between humans and nonhumans. In the nonmodern

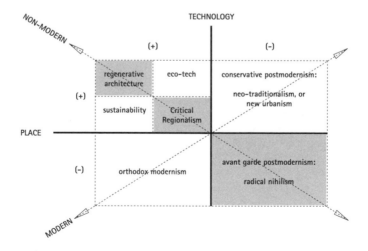

Fig. 3

view, we are no longer subjects empowered to contemplate and order up resources from afar. When we examine how the world really works we are compelled to recognize that we—riders and horses, politicians and voters, bricklayers and bricks—are "quasi-subjects" and "quasi-objects."[23] These terms suggest that what distinguishes a subject from an object at any given moment in time is only a temporary advantage in power relations. At one moment we are in control, and at the next moment we find ourselves being ordered about by the digital logic of machines that determine our health-care benefits or which telephone company will bill us each month. My point here is that in a nonmodern world, humans and nonhumans have more in common than they don't. In such a world, places show up as place-making is practiced. In other words, it is hard to distinguish between the qualities of a place and the technologies employed to make them.

This nonmodern logic further suggests that there is no effective distance between culture and nature. If there ever was such a thing as primeval nature—nature untouched by human invention—it has long ago disappeared. Far from lamenting the lost garden of human origins, nonmoderns see not ruination but increasing opportunities in which human institutions can creatively participate in the cycles of natural systems. Participation in nature just might produce life-enhancing conditions that will benefit all us quasi-objects.

Just as critical regionalism constructs a positive nonmodern synthesis, a negative nonmodern synthesis resolves the modern dilemma equally well—at least from a purely rhetorical point of view. The position that I label as "radical nihilism" in Figure 3 is, I think, best exemplified by the projects of Rem Koolhaas and the Office for Metropolitan Architecture. Koolhaas and those who see the world through similar lenses are simply disinterested in the project of regionalism.

Koolhaas's projects and those related to "sustainability" and "eco-tech" are well documented elsewhere, so I won't dwell on them here. [24]

"Regenerative architecture," however, describes the heart of the nonmodern thesis. This term is borrowed from the landscape architect John Tillman Lyle. I propose substituting it for Frampton's "critical" because "critical" must always refer back to the modern dialectic assumptions embraced by "critical theory." Just as Jameson would renovate critical regionalism as a postmodern doctrine, I propose renovating it as a nonmodern doctrine. [25] The philosophical trajectory of critical regionalism is best understood not in its modernist origins, nor in postmodern Marxism, but within a nonmodern, dialogic future.

Lyle defines a "regenerative system" as one that "provides for the continuous replacement, through its own functional processes, of the energy and materials used in its operation." [26] In this definition, the notion that technology might provide such continuous replacement does not mean that architecture might overcome the second law of thermodynamics, and thus escape the concept of entropy. While it is not possible for any technological system to reconstitute all of the energy consumed in its own creation, architecture—or "place-forms," as Frampton would have it—can certainly participate far more effectively in the natural energy flows of a place than current technological practices do. It is through such participation that entropy might be radically reduced.

Lyle offers the concept of "regeneration" as an alternative to the now-common term "sustainable" because, in his view, to simply sustain current entropic conditions is inadequate. I agree; to merely maintain the status quo of material systems is a necessary, but insufficient, strategy to achieve life-enhancing conditions. It is equally necessary to recognize, as does Latour, that all material systems are technological networks in the sense previously defined. In other words, they are politically constituted. This political recognition requires that we reject the status quo of social systems as equally entropic. It is simply a passive form of positivism (traditional science by another name) to imagine that ecologists can repair the ecosystem in isolation from political processes. Lyle's definition of a regenerative system, then, is flawed because it ignores the social and political constitution of an ecosystem.

Rather than attempt a comprehensive redefinition of what a regenerative architecture might be in this short essay, I'll simply add the following to Lyle's definition: A regenerative architecture will seek to engage human institutions in the democratic reproduction of life-enhancing places. While not yet adequate it does point toward a cultural horizon where the dialogic relationship between technologies and places can be better understood.

Having defined place and technology as the core concepts upon which regionalist architecture depends, I conclude by summarizing this discussion in three propositions followed by eight summary points that are meant to serve as a renovation of Frampton's critical regionalism hypothesis:

First, it is politically desirable and ecologically prudent to reproduce regionalism as a practice relevant to contemporary conditions. Regenerative or sustainable architecture provides a framework through which we might reconstruct and extend that discourse.

Second, to do so we must understand the historic uses and abuses of regionalism, with particular attention paid to the geography of power relations. It is both possible and desirable to make places that relate human institutions to the natural cycles of a region without resorting to appeals that authenticate, and thus legitimize, the authority of entrenched social networks. Rather, a regenerative regional architecture might consciously, and democratically, construct places that relate humans and nonhumans in life-enhancing and ever-changing practices.

Third, although critical regionalism offers a positive direction for architectural practice, its own assumptions are philosophically conflicted and require renovation as a nonmodern polemic for architectural production. The articulation of regenerative regional architecture is a first attempt to meet this challenge.

Toward that end, I must agree with Fredric Jameson that Frampton's discussion of projects by Mario Botta, Jørn Utzon, Alvaro Siza Vieria, or Glenn Murcutt is largely aesthetic in character. To expand this too-narrow interpretation I have engaged two additional issues—the political and the ecological—that are, I believe, essential characteristics of any architecture that aspires to be regenerative. The demand for an overtly political program comes not only from Jameson, but also from the advocates of social ecology. These observers require that architecture be understood not in the aesthetic terms of high culture, but in the social and material context of everyday life. The demand that regenerative architecture engage the ecology of places comes from the ecologists. These observers require that architecture be understood as the transformation of nature. The limits of a purely aesthetic discourse, critical though it may be, are that it remains outside the social and biological conditions that describe normative practices.

As I have implied throughout this essay, the nonmodern dialogic requires that the discipline of architecture be reconstituted as a political, rather than an aesthetic, practice. Through this reconstitution the canon of architecture would be reconceived as not a set of heroic objects, but as the material narrative. This proposal suggests that architects would no longer design "things" per se. Rather, we would design the political processes embodied in technological and topological choices.

The points that follow are generalizations stated as practice-based *attitudes*, not as deductive propositions.

Eight Points for Regenerative Regionalism: A Nonmodern Manifesto

1) *A regenerative architecture will construct social settings that can be lived differently.* This point rejects the notion that technology in itself might be an autonomous agent capable of liberating humans from the oppressive natural and/or social conditions of place. Rather, it suggests that human institutions are both affected by and, in turn, affect the social construction of technological networks. Humans might, then, rationally and democratically construct regenerative technologies as the engaged agents of the humans and nonhumans that collectively inhabit a place.

2) *So as to participate in local constellations of ideas, a regenerative architecture will participate in the tectonic history of a place.* Participation in the tectonic history of a place requires that the interventions of architects be, first, intelligible to local citizens and, second, perceived as relevant to the material conditions of everyday life.

3) *Rather than construct objects, the producers of regenerative architecture will participate in the construction of integrated cultural and ecological processes.* Historically, architects have tended to claim sole authorship for places and thus obscure the complex social and ecological processes in which buildings participate. A regenerative architecture will de-emphasize the significance of objects and emphasize the construction of processes that relate social activity to ecological conditions.

4) *A regenerative architecture will resist the centers of calculation by magnifying local labor and ecological variables.* The overt political program of regenerative architecture will include two

STEVEN A. MOORE · 379

principal strategies. First, the producers of regenerative architecture will consciously subvert the universalizing and optimizing measures of objective building performance. These are typically promoted by such technological networks as the air-conditioning industry and measured in BTUs, calories, and watts. This strategy should not be construed to mean that human comfort is to be devalued or energy squandered. Second, regenerative architecture will rely upon technologies that reveal the manner of their making to magnify local labor knowledge and local ecological conditions.

5) *Rather than participate in the aestheticized politics implicit in technological displays, regenerative architecture will construct the technologies of everyday life through democratic means.* The market has increasingly manipulated architectural technology in order to stimulate those consumers whose appetites have become dulled by the ever-increasing rates of production and consumption. A regenerative architecture will subvert the power of market-driven technologies by engaging citizens in decision making about the technologies that enable everyday life.

6) *The technological interventions of regenerative architecture will contribute to the normalization of critical practices.* Rather than construct critical objects that inform viewers of how history might have been different, regenerative architecture will strive to influence normative construction practices. This proposition recognizes that the ontological dimension of building takes precedence over the representational—that the repetitive material practices of construction do more to influence the operation of society than do singular aesthetic critiques. In this sense, the reproduction of life-enhancing practices is preferred over aesthetic commentary.

7) *The practice of regenerative architecture will enable places by fostering convergent human agreements.* A durable architecture need only delay the inevitability of decay. A *sustainable*

architecture need only maintain the status quo of natural carry-ing capacity. A *regenerative* architecture, however, must concern itself with the reproduction of the institutional agreements that tie humans to the ecological conditions of a place. This suggests that architecture itself must facilitate democratic consideration of the tidal cycle, of prevailing breezes, or of the coolth of the earth itself. This is a matter of democracy and technological development.

8) *A regenerative architecture will prefer the development of life-enhancing practices to the creation of critical and historically instructive places.* The *critical place* helps society to understand that the social construction of places and technologies might have been different. Such a place is a memorial to the forgotten or as yet untried modes of non-capitalist production that would transform nature in some other way. My final point is that criti-cal places are not in themselves productive. Better yet, a critical place can become regenerative only through the production and reproduction of democratic, life-enhancing practices.

Notes

1   John Agnew, *Place and Politics* (Boston: Allen & Unwin, 1987), 62.
    Agnew also discusses the theme of the historic devaluation of place in
    "Representing Space: Space, Scale and Culture in Social Science," in
    Place/Culture/Representation, ed. James Duncan and David Ley (New
    York: Routledge, 1993), 251–71. Agnew interrogates the concept of
    place. I use the terms "place" and "region" interchangeably in this
    text; although they do not mean the same thing, for the purpose of this
    discussion I conflate them.

2   For example, crime statistics reveal that the murder rate in New
    York City is dramatically lower than that of rural Arkansas. See Fox
    Butterfield, "Nationwide Drop in Murders is Reaching to Small
    Towns," *New York Times*, May 9, 2000.

3   Karl Marx, *The Manifesto of the Communist Party*, trans. Samuel Moore
    (London, 1848), 36.

4   Although Max Weber is commonly credited with coining these terms,
    Ferdinand Tonnies actually first used them, in 1887. See Ferdinand
    Tonnies, *Community and Society* (New York: Harper & Row, 1963).

5   Agnew, *Place and Politics*, 231.

6   Soja's position is associated with the tradition of critical theory,
    however his intention is revisionist. See Edward Soja, *Postmodern
    Geographies: The Reassertion of Space in Critical Social Theory* (London:
    Verso, 1989), 120.

7   I am indebted to my colleague Stephen Ross for this insight.

8   Anna Bramwell, for example, has argued that German anti-Semitism
    arises from the multiple doctrines of environmental determinism.
    To generalize that all Germans share a genius that originates in the
    forest and that wandering Jews share a rootlessness that originates
    in the desert is a classic example of determinist, reductivist logic. See
    Anna Bramwell, *Blood and Soil: Richard Walter Darre and Hitler's Green
    Party* (Abbotsbrook, U.K.: Kensal House, 1985). See also Jeffery Herf,
    *Reactionary Modernism: Technology, Culture and Politics in Weimar and
    the Third Reich* (Cambridge, U.K.: Cambridge University Press, 1984).

9   Agnew's concern is apparently that those of us who are most
    concerned with the physical world—architects and physical
    geographers among the chief suspects—are prone to fall into the trap
    of environmental determinism.

10   Agnew, *Place and Politics*, 28. The definition of these terms is further
      amplified in his essay "Representing Space," in *Place/Culture/
      Representation,* ed. James Duncan and David Ley (New York and
      London: Routledge, 1993), 253.

11   Thomas Misa, "Retrieving Sociotechnical Change from Technological
      Determinism," in *Does Technology Drive History,* ed. Merritt Roe Smith
      and Leo Marx (Cambridge, Mass.: MIT Press, 1994), 115–42.

12   Reductive, materialist definitions of technology tend to be less
      sophisticated in their understanding of the social construction
      of artifacts. However, in his essay "Three Faces of Technological
      Determinism" in *Does Technology Drive History,* ed. Merrit Roe Smith
      and Leo Marx (Cambridge, Mass.: MIT Press, 1994), 79–100, Bruce
      Bimber develops a very scholarly yet reductive definition of technology
      as limited to apparatus. Bimber's project leads to other ontological
      problems, which are beyond the scope of this study.

13   For more on the various traditions within science and technology
      studies see my "Technology and the Politics of Sustainability at
      Blueprint Demonstration Farm," *Journal of Architectural Education
      51,* no. 1 (September 1997): 23–25, and my *Technology and Place:
      Sustainable Architecture and the Blueprint Farm* (Austin, Tex.: University
      of Texas Press, 2001).

14   Donald MacKenzie and Judith Wajcman, "Introduction," in *The Social
      Shaping of Technology* (Philadelphia: Open University Press, 1985), 3.

15   Bruno Latour, *We Have Never Been Modern* (Cambridge, Mass.: Harvard
      University Press, 1993), 117.

16   Ibid. and Bruno Latour, "Visualization and Cognition: Thinking with
      Eyes and Hands," in *Knowledge and Society: Studies in the Sociology
      of Culture Past and Present,* ed. Henrika Kuklick and Elizabeth Long
      (Greenwich, Conn.: JAI Press, 1986), 1–40.

17   Implicit in this point is the claim that original nature, if it ever existed
      at all, has long ago been incorporated into second nature, which
      is a work of society. See Henri Lefebvre, *The Production of Space,*
      trans. Donald Nicholson-Smith (1974; reprinted Cambridge, Mass.:
      Blackwell, 1991), 190.

18   Ibid., 31.

19   In constructing this dialogic relation between place and technology,
      I should make clear that I am not building a case for environmental
      determinism, which would be to say that places *cause* technologies.

Given different cultural conditions, the sets of objects that dominate any particular place might be different. Given constant environmental conditions, the interpretive flexibility of culture is entirely contingent. I want to argue that environments do shape technologies but are in turn shaped by them. As a corollary, I am not building a case for technological determinism, which would be to say that technologies *cause* places. The same logic holds that technologies do shape places but are also shaped by them. The point here is that the relation of place and technology is both spatial and discursive. It is a dialogue of cause and effect, means and ends. They are inseparable but contingent concepts that lead inhabitants of a place to a dialogic narrowing of cultural horizons.

20 I want to stress that I am not making a claim in this diagram that modernism or postmodernism can be described entirely within the limits of these two concepts. Rather, I only suggest that these concepts are particularly helpful as heuristic devices to get at those qualities of our time that are relevant to a discussion concerning regionalism.

21 In philosophical discourse Herbert Marcuse attempted a similar blending of Heidegger and Marx. In Marcuse's case, however, the project was further confused by the inclusion of Freud as a third pole. To be clear, I am not suggesting that such hybridized texts are unhelpful, only that their confused assumptions lead to previously unrecognized possibilities.

22 Latour, *We Have Never Been Modern*.

23 Ibid., 51–55.

24 The term "sustainability" is much used and much contested. For an analysis of the term, see *Sustainable Architecture: Natures and Cultures in Europe and North America*, ed. Simon Guy and Steven A. Moore (London and New York: Spon Press, 2005).

   The term "eco-tech" has come into use to describe the environmentally responsible projects of those firms like Sir Norman Foster & Partners that were previously described as "high-tech" practitioners. For more, see Catherine Slessor, *Eco-Tech: Sustainable Architecture and High Technology* (London: Thames & Hudson, 1997), 7.

25 Fredric Jameson, *Seeds of Time* (New York: Columbia University Press, 1994), 194.

26 John Tillman Lyle, *Regenerative Design for Sustainable Development* (New York: Wiley, 1994), 10.

INTRODUCTION
Raised to Observe: Glenn Murcutt /
Glenn Murcutt, interviewed by Cynthia Davidson

Throughout his career, the architect Glenn Murcutt has focused on the specificities of the region in which he builds: his native land of Australia. Without the use of computers or employees, Murcutt designs homes and other smaller-scale structures using a modernist language composed of local, sustainable, and reusable materials. His work is intimately informed by the Australian geography, topography, and climate, employing natural heating, cooling, and ventilation techniques to create buildings that are conditioned for and by their environment. Despite building only in Australia—and this is intentional, as he feels it is necessary to build only for areas one knows—Murcutt has traveled, lectured, and taught extensively, thus spreading his philosophy of practice throughout the architectural community. Indeed, his humble and ecologically minded message has clearly resonated beyond the Australian continent; he received the Pritzker Prize in 2002 and the American Institute of Architects' Gold Medal in 2009.

Cynthia Davidson, the editor of *Log* (an architectural journal launched in 2004), former editor of *ANY*, and the wife of architect Peter Eisenman, has been an influential voice within the architectural discipline during the past few decades. In the winter of 2005 she met with Murcutt during his time as a visiting professor at the Yale School of Architecture in New Haven, Connecticut. Davidson's interview with Murcutt offers insight into his particular method of practice, the value he places on sustainability, and the regional tendencies that have been admired by critics worldwide.

GLENN MURCUTT, INTERVIEWED BY
CYNTHIA DAVIDSON

RAISED TO OBSERVE:
GLENN MURCUTT

First appeared in *Log* 8 (Summer 2006), 31–39. Courtesy of
Cynthia Davidson.

**Cynthia Davidson: What does "sustainable" mean to you,
especially with regard to your work?**

Glenn Murcutt: It is to maintain or keep going; to continue.
Living things can be sustainable if allowed to grow in balance
with other organisms and not to consume at a greater rate than
is sustainable, as we currently do when we overharvest or poison
the land. We don't plan adequately for the future. Australian
aboriginal people have the longest continuous recorded culture on the planet. They have survived for at least 40,000 years—
not through competition but rather through cooperation; they
worked with the land and not against it. Traditional aboriginal
peoples have been living and working in a very sustainable way.

Today, many of us wake up in our air-conditioned houses,
drive to work in our air-conditioned vehicles; we look at the TV
news to see what the weather is like rather than *experiencing* it.
We have become alienated from our environment and no longer

learn about it from deep observation. In our idea of sustainability we have resorted to instruments of all kinds to measure the environment's physical aspects, ignoring its psychological aspects. I have learnt most things through observation, questioning, and understanding. Take, for example, clothing, how we dress. When it's cold we add layers and when it's hot we remove layers. In this way we do, in fact, respond to our various climates and seasonal changes quite well. So the question is: Why do we not design buildings that we can adapt to climate variations in the same way as we adapt our clothing? Why should we not involve ourselves with operating our environments by making adjustments to the cooling winds, the sunlight, and the humidity?

So do you see your buildings as machines, devices, or instruments that perform and adapt?

I'm suggesting that when you think of music and a composer, the mind of the composer through the conductor, then through the orchestra to the audience, it results in this terrific music that we perceive. Well, I look at a building as the instrument that makes this experience possible. We have around us the beautiful flowers and their spring perfumes. I can put scented flowering plants to the northeast of my building: lemon trees, orange trees, or water lilies, and in the summer, on the shore, northeast breezes pick up these scents, and bring them into the building. Then there are light and shading techniques and air-cooling techniques. My buildings open and close—like an instrument. I'm conscious when I'm designing to include prospect, refuge, observation, and reception. One designs buildings to perceive the changing light levels, temperatures, wind patterns, and sun positions; to perceive all these things so that the building performs as an instrument of the cycles of the day and year. For example, I have designed sunscreens with angled, fixed slats fitted to external roof glazing that include the winter sun and exclude the summer sun. Each slat is three millimeters thick; they are spaced 25 millimeters apart and are angled to the winter sun, overlapping to the sun's angle at equinox. At the midwinter solstice, the slat makes a shadow of three millimeters at noon. As the shadow gets wider you know it is getting closer to the summer equinox. Then at the summer equinox the direct summer sunlight is completely excluded. In midwinter, when it's fully included, you can have a blind underneath the glass roof if you don't want so much light, without diminishing the warmth. So the system, in a sense, becomes the modifier of light and warmth according to the seasons—an instrument— and we're the preceptors, as we are when we hear music, as we are in the landscape, as we are in our climate. These are important things to me.

Has this always been your attitude?

Yes, I was raised to observe. My father was a builder. He designed very good buildings and he imparted to me the importance of senses of light and the scents of native flowering plants. When I was very young, my father would bring me onto our neighbors' properties at night and take small pots of soil from their properties. The soil, you see, had too many nutrients in it for the local plants to grow because of the septic tanks that served the area. We would then propagate native plants that would withstand the high nutrients by firing the seeds in the oven or pouring boiling water over some hard-shelled seeds. We'd then plant the seeds in the high nutrient soil. A catalogue of where all this soil came from was kept. We would have had at least 150 pots. Then, we'd go back out at nighttime with the young plants and sticks for labels saying what the plants were and return to the neighbors' properties to plant the tube stock we had propagated. People had no idea where the plants came from, but today there are 20-meter-high trees growing on the hillsides around our old house. It was very eccentric for me, but in 1946 those were very important things. My father was very interested in reducing pollution. We had our own composting and vegetable garden. If he saw people throwing stuff out of their car, he'd pull up to gather their rubbish and then he'd give chase. He'd pull them over and say, "Look, you've dropped this rubbish," and they'd say, "No, we didn't want it," and then he'd say, "And nor does the planet want it," and he'd give it back to them. As children, we were so embarrassed by his forthrightness. But this was the childhood I had, and I can't help but be affected by it. And eventually you become a little bit like it yourself.

Why do you build only in Australia?

To know your own place is to know how to build; how to work with the culture. Through observation I've learnt much from scrutinizing the Australian land, its flora and fauna. The flora is tough and durable, yet supremely delicate. It's so light at its edges that it connects with the deep sky vault. The sunlight is so intense in Australia that it separates the elements in the landscape. The native trees read as groupings of isolated elements rather than interconnected elements. With the high oil content of so many of the trees and the strong sunlight, the foliage ranges in color from silver to weathered grays and from pink-browns to olives. The foliage outside the rainforests is not dense and so casts dappled shadows.

My architecture attempts to convey something of this discrete character of elements in the Australian landscape. I attempt to interpret some of the characteristic elements in our landscape in built form: the legibility of structure, transparency, dappled shadows, and the lightness of all the elements toward the edges. I often think of something Juhani Pallasmaa once wrote about Ecological Functionalism:

"After decades of affluence and abundance, architecture is likely to return to the aesthetics of necessity in which elements of metaphorical expression and practical craft fuse into each other again." ["From Metaphorical to Ecological Functionalism," *The Architectural Review,* June 1993.]

What are the native building materials of Australia?
We have huge reserves of iron ore, so steel is a material that is produced locally. Then timber, which is a marvelous, renewable resource. For the first twenty years of its life a tree takes in carbon dioxide and produces an excess of oxygen. After about another twenty years the carbon/oxygen ratio is about equal because the fallen old bark and leaves require oxygen to decompose, which cancels out the oxygen excess the tree initially produced. The decomposing bark and leaves produce compost for soil and nutrients for future plants.

What about the energy required to build your buildings?
I use lots of timber. Timber can be a truly sustainable resource, because the materials I'm using I put together in a way that they can be taken apart. I use bolted connections so that we can pull the elements apart and put them together again in another way. For example, in the Boyd Center all of the columns and beams are Australian hardwood—brush box (Tristania). This material would have been cut from the wet chlorophyll forests of the north coast of New South Wales about a hundred years ago and now it's recycled. All the plywood I use is plantation-grown material; in using new timbers it is important to know its source. The timber floors I lay are screwed, because if you nail them you can't reuse them. I use lime mortar in brickwork because it can be scraped off and the bricks can then be reused. I did this in my own house. All the paving bricks are laid on a sand bed with only the outer bricks laid on mortar. The bricks set between those

edges can be relocated or reused. If one brick is removed, they all fall apart because they rely on one another for support rather than on a cement mortar bed.

I designed a house for a client, which I bought ten years later. I needed to alter it, and because I had thought about the reuse of materials and methods of assembly at the time of designing the house, I was able to take the external timber veranda, 20 feet by 15 feet, and roll it out into a new position on 44-gallon drums. I took the gable end and put that in a new position and brought out the sliding and louvered glass walls—reusing all the old louvers. Even the timber stairs and stringers linking the ground to the veranda were relocated. I was testing myself during the whole thing as to how much I could reuse and how seamless I could make the reworking of the elements. Not a single building component was lost. It's a way of thinking. The process for determining how elements are connected is also knowing how they can be retrieved and how they can be reused. I'm interested in that because there's very little embodied energy lost in reworking the building material elements. I think that's sustainable.

I have to say, though, that humans are probably not sustainable because we're such destroyers of our environment. If our populations consumed and polluted the earth's resources in balance with the ability of nature to renew, then we'd be sustainable. But we're not sustainable. We destroy. The fact that the planet is in such difficulties shows that we're simply not, as a species, sustainable. Native animals of Australia have soft, padded feet. Domestic sheep, however, are cloven footed animals. Their cloven hooves cause soil compaction and erosion. This occurs because our soils are shallow. The ground becomes compacted, and with the addition of oil from the sheep and tremendous heat and sunshine, a crust forms on the groundplane, so water and wind erode the soil. The rabbit is another introduced species in Australia that is out of balance with its environment.

The rabbit creates erosion by burrowing, and when it rains—an inch and a half of water in half an hour is not uncommon—the burrows start deep erosion with a resulting huge loss of soils.

The rain in Australia is really incredible; when it falls it is heavy. My buildings have pitched roofs because of this heavy rain. My early buildings had flat roofs, but I learnt early that water has to be shed quickly, and in remote areas it has to be collected in water storage tanks for later use.

Do you design rain catchments?
Sure, the roofs of my rural buildings are designed to catch rainwater for use: for drinking, extinguishing fire, flushing the toilets, and watering the garden. In some remote, larger projects waste water is processed for reuse in gardens through rotating biological digesters, an aerating system for gray and black water, which releases the nutrients during aeration—not carried into the groundwater. This system delivers pretty clean water, which can be stored in a lake where ultraviolet light and reed beds continue the purification process. The purified gray and black water can be returned to wet toilets, so there is no need to add fresh water to the toilet system.

How do you approach all these issues when making a building? Are there hierarchies of importance?
There are so many issues that need to be considered simultaneously in making architecture, especially an architecture responsive to a specific place: the geomorphology of a region, the geology and hydrology and topography, which affect water drainage; the latitude and altitude, which define the sun position and influences temperature; the relationship to the coast, which influences humidity, dryness, temperature, rainfall, and snowfall; the flora, which respond differently to different soils and climates; the fauna, which respond to the flora as well as to

the soils and climate; the water, which differs in availability; the waste, which needs management; the materials, their ability to mediate the environment, and their methods of production and assembly, which impact the environment; the structure and its appropriateness; the space and its qualities; the natural heating, ventilating, and cooling strategies; the local culture and how one works with the needs and aspirations of the people one is designing for. All these issues must be included in the thinking about an architecture that is responsive to place—an architecture of response rather than of imposition.

There has been a resistance by architects to environmental design, as many regard climate-responsive architecture as being unable to create beautiful work; they see much of the work as ugly. Working with the environment is viewed as a negative constraint. However, from my experience, and by understanding my imposed limitations, I have found that the opportunities have increased.

INTRODUCTION
On Criticality / *Arie Graafland*

The state of architectural theory and notions of projective practice have been widely debated in the Netherlands by figures
such as Arie Graafland, an educator and a principal of Kerssen
Graafland Architects in Amsterdam. As the director of the Delft
School of Design (DSD), a recently founded doctoral program
at Delft University of Technology dedicated to "the exploration of
the fields of architecture and critical thinking," it is not surprising
to find Graafland involved in this current theoretical discourse.
His essay "On Criticality" originally appeared in the DSD's first
publication, *Crossover: Architecture /Urbanism /Technology*, a
conglomeration of texts concerned with the "emerging 'condition'
of architectural knowledge in both the academic context and
professional practice."[1]

In "On Criticality," Graafland questions Michael Speaks's
argument for an intelligence-based organizational model for
architecture, calling instead for a "'reflexive architecture,' an
architecture addressing its own foundations reflexively." Such
reflexive architecture, Graafland notes, often evolves from the
interaction between the university and design offices, as generally
the former lacks the means to apply their theoretical constructs
to the real world and the latter lacks "the focus [and] the time for
extended experimentation." Graafland then associates this reflexivity with an "architecture of the street," an outgrowth of the realist
attitude advocated by the philosopher/anthropologist/sociologist
Bruno Latour. Turning to the work of another cultural theorist,
Timothy Luke, Graafland expands upon this notion of "reflexive
architecture in the street." Luke posits three "natures" that inform
the way we occupy and conceptualize space: first nature involves
"terrestriality," the elemental characteristics of the earth; second
nature encompasses "territoriality," the built physical and social

environment; third nature concerns "an informational cybersphere or telesphere" that gives rise to notions of the virtual. With respect to architecture, Graafland connects digital technologies with third nature, which is "largely penetrating first and second nature [and] dissolv[ing] any notion of ground or context." Architecture divorced from ground and context can easily approach an aesthetic formalism disconnected from cultural, historical, and phenomenological concerns. The architectural object thus becomes more important that the experiencing subject, and "we lose the very notions of gender, sexuality, ethnic diversity, uneven distribution of wealth, and class." For Graafland, this is an unacceptable alternative; "in architecture and urbanism," he declares, "we cannot do without 'ground,' nor can we do without critical thought." Thus, "On Criticality" concludes with a reaffirmation of the importance of theory conceptualized as critical thought.

As well as critiquing Speaks's concept of design intelligence and expressing his own thoughts on reflexive architecture, Graafland's article touches on other issues, such as the subject's relationship to architecture, consumerism and "brand-name architecture," the role of digital technologies in design, and the proliferation and materiality of information/communication networks. Consequently, Graafland's meditation on criticality highlights a wide range of topics that inform contemporary theoretical discourse.

Note
1   Arie Graafland and Julie Kavanaugh, "Introduction," in *Crossover: Architecture / Urbanism / Technology* (Rotterdam: 010 Publishers, 2006), 1.

ARIE GRAAFLAND

ON CRITICALITY

First appeared in *Crossover: Architecture / Urbanism / Technology*
(Rotterdam: 010 Publishers, 2006). Courtesy of the author
and the publisher.

The flat screen of my computer has a name of its own. It's called digital life. Is there life inside my computer? Well, sometimes it looks like it. It does things on its own. Indeed, it seems to have its own mind. It shows me lively pictures; it communicates for me all over the planet with its equals. It can drive me mad, actually, but mostly I am quite happy with what it does for me. At least it has changed my working life considerably. And isn't that what most life-forms are about? Changing behavior. But where does that leave me as a person? Am I lost as a mere "interface"?

Quite a few architects and artists will tell me: "You are not lost, you just have to talk back. Communicate!" Communicate with our (plans for) digital architecture and art forms. I am already part of what William Gibson wrote twenty years ago about cyberspace; I am part of that "consensual hallucination" called cyberspace. It also seems to be a lot more than that. Certainly, more than the computer itself. It is about networks, compatibility, architectures, access, non-accessibility;

it is about power, transfers of money, data and information that flow through it. And it is also about new forms of architectural practices, office organizational strategies, and profiling.

Enabled by the new information and communication technologies, Michael Speaks[1] writes that network practices in the 1990s became communities that are more powerful than any single studio or office. Speaks explores the organizational structures of a few offices that, like academic research groups in the same period of time, became more internationally oriented, using each other's networks and expertise. For example, the Amsterdam based UNStudio (United Network Studio) of Ben van Berkel and Caroline Bos organized their office as a "network studio." These network firms proliferated in the 1990s, reflecting the need for small, innovative studios to create working partnerships. Speaks focuses on organization and economic change, indeed, his vocabulary is on "innovation." The central idea of this innovation is a highly organizational one. Speaks talks about "knowledge based services" and refers to "cultural intelligence." In referring to SHoP (Sharples Holden Pasquarelli), a young firm in New York, he quotes Gregg Pasquarelli who was looking for a new way of practice, in which design was not just handed off, but was part of an entire approach. SHoP to him is unlike most architectural offices—the model is a consultant firm, not the traditional master-builder type office. He stresses the combination of design intelligence with computer design technology and a sophisticated approach to marketing, public relations, and other aspects of the business of architecture in order to create that "truly innovative" practice.

Speaks is in fact referring to the transition from Fordism to *flexible accumulation*, described by David Harvey and others[2] in the 1990s. This more flexible form of capital and organization emphasizes the new as a category, a recurring term in these accounts on the benefits of computerization. It is the fleeting, the ephemeral, the fugitive and the contingent in modern life, rather than the more solid values implanted under Fordism[3] that becomes paramount. Harvey discusses three accounts from that period of time, all dealing with the same economic and organizational issues. The rather celebratory account by Halal[4] of new capitalism, emphasizes the new entrepreneurialism. The second is Lash and Urry's *The End of Organized Capitalism*[5], and the third is a book by Swyngedouw from 1986[6] providing in great detail the transformations in technology and the labor process. Many of Speaks' arguments are similar to Harvey's in theorizing this transition.

The period from 1965 to 1973 was one of the inability of Fordism and Keynesianism to contain the inherent contradictions of capitalism. On the surface, Harvey writes, these difficulties could best be captured by one word: rigidity. There were problems with the rigidity of long-term and large-scale fixed capital investments, in labor markets, labor allocation and contracts. The 1970s and 1980s have been a troubled period of economic restructuring, and social and political readjustment. This shift to flexible accumulation rests on flexibility with respect to labor processes, markets, products and consumption patterns. Furthermore, the shift is characterized by the emergence of entirely new sectors of production, new ways of providing financial services, new markets and above all, greatly intensified rates of commercial, technological and organizational innovation.

According to Speaks, even the most forward-looking members of the architectural establishment have ignored these innovations. And for sure, for some of the offices their way of working is new. Greg Lynn (Los Angeles), Douglas Garafalo (Chicago) and Michael McInturf (Cincinnati), mostly architects with smaller offices in different cities, took advantage of electronic imaging and new communication technologies. Together they realized the Korean Presbyterian Church of New York.

Stan Allen and James Corner—one in New York, the other in Philadelphia—collaborated in architectural thinking, research and landscape architecture. Also the Dutch firm MVRDV is into research of datascapes, urban design/decision-making models like Regionmaker and publishing office work as research-related. An important aspect of this innovation is the fact that the principals were far more involved in academic research-related work than the majority of their colleagues ever were. Their colleagues are still more interested in publishing their completed office work. Mostly built work, they do not make that step back, there is virtually no distance from their design production. Probably Rem Koolhaas is the inspiring figure here, his first form of "practice" being, so to speak, a book on Manhattan. Later publications show more of the tendencies Speaks indicates—writing about architecture and urbanism, a clever mix of proposed and executed office work, critical articles, and a surplus of photographic material combined with an ingenious way of presenting, made possible by advanced digital assembling techniques and the design skills of Bruce Mau and the like. In the 1990s AMO, an offshoot of OMA, was set up when principals Rem Koolhaas and Dan Wood, then project architect for OMA's abandoned Universal Studios Project in Los Angeles, decided to begin this theoretical arm together. At the moment, Reinier De Graaf heads AMO.

Another example of Italian origin is Stefano Boeri[7], exploring urban projects, doing design research, and with an architectural practice in Milan. For some architecture schools, this new methodology meant new forms of architectural research. Koolhaas started his "Project for the City," an immensely influential and fast paced project at Harvard School of Design. In Rotterdam, the Berlage Institute is always on the cutting edge of design and architectural thinking and has established a name for itself. More recently, the TU Delft established its Delft

School of Design, an internationally oriented research laboratory at the Architecture Faculty. They all have in common the exploration of the fields of architecture and critical thinking.

Nevertheless, for Speaks, the times of "critical theory" are past. At stake here was more than the transition to flexible accumulation in Western economies as proposed by Harvey. Instead, this new flexible accumulation of architectural image and practice, as well as forms of management, is the new successor to the so-called exhaustion of primarily Continental theory. In this depletion, Speaks sees the failure to recognize the important shift in the relationship between thinking and doing that occurred in architecture in the 1990s. Consequently, the more recent focus is on American pragmatism and on these "newly emerging forms of practice." For him the new challenge for architecture is to develop forms of practice able to survive the fiercely competitive global marketplace. The idea is that architects use "intelligence" in a twofold way: as a specific form of practical knowledge characteristic for the profession, and in the practical way the American CIA or military might want to use "intelligence." Architects should be able to think ahead and visualize ahead—a form of fore-knowing the effects and, at the same time, the social impacts of their proposals. Yet, in order to be able to do so, they must employ "intelligence" like the military, be able to work from seemingly endless fragments of "information," rumours even, and disinformation. The "chatter" of the outside world should be related to the projective capacity of the profession. The way to do it is just to use your imagination and to play along.

The question is, however, are there other ways to deal with projective practice and how can critical thinking be involved in this procedure? Or is critical thinking, indeed "exhausted"? The first thing to be said is that virtually no office in the past has been interested in critical thinking; this investigation has always been solely the domain of philosophy and sociology in the universities. Certainly, critical theory was not a field of interest that played any role in actual office work. The link Speaks makes between modernization of the work process in architectural offices, and "the exhaustion of Continental theory" is questionable in itself since Continental theory never played any role in daily office practice in Europe and America. Architects get their ideas elsewhere—from confrontation with the specificity of site and program, from work of other architects, from periodicals and professional literature. The discourse on theory, in fact, streams along in all of its convoluted complexity, largely unnoticed by the average practitioner of architecture. If the articles get too complex, simply no one will read them. Indeed, there has always been "chatter"; and in fact, there will probably always be "chatter" in the architectural office with its chaotic work processes, and also in the Universities where different interests and ideas have to work together or at least tolerate each other. Speaks' argument runs two ways: firstly promoting flexible and internationally oriented office practices, and secondly announcing the "exhaustion" of critical thinking in the Universities. I argue that although the two are substantially unrelated practically speaking, they are both relevant questions for architecture and especially for architectural education.

What other ways are there to approach this question? What is needed here, in my opinion, is what I would like to call a "reflexive architecture," an architecture addressing its own foundations reflexively, paired with the digitalized work processes on a larger scale than the traditional office practices employed until recently. To be clear, in the end I do not think that the offices can do this reflexive architecture on their own. Most of them will have neither the focus nor the time for extended experimentation. A studio setting is necessary in order to be able to get the desired focus. The designs in my *Socius of*

Architecture[8] were made in our office, but the text came from my work in the University. "Reflexivity" is an activity mainly in Universities since it relates to "critique" and to contemporary notions of time and space. If this split between office practice and University research remains, it will leave the historians and critics on the safe side, they won't have to bother with the messy daily practices in the offices where negotiating and adapting are more common than the grand design. However, I think the research groups in Universities cannot do reflexive architectural research without the offices involved. They lack the much needed pragmatic context and client. What is happening in Speaks' discourse is the effort to promote a few American and Dutch offices to the forefront of contemporary architectural practice. His main argument being an organizational and instrumental one, a position of instrumentality covered by a "pragmatic" stance no longer assessing the outcome of the designs. Not quite a new position.

This "obsession with instrumentality," as Alberto Pérez-Gómez[9] writes, rages unabated in architectural practice and almost always underscores the "leading edge" positions. He traced the instrumental obsession in mid-eighteenth-century technical theories in order to probe their myths of rationality. His focus was on pre-modern architecture where essential aspects of architectural knowledge were defined as *techne* founded on *mathemata* that could be transmitted through a "scientific" treatise. Pérez-Gómez examined the polemic between two instrumental theories in late seventeenth- and eighteenth-century France, the work of Charles Étienne Briseux and his criticism of the earlier writings of Claude Perrault.[10] The contemporary "obsession with instrumentality"' encourages fashionable architectural projects that are oblivious to their cultural context, to their intended programs, to their historical roots, to ethical imperatives and to our experiencing body.

Although Pérez-Gómez is correct, in my opinion the problem is that today's architectural practice is no longer on the level of historical consciousness, or even managerial and organizational levels as Speaks suggests, no longer on a cognitive or historical level, but on the level of a software-driven flattened out aesthetic reflexivity.

This kind of aesthetic reflexivity has more recently found an important place in the production and consumption of the culture industries. Architectural books and magazines are also a part of this mechanism. Treatises are no longer an option for an architect, rather a necessity. For the offices it will be hard, if not impossible, to step back from this aestheticization. The conditions under which they work are in a sort of symbolic flow, cultural capital creation and aesthetically cast expert systems that are intrinsic to the current profession. Whereas intellectual property rights are the main form of capital in the culture industries, in architecture what is sold is not the intellectual rights since it is a singular operation, but the "product," the architectural project, and especially the "name" the firm or architect has managed to make for himself by way of publishing. Quite a lot of the smaller firms Speaks mentions do niche marketing, finding holes in a major markets of building practices. What some of them have invented are not so much an economic and managerial innovation as well as a strategic aesthetic innovation in profiling and image production. This invention/promotion of course has been the case for longer periods of time in the twentieth century, and was always followed by a critique from both Marxist and conservative sides. Nevertheless, the critique is also getting more and more complex. In Marxist critique, at least there was always a stronghold, a form of resistance with aesthetic depth, as in for example, Tafuri or Adorno. But what is happening now is the disappearance of that subject of resistance in the circulation of images in contemporary information and communication structures. This very disappearance, however, is what Speaks characterizes as the "exhaustion of Continental theory."

We are no longer dealing with reflexive subjects, but reflexive objects, as Lash and Urry[11] argue. They have argued that the current cultural artefacts in the music industry, to use one example, are no longer transcendent as representations, but that they have become immanent as objects amongst other objects circulating and competing in information and communication structures of popular culture. Music has become a lifestyle. Their claim is that with modernization and autonomization, hence differentiation of the cultural, culture became primarily representation. More recently we have seen representations taking up the functional position of objects, objects which only differ from other objects of everyday life in their immaterial form and aesthetic character. Madonna as a star is not just an image, but a representation. She has become a cultural object in the anthropological sense of culture. With the declining significance of social structures and their partial displacement by information and communication structures the aestheticization of everyday life becomes possible. Our current condition of postmodernity is in effect the generalization of aesthetic modernism to not just an elite, but the whole of the population. Aesthetic modernism, however, presupposed that autonomous subject with depth and reflection. It assumes an aesthetic expressive subject. Lash and Urry argue that the circulation of images in contemporary information and communication structures entails not an aesthetic subject, but these reflexive objects.[12] Although their observations might be too close to Baudrillard's notion of dystopia[13] here, it is true that the subjects tend to be flattened out in the ongoing proliferation of digitalized images. But to me this process is not yet completed, not yet exhausted, there are still critical possibilities left. For sure this flexible accumulation is much more than a merely economic managerial flexibility as suggested by Speaks. In our digital world, contemporary architectural image production is replacing modernistic aesthetics for an "anaesthetics" as Neil Leach[14] has recently suggested.

Record companies are not so much selling the record, but the artist. For architecture this is not the same situation; architecture does not command that kind of widespread interest in society, although interest is growing rapidly in magazines originally not dealing with architecture. But for the architectural in-crowd, Rem Koolhaas and Frank Gehry are functioning in a comparable way. It is not so much the building, but a "Koolhaas" as a brand name, reinforced by his own publications and the OMA/AMO office, and even more by the endless publications on his work in books and magazines. Many culture sector firms have become like advertising agencies, and advertising itself has become more like a culture industry, Lash and Urry have argued. For example, the PR firm of Saatchi in London profiles their advertising business as "commercial communication." The AMO office is not too far away from the same practice. OMA/AMO's research into Shopping more or less coincided with their Prada account. The office not only designed the shops, but took care of the corporate identity of the company in advertising and publicity.

I am avoiding the already obsolete terms "innovative" and even the terminology of "critical architecture" since I am also of the opinion that "critical" in social theory and philosophy is indeed problematic and cannot easily be related to a projective aesthetic practice like architecture. Nevertheless, in saying "critical" we must be precise. Certainly "critical" can be related to "retrospective," historical, and critical analyses. Critical itself is either under a lot of pressure or it is fading away completely in social theory and philosophy since for many it seems to have lost the much needed critical subject. There is certainly much more at stake here than the mentioned shift to a new organizational model. It is also a matter of knowledge as Speaks suggests. Philosophical, political, and scientific truths have fragmented into proliferating swarms of "little truths," appearing and disappearing so fast that ascertaining whether they are really true is impractical if not altogether impossible, he writes.[15]

Yet his altogether too hasty conclusion is a farewell to critical theory; ideas or ideologies are no longer relevant, but *intelligence* is. The "critical architectures" of the 1960s and 1970s had none of the theoretical, political, or philosophical *gravitas* of their early twentieth century predecessors, he writes. On top of that, Post Modernism, Deconstructivism, Critical Regionalism, and many others in the late 1980s and 1990s posed as false pretenders to Modernism. The opposition Speaks is laying out here is about different forms of theoretical and aesthetic practices. His claim is that "vanguard practices" are reliant on ideas, theories, and concepts *given in advance* (my italics), and that "post-vanguard" practices are more "entrepreneurial" in seeking opportunities for innovation. That is to say, practices that cannot be determined by any idea, theory, or concept.[16]

I think it is here where the misunderstandings are in danger of arising. To my mind, architecture as a projective and creative aesthetic practice can never be both solidly and safely guided by critical theory which is retrospective by definition. The *projection* of architectural thought into a building and its *prospectively* hoped-for aesthetic effects will always be an uncertain stab in the dark, whether it comes from "entrepreneurial opportunities for innovation," or from "critical" intentions. It has nothing to do with the idea of "stable theories" given in advance, or with the inventions of entrepreneurial practices. I will stress the aesthetic side of this projective process; it certainly does not mean an "anything-goes." There are many stable ways to analyze and organize the context, the program, the construction, the budget, etc. But in many cases, it is this aesthetic effect that is discussed at length beforehand in both educational and practical settings. Philosophy in this context easily leads to a confusion, in many cases coming from Eisenman's writings and especially his linking up with philosophical partners like Derrida and Rajchman where, at least to my mind, there is a false suggestion of *projective* archi-philosophy. Whether this is due to the way Eisenman always publishes his projects or whether it comes from a genuine philosophical interest in the projects is hard to decide. I think it is possibly both, but what seems to be certain is that it is confusing the American discourse on "criticality."

Speaks himself seems to be "exhausted" by this discourse, but that does not mean that we are completely at a loss here. Certainly it is possible to say something intelligible about economic conditions in design practice, about political choices and decision making in urbanism, about territorial conditions or "terrestriality," about design ideologies and managerial relations. In the end, architecture and urbanism are about our lives and the way we experience our world. Nevertheless, the comments of Speaks, although I do not agree with his argument, no doubt confront us with the more serious problem, that of critique itself. The argument presents us with yet another opportunity to question the status and usefulness of deconstructionism, critical theory, and our ideas about society and nature.

Indeed, Bruno Latour writes, "it has been a long time since the very notion of the avant-garde—the proletariat, the artistic—passed away, pushed aside by other forces, moved to the rear garde, or may be lumped with the baggage train."[17] It looks like we are still going through the motions of a critical avant-garde, but is not the spirit gone, he asks? Staying with the idea that critical thought is a weapon, a *"Waffe der Kritik"* as it was once called, Latour writes that we have to re-think our critical strategies and instruments. The actual threats might have changed so much that we might still be directing our entire arsenal east or west while the enemy has now moved to a very different place. Our critical arsenal with the neutron bombs of deconstruction, with the missiles of discourse analysis, might all be misdirected. And yes, we might be using the wrong arsenal, we will have to go back again to deconstructivist architecture and our newly established digital architectures to see what went wrong. And at the same time come up with alternatives, the latter more imperative than the former.

At first sight there might be a correspondence between Speaks' notions and Latour's. But in fact their positions are very different. Latour's plea is to get closer to the facts, not fighting empiricism, but on the contrary renewing empiricism. The new critical mind for him is to be found not in *intelligence*, but in the cultivation of a stubbornly realist attitude, to speak like William James, a realism dealing with what he calls *matters of concern*, not matters of fact.[18] Instead of moving away from facts, we have to direct our attention toward the conditions that made them possible. For architecture it implies the redirection of our thoughts to what I would call *an architecture of the street*. A reflexive architectural way of proceeding, renewing empiricism, and addressing the sophisticated tools of architectural deconstruction and its inherent construction—or better, the lack of—social construction. The desired outcome of architectural practices discussed at length in architecture schools, books and magazines can never be guided by a rhetoric of "entrepreneurial architecture," or "design intelligence." A discourse which only focuses on organizational questions, and is referring to "critical" architectures as lost cases, is in fact a hastily post-modern and post-political manoeuvre that needs to be addressed. It is still possible to think of critique in other ways. Not so much in the exclusive Marxist way which I will briefly explain a little further on, but in a way Latour and Lash suggest. Not as the critic who debunks, but the one who assembles. The critic in his thinking is not the one who pulls the rug from under the feet of the naïve believers, but the one who offers the participants arenas in which to gather, Latour writes. That is to say, generating more ideas than we have received, not being purely "negative," but in fact productive.

In order to explicate this progression in the field of architecture, I will relate to an earlier publication where I tried to show both relation and ruptures between architecture and 'critical' theory.[19] In an insightful article in *Harvard Design Review*[20], George Baird sketches out the American discussion on "criticality," which has its origin in Europe in Marxist and Kantian thinking. The lineage of criticality in architecture more or less starts with Peter Eisenman, accompanied by Michael Hays, who has developed a position consistently focussed intellectually on concepts of "resistance" and "negation," Baird writes.[21] Both refer to the Italian historian and critic Manfredo Tafuri. To my mind, one of the crucial notions on criticality is to be found in Hays' book on Hannes Meyer and Ludwig Hilberseimer[22], which is heavily indebted to the work of the Marxist thinker Fredric Jameson.[23] For Hays—following Tafuri[24]—Mies van der Rohe was the paramount exemplar of negation in late Modernism. The work of Mies is examined as critical, or resistant and oppositional. In another writing,[25] Hays addresses the surface distortions and formal inscrutability of the 1922 skyscraper project published in the second issue of *G* magazine. Mies insists that an order is immanent in the surface itself and that the order is continuous with and dependent upon the world in which the viewer actually moves. Hays puts the building into the context of the German city at the time, referring to Georg Simmel's ideas on the blasé individual. This sense of surface and volume in fact wrenched the building from the atemporal, idealized realm of autonomous forms, in order to install it in the historical world of that time. The design, then, becomes open to the chance and uncertainty of life in the metropolis. The moment of resistance is that it is not subsumed in the chaos of the metropolis, but rather seeks for another order through the systematic use of the unexpected mirroring of surfaces. Hays addresses the building, not the architect's intentions or oeuvre.

Other later works of Mies, like Alexanderplatz in Berlin and the Adam building on Leipzigerstrasse, do not fall under the same category; it all depends on how the buildings can be related to a focused and critical assessment from sociology or philosophy. Instead of Simmel, one could also argue from Walter Benjamin's work. The main question is how the relation is assessed between project and city. Not in the sense most urbanists discuss this relation as a fitting-in with the site, but as a critical reading of both city and architecture at the same time. The later projects abstain from any dialogue with the physical particularities of their contexts; the glass walled blocks could be reproduced on any site. The sameness of the units and undifferentiated order tend to deny the possibility of attaching significance to the arrangements. Yet, Hays argues, it does not mean that these later designs are unrelated to the 1922 skyscraper designs. It is the repudiation of an *a priori* logic as primary focus of meaning that ties them together. Mies' achievement in the Alexanderplatz design was to open up a clearing of silence in the chaos of the nervous metropolis; it is silence that carries the burden of meaning in this project.

Interestingly enough, the new position of "criticality" seems to be with Elizabeth Diller and Ricardo Scofidio, since Michael Hays' first act as curator of New York's Whitney Museum was to give them a major exhibition. But even more interesting is that they chose to exhibit many of the museum gallery projects that have made them famous, Baird writes.[26] None of the building projects on which their recent design practice has focused was shown—projects that will have to meet the more difficult test of being critical "in the street." To be able to relate to notions of "lived space," which is part of this criticality in the streets, we will have to relate to the ideas of a critical theory, and especially projective thinking as in *reflexive architecture* (not to be confused with "critical architecture"). "Critical" can only be used for theory, not for architecture. In the projects in the *Socius* book[27], it is directly related to an "architecture in the streets." Remarkably, the earliest and most severe critique on Eisenman's work came from Tafuri, where Eisenman's work was considered to be fit for the *boudoir*, and *not for the street*.[28] So let us turn to that "reflexive architecture in the street" and see what it has to offer.

The Human Body and its Ground

Before we go back to the architectural discourse, we first have to address more general notions of (human) nature, sustainability, bio-sphere, and information society. How do we address these questions? The concept of human nature is highly complex; I will not strictly follow the problem of what is called "the post-humanist subject" as it is already well presented in current cultural discourse or theory.[29] I will address the problem of "digital worlds" from the problem of "*grounding*," and the necessity of a spatio-temporal "*re-framing*" of architectural thought in terms of the organic and inorganic in order to get at ways in which we may rethink the possibility of sustainable action and agency in our times. Cyberspace in particular, Timothy Luke argues[30], forces human beings to re-conceptualize their spatial situation inasmuch as they experience their positions in cyberspace only as simulations in some "virtual life" form. His argument is that we might need another reasoning to capture these digital worlds. The epistemological foundations of conventional reasoning in terms of political realism are grounded in the modernist laws of second nature, he writes. We might need another epistemic notion on what is *real* and what is *virtual*. In taking up the notions of "first" and "second" nature, Luke defines the "third nature" as informational cybersphere/telesphere.

Digitalization shifts human agency and structure to a register of informational bits from that of manufactured matter. Human presence gets located in the interplay of the two modes of nature's influence. First nature, according to Luke, gains its identity from the varied terrains forming the bioscape/ecoscape/geoscape of "*terrestriality*." Earth, water and sky provide the basic elements mapped in physical geographies of the biosphere that in turn influence human life with natural forces. Yet a large part of the biosphere is polluted beyond recovery. For example, car and air traffic are jointly responsible for some 40% of the USA's annual energy consumption, but the built environment consumes an equal amount, the rest taken by industry. Urban sprawl in the USA is one of the major problems of energy consumption. Subsidized gas, relatively low taxes on cars, high accessibility by car, and low land prices guarantee more and more sprawl every day. Of course the problem is far more complex than what can be briefly described here in a few lines. My main concern is how to understand our own actions in relation to nature and the possible architectural and urban solutions.

Both architecture and urbanism play an important role in the understanding of digitalized work processes and digital architecture, and the relation to *bioscape*, *ecoscape* and *geoscape*. It is difficult, if not impossible to say where these systems begin or end, where solutions to the environment might be found, what kind of agreement we might reach to solve architectural and urban problems. There is indeed a witches' brew of political arguments, concepts and difficulties that can conveniently be the basis of endless academic, intellectual, theoretical and philosophical debate, as David Harvey writes.[31] Some common language has to be found, according to Harvey, or at least an adequate way of translating between different languages. His common ground is in "the web of life" metaphor; it might indeed help us to filter our actions through the web of interconnections that make up the living world.

In addition, Luke's definition of the nation state, mass society and global geopolitics as historical artefacts used for constructing and conquering the built environments or social spaces of second nature can help us along this path. It is a domain historically described for architecture by Richard Sennett in his book *Flesh and Stone*.[32] Second nature is discussed in the sense of the technoscape/socioscape/ethnoscape of *territoriality*. Luke might be right that many of the changes today cannot be fully understood with these two concepts alone. The elaborate human constructions become overlaid, interpenetrated and reconstituted with a "third nature" of an informational cybersphere or telesphere, he argues. As a new concept we might want to see this in a Deleuzian way of a contour, a configuration, a constellation of an event to come. It will also have more and more implications for the way we deal with architecture and urbanism. Architectural and urban design are deeply involved in "third nature." Until recently, design was involved in first and second nature, but with digitalization it has entered a third nature. This is not only a question of the "means" of designing, it has—and will—influence our ways of seeing and experiencing architecture.

On the other hand, Peter Eisenman writes, architecture traditionally was place-bound, linked to a condition of experience.[33] Eisenman refers to the comparable notions Luke is writing about, mediated environments challenging the givens of classical time, the time of experience. Writing about his Rebstock Park project for Frankfurt, Eisenman writes that architecture can no longer be bound by the static conditions of space and place. To his mind architecture must deal with new conditions like the "event."[34] Rebstock is seen as an unfolding event—events like a rock concert where one becomes part of the environment. Yet architectural theory has largely ignored this idea. Instead, theory has focussed on notions of figure and ground, according to Eisenman. There seem to be two ways of dealing with this conceptual pair; one leading to contextualism, and one leading to a *tabula rasa* such as the modern movement imagined. With architectural modernism there is no relationship between old and new, or between figure and ground. Ground, or territoriality in Luke's terms, is seen as a clear neutral datum, projecting its autonomy into the future. I think both Luke and Eisenman are right in detecting a "third nature," but where it will lead is still not clear.

Critical Theory in Brief: the Aesthetic Mode of Writing
Theory has to be grasped in the place and time out of which it emerges. These situations are constantly changing. In that sense, Scott Lash's use of "*allegory*" is an interesting thought that I would like to pursue for a moment. He distinguishes two types of modernism in social theory: on the one hand, positivism, and on the other "*Lebensphilosophie*." Positivism he understands as structured along the lines of "system," and *Lebensphilosophie* along the principle of "symbol." The forerunner of positivism, whose paradigmatic system building figures run from Rousseau/ Condorcet, through Comte, the late Marx, Le Corbusier and more recently Habermas's later work, is French humanist classicism. Lash refers to the not unproblematic opposition of "*Zivilisation*" and "*Kultur*" in Norbert Elias' work.[35] Lash's main reference here is Simmel, who worked more in the idiom of symbol than system. Simmel also began to work in a different register, the register of allegory. Lash describes it as a deepening of Goethe's notion of symbol in contrast to French classical allegory which was superficial and ornamental, as it was associated

with the salons and the manners of court society. Lash shifts the notion of symbol from the classical to the baroque allegory, from French court society to Spanish absolutism and thus to baroque allegory. For Lash it consists of a completely different register from the original juxtaposition of symbol and allegory, it has to do neither with *Zivilisation* nor *Kultur*. Concepts seem to partially lose their original meaning here, in fact Lash is laying out a different "plane of immanence"in the Deleuzian sense.

Second and third nature as newly established concepts would need a different laying out of the plane that holds them together. Classical allegory proffers a point for point homology between two narratives; his baroque version posits a significant absence, a "hole" in the underlying narrative. If the original, "true" story somehow is not quite right, then the point to point homology between the second narrative and the first is no longer possible. Baroque allegorists such as Nietzsche, Simmel, Benjamin, Adorno and Karl Krauss write in the form of an essay, Lash maintains. The essay might well look "*wissentschaftlich*," but instead emerges in an aesthetic mode—serious and at the same time superficial, light, ornamental.

Baroque allegory is, in fact, opposite to a Marxist explanation. Michael Hays refers to Louis Althusser, the French Marxist, with regard to his idea of "relative autonomy."[36] At the other end of the line, then, might be the Frankfurt School of Horkheimer and Adorno. In the American debate on "critical," the term is used many times by different authors with often divergent meanings, but it might be good to remember that Parisian Marxism in the sixties and seventies was never interested in a "critical" but in a Marxist "scientific" way of proceeding. My first two books on the architectural body, were written as an essay in that aesthetic mode to which Lash refers—a seemingly 'light,' sometimes 'ironic' architectural critique as in my analysis of Rem Koolhaas' Downtown Athletic Club and Duchamp's

Large Glass.[37] Yet the allegorist is, while looking ornamental, simultaneously deadly serious. In Lash's formulation, the allegorist is the father of the illegitimate child of modernity's other.

Conclusion

With many of the contemporary architectural electronic imaging techniques and communication technologies, we arc in the end loosing all ground. My claim is that we need more ground and permanence in architecture instead of "folds." Seen from an architectural perspective, it means that blobs and folds take the city as an additive texture without any coherence; they consume too much space since they want to stand on their own imagined pedestals. They reinforce urban sprawl. Instead of more compact building, they spread out. There is indifference to the environment, grounding is no issue. I think I can agree with Lash's critique. Although I do not think his critique works in the instance of Koolhaas as he suggests, it does work very well for digital architectures: speed supersedes space as indifference supersedes difference.

The source for these digital designs is third nature. Third nature here is largely penetrating first and second nature; it dissolves any notion of ground or context. It is here where my doubts for a possible application to architecture and urbanism begin. Like second nature, third nature is no doubt a social product. Eisenman's Rebstock Park shifts the notion of figure/ground to one of assumed Deleuzian folding. This shift has direct consequences for the grounding of design. We should realize that all spaces are *constructs* and *real*, including our digital worlds. Virtual space in Deleuze's sense is not an unforeseen possibility in the design, to be realized in a certain framing. It is about a question that will open up new uncharted territories. First and second nature do not have more materialized substance; it is indeed more than a collective hallucination restricted to the symbolic domains of social superstructures. It has an immense material base in communication satellites, and fibre optic networks as Manuel Castells has analysed.[38]

In architecture and urbanism, we cannot do without "ground," nor can we do without critical thinking. I think Deleuze and Guattari are very right in saying that thinking takes place in the relationship of territory and earth. If we lose first and second nature, we lose the very notions of gender, sexuality, ethnic diversity, uneven distribution of wealth, and class. Too easily, the shift from harsh reality into the seemingly endless possibilities of the computer programmes is made, made without much interest for these categories. The location of most of Lynn's constructions is nowhere; they might be anywhere. Just like the complexity of movement in Koolhaas' international airports, they are for the greater part interchangeable. In architecture and urbanism, we can never lose ground; third nature won't be enough. Thinking, in the end, always takes place in relation to territory and earth. We need first and second nature too.

Notes

1 Michael Speaks, "Design Intelligence and the New Economy," in *Architectural Record* (01–2003), 72.

2 See for example, David Harvey, *The Condition of Postmodernity: An Enquiry into the Origins of Cultural Change* (New York: Blackwell, 1990).

3 Ibid., 171.

4 William E. Halal, *The New Capitalism* (New York: John Wiley & Sons, 1986).

5 Scott Lash and John Urry, *The End of Organized Capitalism* (Cambridge: Polity Press, 1987).

6 E. Swyngedouw, "The Socio-spatial Implications of Innovations in Industrial Organization." *Working Paper* no 20, Johns Hopkins European Center for Regional Planning and Research (Lille: 1986).

7 Stefano Boeri, Arturo Lanzani, and Edoardo Marini, "Ambienti, paesaggi e imagine della regione Milanese," in *AIM, Associazione Interessi Metropolitani* (Milan: Editrice Abiare Segeta spa, 1993).

8 Arie Graafland, *The Socius of Architecture: Amsterdam, Tokyo, New York* (Rotterdam: 010 Publishers, 2000).

9 Alberto Pérez-Gómez, "Charles-Étienne Briseux: The Musical Body and the Limits of Instrumentality in Architecture," in *Body and Building: Essays on the Changing Relation of Body and Architecture,* ed. by George Dodds and Robert Tavernor (Cambridge, Mass.: MIT Press, 2002), 164 ff.

10 Ibid., 164.

11 Scott Lash and John Urry, *Economies of Sign and Space* (London: Sage Publications, 1994).

12 Ibid., 132.

13 Jean Baudrillard, *Simulation and Simulacra,* trans. Sheila Faria Glaser (Ann Arbor, Mich.: University of Michigan Press, 1995).

14 Neil Leach, *The Anaesthetics of Architecture* (Cambridge, Mass.: MIT Press, 1999).

15 Michael Speaks, "Design Intelligence" in *A+U* (2002:12 December), 12.

16 Ibid.

17 Bruno Latour, "Why has critique run out of steam? From matters of fact to matters of concern," in *Critical Inquiry* (Winter 2004): 226.

18 Cf. Bruno Latour, *Reassembling the Social: An Introduction to Actor-Network-Theory* (Oxford: Oxford UP, 2005).

19 Arie Graafland, op. cit.

20 George Baird, "'Criticality' and its Discontents," in *Harvard Design Magazine, Rising Ambitions, Expanding Terrain, Realism and Utopianism* (Fall/Winter 2004).

21 George Baird, op. cit., 16ff.

22 K. Michael Hays, *Modernism and the Post Humanist Subject* (Cambridge, Mass.: MIT Press, 1992).

23 See Fredric Jameson, *The Political Unconscious: Narrative as a Socially Symbolic Act* (New York: Cornell University Press, 1981) and "Postmodernism, or the Cultural Logic of Late Capitalism," in *New Left Review* 146 (July–August 1984), 63ff.

24 Manfredo Tafuri, *Theories and History of Architecture* (London: Granada Publishing, 1980).

25 K. Michael Hays, "Critical Architecture, Between Culture and Form," in *Perspecta 21, The Yale Architectural Journal* (Cambridge, Mass.: MIT Press, 1984).

26 George Baird, op. cit.

27 Arie Graafland, op. cit.

28 Manfredo Tafuri, "L'architecture dans le boudoir," in *The Sphere and the Labyrinth: Avant-gardes and Architecture from Piranesi to the 1970s* (Cambridge, Mass.: MIT Press, 1987), 267ff.

29 cf. Michel Foucault, *The Archaeology of Knowledge* (Great Britain: Tavistock Publications Limited, 1972) and *The Order of Things* (Great Britain: Tavistock Publications Limited, 1970).

30 Timothy W. Luke, "Simulated Sovereignty, Telematic Territoriality: the Political Economy of Cyberspace," in *Spaces of Culture*, ed. Mike Featherstone and Scott Lash (London: Sage, 1999), 28ff.

31 David Harvey, *Spaces of Hope* (Los Angeles: University of California Press, 2000), 215.

32 Richard Sennett, *Flesh and Stone: The Body and the City in Western Civilization* (New York, London: Norton & Company, 1994).

33 Peter Eisenman, "Unfolding Events: Frankfurt, Rebstock and the Possibility of a New Urbanism," in *Unfolding Frankfurt* (Berlin: Ernst & Sohn, Verlag fur Architektur und Technische Wissenschaften GmbH, 1991), 9.

34 Eisenman's critique is on architecture theory's neglect of the event structure in architecture. He might be right there, but I think it is not

only a question of addressing the topic of the event structure, but also the way we write about it. It is not only about an open mind for fleeting events, but very much about a fleeting way of writing about these events. For a large part, architecture history has been focused on what Eisenman calls the figure-ground relationship. Events however go further than just the 'function' of a plan. Events go deeper into the structure of a plan; indeed, they form it for the most part as I tried to show in my Versailles analysis. See my [A. Krista Sykes] *Versailles and the Mechanics of Power. The Subjugation of Circe. An Essay* (Rotterdam: 010 Publishers, 2003), 54 and note 86.

35 Daniel Gordon in his *Citizens Without Sovereignty: Equality and Sociability in French Thought, 1670–1789* (Princeton: Princeton University Press, 1994) draws attention to the influence of Thomas Mann's criticism of French 'civilization.' In his *Betrachtungen eines Unpolitischen* of 1918, Mann makes the same distinction Lash makes between 'civilization' and 'culture,' whereby Germany for Mann was more subjected to the latter and France to the former. Gordon's book deals with the to his mind uncritical antithesis as used by Elias to argue about cultural history. Gordon shows that Elias's 'spatial axis'— the difference between France and Germany—is not convincing. See my *Versailles and the Mechanics of Power. The Subjugation of Circe. An Essay* (Rotterdam: 010 Publishers, 2003), 54 and note 86.

36 K. Michael Hays, "Ideologies of Media and the Architecture of Cities in Transition," in *Cities in Transition*, ed. Arie Graafland and Deborah Hauptmann (Rotterdam: 010 Publishers, 2001), 263ff.

37 Arie Graafland, "Artificiality in the Work of Rem Koolhaas," in *Architectural Bodies* (Rotterdam: 010 Publishers, 1996), 39ff.

38 Manuel Castells, *The Informational City: Information technology, Economic Restructuring and the Urban Regional Process* (London: Blackwell, 1989).

INTRODUCTION
Metaphysics of Genetic Architecture and Computation /
Karl S. Chu

In "Metaphysics of Genetic Architecture and Computation," the
architect and educator Karl S. Chu discusses the ways in which
our world, and our conception of our past, present, and future,
are changing in response to the fields of computation and genetics. Advances in computation—for example, the growth of the
internet—have an undeniable impact on daily life. The same can
be said for developments in genetics, which affect everything from
the food supply to the types of pets available. According to Chu,
"the evolution of life and intelligence on Earth has finally reached
the point were it is now deemed possible to engender something
almost of out nothing." This widespread upheaval, fueled by the
reach and transference of information, is ushering us toward what
Chu describes as the "so-called Post-Human Era, which will
bring forth a new kind of biomachinic mutation of organic and
inorganic substances."

   In Chu's opinion, architects have yet to grasp this shift. "In
order to break through the barrier of complacency and self-
imposed ignorance on the part of the discipline, what is needed,"
he asserts, "is a radicalisation of the prevailing paradigm of
architecture...by developing a new concept of architecture that
is adequate to the demands imposed by computation and the
biogenetic revolution." Importantly, this is *not* an architecture that
imitates or copies biological form. Rather, Chu calls for "a monadology of genetic architecture that deals with the construction of
possible worlds," in which the monad is the single bit of information, capable of replicating and organizing itself into increasingly
complex networks of relations that reflect the order of its world.

KARL S. CHU

METAPHYSICS OF GENETIC ARCHITECTURE AND COMPUTATION

First appeared in *Architectural Design* 76, no. 4 (July/Aug. 2006), 38–44. Courtesy of Wiley Publishing.

"All is algorithm!"
—Gregory Chaitlin[1]

With the dissolution of the last utopian project of Man in the name of Communism, the great spectre that once haunted Europe and the rest of the world has all but vanished, leaving in its wake an ideological vacuum that is now being filled by the tentacles of globalisation with its ecumenical ambition. As humanity has become mesmerised by the triumphant spell of capitalism, what remains less apparent in the aftermath of this dissolution is that the world is moving incipiently toward a threshold that is far more radical and fantastic than any utopic vision since the dawn of the Enlightenment. Once again, the world is witnessing the rumblings of a Promethean fire that is destined to irrupt into the universe of humanity, calling into question the nature and function of life—world relations as

422

they so far have existed. These rumblings, stemming in large measure from the convergence of computation and biogenetics in the latter part of the twentieth century, have already begun to invoke gravid visions of the unthinkable: the unmasking of the primordial veil of reality.

The evolution of life and intelligence on Earth has finally reached the point where it is now deemed possible to engender something almost out of nothing. In principle, a universe of possible worlds based on generative principles inherent within nature and the physical universe is considered to be within the realm of the computable once quantum computing systems become a reality.[2] For the first time, humankind is finally in possession of the power to change and transform the genetic constitution of biological species, which, without a doubt, has profound implications for the future of life on Earth. By bringing into the foreground the hidden reservoir of life in all its potential manifestations through the manipulation of the genetic code, the unmasking or the transgression of what could be considered the first principle of prohibition—the taking into possession of what was once presumed to be the power of God to create life—may lead to conditions that are so precarious and treacherous as to even threaten the future viability of the species Homo sapiens on Earth. At the same time, depending on how humankind navigates into the universe of possible worlds that are about to be siphoned through computation, it could once again bring forth a poetic re-enchantment of the world, one that resonates with all the attributes of a premodern era derived, in this instance, from the intersection of the seemingly irreconcilable domains of logos and mythos. Organically interconnected to form a new plane of immanence that is digital, computation is the modern equivalent of a global alchemical system destined to transform the world into the sphere of hyper-intelligent beings.

The power of computation is already evident: in the last 70 years since the inception of the Universal Turing Machine,[3] it has ushered in the Information Revolution by giving rise to one of the most significant and now indispensable phenomena in the history of communication: the Internet or what could also be characterised as the universe of the Adjacent Possible. Stuart Kauffman defines the Adjacent Possible as the expansion of networks of reaction graphs within an interactive system into neighbourhood domains of connectivity which until then remain in a state of pure potentiality. He suggests that: "The Universe has not explored all possible kinds of people, legal systems, economies or other complex systems," and that "autonomous Agents tend to arrange work and coordination so that they are expanding into the Adjacent Possible as fast as they can get away with it."[4]

Like every phase transition, the Internet marks a new world order by reconfiguring the planet with a virtual, albeit an interactive, matrix that is becoming increasingly spatial, intelligent and autonomous: a global self-synthesising organ bustling with neural intelligence feasibly detectable from every corner of the Milky Way and beyond. The implications for architecture are most pronounced at the level of construction of possible worlds. The thesis this paper advances is that architecture is becoming increasingly dependent on genetic computation: the generative construction and the mutual coexistence of possible worlds within the computable domain of modal space.

Yet, what is the nature of computation that is destined to change the world, including architecture? No instrumental concept or logic of implementation since the invention of the wheel has fostered so much enthusiasm and promise as computation. Beyond the normative conception of computing machines as mere instruments for calculation, fabrication and communication, it is important to recognise the nature of the underlying ambitions of computation and its relation to architecture.

As controversial and provocative as it may seem, the underlying ambitions of computation are already apparent: the embodiment of artificial life and intelligence systems either through abstract machines or through biomachinic mutation of organic and inorganic substances and, most significantly, the subsequent sublimation of physical and actual worlds into higher forms of organic intelligence by extending into the computable domain of possible worlds. At the most prosaic level, however, computation, like natural languages, deals with information in its most general form. Computation functions as manipulator of integers, graphs, programs and many other kinds of entities. But in reality, computation only manipulates strings of symbols that represent the objects.

It should also be pointed out that, according to the late Richard Feynman, computing systems could be constructed at the atomic scale: swarms of nanobots, each functioning in accordance to a simple set of rules, could be made to infiltrate into host organisms or environments including the human body. In its simplest form, computation is a system that processes information through a discrete sequence of steps by taking the results of its preceding stage and transforming it to the next stage in accordance with a recursive function. Such an iterative procedure based on recursion has proved to be astonishingly powerful and is classified as belonging to a class of machines having universal properties.

It is not surprising that the origin of computation lies in an attempt to embody instrumental reason in an abstract machine with the attendant drive to encode the logic of life and the world around us in all its manifestations. The quest for a Universal Language[5] that could encapsulate all the attributes and functions necessary to inscribe the form and structure of all computable worlds is becoming one of the most persistent endeavors in the short history of computation. Since computation is about information processing at the most fundamental level, John Wheeler, the prominent American scientist influential to a whole generation of physicists in the latter half of the twentieth century, initiated an information-theoretic conception of the world by stipulating that every item in the universe has at bottom—at a very deep bottom, in most instances—an immaterial source and explanation that is information-theoretic in origin.[6] The fact that computation is a physical process further stipulates the existence of a self-consistent logical loop: the laws of physics define the allowed mechanical operations and the possible activities of a Universal Turing Machine, which in turn determine which mathematical operations are computable and define the nature of solvable mathematics. In other words, the laws of physics generate the very mathematics that makes those laws computable. The discovery of this inextricable linkage between computation and physics has led to the awareness that physical processes are in fact forms of computation, and nowhere is this understanding made more explicit than in Stephen Wolfram's formulation of the Principle of Computational Equivalence. Wolfram remarks: "All processes, whether they are produced by human effort or occur spontaneously in nature, can be viewed as computations."[7]

This proposition reflects a fundamental shift in the way we think about the nature of the physical universe; it is nothing short of a paradigm shift, which would not have been conceivable without an underlying thesis that enables the construction of such a world view: the Church-Turing Thesis, as formulated by Alfonso Church and Alan Turing in the early part of the twentieth century. According to Turing: "Every 'function which would naturally be regarded as computable' can be computed by the Universal Turing Machine."[8]

Although the absolute veracity of the thesis cannot be decided by logical means, all attempts to give an exact analysis of the intuitive notion of an effectively calculable function have turned out to be equivalent. Each analysis offered has proven to pick out the same class of functions, namely those that are computable by the Turing machine.

Parallel to the development of computation is the discovery of the DNA code in the early part of the twentieth century, the significance of which has only begun to be realised with the completion of the Human Genome Project. Finally, with the convergence of computation and biogenetics, the world is now moving into the so-called Post-Human Era, which will bring forth a new kind of biomachinic mutation of organic and inorganic substances. Information is the currency that drives all these developments, and nowhere is this more apparent than in the words uttered by Craig Venter, the ex-CEO of Celera Corporation which completed the human genome sequence: "The goal is to engineer a new species from scratch."[9]

Notwithstanding theological implications, this statement bluntly announces the unadulterated ambition of the biogenetic revolution. It is only a matter of time before the world will witness biomachinic mutation of species proliferating into every facet of what so far has been the cultural landscape of humanity. Architects take note: this is the beginning of the demise, if not the displacement, of the reign of anthropology, which has always subsumed architecture. Architecture, especially from the standpoint of its mythical inception, has always been a subset of anthropology: the expulsion of Minotaur, the beast, by entrapping it in the labyrinth built by Daedalus, the mythical architect at Knossos. The potential emancipation of architecture from anthropology is already enabling us to think for the first time of a new kind of xenoarchitecture with its own autonomy and will to being. In order to break through the barrier of complacency and self-imposed ignorance on the part of the discipline, what is needed is a radicalisation of the prevailing paradigm of architecture, beyond retroactive manifestos, by developing a new concept of architecture that is adequate to the demands imposed by computation and the biogenetic revolution.

Even though architects have incorporated computing systems in the design and construction of buildings and environments, the phase of transmodernity that we are now in is perhaps best characterised by the use of computation still operating under the vestiges of the old paradigm. In other words, architecture has still yet to incorporate the architecture of computation into the computation of architecture. Within the contemporary landscape of architectural discourse there are two divergent trends with theoretical motivations: the morphodynamical and the morphogenetic systems' approaches to the design and construction of buildings. These two systems are reminiscent of a strikingly similar problem that exists in modern biology, which is still attempting to synthesise the differences that exist between molecular biology, on the one hand, and developmental biology on the other. What is needed in architecture also is a similar synthesis of the two. After more than half a century of engagement with the avant-garde, the practice of architecture has become increasingly conscious of its embeddedness within the general economy of forces, relationships and the global economy. The morphodynamical approach, which has spurred two different methodological orientations in dealing with programmatic issues, is the more dominant of the two at the moment. The morphogenetic system is still more or less in its embryonic stage, even though it is by far the more fundamental and necessary since it deals with the construction of objects directly.

Having identified some of the salient features that are integral to dominant trends within contemporary architecture, as well as the nuanced relations that each of these trends have with regard to the phenomenon of globalisation, which is increasingly augmented and driven by the gift of Promethean fire that is now saturating the cultural universe of humanity with all forms of transgenic mutation, we are now in a position to articulate a more comprehensive theory of architecture, one that is adequate to the demands imposed by the convergence of computation and biogenetics in the so-called Post-Human Era: a monadology of genetic architecture that deals with the construction of possible worlds. As we now approach what Ray Kurzweil refers to as the Singularity,[10] the myth of matter, which underlies most theoretical and practical discussions of architecture, is about to be displaced by the myth of information. Contrary to Mies van der Rohe's oft-quoted remark that architecture is the art of putting two bricks together, the emerging conception is that architecture is the art of putting two bits together, at least bits that are programmed to self-replicate, self-organise and self-synthesise into evermore new constellations of emergent relations and ensembles.

The use of the term "monadology" is based on the fact that genetic architecture is an extension and transformation of some of the propositions, especially those that define attributes and properties of relationships among monads, contained in Gottfried W. Leibniz's *Monadology* (1714),[11] albeit without its theogony, into an architectural theory of world-making. *Monadology* is one of the earliest attempts in sketching out a system of principles that generalises the nature of the world from an abstract point of view; it shares conceptual properties that are now deemed to be fundamental to the science and philosophy of computation. Even though Leibniz was impeded by the lack of conceptual and technical resources at the time,[12] his ideas nonetheless paved the way for the subsequent development of computation and, according to Gregory Chaitin, Algorithmic Information Theory[13] in the twentieth century.

Leibniz's *Monadology* is arguably the earliest endeavour to propose what is now known as an open-source architecture based on the principles of philosophical genetics: the principle of generative condensation, the principle of combinatorial expansion, and the principle of the conservation of information. *Monadology* is a metaphysical treatise; Leibniz defines each monad as a metaphysical point, an irreducible concept of an atomic entity that is endowed with an immaterial substance. Contrary to Leibniz and without the reference to God as the supreme creator of monads, a computational theory of monadology would instead qualify each monad as one BIT of information at the most irreducible level, and by extension a unit of a self-replicating system. It is based on this conception of a monad as a minimal unit of a self-replicating system that a monadology of genetic architecture is developed here.

Historically, genetic architecture can be seen as an extension and transformation of utopic ideas implicit within the avant-garde to create new worlds by drawing on new sciences and technologies. Genetics is a term coined by William Bateson in 1905 to encompass the study of heredity, and "gene" was introduced around the same time by the Danish botanist Wilhelm Johannsen, to account for the units within sex cells that determine the hereditary characteristics. The meanings of both terms, "genetics" and "gene," are sufficiently abstract and general to be used as concepts that have logical implications for architecture without being anchored too explicitly to biology. Implicit within the concept of genetics is the idea of the replication of heritable units based on some rule inherent within the genetic code, and embedded within the mechanism for replication is a generative function: the self-referential logic of recursion. Recursion is a function or rule that repeatedly calls itself or its preceding stage by applying the same rule successively, thereby generating a self-referential propagation of a sequence or a series of transformations. It is this logic, encoded within an internal principle, that constitutes the autonomy of the generative that lies at the heart of computation.

Even though genetic is a term derived from biology, it is used here as a generic concept based on the interconnected logic of recursion and self-replication whose philosophical underpinnings go far beyond the confines of molecular biology. It should therefore be noted that genetic architecture is neither a representation of biology nor a form of biomimesis; instead, its theoretical origins, insofar as genetic architecture is concerned, can be traced to John von Neumann's invention of the cellular automaton and his "von Neumann architecture" for self-replicating systems. From the early stages of the development of modern computing systems, von Neumann was proposing the idea of self-replication. Even though he participated in discussions, leading to the development of the first electronic computer ever built—the ENIAC—von Neumann eventually came up with what is now known as the von Neumann architecture—the prototype for modern computing systems with its stored memory program. This addressed the idea of a machine that could manufacture itself: a robot that self-replicates and self constructs copies of itself,[14] a notion that lies at the heart of biology: the essence of self-reproduction is organisation—the ability of a system to contain a complete description of itself and use that information to create new copies.

The von Neumann architecture for a self-replicating system is the ancestral and archetypical proposal, which consisted of two central elements: a Universal Computer and a Universal Constructor. The Universal Computer contains a program that directs the behaviour of the Universal Constructor, which, in turn, is used to manufacture both another Universal Computer and a Universal Constructor. Once finished, the newly manufactured Universal Computer was programmed by copying the program contained in the original Universal Computer, and program execution would then begin again. The von Neumann architecture is, therefore, a precursor to the architecture of a genetic system.

Notes

1   Gregory Chaitin, *Leibniz, Information, Math and Physics*, http://www.cs.auckland.ac.nz/CDMTCS/chaltin/kirchberg.pdfl, 2003, 9.

2   David Deutsch, "Quantum Theory, the Church-Turing Principle and the Universal Quantum Computer," in *Proceedings of the Royal Society of London* A 400, 1985, 3.

3   Alan Turing, "On Computable Numbers with an Application to the Entscheidungsproblem," *Proceedings of the London Mathematical Society*, Ser 2, Vol 42, 1936. Alan Turing developed the Universal Turing Machine, an abstract machine in the logical sense of the term, in response to David Hilbert's call for the resolution of the decision problem, or Entscheidungsproblem, in mathematics.

4   Stuart Kauffman, *Investigations* (New York: Oxford University Press, 2000), 142–44. Kauffman's concept of the Adjacent Possible was applied in the context of his investigations into the origin of life based on autocatalytic systems, which are derived from random interactions of nodes within Boolean networks. See http://www.paulagordon.com/shows/kauffman/.

5   Paolo Rossi, *Logic and the Art of Memory: The Quest for a Universal Language* (Chicago: University of Chicago Press, 2000), 145–94.

6   John Wheeler, "Information, Physics, Quantum: The Search for Links," in *Complexity, Entropy and the Physics of Information*, ed. Zurek Wojciech (Santa Fe Institute Studies in the Sciences of Complexity Proceedings), Vol VIII, (Reading, Mass.: Addison-Wesley, 1989), 5.

7   Stephen Wolfram, *A New Kind of Science* (Champaign, Ill.: Wolfram Research, 2002), 41.

8   Alan Turing, op cit. Note: Apart from the analyses defined in terms of lambda-definability and recursiveness by Alonzo Church, there are analyses in terms of register machines by John C. Shepherdson and Howard E. Sturgis, Emil L. Post's canonical and normal systems, combinatory definability by Moses Schönfinkel and Haskell B. Curry, Markov algorithms and Gödel's notion of reckonability.

9   Craig Venter, "Supermicrobe Man," *Wired*, no. 10, 12 December 2002, 191.

10 Ray Kurzweil, "The Singularity," in John Brockman, *The New Humanists: Science at the Edge* (New York: Barnes & Noble, 2003), 215–32.

11 G.W. Leibniz and Nicholas Rescher, *G.W. Leibniz's Monadology: An Edition for Students*, (Pittsburgh, Pa.: University of Pittsburgh Press, 1991).

12 Martin Davis, *The Universal Computer: The Road From Leibniz to Turing* (New York: W.W. Norton, 2000), 180–87.

13 Chaitlin, op cit.

14 William Poundstone, *The Recursive Universe: Cosmic Complexity and the Limits of Scientific Knowledge* (Chicago: Contemporary Books, Inc., 1985). See also: http://www.zyvex.com/nanotech/selfRepJBIS .html#vonNeumannArchitecture.

INTRODUCTION

Introduction to *Atlas of Novel Tectonics* /
Reiser + Umemoto

In 1986, architect/educator Jesse Reiser and architect/landscape architect Nanako Umemoto founded their New York–based design firm Reiser + Umemoto. Since then, this husband–wife team has developed a design philosophy that is expressed in their book published two decades later, *Atlas of Novel Tectonics*. As the title implies, Reiser + Umemoto's architectural approach hinges on innovation, materiality, and a certain brand of practicality that (in keeping with the image of an "atlas") incorporates a matter-of-fact attitude toward architectural design. Indeed, as they clearly state in their introduction to the *Atlas*, "the primary and necessary conceit of this work is that beneficial novelty is the preferred condition to stability and the driving agenda behind architectural practice." This makes sense, as they view "architectural design as a series of specific problem situations," where the "design process allows openings and advances to occur," generating a practice "agile enough to avoid getting stuck." The novel provides room to maneuver, space for architecture to evolve.

Architecture, as Reiser + Umemoto declare, is constantly faced with new challenges due to changing methods of inhabitation. A building erected to address one problem will, most likely, find itself asked to accommodate others after its completion. It is this unpredictability, this volatility that pushes the discipline toward the novel. This inherent instability can give rise to a dynamic architecture—not in the sense of an architecture that actually moves or modifies its form, but rather an architecture that is simultaneously "matter" and "atmosphere," "structure" and "effects." The authors feel that such an architecture derives from an emphasis on a material practice that erodes the opposition of

434

architectural object and field, permitting "a notion of space and matter as one."

Reiser + Umemoto's appreciation for "beneficial novelty" does not preclude more conventional or accepted aspects of the discipline. Thus they do not shy away from the architecture of the past, nor do they shun traditional architectural concepts, which provide a platform from which invention can emerge. This notion sets the path for the successive discussions within the *Atlas of Novel Tectonics*, which read as brief commentaries and occasionally parables on issues of concern within architectural practice.

INTRODUCTION

First appeared in *Atlas of Novel Tectonics* (New York: Princeton
Architectural Press, 2006), 17–35.

The most attentive study of the most homogenous milieu,
of the most closely woven concatenation of circumstances,
will not serve to give us the design of the towers of Laon.
—Henri Focillon, *The Life of Forms in Art*

It may seem a strange contradiction in a book devoted to concepts to put forward a call for the specific, but all the concepts,
all the models presented here, are meaningless to the architect
if the specific reality of the project is absent. For unlike planning, the success or failure of architecture rests finally on its
specificity, and no account of circumstances will ever account
for the work as such.

In a time so obsessed with establishing the value of works
as the products of contexts and conditions, the architect may
take solace in the fact that the corrosive relativism that plagues
the historian will not plague the architect who curiously traffics
in products that, if not permanently fixed, and however formed
around the flux of matter, nevertheless rest on the side of persistence. They are never reducible to the fleeting interpretations—

436

or, for that matter, practices—projected onto them. Thus, architecture is the substrate for the accidents of history rather than its embodiment.

This persistence gives us pleasure precisely because of the other developments that go with it.

The historian, and the critic, bear an imperative to contextualize and establish meaning, which stands them in opposition to the practice of architectural design. History, merely as a form of consciousness, is not sufficient to give rise to the architectural project. This is not to deny the importance of histories, texts, and conditions but to point out a property of the architectural artifact. The history, conditions, and time of formation of any project are distinct from the effects of the project itself, which has its own particular way of influencing histories as it mobilizes effects. Indeed, as Friedrich Nietzsche points out in his 1874 essay "On the Uses and Disadvantages of History for Life," there is always an element of the unhistorical in any act of creation.[1] This is not only a vital precondition to creating anything new but also adheres to the object of architecture itself, which, after all, will always exceed the words that order architectural programs. Just as Jorge Luis Borges suggests that an author creates his own precursors, new architecture fundamentally reorganizes the canon. Architecture makes a new history; history doesn't make a new architecture.

The primary and necessary conceit of this work is that beneficial novelty is the preferred condition to stability and the driving agenda behind architectural practice. This in no way requires us to reject traditional practices or the pragmatics of architecture. In fact, we consider it doubly incumbent upon those pursuing the novel to embrace these fields.

The naturalist polymath D'Arcy Thompson modestly states in his 1917 *On Growth and Form*, "This book of mine has little need of preface for it is indeed all preface from beginning to end."[2] Like Thompson's work, ours is prefatory. Our treatment deals in a qualitative fashion with issues that ultimately require quantitative treatment: the province of our collaborators, engineers.

Like Anthelme Brillat-Savarin's 1825 *Physiology of Taste*, this is not a book of recipes, but in its specificity, it suggests a way of operating within the discipline. Each argument develops around a specific condition or case, but its value lies in its wider application. We see architectural design as a series of specific problem situations that, contrary to the discursive disciplines, cannot be argued away. The architectural design process allows openings and advances to occur before the problem's sheer recalcitrance shuts down development. Thusly, design practice becomes agile enough to avoid getting stuck.

Potential

In his 1981 book *A Scientific Autobiography*, Aldo Rossi makes the relationship of matter and energy a fundamental precondition of architecture. He describes the physicist Max Planck's account of a schoolmaster's story about a mason who with great effort heaved a block of stone up on the roof of a house:

> The mason was struck by the fact that expended energy does not get lost; it remains stored for many years, never diminished, latent in the block of stone, until one day it happens that the block slides off the roof and falls on the head of a passerby, killing him...in architecture this search is also undoubtedly bound up with the material and with energy; and if one fails to take note of this, it is not possible to comprehend any building, either from a technical point of view or from a compositional one. In the use of every material there must be an anticipation of the construction of a place and its transformation.[3]

Rossi's observations are more pertinent today than ever. While matter and energy constitute the vital components of Rossi's formulation, they exist within an essentialist universe of fixed typologies, the potential of which is understood as the anima that surrounds objects of perfect stillness. And yet, the same actors are in play: energy, matter, and potential, but their roles have been reversed. Rossi delights in "the double meaning of the Italian word *tempo*, which signifies both atmosphere and chronology."[4] The mist that daily glides into the galleria animates its vast silent form with the life that has animated architecture since the advent of classicism. But we have other ambitions for this vitality, which now must enter and find expression in the fabric of matter itself. Let's be clear: it is not the vulgar misconception that architecture must be literally animate, nor that processes illustrated by animation software guarantee dynamic architecture. It need not move, but its substance, its scale, its transitions and measurement will be marked by the dilations and contractions of the energy field.

A universe defined by a fixed field and unchanging essences has been superceded by a matter field that is defined locally only in and through its own interactions. This architecture is about speeds rather than movements. Speed is understood as an absolute, therefore this architecture's fabric may register speeds from very fast to very slow while remaining essentially in place. Architecture thus is no longer the brooding and silent witness to the flux of tempo but is as much matter and structure as it is atmosphere and effects. We've gone from seeing temporal work in contrast to permanent architecture to seeing the temporal entering into the very fabric of the architecture itself, rendering it ambient.

In contrast to Rem Koolhaas's notion that freedom is an absence of architecture —as, for example, when he describes the open space of a town square as embodying the greatest possible freedom—we side with Rossi's belief that freedom in Koolhaas's sense is vacuous; that, in fact, it is the constraints of architecture, its formal particularity and persistence beyond any functionalist determination, that truly embodies freedom. For in being neither uniformly open nor uniformly closed, it lies open to the unforeseen as it works on our changing activities over time.

We assert the primacy of material and formal specificity over myth and interpretation. In fact, while all myth and interpretation derives from the immediacy of material phenomena, this equation is not reversible. When you try to make fact out of myth language only begets more language, with architecture assuming the role of illustration or allegory. This is true not only of the initial condition of architecture but actually plays out during the design process in a similar way. Material practice is the shift from asking "what does this mean?" to "what does this do?"

From Extensive Field/Intensive Object To Intensive Field-Object

In response to the perceived sterility and homogeneity of modern architecture, figures of the last generation as varied as Robert Venturi and John Hejduk selected and developed highly specific elements of the movement. This extraction of (generally figurative) motifs from the more systematic, Cartesian field they had occupied in high modernism was seen as a promulgation of uniqueness and variety in architecture. With equal ease, it could be defined through the development of a singular volume or figure or, in more discontinuous fashion, the collage technique. But this selective approach carried liabilities as well, for it dispensed with the grand systematic ambitions of modernism in favor of an idiosyncratic approach and concentrated on a revision of modernism that foregrounded the object divested of its field.

For architects, notions of space, until recently, remained trenchantly Cartesian, whether the field was recognized or the object premiated. The big shift, in which our work participates is the removal of the fixed background, of ordinates and coordinates, in favor of a notion of space and matter as being one. This shift is not simply one in concept or belief that would leave the architecture unchanged; at a fundamental level, it changes the way architecture is thought about and designed, and the way it emerges as a material fact.

Apologists for modernism—or those who simply want to extend the modernist project by updating their arguments while leaving the architecture unchanged—are in grave error. In their minds, the shifting paradigm is simply yet another shift in discourse, it doesn't affect the object, and the object has no effect on it. Discourse alone merely becomes a more fashionable view of the same universe, thus implying that the early model is but a failure of interpretation.

The Cartesian paradigm, long discredited in the sciences, has lost its hold on architectural thinking. In fact, it was always a special case of a larger universe, the potential of which lay untapped and unrealizable before the advent of new paradigms. You need the new model to think the new work. And so we are not denying the existence of universal space, we are suggesting that the universal is not coordinates without qualities but rather a material field of ubiquitous difference.

Any serious project today must nevertheless contend with the force of the modernist canon and its outgrowths. We see our project not as a completion of universal models such as those devised by the modernists, nor as a counter-model to them, but rather as an excursion into new territory. Some baggage must be dropped along the way, or like the Argo, become a vehicle transfigured by the journey. This book is part of the critical project, but it aspires to an affirmative criticality. We seek to dispel the essentialist assumptions about universality, solidified notions about historical models, and even the irreducibility of the authors themselves. For it becomes surprisingly evident that the canonical works display a profound impersonality; they are, in fact, the most comprehensive confrontations with a problematic that only later acquire an authorial stamp.

This tension among classical models, structural honesty, and compositional formalism constitutes a "both-and" argument in the Venturian sense.[5] But in contrast to Venturi's formulation, our project understands this dynamic not as a play of signifiers to be "read" (and thus, fixed in issues of meaning) but as a properly material contest in material logics. We would postulate an "and and and" argument—neither pure classical models, nor pure structural honesty nor pure compositional formalism, implying a more open-ended process.

Venturi's "both-and" is a mannerist hierarchy that attempts to regulate complexity and contradiction as a comprehensive whole as a legible dimension of the building. "And and and" pushes multiplicity to a level of depth that isn't present in the purely semiotic arguments of Venturi. For while all architecture can be read, it is only the postmodernists who reduce both process and reception to a semiotic game. This architecture of multiplicities operates as much with the visible conditions of architecture as the invisible processes of, for example, structure and program. This is, in a sense, more closely connected to a modernist depth than a mere play of surfaces and signifiers.

For example, the Miesian project in its most impersonal and "universal" sense may thus be resituated. As a special case within a much larger and more varied universe. We see a systematicity to endeavors such as Mies's which can be exponentially expanded through modes that allow for emergence rather than merely extension.

This therefore is not yet another plea for eclecticism but a shift for modernism into new and unforeseen territories. This is a critical stance that can only be worked out architecturally. Taking the specific problematic as a starting point, how does one produce multiplicities in formal arrangements? How does one produce multiplicity in structure? How does one produce multiplicity in function? This is the content of this book.

Constraints

> It will be remembered that the principle of exclusion is a very simple, not to say primitive, principle that denies the values it opposes. The principle of sacrifice admits and indeed implies the existence of a multiplicity of values. What is sacrificed is acknowledged to be a value even though it has to yield to another value which commands priority.
> —Sir E. H. Gombrich, "Norm and Form"

Sir E. H. Gombrich's 1966 essay "Norm and Form" serves as an instructive way to navigate both our attraction to Mies's classical solutions and the desire for the resolution, or adjudication, of competing and conflicting demands. Gombrich first makes the claim that there are indeed classical solutions. For example, the resolution of the conflict in painting between balance and symmetry—once symmetry is challenged—is arrived at through "an ideal compromise between two conflicting demands."[6] This compromise is thought to be classical in the sense of presenting an unsurpassed solution that could only be repeated, not improved upon. Deviation on the one side would threaten the correctness of design; on the other, the feeling of order. Seen from this point of view, the "classical" solution is indeed a technical rather than a psychological achievement.

The classical is what Sir Gombrich calls a "norm," which embodies an "essence" that "permits us to plot other works of art at a variable distance from this central point."[7] The art historian distinguishes such genealogies as classicism and its descendents from mere series of morphological distinctions. It is only when distinction is defined by its correspondence with and deviation from certain norms—that is, its response to human aims and human instruments—that, to use polymath Gregory Bateson's term, they embody a "difference that makes a difference."[8]

There is a kind of paradox in that, one could argue, there is a greater stability to something like painting, where aside from the developments of interpretation and practice, the form and program of any particular painting remain fixed forever in their time, whereas in architecture, ever-changing demands and uses are either accommodated or resisted by the building. But the very instability of the temporal inhabitation of buildings, per se, is a part of the force that drives the discipline as a whole to novelty, in that it is constantly being asked to address new and changing problems. And while such demands can never be finally addressed, they serve as a heuristic device to invention.

What is of interest to us is distinguishing between the place of the norm in the perpetuation model of the classical and the novelty that emerges when architecture addresses evolving demands. This issue of the norm, in some sense, is related to the issue of difference, as for example when a normative model is so elaborated upon and it departs so much from the model from which it was derived that it shifts from being a difference in degree to a difference in kind. Such extreme elaboration, in the minds of conservative critics and architects, has the unfortunate effect of shutting down highly profitable areas of invention in a call for a return to order.

They, in effect, operate under what Gombrich characterizes as an exclusionary principle—a reductive operation, as common in criticism as it is in manifestoes. Under exclusionism, the specificity of what is being excluded is not engaged but rather dismissed out of hand. In functionalism, for instance, any element that would be deemed ornamental is systematically excluded.[9]

We see that the norms themselves, in so much as they are understood as demands and necessities, are instable. They come in and out of being and change over time. Extreme elaboration can produce demands that never existed before. Thus, inventions may lay fallow for a time, until they are pulled in to the social field when a receptive context for them comes about. In this way, invention actually forms a norm.

Architectural solutions are never free of the categories they dismiss. There is a decorative element to functionalism that exists even when all ornament has been stripped away. Within what Gombrich calls the sacrificial mode, by contrast, conflicting demands are more gradually worked out through emphasis and exchange, leaving open such possibilities as decorative function. The principle of sacrifice "admits and indeed implies the existence of a multiplicity of values. What is sacrificed is acknowledged to be a value even though it has to yield to another value which commands priority."[10]

Since what is built and inhabited often persists beyond the social practices that define its use, there nevertheless exists a hierarchy of forms and arrangements of the gross form of architecture, which indirectly work on the more temporal arrangements that go on within it. This relationship is at best probabilistic, like the continuously changing arrangements of office furniture governed by the market forces at work in high-rise buildings. We hold to the idea that architecture is not simply reducible to the container and the contained but that there exists a dynamic exchange between the life of matter and the matter of our lives.

Notes

1   Friedrich Nietzsche, "On the Uses and Disadvantages of History," in *Untimely Meditations*, ed. Daniel Breazeale, trans. R. J. Hollingdale (Cambridge, Mass.: Cambridge University Press, 1997), 57–124.

2   D'Arcy Thompson, *On Growth and Form*, rev. ed. (New York: Dover, 1992), prefatory note.

3   Aldo Rossi, *A Scientific Autobiography*, trans. Lawrence Venuti (Cambridge, Mass.: MIT Press, 1981), 1.

4   Ibid.

5   Robert Venturi, *Complexity and Contradiction in Architecture* (New York: Museum of Modern Art, 1966), 30.

6   E. H. Gombrich, "Norm and Form," in *Studies in the Art of the Renaissance*, second ed. (New York: Phaidon, 1971), 95.

7   Ibid., 96.

8   Gregory Bateson, *Steps to Ecology of Mind* (Chicago: University of Chicago Press, 2000), 459.

9   Gombrich, "Norm and Form," 97.

10 Ibid.

INTRODUCTION
Practice Makes Perfect / *Sylvia Lavin*

In "Practice Makes Perfect," originally a lecture given at the
Berlage Institute in Rotterdam in March 2006, the architectural
historian, theoretician, and educator Sylvia Lavin boldly asserts:
"Architecture has no contemporary theory of practice. There
are theories of architecture but only shoptalk about buildings."
To assess how this situation arose, she explores the role of representation in architecture during the past four decades, from
the "era of representation" to the "space of representation."
According to Lavin, during the era of representation—which
accompanied and responded to strident critiques of structuralism
and language—architecture for various reasons became a representation of the societal ills modern architecture failed to cure,
and architects enacted a purge of sorts via conceptual and actual
violent maneuvers carried out on architectural objects. Explained
by Lavin in psychological terms, this necessary stage segued
into a permanent attitude of martyrdom no longer appropriate
for or relevant to the discipline's cultural situation. Architecture
entered the space of representation, where representation served
as a refuge for architecture, "a hideout instead of a means of
attack." Thus architecture arrives in the twenty-first century, where
we discover Norman Foster's Swiss Re Tower (now 30 St. Mary
Axe), a work restrained by the "stiff logic of representation," the
inescapable image of tower-as-dildo. At this point, Lavin concludes, representation for architecture is more of a prison than a
sanctuary.

With this explanatory narrative as a platform, Lavin's main
directive—delivered through an entertaining analogy between
architecture and sex toys—is for architecture to "focus less on
representation and more on practice." As to how this might be
accomplished, Lavin offers the logic of the pet rock as a model for

447

an architecture that escapes the dichotomy of good-versus-bad in favor of an architecture that traffics in novelty and pleasure. It is interesting to note that the architectural project Lavin aligns with the pet rock is yet another, albeit earlier, Foster design—the Willis, Faber, and Dumas Building of 1970.

SYLVIA LAVIN

PRACTICE MAKES PERFECT

First appeared in *Hunch* 11 (Winter 2006/7), 106–13. Courtesy of
Sylvia Lavin and Penelope Dean.

Alejandro Zaera-Polo likes Norman Foster's Swiss Re
Headquarters. He thinks there is much to learn, almost admire,
from this building—how it circulates through the world to how
it has captured popular appeal: the British have named it as they
would a pet (the "gherkin"). Above all, Alejandro offers it and its
architect as models for new forms of achievement and success
in architecture. And Alejandro has speculated that many of these
qualities stem from the building's representational character,
from what Charles Jencks has called its iconicity or what Kevin
Lynch would have called its imageability. In other words, it's a
simple sign that everyone can read but is not overly literal allowing personal projections to take place, an understandable image
waiting to be customized: the British like gherkins, Americans
like pickles, and the building is generic enough to stand in for
either condiment. And, again according to Alejandro, it's an
image abstract enough not only to allow customization but to
serve the architect as camouflage as well, allowing him to slip

449

in ulterior meanings, motives, and complexities that have nothing at all do to with side dishes, but rather that use side dishes as cover for architectural agendas, ideas that are contraband and must be smuggled into architecture because they would be unpalatable to the client, the city, or the public in a more direct state. Clients like pickles but architects use pickles to camouflage their cucumbers, which they prefer to offer raw to anyone who will bite.

Leaving aside for the moment just what a cucumber decoder might be and what kind of architectural secrets a cucumber can hide, once the idea of building-as-sign is invoked, a slippery slope appears heading straight for understanding architecture in terms of less fluid forms of signification, toward what Erwin Panofksy called its symbolic form, what Robert Venturi would have called its iconography, what Jencks used to call its meaning, and what Freud would have called its dream wish. In this land of signs and semiotics, of metaphors and imagery, symbolic representations tend to stabilize interpretation providing not blank slates on which anything can be projected and through which covert intentions can be slipped, but rather acting as security checkpoints that insist on a one-to-one identification between your papers and your image making sure that you are who and what you appear to be. The logic of representation is difficult to outwit or double-cross. As a result, chances are that using representation as a mere expedient will entangle the architect in an ever more rigid understanding of how images communicate. That Andy Warhol's witty soup full of double entendres did in fact lead to Charles Moore's Piazza d'Italia and then to Daniel Libeskind's 1776 Tower of Freedom is not just the story of the dumbing-down of representation by architecture but of the inevitable trajectory of representation. There is little room for innuendo or coyly flirtatious evasiveness once representation takes control. Instead, the stiff logic of representation makes it necessary to conclude, in the case of the Foster tower, that whatever double meaning it may have, whatever secret architectural code Alejandro thinks is in there doing the work of mole, spy, and secret agent, its image ultimately conflates with and in a single overt meaning. Face it: what the British with their so quaint, quirky, and secretly demented euphemisms call the erotic gherkin, looks like a penis, or a substitute penis, what we vulgar Americans call a dildo.

This is where and why the building's interest begins to detumesce. It's not that I have a puritanical resistance to the idea of arousing buildings; quite the contrary. The problem, once that I've been led into the land both of look-a-likes and lookie-loos, is what kind of dildo the gherkin resembles. Advanced dildos, or at least those that are voted most popular and best designed, don't look like penises anymore. Sex toys have learned the lesson that signifiers and signifieds have loose connections that can be exploited: sex toys revel in the idea that the penis and the phallus are separable. Sex toys know that imageability is best understood not as an element of meaning but as a functional part of performance—looking sexy rather than like a penis enhances the performance of a dildo. Furthermore, historically speaking, penis buildings as a typology, and it is one, have been something of a flop, one-liners that can't make it for the long haul, which leads to the conclusion that we really don't need any more penis buildings.

Instead of going to learn from Las Vegas, architecture needs to get some "sex ed" at Agent Provocateur. Letting go of the iconography of the penis has permitted dildos to perform in ways that expose a penis as, well, lacking. Dildos have become more visually provocative and more performatively effective than architecture. So the lesson of Agent Provocateur is: focus less on representation and more on practice. And speaking of sex toys and performance, practice makes perfect as any woman can tell you. Architecture doesn't get enough practice these days, not because it doesn't like to mix business with dildos but rather because it has forgotten how to mix pleasure with practice.

Architecture has no contemporary theory of practice. There are theories of architecture but only shoptalk about buildings. In fact, most architects think of professional practice as antithetical to theorization and resistant to being construed as a theoretical object. As a result, the construction explosion is causing a free-fall from high-concept work down toward concrete blocks and architecture has no strategy for landing. Alejandro is one of the few contemporary architects who is both getting caught up in the building boom yet working hard to be intelligent and deliberate about being ensnared. Nevertheless, how to talk to clients is not a question reducible to representation. For example, Elizabeth Diller is also looking for ways to reflect on communication in practice yet she insistently avoids the use of iconic images to collapse all of a project's complexities into a single package. Instead, she is exploring a double, triple, and quadruple-speak, a plurality of discursive genres, each highly specific and tailored to a particular audience and constituency. The point is not that D+S and FOA have differing opinions about representation. The point is that they are both confronting a historical shift into practice.

Practice is booming today, and not just because the young are older, the small are bigger, and more money is available. That is always the case. Instead, the building boom reflects the fact that the historical circumstances of architecture—its place in the geography of contemporary culture—are fundamentally different today than they were thrity years ago and have been changed by significant pressures exerted from within the discipline. An actual history has unfolded and is unique to the last several decades; it's a particular history of architecture of what I will call the era of representation and of how that era structured itself in relation to professionalism, practice, and disciplinarity.

The era of representation began when philosophy came to recognize that its traditional study of truth and knowledge was in fact a study of the language used to represent ideas about truth and knowledge. The way architecture worked through this bite of the apple and expulsion from philosophical paradise constituted an enormous intellectual effort that led to the radicalization of the field in the 1960s. Many of the ontologically confusing phenomena of that period—confusing in scale, in function, and in duration—were the tools used by architecture to think how building would have to change in the face of the problem of language and the epistemological uncertainties thereby produced. At the same time, however, the confidence in building that typified the pre-war architect, that gave him the fantastic hubris necessary to imagine things like the *Plan Voisin*, was shaken by the idea that buildings are not things but rather are mediated representations, and a self-assured building profession became instead a suspicious and critical set of discourses.

The beginning of the most radical phase of this era of representation is often dated to between 1966 and 1970 when Jacques Derrida delivered and published *Structure, Sign, and Play in the Discourse of the Human Sciences*. During these years, Derrida's attack on structuralism expanded to become a critique of structurality itself and of the understanding of the center as not only a repressive concept but an impossible one at that—both bad and false at the same time. This expansion coincided with and is the philosophical armature of the student protests against the war and the many institutions, equally repressive and of centralizing power, that supported it. Both of these uprisings, the one led by students, the other by philosophers, identified buildings, which usually contain both structure and centers, as the most formidable and obdurate instantiation of the problem of intellectual and political authority. Architecture's objecthood, its literal physical matter and body, geometry and structure, made it an ideal target. But not because architecture is in fact more complicit or exploitive than other institutions or disciplines, although these were all given as reasons. It was an ideal target because its buildings sat still and were easy to hit and hitting something—anything—made escaping complicity seem possible. By the late 1960s, it had become necessary, not anecdotally but historically and theoretically, to believe that one could not build one's way out of political inequity, as the early modernists had, and to think that architecture could never offer a solution to housing, as even the immediate post-war architects had. Architecture had become the problem, not a solution, and a straw figure used as a sitting duck in the war against "the man."

Another name for a sitting duck is a bad object, which is something that isn't really bad and isn't really an object. Instead, a bad object is a representation, a psychic image that is used to hold and contain all bad things, bad feelings, and indeed badness itself. A less technical term is scapegoat. The benefit of producing this bad object is that it makes good objects possible. Good objects and bad objects are equally fictitious: one totally idealized, the other absolutely demonized. Pre-war modernists operated within an era of truth and in a culture that perceived architecture as a good object. As such, architecture was idealized and therefore over-promised and under-delivered. In contrast, by the late 1960s, belief in "the facts" had become the anxious suspicion that necessarily accompanies the regime of representation where nothing can be as it seems. In order to find a significant role in this era, architecture voluntarily committed ritual suicide and provided the social and cultural landscape with a collective bad object.

A good demonstration of how this worked are statements by Julian Beck, the founder of the Living Theater, an experimental group that ultimately exiled itself to Europe because its original venues in New York were closed again and again by various government agencies, including the fire department and the Internal Revenue Service. When the NYC building department stepped in, however, Beck's justifiable rage against yet another bureaucracy turned into a rage against architecture itself. The statement was made in the context of a discussion of the 1970 trial of the Chicago Seven, which had become a spectacular event that staged the splitting of the good counter-culture against the bad "man." For Beck, architecture organized this split and what might have been an indictment of the legal system used Mies and his architecture quite literally as a theater on which to stage an attack on repression itself. Beck writes:

> during the trial, the judge is annoyed with the defense attorney's unwillingness to sit still. And the judge says, there is a great architect, Mies van der Rohe, who designed that lectern as well as the building, and it was a lectern and not a leaning post. I have asked you to stand behind it when you question the witness.
>
> Pomposity, inflexible, rampant, the tall straight rigid buildings, with the straight proud men, the ramrod spines, not bent by labor...repressive architecture is rampant...The Parthenon? Its geometry? Beauty and Philosophy are not enough. Who lugged the stones? Who smelted the bronze for van der Rohe's whiskey building?

Over the course of these few sentences, a lectern is transposed into architecture and then into geometry itself, which in turn becomes a system for maintaining not only a repressive legal structure but for social inequity as far back as ancient slavery. In this hysteria, any thought of Mies as a force for good is erased. Such a ramrod slave master could not have been a director of the Bauhaus, a champion of collective housing, a Jew in 1930s Germany who escaped and brought gifts like the Resor House to the U.S. There is no nuance in Beck's diatribe, no sense of the complexities that make up either a person or a building. Mies and his building do not in fact exist for Beck but rather are psychological projections and representations pressed into service as bad objects.

1970 was a good year for being a bad object. Architecture attracted widespread attention for its badness as it became the thing everyone loved to hate. Superstudio thought you could only save architecture by killing it. In a gesture of utopian mercy, they drowned the monuments of Italy. The Austrians and the French preferred to blow things up. Architects willingly served up architecture as a kind of noble sacrifice to the cause. Cutting was a favorite way to demonstrate the badness of the architectural object. Architects transformed the traditional understanding of buildings as bodies into bodies as sites of ritualistic self-mutilation. Peter Eisenman not only sheared building from architecture and the profession from the discipline but literally cut the Frank House to shreds. The best cutter of them all was Gordon Matta-Clark, who in this same pivotal year of 1970 sliced up a suburban house.

Splitting is not only Matta-Clark's most influential work, it is also the psychoanalytic term for dividing things into absolute good and bad objects. Splitting is a primitive form of defense, useful for infants (and the historical avant-garde), but generally associated with borderline personalities in adults who presumably should be better able to manage a more integrated sense of both good and bad. Splitting is a way of managing the world that starts off useful and ends up a problem. In 1970, it was good for buildings to get sliced, attacked, blown to bits, hidden, and drowned, since the attacks on these bad objects made good political action seem possible. Splitting architecture into a bad object had good purposes, and the structure of representation that made the splitting possible was a needed weapon in a justified war. The refusal to build and the containment of architecture within representation, such as in the work of John Hejduk, was thus not a matter of insufficient opportunity but a matter of principal.

But as is always and inevitably the case, exaggerated moral principles turn into dogma just as in warfare, confusion reigns on the battlefield, friendly fire goes off, and the difference between foe and ally gets slippery. Splitting moved from a necessary psychological stage into a pathological condition. Instead of engaging representation as a philosophical question it became an architectural strategy, a space into which architecture moved. By the 1980s, when it became conceivable to some that, for example, Hejduk's Bye House should actually get built, architecture had left the era of representation, in and through which Hejduk had conceived the house, to enter a commodified and fetishized space of representation. At this point, representation became a hideout instead of a means of attack.

Today, we can perversely say that we are lucky enough to once again have enemies. The psychological terrain of contemporary culture has shifted: bad objects are everywhere and we don't need to make them up. In fact, we need some, any, good objects. Popular culture is way ahead of architects in recognizing and acting on this need. Culture at large is eager to love architecture, is desperate to perceive it as a good object that always delivers, while architects still tend to be self-loathing, ready to reject every accomplishment, embarrassed and perplexed that anyone would think building useful, humiliated and condescending to its own success. That everyone in the world wanted to attribute the Bilbao effect to the architect, except architects, is a good case in point (whatever the facts may be).

Architects must return to building as a matter of principal, not as a matter of accident or anecdote. The building boom is not only the result of extra-architectural phenomena but an indication that architecture is ready to emerge from its hideout in the space of representation: not to return to the impossible ideals of the good object, but to forgo the by-now masochistic pleasure of being a bad object. Psychoanalysis offers as a solution what it calls the good-enough object, which is good at some things in some contexts for some period of time for particular purposes. 1970 was a good year for cutting up buildings because architecture hadn't yet been fully subjected to the regime of splitting. But by the same token, 1970 was a good year for finding buildings that didn't need to choose between being good and bad, but rather still had available the option of being just good enough. Foster himself did not always work through the logic of representation and with the goal of being an over-idealized object waiting to be worshipped. Unlike the gherkin, which imagines itself to be a good object but is just a disappointing penis, Foster's Willis, Faber, Dumas Building of 1970 is more like a pet rock.

If dildos are useful for thinking through the failure of the good object, novelty items make good models for good-enough architectural objects. The pet rock, a product of the 1970s, is the most perfect novelty item ever: nothing more than an advertising gimmick and the total collapse of packaging into package. Pet rocks are, ontologically speaking, undecidable kinds of objects—ridiculous, but also seriously good at doing what they set out to do. The fad lasted less than a year and reached its apogee in 1975 when it was the Christmas gift to give. Pet rocks were desirable because they exemplified newness, which is the temporal equivalent to the "good enough." Novelty does not operate within the stabilizing economy of opposites like good and bad but generates a more quixotic logic of newness. Novelty works as a shifter within the ephemeral economy of information flows and therefore, unlike originality, has a wily and cunning quality that makes it hard to pin down. Because novelty is fickle and short-term, it cannot acquire authority and certainly no gravitas: it can make no big promises and therefore can never under-deliver or disappoint. Without either use or exchange value, novelty can only be measured by the pleasure it provokes. Generic yet different, mass-produced yet found, perfectly unjustifiable yet able to capture popular affection in entirely unprecedented ways, novelty items are good enough models for contemporary architecture.

So rather than try to use representation as a way to dupe clients into building something they don't want, why not sell them something they desire. The pet rock as an architectural diagram is more compelling than a penis or a palm tree: it generates neither original nor copy, comes with little self-importance and exploits its very frivolity. Utterly beneath contempt, pet rocks are oblivious to legislation and restrictive scrutiny. Ontologically and functionally unstable, it is impossible to fall into the false positivism of conventional architectural discourse, or what Philip Johnson called crutches, when talking about them. The pet rock demands inventive response, since to say your pet rock was bad today or your pet rock was good today would mean nothing. The pet rock cannot be cut, or drowned, or split in two: it is not susceptible to either idealization or demonization. It contains no secret messages, has nothing to decode, but it moved through the world with incredible if unsuspecting power and, as a model, is exactly good enough.

INTRODUCTION
Ru(m)inations: The Haunts of Contemporary Architecture /
John McMorrough

In this text, John McMorrough crafts the term "ru(m)ination" to characterize the convergence of the words "ruination" and "rumination," and conceptually circumscribe the history of recent architectural thought. As an architect, historian, theorist, and educator, McMorrough occupies a privileged position from which to comment on the discipline, which he presents as calcified by (an unconscious) adherence to an outdated architectural logic. Despite the destructive operations and obsessive musings that have appeared since the 1960s, attempts to supersede the perceived failures of modern architecture and subsequent thoughts of the critical, architects remain inexorably wed to the disciplinary justifications against which they rebel. McMorrough equates this mentality with that of zombies who, in their single-minded quest to eat brains, repeat the paths traveled in their previous lives. Likewise, he proposes that architects, nourished by the "intelligence of previous generations," unthinkingly—even instinctively—trace their predecessors' footsteps. Thus, seemingly new architectural maneuvers, most recently the focus on performative architectures and generative practices, are ultimately undermined by the lingering phantom of autonomy.

What, then, are zombie-architects to do? How might they move beyond this impasse? McMorrough locates hope in the very lack of theoretical framework for appraising the contemporary architectural forays into the creation of form. Such mental tools would surely depart from the "ru(m)inations" of the immediate past, but would no doubt build upon a reconsideration of that past, of the inherited material that gave rise to our current situation.

460

The value of McMorrough's conclusion rests in his mandate to rethink and reveal the potential, and limits, of the architectural discipline. For a population mired in the theory-versus-practice debate, McMorrough emphasizes that the two are truly inseparable, shifting the focus from "theory or practice" to "theory and practice," or even "practice through theory." Indeed, how can one operate within a discipline without an awareness and understanding of what that discipline can be?

JOHN McMORROUGH

RU(M)INATIONS:
THE HAUNTS
OF CONTEMPORARY
ARCHITECTURE

First appeared in *Perspecta* 40 (Sept. 2008), 164–69. Courtesy of the author and the Yale School of Architecture.

As an activity that defines itself through its definitions (of spaces, of uses), the history of architecture is full of wholes—provisional totalities conceived to give coherence to an activity caught between the conflicting compulsions of necessity and frivolity. Whether in relation to capital, capacity, structure, or symbolism, architecture's history and legacy—maybe its very meaning—is to be found in the creation of reasonable explanations for its existence, its *raison d' être* made in the midst of a series of preservative justifications, in leaps of faith and defensive postures. This realm of shadow (formerly known as ideology), stories, fables, and superstitions is part of the logic of architecture itself. These manifestations of collective imagination are narrations that embody aspirations of society at large, and of architects themselves.

One instance of this phenomenon, in the tales of architecture's transmogrification over the last forty-odd years, is sublime: inspiring and, in a sense, terrifying. Regarding this period, which generally falls under the auspices of the Post-Modern (widely defined), the following is a sketch of a particular trajectory for how at a specific historical juncture architecture entered into a problematic relationship with the capacity to make proposals and instead focused on issues of signification. The ramifications of this are still felt, if not always fully acknowledged. It was (and is) a systematic avoidance through which architecture defined itself as a discipline. To give this phenomenon a name, we can consider the conceptual adjacency between two terms—ruination and rumination—that mark the period. While ruinations can be considered as both the causes and effects of demise (for this use, literally, ruins in appearance and ruinous in motivation), ruminations are lengthy considerations, negative cyclic thinking, persistent and recurrent worrying or brooding, obsessive-compulsive behavior—and in bovine usage, nonnutritious consumption. The oscillation between the modalities of ruination and rumination, between form and thought, in their multiple and paradoxically connected meanings, encapsulates the framework that spooks architecture to this day. Together these ru(m)inations define the twists and turns of architecture's epistemological machinations, and at this point are synonymous with the very idea of architectural disciplinarity, then and now.

The Act of Ruining or the Condition of Being Ruined[1]
The ruin strikes us so often as tragic—but not as sad—
because destruction here is not something senselessly
coming from the outside but rather the realization of a tendency inherent in the deepest layer of the existence of the
destroyed.[2]
—Georg Simmel

The ruin has been alternately inspiration, model, embarrassment, and legitimization; and its reenactment is an appeal both to the pictorial form of architecture's legacy and to its conceptual history. More than the simple pleasure of the ruin as pastoral fragmentation, it has continually been rethought as an end in itself, and even from its antiquarian origins has been a persistent figure of the architectural imagination, a source of material and inspiration.[3] Architects of the 1970s continued this trajectory by incorporating the image of ruin into their work. As embodied by the etymology of ruin, in the Latin root verb *ruere* ("to fail"), in versions ranging from collisions literal, denoted, and notational, architects inscribed the failure of architecture into its form. The relation of this expression to forces both external and internal to architecture explains the occurrence.

Failure that Results in a Loss of Position or Reputation[4]

Happily, we can date the death of modern architecture to
a precise moment in time.[5]
—Charles Jencks

Like all Gothic tales, this one is borne of tragedy and accident. For the sake of narrative we can presuppose that the ideal of architecture (modern architecture, more exactly) came to a full stop at some point in the 1970s. As an initial premise it is an inauspicious start, but even cursory examination of this period's cultural artifacts finds the idea in a variety of depictions in both its high and low forms. It is most notably embodied in the description of the city, which according to the prevalent options had suffered the ignominies of an urban renewal that meant a qualitative loss with not only demolition of the existent city fabric but also the legacy of failed renewals. Add to this other more spontaneous demolitions, both accidental and malicious, and the result was an image of the city literally and figuratively in ruins.

The reported causes for this [now] seemingly preemptive devaluation ranged from the failure of modern housing and the perceived rise of criminality within its domain to the energy crisis and the slowdown of the building industry, to the abstraction of modern architecture and the semantic opacity of transparent modern buildings. These were more than a general suspicion of the authority of architecture per se; they were an indictment of the modernizing impulse of architecture to fix the whole of society's problems: an overestimation of efficacy in the first case, and an underestimation of potential in the second. What links these images of destruction, of buildings in decline or in a state of demolition, is a general malaise—an atrophy of architecture's constructive capacities.

It was thought that architecture might have promised too much. With the twin impulses of technical inevitability and social contract, architectural modernism had come to represent a tangled web of motivations that were held simultaneously as style, politics, and zeitgeist. Once the limits of this were identified, architectural historians and critics commented prolifically with whole series of books and articles focusing on architecture's failure to deliver upon its social goals. Their diagnoses were quick to pronounce the deceased, with the death of "the street,"[6] "the city,"[7] and finally "modern architecture" itself.[8] In such a ruinous state, the answer was found paradoxically in the potential of ruin itself.

> **To meditate or muse; ponder[9]**
> No longer enabled to present itself as utopia, ideology
> indulges in nostalgic contemplation of its own outmoded
> roles, or disputes with itself.[10]
> —Manfredo Tafuri

The "death of" theses have yielded opposing reactions in the cases of painting and architecture. In painting it was a move to other media; in the case of architecture, an entrenchment into its own codes within the forms of autonomy. The significance of the ruin applies not only to its appearance (as an image) but also to the status of its continuation (as a thought). And its appeal lies in its simultaneous embodiment of demise and preservation of the idea of architecture, not only in appearance but as an implied system. The ruin represents strategies that denote a shared practice, the *lingua franca* of a common pursuit. Both deified and secularized, autonomy no longer argued for architecture's abilities; it articulated a definition of architecture in and of itself. As geometry was no longer spiritual, it was rendered as form; and structure was no longer efficient but was a signification of construction itself—as tectonics. No longer anything other than itself, architecture was now a representation of itself: a representation of representations no longer to be understood in relation to the exigencies of its own creation.

> To chew again or over and over[11]
> Repetition is the thought of the future.[12]
> —Gilles Deleuze

This all seems to be of only anecdotal interest, and certainly not a concern of the moment, for in the current prevalence of architecture's ascension to the embodiment and ennoblement of global capital (think Dubai, China, Moscow, and Bilbao), the idea of (modern) architecture's death must surely reside in the past. Yet, improbably, it is out of that previous malaise that the architecture of today, in its seemingly robust constitution, has grown.

The roots of this are generational. Architecture, caught in a period "after meaning," was (and perhaps is perpetually) in a quandary as to how to position its production both within the cultural field at large and within the logic of its own development. After the rejection of the semiotic enthusiasms of Post-Modernism, and its negation by deconstruction (after all, they are two versions of the same project to denote the possibility, or impossibility, of meaning), the aporias of indexicality and commentary seem to be equally exhausted. Contemporary architects have become educated in a context of hyperarticulated theoretical discourses (those that were at one level representational projects) but look in a different direction, rejecting the possibility of signification in the widest possible sense. These architectural *Trummerkinder* ("children of the ruins") are unified in their explicit rejections of semiotic models, only to find that replacement models offer a particular and tenuous relation to the real (both an under- and overestimation). As research replaces theory the idea of project is now replaced with that of scheme (both as design and as a plan of action that is especially crafty). A scheme makes itself valid, not as ideal but as particularity—as the frameworks, arguments, and illustrations that constitute the work—and there is no object. The scheme is not a residue, an index, a palimpsest, or a text at all; it is a description of actions, and it is in fact the diagram.

After the labors of architecture as code and the difficulties of such extended problematics, architecture—now in its post-ideological (post-Post-Modern) turn—seeks terra firma in all manner of the explicit: in technology with fabricators, with sensation for the neominimalist, and in information with the bureaucratic-pragmatists. Common to all this we see the interest in emergence and other forms of self-organization, a trial-and-error approach, an open-ended experimentation—it is architecture seemingly without motivation. The opacity of this post-indexical work seeks to move past the legibility that comes from concerns with the text and takes pains not to reveal the process of its formation. In spite of the recasting of the architectural project from one widely considered to be representational to one particularly focused on performance, architecture returns frequently to favored terms. Whether to form, to space, or construction (or tectonics, or in even more recent parlance, fabrication), each makes sense insofar as they are understood as elaborations of a disciplinary problematic. Project-based processes may define the work in its individuated substantiation, but it is the discipline-based justifications that define the work as architectural. Projects are presented in terms of their emergence, but understood in terms of the ideation of historical issues. As one can see in example after example of contemporary work, the logics of archaic construction underwrite the arguments for advanced computational geometry. Such elaborations make the labors of the discipline simply laborious, making difficulty its own value—the images of fabrication (again both literally and figuratively) are nothing if not the quantification of the time and effort spent. No longer spoken as such, autonomy still regulates a variety of these developments through reasons that appear to be motivated by patterns occurring only within some reptilian unconsciousness of the practice; with arguments of architectural autonomy rendering the formulas of cellular automata, the autonomous has become the automatic.

Replacing the relatively decrepit repertories of the ruin is a more monstrous menagerie of the mutant, the viral, the alien, the blob (the list goes on). What unifies these appellations is their desire for an alternative to the reification of the inorganic with the vitality of animation. If the ruin is the inert figure adequate to the representation of architecture in decline, then perhaps the zombie is the mobile figure of architecture, disciplinary continuity in the form of nonorganic self-organization and emergent intelligence. Zombies, after all, are materialist images par excellence. As exemplified in the films of George A. Romero, zombies are slow, single-minded, and incapable of thought, their ominous status achieved by sheer multiplicity and singlemindedness, their effectiveness based on the uncontrolled yet driven mass. Singularly motivated—to eat brains, a motivation that is sufficient for them to operate—their actions are dictated by patterns of habit. In Romero's classic "Dawn of the Dead," the zombies returned to the mall because of "some kind of instinct. Memory...of what they used to do."[13] As the architectural zombies of today consume the intelligence of previous generations, they return to favored terms again and again—architects enacting and reenacting certain patterns of behavior. The recent interest in so-called "generative" models is not an overcoming of the mourning of architecture but its enactment; for in these various evocations of life, we find that the animations of the architectural body are in fact compensatory metaphors for its moribund status.

Afterthoughts

Are we not in a period in which a number of approaches
that have 'died' seem to have a surprisingly robust afterlife?[14]
—Rem Koolhaas

The necrotic condition of architectural possibility today is not only a function of one style or a subset of concerns; it is pervasive within a variety of means by which the defining terms of architectural coherence (its unspoken justifications) are formulated today. Once a discipline is defined in relation to its preservative rather than its performative attributes, it is a constraint rather than an opportunity. While at one point such preservations were a necessity, they have now outlived their initial use. At this point the disciplinary conception of architecture concretizes the formats of practice as a rite: what was once the saving grace is now the problem itself. The impulse that originated as a mechanism of preservation has now been transposed into meaning—the defense mechanisms of architecture have become its content; the fort becomes a prison.[15]

The disciplinary argument is no longer capable of sustaining the development of architecture and should no longer be continually propped up. It is not a matter of choice since the options for architecture to correct its course—to move to technology or economics (pragmatism), or perhaps retire further into its own dogma (utopia)—are all too familiar, each an individual manifestation of a collective amnesia regarding the impossibility of such facilities. It is not possible to simply forget or ignore these constructions. Instead architecture needs to creatively dismantle its own fortifications, to try yet again a new ru(m)ination.

Proposing the zombie as the figure of architecture today clearly has pejorative connotations; however, the zombie also has a certain kind of freedom. In the sheer multiplicity of its explorations of options, its systems have facilitated (by the parallels developed in their enabling technologies) new avenues of form generation. The promise of these conditions is the articulation of new possibilities, of ways of arranging circumstance. The opportunity and limit of this juncture is the lack of a critical apparatus to evaluate the demands of this new intelligence on its own terms rather than with the criteria of older models. Attention to date has been on the degree to which these efforts generate unexpected results, though its possibilities are perhaps less significant for the generation of novel form and much more useful for questioning inherited conceptual strictures. These are questions not about the limits of architectural styles but that of one discipline, and perhaps the beginning of another. What is necessary is a rearticulating of the capacities of architecture, in order to retest the historic legacies of the architectural and to re-engage an understanding of these as means, not ends.

Notes

1 "Ruination." Dictionary.com. The American Heritage® Dictionary of the English Language, Fourth Edition (New York: Houghton Mifflin Company, 2004). http://dictionary.reference .com browse/ruination (accessed August 03, 2007).

2   Georg Simmel, "The Ruin" [1911], in *Essays on Sociology, Philosophy, and Aesthetics*, ed. Kurt H. Wolff (New York: Harper and Row, 1965), 263.

3   See Brian Dillon, "Fragments from a History of Ruin," *Cabinet* 20 (Winter 2005/6).

4   "Ruination." Dictionary.com. WordNet® 3.0, Princeton University. http://dictionary.reference.com/browse/ruination (accessed August 03, 2007).

5   Charles Jencks, "The Death of Modern Architecture," in *The Language of Post-Modern Architecture* (New York: Rizzoli, 1977), 9.

6   Vincent Scully, "Death of the Street," *Perspecta* 8 (1963): 91–96.

7   Jane Jacobs, *The Death and Life of Great American Cities* (New York: Random House, 1961).

8   See Jencks, ibid.

9   "Rumination." Dictionary.com Unabridged, Vol. 1.1 (New York: Random House). http://dictionary.reference.com/browse/rumination (accessed August 03, 2007).

10 Manfredo Tafuri, "Architecture and Its Double: Semiology and Formalism," in *Architecture and Utopia: Design and Capitalist Development* (Cambridge, Mass.: MIT Press, 1976), 163.

11 "Rumination." Dictionary.com Unabridged, Vol. 1.1 (New York: Random House) http://dictionary.reference.com/browse/rumination (accessed: August 03, 2007).

12 Gilles Deleuze, *Difference and Repetition* (New York: Columbia University Press, 1995), 7.

13 George A. Romero, "Dawn of the Dead" (1977), Scene 167.

14 Rem Koolhaas and Hans Ulrich Obrist, "Relearning from Las Vegas: An Interview with Denise Scott Brown and Robert Venturi," in *Harvard Design School Guide to Shopping* (Cologne: Tashen, 2002), 595.

15 Another name for this position is the "critical," which, at this point in architectural discourse represents a mélange of Kantian, Marxist, and reactionary positions that have coalesced into a presumptive mental disposition as well as a recurrent formal and conceptual strategy of inversion. The question of the day is not only the identification of the potential and limitations of criticality, but the degree to which it is even possible to de-define architecture's relationship to it.

AFTERWORD
K. Michael Hays

Architecture is a specific kind if imagination—an intimate blend of sensing, imaging, and conceptualizing—that organizes the world in categories of space and time. Architecture's object is not nearly so simple as a building. The most complexly negotiated and contested of all cultural productions and representations, architecture involves issues of perception, subject formation, image, system, and code; it shares domains with ethics and jurisprudence, gravity and weather. The determinate context of a single instance of architecture involves all the technological, aesthetic, economic, juridical, and psychological forces that drive social production and indeed in some ways articulate history itself. And the conflicting overdetermined claims and demands placed on architecture by society—its patrons, producers, and publics—are both figured and repressed in its very form.

Yet it is writing that produces the object of architecture, or more precisely, writing makes the object of architecture thinkable as such. Writing organizes architecture's myriad vectors of identification and influence into thinkable wholes, perceptible scenarios, reaching backward in time to find precedents, projecting forward to predict consequences, producing connections and patterns where before there were only isolated items.

In the 1970s and '80s architecture attempted to become writing. First it claimed to be a language. But language is a system shared, with built-in preconceptions and associations; any individual instance of the generalized system uses parts—call them types, codes, or styles—that have been used already; so all individual examples of the architectural language are inescapably ideological. Architectural writing, architecture as writing, is a third term that works in the distance between the social horizon of the generalized language and the particular, personal depths

472

that determine individual style; it opens a space (the *only* space) where the ideologies and assumptions of architecture can be scrutinized, reflected upon, transgressed, and transcended. Thus the ideal project of the 1970s and '80s departed from the world of ordinary objects and individuals around it, was not constrained by the rule of representation, and exercised its reflexive, critical vocation in an intransitive mode normally reserved for writing alone. The much sought after autonomy for architecture, as well as its possible resistance to or critical distance from the status quo, depended on its linguistic and discursive formulation.

But all that changed somewhere around the time Krista Sykes's present collection begins. Were an architectural ontology of the nineties and naughts possible, it would not be of the linguistic; it would have to be an ontology of the atmospheric— of the only vaguely defined, articulated, and indeed perceptible, which is nevertheless everywhere present in its effects. The new paradigm is of course integrally tied to digital design technologies (generic ones of *design*, not specific to the language of architecture) and computer programs that coordinate and synthesize multiple parameters and different sorts of data into smooth, frictionless flows. At times the visual results of these technologies appear as little more than hovering wisps spun out of a software package. At other times, they are almost too vivid, too present, overly real—a multimedia fusion of graphic devices collected on an animated, alloyed wrapper of texture and pattern that can be scanned for information, that seems to send out references, at one scale, to molecular, biological, informational systems and, at another scale, to the global urbanization of the planet, joining those two poles with a representation that contains but exceeds the information that produced it. The production of this architecture explicitly refuses any professionalism or disciplinary partitioning; no more struggle for autonomy or resistance to its social surround. So it is consistent that the conventions of reception produced by the new architecture will be woven into the same general media fabric as video games, social networking websites, and televisual leisure. Architecture is now part of the smooth media mix; its visage and function can drift and expand in culture in unprecedented ways, spreading laterally in a stretched-out mixed-media experience. It no longer corresponds to a particular social public or locale, neither the street nor the strip, Las Vegas or Venice, which is perhaps what gives it its slightly surreal quality: duplicitous in its matter, even though exaggerated in its thingness. Whereas the architecture of the 1970s and '80s was algebraic—its types and elements gained their significance only relationally—the new architecture is topological: a condition of field rather than object, of continuity rather than closure, of blur rather than calibration. Its iteration is one of a complex, metonymic series of blobs, corpuscles, wrappers, shingles, and facets that exist in a continual process of differentiation and mutual exchange, an emulsification so complete that surface, shape, and pattern take over, often leaving issues of typology and tectonics to float in the theoretical backwater.

Architecture, as we are so ceaselessly reminded, is experienced in distraction. The architecture of atmosphere raises this intrinsic ambience to a new level; it seeks to be a direct stimulation of the sense organs, shunting around critical consciousness altogether. Which makes writing about it all the more imperative. But writing the new architecture means writing with the body as much as the mind, apprehending the atmospheric and the ecological as feeling and affect as well as thought—folding and refolding the situation, thickening and articulating it into narrative structures, squeezing it to yield its social precipitate. The mode of writing we now have recourse to is not inscription (with its implication of certainty) but diagramming. To write diagrammatically means making visible the connections of architecture to other practices and modes of thought, scanning for its preconditions and operative assumptions, its power centers and movements, tracking the consequences as its effects multiply then split apart and disperse to find other alliances. Diagrammatic writing emphasizes connection, choice, and change. And this, all the while pondering the internal limits on the representability of (or the very possibility of writing about) the specific historical moment. If I insist that all writing about architecture should have on its horizon, as its ultimate albeit impossible goal, a vision of history itself, it is because I believe historicizing is an expansion, not a reduction, of its object.

Constructing a New Agenda registers the range of ambitions and styles in recent writing about architecture. The best of the articles exploit a productive tension between the contingencies of the specific situations of their emergence and the more global reach of a particular commitment, vision, and theory. The common thread running through the collection is the conviction that architecture is a cultural response to a situation (often regarded as unsatisfactory or incomplete), which then enables writing the architecture as action and practice rather than inert thing. This makes for a great richness as well as sheer reading pleasure. It also attests that the present situation continues to demand new formats, new styles, new modalities of writing—some quicker, some slower, some smaller and more concise, some larger and more encompassing. We must write more and better. For whatever objective transformations we might achieve in the form of our buildings, they will never be secure until they are accompanied by a whole collective reeducation that develops new reading habits, thought processes, and practices, and constructs a new consciousness capable of matching the new situation.

CONTRIBUTORS' BIOGRAPHIES

Stan Allen directs the design firm Stan Allen Architect, located in Brooklyn, New York, and is professor and dean of the School of Architecture at Princeton University. Formerly Allen was a principal in Field Operations with landscape architect James Corner. Allen's publications include *Points + Lines: Diagrams and Projects for the City* (1999) and *Practice: Architecture, Technique and Representation* (2000). Allen received undergraduate degrees from Brown University and The Cooper Union, and he recieved a master of architecture from Princeton University.

Deborah Berke is the founder and principal of Deborah Berke & Partners, and professor of architecture at Yale University. She has taught at various institutions, including the Rhode Island School of Design (RISD) and the University of Miami, served as the chair of the Buell Center for the Study of American Architecture at Columbia University, and is a founding trustee of the Design Trust for Public Space in New York City. In 1997 Berke co-edited *Architecture of the Everyday* with Steven Harris, and in 2008 with Tracy Myers she authored *Deborah Berke*, a book on her firm's work. Berke received her degrees in architecture and urban planning from RISD and The City University of New York.

Michael Braungart is professor of process engineering at the Technical University of Northeast Lower Saxony.

He is the founder of the Environmental Protection Encouragement Agency in Hamburg and a co-founder and principal of McDonough Braungart Design Chemistry with William McDonough, with whom he wrote *Cradle to Cradle: Remaking the Way We Make Things* (2002). Braungart received a doctorate in chemistry from the University of Hannover.

Karl S. Chu is adjunct associate professor of architecture at the Graduate School of Architecture, Planning and Preservation (GSAPP) at Columbia University and principal of METAXY, an architecture studio based in Los Angeles. He is the founder and co-director of the Institute for Genetic Architecture at the GSAPP, as well as the director of the program for Metaphysics of Architecture and Computation at ESARQ, Internacional de Cataluyna, Barcelona. Chu has taught at the Otis Art Institute, Auburn University, Georgia Institute of Technology, and Southern California Institute of Architecture, and he has lectured and published widely on the union of computation, genetics, and architecture. Chu received a bachelor of architecture from the University of Houston and a master of architecture from the Cranbrook Academy of Art.

The Congress for the New Urbanism (CNU) is an organization dedicated to the creation of human-friendly and ecologically sensitive built environments, from the local through the regional scale. In 1993 a group of architects, including Peter Calthorpe, Andrés Duany, and Elizabeth Plater-Zyberk, founded the CNU and established an annual meeting, or "Congress," to address issues of urbanism and urban development. CNU membership extends beyond the disciplines of architecture and planning, including individuals from fields such as economics, law, government, and education. Based in Chicago, the CNU has become an international movement, influencing the discussion and creation of multiple projects in the United States and abroad.

Cynthia Davidson is the director of the Anyone Corporation (responsible for the ANY publications and conferences), the editor of the journal *Log* and *ANY Magazine*, and a member of the MIT Press's editorial board for the Writing Architecture series. She studied journalism and art history at Ohio Wesleyan University and was a Loeb Fellow in Advanced Environmental Studies at Harvard University.

Norman Foster is the founder of Foster + Partners. He has received a number of honors, including both the Pritzker Prize and a British Life Peerage. His firm is responsible for works such as the Swiss Re Tower (2004) in London and the Hearst Headquarters (2006) in New York. Foster attended the Manchester University School of Architecture and City Planning before earning a master of architecture from Yale University.

Arie Graafland is Antoni van Leeuwenhoek Professor of Architecture Theory at the Faculty of Architecture at Delft University of Technology, where he founded and directs the Delft School of Design. He is a principal of Kerssen Graafland Architects in Amsterdam, the editor of the Delft School of Design Series on Architecture and Urbanism, and has published and lectured widely on architecture and urbanism. He studied at Rotterdam Polytechnic, the University of Amsterdam, the Royal Academy of the Arts in Amsterdam, and Vrije Universiteit in Amsterdam before receiving a doctorate from Delft University of Technology.

K. Michael Hays is Eliot Noyes Professor of Architectural Theory and co-director of doctoral programs at Harvard University Graduate School of Design. In 2000, he became the first adjunct curator of architecture at the Whitney Museum of Modern Art. Among other accomplishments, Hays is the founder of the journal *Assemblage: A Critical Journal of Architecture and Design Culture*, editor of *Architecture Theory since 1968* (1998) and the author of *Architecture's Desire: Reading the Late Avant-Garde* (2009). He received a bachelor of architecture from Georgia Institute of Technology and a master of architecture and a doctorate from the Massachusetts Institute of Technology.

Thomas Herzog, former dean of the Faculty of Architecture at Technical University Munich, is a principal of Herzog + Partner. He has taught at a number of institutions, including the University of Kassel, the University of Pennsylvania, and Tsinghua University Beijing in China. Herzog has received numerous honors and awards, and he has published extensively on issues of technology and sustainability, most recently editing the "European Charter for Solar Energy in Architecture and Urban Planning" (2007), based on the book *Solar Energy in Architecture and Urban Planning* (1996) and its parent conference in Berlin. He studied architecture at Technical University Munich and earned a doctorate from the University of Rome, La Sapienza.

Fredric Jameson is William Lane Professor of Comparative Literature and Romance Studies at Duke University where he focuses on nineteenth- and twentieth-century French literature and Marxist literary theory. He has taught at Harvard University, Yale University, and the University of California, among other institutions. His numerous publications include *Postmodernism, or, The Cultural Logic of Late Capitalism* (1991), *The Cultural Turn* (1998), and *A Singular Modernity* (2002). Jameson received a bachelor of arts from Haverford College and a master of arts and a doctorate from Yale University.

Jan Kaplicky was the founder and principal of Future Systems, based in London. As an educator he was affiliated with the Architectural Association as well as other architectural programs. Future Systems's most notable works include the Media Center for Lord's Cricket Grounds (1999) in London, and the controversial competition-winning design for the National Library of the Czech Republic (2007). Kaplicky received a diploma in architecture from the College of Applied Arts and Architecture in Prague.

Jeffrey Kipnis, professor of architecture at the Knowlton School of Architecture at Ohio State University and Distinguished Visiting Professor at Angewandte Kunst, Vienna, has taught at various institutions, including Harvard University, the Architectural Association in London, and Columbia University. He is responsible for a number of exhibitions, writings, and an award-winning film (*A Constructive Madness*, 2003, with Tom Ball and Brian Neff) that address facets of contemporary architecture. Kipnis attended Georgia Institute of Technology and Georgia State University, where he earned a master of science in physics.

Rem Koolhaas is founder and principal of the Office for Metropolitan Architecture and the affiliated firm AMO. As a professor of architecture at Harvard University Graduate School of Design, he has led a series of projects on the nature of the contemporary city. He is the author of multiple publications, such as *Delirious New York* (1977) and *SMLXL* (with Bruce Mau, 1995); his many built works include the Seattle Public Library (2004). Koolhaas was awarded the Pritzker Prize in 2000. He received a degree in architecture from the Architectural Association in London.

Sanford Kwinter is visiting associate professor of architecture at Harvard University Graduate School of Design. He previously taught at the Massachusetts Institute of Technology, Columbia University, and Rice University, and he co-founded the influential Zone Books. He has written and lectured extensively about architectural theory and design and was involved in an editorial capacity with the journal *Zone, Assemblage*, and the ANY conferences and publications. Kwinter's books include *Architectures of Time: Toward a Theory of the Event in Modernist Culture* (2001) and *Far From Equilibrium: Essays on Technology and Design Culture (2008)*. He received a doctorate in comparative literature from Columbia University.

Sylvia Lavin is professor of architectural history and theory at the University of California, Los Angeles. She has taught as a visiting professor at numerous institutions, including Princeton, Harvard, and Columbia universities. She has written and lectured widely on contemporary architectural history, theory, and criticism. Her publications include *Form Follows Libido: Architecture and Richard Neutra in a Psychoanalytic Culture* (2005), *Crib Sheets: Notes on Contemporary Architectural Conversation* (2005), and *The Flash in the Pan and Other Forms of Architectural Contemporaneity* (2009). Lavin received a bachelor degree from Barnard and master and doctoral degrees from Columbia University.

Greg Lynn is the principal of Greg Lynn FORM in Los Angeles. He is master professor at the University of Applied Arts in Vienna; studio professor at the University of California, Los Angeles, Department of Architecture and Urban Design; and Davenport Visiting Professor at Yale University. His most recent book is *Greg Lynn FORM* (2008), and his current projects include

private residences in Los Angeles and two public housing developments in Europe. He received undergraduate degrees in architecture and philosophy from Miami University of Ohio and a master of architecture from Princeton University.

Reinhold Martin, partner in the firm Martin/Baxi Architects, is associate professor of architecture and director of the Doctoral Program in Architecture and the Master of Science Program in Advanced Architectural Design at Columbia University. He is a founding co-editor of the journal *Grey Room* and the author of many publications on modern and contemporary architectural history and theory, including *The Organizational Complex: Architecture, Media, and Corporate Space* (2003) and *Multi-National City: Architectural Itineraries* (2007). Martin received an undergraduate degree from Rensselaer Polytechnic Institute, a graduate degree in architectural history and theory from the Architectural Association, and a doctoral degree from Princeton University.

William McDonough is the founder and principal of William McDonough + Partners, as well as a co-founder and principal of McDonough Braungart Design Chemistry with Michael Braungart, with whom he wrote *Cradle to Cradle: Remaking the Way We Make Things* (2002). He has earned an international reputation as an ecologically minded architect, co-authoring *The Hannover Principles: Design for Sustainability* (1991) to help govern the development of the city's 2000 Expo. McDonough formerly was Edward E. Elson Professor of Architecture and dean of the School of Architecture at the University of Virginia. He attended Dartmouth College and earned a master of architecture from Yale University.

John McMorrough is assistant professor of architecture at the Knowlton School of Architecture at Ohio State University and principal in the firm studioAPT, based in Columbus, Ohio. He has taught at Yale, Harvard, and Northeastern universities as well as the Massachusetts Institute of Technology. McMorrough has published on architectural theory and criticism in journals such as *Hunch*, *Praxis*, and *Perspecta*, and he has served as an invited critic and lecturer at multiple venues. McMorrough received a bachelor of architecture from the University of Kansas and a master of architecture and a doctorate from Harvard University.

William J. Mitchell is professor of architecture and media arts and sciences at the Massachusetts Institute of Technology, holding the Alexander W. Dreyfoos Jr. professorship and heading the Program in Media Arts and Sciences. He formerly served as dean of the School of Architecture and Planning at MIT and taught at Harvard University; the University of California, Los Angeles; and the University of Cambridge. Mitchell is the author of several articles and books, including *City of Bits: Space, Place, and the Infobahn* (1995), *e-topia: Urban Life, Jim—But Not As We Know It* (1999), and *Placing Words: Symbols, Space, and the City* (2005). He received a

bachelor of architecture from the University of Melbourne, a master of environmental design from Yale, and a master of arts from the University of Cambridge.

Samuel Mockbee, a native of Mississippi, left his successful architectural practice—Mockbee Coker Architects—in 1991 to become a full-time professor at his alma mater, Auburn University. There, with D.K. Ruth, Mockbee co-founded the Rural Studio, a student design-build initiative that assists underprivileged communities. The award-winning work of the Rural Studio has been published and exhibited both nationally and abroad, attracting attention as an alternative model for architectural education and practice.

Steven A. Moore is Bartlett Cocke Professor of Architecture and Planning and director of the Sustainable Design Program at the University of Texas at Austin. Previously he taught at Texas A&M University and practiced architecture in Maine. He has published widely on sustainability and regionalist design, including *Technology and Place: Sustainable Architecture and the Blueprint Farm* (2001) and *Alternative Routes to the Sustainable City: Austin, Curitiba, and Frankfurt* (2007). He received a bachelor of arts in architecture from Syracuse University and a doctorate from Texas A&M University.

Glenn Murcutt practices architecture in Australia and has gained widespread recognition for his small-scale, ecologically sensitive, vernacular designs. He has served as a visiting professor at a variety of institutions, such as Yale University, the University of Virginia, and Montana State University, and he has lectured throughout the world. He has received a number of honors and awards, including the Pritzker Prize in 2002. Murcutt received an architecture degree from the University of New South Wales.

Antoine Picon is professor of the history of architecture and technology and co-director of doctoral programs at Harvard University's Graduate School of Design. In addition to numerous articles, his publications include *French Architects and Engineers in the Age of Enlightenment* (1988) and *La ville territoire des cyborgs* (1998). He received degrees in engineering from the Ecole Polytechnique and the Ecole Nationale des Ponts et Chaussees, a degree in architecture from the Ecole d'Architecture de Paris-Villemin, and a doctorate in architectural history from the Ecole des Hautes Etudes en Sciences Sociales.

John Rajchman is a philosopher who focuses on theory and criticism of twentieth-century art and architecture. He has taught at a variety of institutions, including Columbia University, the Collége International de Philosophie in Paris, and The Cooper Union. Among other publications, he is the author of *Constructions: Writing in Architecture Series* (1998) and *The Deleuze Connections* (2000), as well as the co-editor of *French Philosophy Since 1945: Problems, Concepts, Inventions—Postwar French Thought, Volume IV* (2009). Rajchman received a doctorate from Columbia University.

Reiser + Umemoto is a New York-based firm lead by architects Jesse Reiser and Nanako Umemoto. Reiser is also an associate professor of architecture at Princeton University, and the pair has taught and lectured throughout the United States, Europe, and Japan. Reiser + Umemoto has won a number of design competitions and their work has been featured in multiple exhibitions and publications. They authored the *Atlas of Novel Tectonics* (2006), and recent designs include Office Tower O-14 in Dubai (2009). Reiser earned degrees from The Cooper Union and Cranbrook Academy of Art; Umemoto studied at the School of Urban Design at the Osaka University of Art and graduated from The Cooper Union.

Richard Rogers is a principal of Rogers Stirk Harbour + Partners. Since pairing with Renzo Piano to design the Centre Pompidou in Paris (1976), Foster has received multiple awards and honors, including a British Life Peerage and the Pritzker Prize. Among his office's recent works are Terminal 4 at Madrid Barajas Airport and one of the towers on the World Trade Center site. Rogers studied at the Architectural Association in London and received a master of architecture from Yale University.

Saskia Sassen is Robert S. Lynd Professor of Sociology at Columbia University and Centennial Visiting Professor at the London School of Economics. She has published widely on issues related to globalization and networked technologies, including *The Global City* (1991) and *Territory, Authority, Rights: From Medieval to*

Global Assemblages (2006). Sassen is active in a number of national and international organizations and has received many honors and awards. She holds master and doctoral degrees from the University of Notre Dame, Indiana.

Robert Somol is director and professor of the School of Architecture at the University of Illinois, Chicago. He has taught at Ohio State University, Princeton University, and the University of California, Los Angeles, in addition to other institutions. Somol is the editor of *Autonomy and Ideology* (1997) as well as many articles on modernism and contemporary architecture. He received a bachelor of arts from Brown University, a law degree from Harvard Law School, and a doctorate from the University of Chicago.

Michael Speaks is dean of the College of Design at the University of Kentucky and leads the urban research group Big Soft Orange, based in Los Angeles and Rotterdam. Previously Speaks was the director of the Graduate Program and founding director of the Metropolitan Research and Design Postgraduate Program at the Southern California Institute of Architecture in Los Angeles. He also taught at Yale, Harvard, Columbia, The Berlage Institute, and the University of California, Los Angeles. He is the founding editor of *Polygraph*, a contributing editor for *Architectural Record*, and a former editor at *A+U* and *ANY*. Speaks earned a bachelor degree from the University of Mississippi and a doctoral degree from Duke University.

Roemer van Toorn is professor at the Berlage Institute, where he directs the Projective Theory Program, and a researcher at Delft School of Design at Delft University of Technology, where he is pursuing his doctoral degree. Van Toorn has been involved with a number of publications, including *Architecture in the Netherlands* and the journals *Archis (Volume)*, *Hunch*, *Domus*, and *Abitare*. He co-edited *The Invisible in Architecture* (1994).

Anthony Vidler is dean and professor of the Irwin S. Chanin School of Architecture at The Cooper Union. He previously taught at Princeton University School of Architecture, where he chaired the PhD committee, was director of the Program in European Cultural Studies, and was appointed William R. Kenan Jr. Chair of Architecture. He also taught at the University of California, Los Angeles, where he served as professor and chair of the Department of Art History and professor of the School of Architecture. His numerous publications include *The Architectural Uncanny: Essays in the Modern Unhomely* (1992), *Warped Space: Architecture and Anxiety in Modern Culture* (2000), and *Histories of the Immediate Present: Inventing Architectural Modernism* (2008). Vidler received undergraduate and architecture degrees from Cambridge University, and a doctorate from Delft University of Technology.

Sarah Whiting is dean of the Rice School of Architecture and principal and co-founder of the architectural firm WW. She has held teaching positions at Princeton University, Harvard

University, the University of Kentucky, the Illinois Institute of Technology, and the University of Florida. She has published extensively on architectural and urban theory and is the author of *Superblock City* (forthcoming). Whiting holds a bachelor of arts from Yale University, a master of architecture from Princeton University, and a doctorate from the Massachusetts Institute of Technology.

Ken Yeang is a principal of Llewelyn Davies Yeang in London and its partner firm Hamzah & Yeang in Malaysia. He has taught at multiple architectural programs, such as at Texas A&M University, the University of Malaya, the University of Hawaii, and the University of Illinois, where he served as Distinguished Plym Professor. Yeang focuses on ecological design and has written a number of texts on the subject, most recently *Ecomasterplanning* (2009). He received an architectural degree from the Architectural Association in London and a doctorate from Cambridge University.

SELECTED
BIBLIOGRAPHY

Allen, Stan. *Practice: Architecture, Technique, and Representation.* Amsterdam: G+B Arts International, 2000.

ANY 1/0: Seaside and the Real World: A Debate on American Urbanism (July/August 1993).

ANY 23: Diagram Work: Data Mechanics for a Topological Age (December 1998).

Assemblage 41 (2000).

Bouman, Ole, and Roemer van Toorn, eds. *The Invisible in Architecture.* London: Academy Press, 1994.

Davidson, Cynthia C., ed. *Anything.* Cambridge, Mass.: MIT Press, 2001.

———. *Anybody.* Cambridge, Mass.: MIT Press, 1997.

———. *Anyhow.* Cambridge, Mass.: MIT Press, 1998.

———. *Anymore.* Cambridge, Mass.: MIT Press, 2000

———. *Anyplace.* Cambridge, Mass.: MIT Press, 1995.

———. *Anytime.* Cambridge, Mass.: MIT Press, 1999.

———. *Anyway.* New York: Rizzoli, 1994.

———. *Anywhere.* New York: Rizzoli, 1992.

———. *Anywise.* Cambridge, Mass.: MIT Press, 1996.

Dean, Andrea Oppenheimer. *Rural Studio: Samuel Mockbee and an Architecture of Decency.* New York: Princeton Architectural Press, 2001.

Di Christina, Giuseppa, ed. *AD Architecture and Science.* London: Academy Press, 2001.

Duany, Andres. *Suburban Nation: The Rise of Sprawl and the Decline of the American Dream.* New York: North Point Press, 2000.

Eagleton, Terry. *After Theory.* London: Allen Lane, 2003.

Foster, Norman, and David Jenkins, eds. *On Foster...Foster On.* Munich: Prestel, 2000.

Foster, Norman. *Reflections.* Munich: Prestel, 2006.

Hays, K. Michael, ed. *Architecture Theory since 1968.* Cambridge, Mass.: MIT Press, 1996.

———. *Architecture's Desire: Reading the Late Avant-Garde.* Cambridge, Mass.: MIT Press, 2009.

———. "Critical Architecture: Between Culture and Form." *Perspecta 21* (1984): 15–29.

———. *Oppositions Reader.* New York: Princeton Architectural Press, 1998.

———. "Prolegomena Linking the Advanced Architecture of the Present to that of the 1970s through Ideologies of Media, the Experience of Cities in Transition, and the Ongoing Effects of Reification." *Perspecta 32: Resurfacing Modernism* (2001): 100–107.

Herzog, Thomas, ed. *Solar Energy in Architecture and Urban Planning.* Munich: Prestel, 1996.

Hunch 6/7: 109 Provisional Attempts to Address Six Simple and Hard Questions About What Architects Do Today and Where Their Profession Might Go Tomorrow (2003).

Holl, Steven, Juhani Pallasmaa, and Alberto Pérez-Gomes. *Questions of Perception: Phenomenology of Architecture.* San Francisco: William K. Stout, 2007.

Jameson, Fredric. *The Cultural Turn: Selected Writings on the Postmodern, 1983–1998*. New York: Verso, 1998.

———. *A Singular Modernity: Essay on the Ontology of the Present*. New York: Verso, 2002.

Katz, Peter. *The New Urbanism: Toward an Architecture of Community*. New York: McGraw-Hill, 1994.

Kipnis, Jeffrey. *A Constructive Madness*. Directed by Thomas Ball and Brian Neff. Cleveland, Ohio: Telos Video Communications, 2003. Video recording.

———. "Towards a New Architecture." In *Folding in Architecture,* edited by Greg Lynn, 41–49. London: Academy Press, 1993.

——— and Annetta Massie. *Mood River*. Columbus, Ohio: Wexner Center for the Arts, Ohio Center for the Arts; New York: Distributed Art Publishers, 2002.

Koolhaas, Rem, and AMO/OMA. *Content*. Cologne: Taschen, 2004.

———, Jeffrey Inaba, Sze Tsung Leong, and Chuihua Judy Chung, eds. *Great Leap Forward*. Cologne: Taschen, 2001.

———, Jeffrey Inaba, Sze Tsung Leong, and Chuihua Judy Chung, eds. *Harvard Design School Guide to Shopping*. Cologne: Taschen, 2001.

———, Stefano Boeri, Sanford Kwinter, Nadia Tazi, and Hans Ulrich Obrist. *Mutations*. Barcelona: Actar, 2001.

———, and Jennifer Sigler, eds. *Small, Medium, Large, Extra-large: OMA, Rem Koolhaas, and Bruce Mau*. New York: Monacelli Press, 1995.

Kwinter, Sanford. *Architectures of Time: Toward a Theory of the Event in Modernist Culture*. Cambridge, Mass.: MIT Press, 2001.

———. *Far From Equilibrium: Essays on Technology and Design Culture*. Edited by Cynthia C. Davidson. Barcelona: Actar, 2007.

Lavin, Sylvia, Helene Furjan, and Penelope Dean. *Crib Sheets: Notes on the Contemporary Architectural Conversation*. New York: Monacelli, 2005.

Leach, Neil. *Rethinking Architecture: A Reader in Cultural Theory*. London: Routledge, 1997.

Log 5 (Spring 2005).

Lootsma, Bart. *SuperDutch: New Architecture in the Netherlands*. New York: Princeton Architectural Press, 2000.

Lynn, Greg. *FORM*. New York: Rizzoli, 2008.

———. *Animate Form*. New York: Princeton Architectural Press, 1999.

———. *Folds, Bodies & Blobs: Collected Essays*. Bruxelles: La Lettre vole, 1998.

Manifold 1: After Theory (Spring 2007).

Martin, Reinhold. *Multi-National City: Architectural Itineraries*. Barcelona: Actar, 2007.

———. *The Organizational Complex: Architecture, Media, and Corporate Space*. Cambridge, Mass.: MIT Press, 2003.

McDonough, William, and Michael Braungart. *Cradle to Cradle: Remaking the Way We Make Things*. New York: North Point Press, 2002.

Mitchell, William J. *City of Bits: Space, Place, and the Infobahn.* Cambridge, Mass.: MIT Press, 1995.

———. *e-topia: Urban Life, Jim—But Not As We Know It.* Cambridge, Mass.: MIT Press, 1999.

———. *Placing Words: Symbols, Space, and the City.* Cambridge, Mass.: MIT Press, 2005.

Moos, David, ed. *Samuel Mockbee and the Rural Studio: Community Architecture.* Birmingham, Ala.: Birmingham Museum of Art; New York: Distributed Art Publishers, 2003.

Nesbitt, Kate. *Theorizing a New Agenda for Architecture: An Anthology of Architectural Theory, 1965–1995.* New York: Princeton Architectural Press, 1996.

Picon, Antoine. *La ville territoire des cyborgs.* Besançon, France: Editions de l'Imprimeur, 1998.

Rajchman, John. *Constructions.* Cambridge, Mass.: MIT Press, 1998.

Sassen, Saskia. *Territory, Authority, Rights: From Medieval to Global Assemblages.* Princeton, N.J.: Princeton University Press, 2006.

———. *Cities in a World Economy.* 3rd edition. Thousand Oaks, Calif.: Pine Forge Press, 2006.

Saunders, William S., ed. *Commodification and Spectacle in Architecture: A Harvard Design Magazine Reader.* Minneapolis, Minn.: University of Minnesota Press, 2005.

———. *Judging Architectural Value: A Harvard Design Magazine Reader.* Minneapolis, Minn.: University of Minnesota Press, 2007.

———. *Nature, Landscape, and Building for Sustainability: A Harvard Design Magazine Reader.* Minneapolis, Minn.: University of Minnesota Press, 2008.

———. *The New Architectural Pragmatism: A Harvard Design Magazine Reader.* Minneapolis, Minn.: University of Minnesota Press, 2007.

———. *Reflections on Architectural Practice in the Nineties.* New York: Princeton Architectural Press, 1996.

———. *Sprawl and Suburbia: A Harvard Design Magazine Reader.* Minneapolis, Minn.: University of Minnesota Press, 2005.

Silvetti, Jorge. "The Muses are not Amused: Pandemonium in the House of Architecture." *Harvard Design Magazine* (Fall 2003/Winter 2004): 22–33.

Somol, Robert. *Autonomy and Ideology: Positioning an Avant-garde in America.* New York: Monacelli, 1997.

Tschumi, Bernard, and Irene Cheng, eds. *The State of Architecture at the Beginning of the 21st Century.* New York: Monacelli, 2003.

SHoP Architects, ed. *Versioning: Evolutionary Techniques in Architecture.* London: Academy Press, 2003.

Vidler, Anthony. *Histories of the Immediate Present: Inventing Architectural Modernism.* Cambridge, Mass.: MIT Press, 2008.

———. *Warped Space: Architecture and Anxiety in Modern Culture.* Cambridge, Mass.: MIT Press, 2000.

Yeang, Ken. *Designing with Nature: The Ecological Basis for Architectural Design*. New York: McGraw-Hill, 1995.

———. *Ecodesign: A Manual for Ecological Design*. London: Wiley, 2006.

———. *Ecomasterplanning*. Chichester, West Sussex, U.K.: Wiley, 2009.

INDEX

306090, 20

A+U, 134, 136, 204, 206, 247, 418, 486
Acconci, Vito, 242, 322
Adjacent Possible, 424, 432
Adorno, Theodor, 94, 296, 313, 350, 403, 415
aesthetic reflexivity, 403
aesthetics, 148, 165, 193, 241, 288, 290, 310, 323, 331, 347, 355, 359, 390, 405, 471
aesthetics, as politics, 148, 165, 310, 347
Africa, 98
Agent Provocateur, 451
Agnew, John
  Place and Politics; 382, 383
  "Representing Space," 383
AIDS, 305
Al Qaeda, 205, 208
Alaskan tundra, 340
Alberti, Leon Baltista, 107, 120
Alef-Beit, 339
algebra, 132
allegory, 99, 414, 415, 440
Allen, Stan, 61, 362, 399, 476
  "Field Conditions," *Points + Lines*, 116–133
  Korean-American Museum of Art, Los Angeles; 117, 476
  National Diet Library, Kyoto Prefecture, Japan, 117
  "Revising Our Expertise," 312
Alonso, Hernan Diaz, 212
Althusser, Louis, 415
American Civil War, 234
American Institute of Architects (AIA)
  Gold Medal, 385
  "Sustainable Design," 116

Americanization, 253, 259
AMO, 26, 29, 134, 212, 399, 405, 480, 491, 314,
Anderson, David P. and John Kubiatowicz
  "The Worldwide Computer," 244
Ando, Tadao, 163, 294, 363
Andre, Carl, 123, 124
Andrewes, William J. H.
  "A Chronicle of Timekeeping," 243
anexact geometries, 43, 60
anthropology, 14, 427, 199, 297
ANY, 19, 63, 80, 89, 104, 186, 312, 385, 477, 478, 481, 486, 489
Architectural Design, 30–32, 39, 60, 132, 167, 288, 422, 494
architectural form, 42, 53, 120, 277, 328
architectural history, 140, 268, 481, 482, 484
architectural practice, 16, 23, 51, 152, 202, 211, 213, 316, 347, 378, 397–403, 408, 434–437, 483
architectural representation, 33, 268, 269, 271, 273, 278, 283–285
architectural style, 72, 470
architectural theory, 12–17, 30, 260, 324, 332, 334, 394, 414, 429, 478, 481, 482
Architecture Between Spectacle and Use, conference at the Clark Art Institute, 318
Architecture by Numbers, show at the Whitney Museum of American Art at Altria, 332–34
architecture imaginary, the, 343
architecture, American, 14, 114, 476
architecture, autonomous, 350
architecture, digital, 271–277, 396, 408, 412, 416
architecture, everyday, 23, 70
architecture, genetic, 421, 429–431, 477